Financial Markets and Institutions

SCHOOL OF ORIENTAL AND AFRICA

Since the first edition of this book, the world's financial system has been through its greatest crisis for a century. What made this crisis unique is that severe financial problems emerged simultaneously in many different countries, and its economic impact was felt throughout the world as a result of the increased interconnectedness of the global economy. Written for undergraduate and graduate students of finance, economics, and business, the second edition of this successful textbook provides a fresh analysis of the world's financial system in light of the recent financial crisis. Combining theory, empirical data, and policy, it examines and explains financial markets, financial infrastructures, financial institutions, and challenges in the domain of financial supervision and competition policy. This new edition features three completely new chapters: one on financial crises, a second on financial innovation, and, on the policy side, a third on the monetary policy of the European Central Bank.

Jakob de Haan is Head of Research of De Nederlandsche Bank and Professor of Political Economy at the University of Groningen.

Sander Oosterloo is Senior Policy Advisor at the Netherlands Ministry of Social Affairs and Employment.

Dirk Schoenmaker is Dean of the Duisenberg School of Finance, Amsterdam, and Professor of Finance, Banking, and Insurance at the VU University Amsterdam.

Financial Markets and Institutions

A European Perspective

Second Edition

Jakob de Haan

Sander Oosterloo

Dirk Schoenmaker

CAMBRIDGE UNIVERSITY PRESS
Cambridge, New York, Melbourne, Madrid, Cape Town,
Singapore, São Paulo, Delhi, Mexico City

Cambridge University Press
The Edinburgh Building, Cambridge CB2 8RU, UK

Published in the United States of America by Cambridge University Press, New York

www.cambridge.org
Information on this title: www.cambridge.org/9781107635920

First edition 2009
Second edition 2012

Printed in the United Kingdom at the University Press, Cambridge

A catalogue record for this publication is available from the British Library

Library of Congress Cataloguing in Publication data
Haan, Jakob de.
 Financial markets and institutions : a European perspective / Jakob de Haan, Sander Oosterloo,
 Dirk Schoenmaker. – Second edition.
   pages   cm
 Expanded version of the authors' European financial markets and institutions, 2009.
 Includes bibliographical references and index.
 ISBN 978-1-107-02594-3 (hardback) – ISBN 978-1-107-63592-0 (paperback)
 1. Financial institutions.   2. Capital market.   I. Oosterloo, Sander.
 II. Schoenmaker, Dirk.   III. Haan, Jakob de. European financial markets and
 institutions.   IV. Title.
 HG173.H293 2012
 332.1–dc23
 2012013669

ISBN 978-1-107-02594-3 Hardback
ISBN 978-1-107-63592-0 Paperback

Contents

v

Boxes

Figures

Tables

Countries

Member States of the European Union

	Country	Official abbreviation	Year of accession
1	Austria	AT	1995
2	Belgium	BE	1951
3	Bulgaria	BG	2007
4	Cyprus	CY	2004
5	Czech Republic	CZ	2004
6	Denmark	DK	1973
7	Estonia	EE	2004
8	Finland	FI	1995
9	France	FR	1951
10	Germany	DE	1951
11	Greece	EL	1981
12	Hungary	HU	2004
13	Ireland	IE	1973
14	Italy	IT	1951
15	Latvia	LV	2004
16	Lithuania	LT	2004
17	Luxembourg	LU	1951
18	Malta	MT	2004
19	Netherlands	NL	1951
20	Poland	PL	2004
21	Portugal	PT	1986
22	Romania	RO	2007
23	Slovakia	SK	2004
24	Slovenia	SI	2004
25	Spain	ES	1986
26	Sweden	SE	1995
27	United Kingdom	UK	1973

The European Union (EU) consists of 27 Member States as of 2012 (EU 27). Before the accession of the New Member States in 2004 and 2007, the EU consisted of 15 Member States, which are usually indicated by EU-15. The 10 New Member States in 2004 are indicated by NMS-10 and the total of 12 New Member States in 2004 and 2007 are indicated by NMS-12. EU-25 refers to the EU-15 and NMS-10. EU-27 refers to the EU-15 and NMS-12. Croatia is set to become the 28th Member State of the EU in 2013.

There are 17 countries in the euro area.

Countries in the euro area

	Country	Year of accession
1	Austria	1999
2	Belgium	1999
3	Cyprus	2008
4	Estonia	2011
5	Finland	1999
6	France	1999
7	Germany	1999
8	Greece	2001
9	Ireland	1999
10	Italy	1999
11	Luxembourg	1999
12	Malta	2008
13	Netherlands	1999
14	Portugal	1999
15	Slovakia	2009
16	Slovenia	2007
17	Spain	1999

Abbreviations

ABP	Algemeen Burgerlijk Pensioenfonds
ABS	Asset-Backed Securities
ACP	Asset-backed Commercial Paper
ACP	Autorité de Contrôle Prudentiel
AIG	American International Group
ALM	Asset and Liability Management
AMF	Autorité des Marchés Financiers
ATM	Automated Teller Machine
BaFin	Bundesanstalt für Finanzdienstleistungsaufsicht
BHB	Bond Home Bias
BIS	Bank for International Settlements
BME	Bolsas y Mercados Españoles
BoE	Bank of England
CalPERS	California Public Employees Retirement Scheme
CAPM	Capital Asset Pricing Model
CB	Central Bank
CCP	Central Counterparty
CD	Certificate of Deposit
CDC	Collective Defined Contribution
CDO	Collateralised Debt Obligation
CDS	Credit Default Swap
CEA	Comité Européen des Assurances
CEBS	Committee of European Banking Supervisors
CEEC	Central and Eastern European Countries
CEIOPS	Committee of Insurance and Occupational Pensions Supervisors
CEO	Chief Executive Officer
CESR	Committee of European Securities Regulators
CET1	Common Equity Tier 1

CFO	Chief Financial Officer
CLS	Continuous Linked Settlement
CRA	Credit Rating Agency
CRAAC	CRA Assessment Centre
CRD	Capital Requirements Directive
CRO	Chief Risk Officer
CSD	Central Securities Depository
DB	Defined Benefit
DC	Defined Contribution
DG	Directorate General
DTB	Deutsche Terminbörse
EBA	European Banking Authority
EBC	European Banking Committee
EBRD	European Bank for Reconstruction and Development
EC	European Commission
ECB	European Central Bank
ECFI	European Court of First Instance
ECJ	European Court of Justice
ECN	European Competition Network
Ecofin	Economic and Financial Affairs Council
ECSC	European Coal and Steel Community
ECU	European Currency Unit
EDP	Excessive Deficit Procedure
EEA	European Economic Area
EEC	European Economic Community
EFA	European Financial Agency
EFAMA	European Fund and Asset Management Association
EFCC	European Financial Conglomerates Committee
EFR	European Financial Services Round Table
EFSF	European Financial Stability Facility
EFSM	European Financial Stabilisation Mechanism
EHB	Equity Home Bias
EIOPA	European Insurance and Occupational Pensions Authority
EMI	European Monetary Institute
EMS	European Monetary System
EMU	Economic and Monetary Union
EOE	European Options Exchange
EONIA	Euro Overnight Index Average
EP	European Parliament

EPC	European Payments Council
EPM	ECB Payment Mechanism
ERC	European Repo Council
ERM	Exchange Rate Mechanism
ESA	European Supervisory Authority
ESC	European Securities Committee
ESCB	European System of Central Banks
ESFS	European System of Financial Supervisors
ESM	European Stability Mechanism
ESMA	European Securities and Markets Authority
ESRB	European Systemic Risk Board
ETF	Exchange Traded Funds
EU	European Union
Euratom	European Atomic Energy Community
EUREPO	Repo Market Reference Rate for the Euro
EURIBOR	Euro Interbank Offered Rate
FCA	Financial Conduct Authority
FDI	Foreign Direct Investment
FESE	Federation of European Securities Exchanges
FPC	Financial Policy Committee
FRA	Forward Rate Agreement
FSA	Financial Services Authority
FSAP	Financial Services Action Plan
FSC	Financial Services Committee
FSF	Financial Stability Forum
FSOC	Financial Stability Oversight Council
FSR	Financial Stability Review
FTO	Fine Tune Operation
FX	Foreign Exchange
GDP	Gross Domestic Product
GMI	Governance Metrics International
GVA	Gross Value Added
HI	Herfindahl Index
IAS	International Accounting Standards
IASB	International Accounting Standards Board
ICI	Investment Company Institute
ICMA	International Capital Market Association
ICSD	International Central Securities Depository
IFRS	International Financial Reporting Standards

IMF	International Monetary Fund
IOSCO	International Organisation of Securities Commissions
IPO	Initial Public Offering
IRS	Interest Rate Swap
ISD	Investment Services Directive
ISDA	International Swaps and Derivatives Association
IT	Information Technology
LCR	Liquidity Coverage Ratio
LI	Lerner Index
LIFFE	London International Financial Futures and Options Exchange
LoLR	Lender of Last Resort
LSE	London Stock Exchange
LTCM	Long-Term Capital Management
LTRO	Longer-Term Refinancing Operation
LVPS	Large-Value Payment System
M&As	Mergers and Acquisitions
MBS	Mortgage-Backed Securities
MFI	Monetary Financial Institution
MIF	Multilateral Interchange Fee
MiFID	Markets in Financial Instruments Directive
MMF	Money Market Fund
MoU	Memorandum of Understanding
MRO	Main Refinancing Operation
MSCI	Morgan Stanley Capital International
MTF	Multilateral Trading Facility
MTO	Medium-Term Objective
NAV	Net Asset Value
NCA	National Competition Authority
NCB	National Central Bank
NMS	New Member States
NSA	National Supervisory Authority
NSFR	Net Stable Funding Ratio
NYSE	New York Stock Exchange
OECD	Organisation for Economic Co-operation and Development
OFT	Office of Fair Trading
OIS	Overnight Interest Rate Swap
OMX	Options Maklarna Exchange
OTC	Over-the-Counter
PAYG	Pay-As-You-Go

P&C	Property and Casualty
PCA	Prompt Corrective Action
PSD	Payment Services Directive
PvP	Payment versus Payment
RAROC	Risk Adjusted Return On Capital
RBB	Regional Bond Bias
REB	Regional Equity Bias
ROE	Return On Equity
RTGS	Real-Time Gross Settlement
SBA	Stand-by Arrangement
SCP	Structure-Conduct-Performance
SEA	Single European Act
SEC	Securities and Exchange Commission
SEPA	Single Euro Payments Area
SETS	London Stock Exchange's premier Electronic Trading System
SGP	Stability and Growth Pact
SIB	Systemically Important Bank
SIFI	Systemically Important Financial Institution
SIV	Structured Investment Vehicle
SMEs	Small and Medium Enterprises
SMP	Securities Markets Programme
SOFFEX	Swiss Options and Financial Futures Exchange
SPO	Secondary Public Offering
SPV	Special Purpose Vehicle
SRO	Self Regulatory Organisation
SSNIP	Small, but Significant Non-transitory Increase in Prices
SSP	Single Shared Platform
STP	Straight-Through Processing
TARGET	Trans-European Automated Real-Time Gross Settlement Express Transfer System
TEU	Treaty on European Union
TFEU	Treaty on the Functioning of the EU
T2S	TARGET2-Securities
UCITS	Undertakings for Collective Investments in Transferable Securities
UK	United Kingdom
US	United States
VaR	Value-at-Risk

Preface

As a team of authors we have followed the building of the European financial system from different angles. We have contributed to the academic literature on this topic. Moreover, one of us has been teaching a course on European Financial Integration, from which this book has emerged. On the policy side, the authors have been directly involved in the work of national administrations (i.e. the Ministry of Finance, the Ministry of Economic Affairs in the Netherlands, and the Dutch central bank) as well as the European institutions (i.e. the Council, the European Commission, and the European Central Bank). As part of our job, two of us have participated in many meetings in Brussels discussing the future of European financial markets and institutions, and negotiating new European financial services directives.

The authors would like to thank Wilco Bolt, Jean Frijns, Ronald Heijmans, Iman van Lelyveld, Bert Menkveld, Almoro Rubin de Cervin, Martijn Schrijvers and Casper de Vries for their advice on specific chapters.

What is new in the second edition?

Since the first edition of this book, the world's financial system has been through its greatest crisis for a century. What made this crisis unique is that severe financial problems emerged simultaneously in many different countries, and its economic impact was felt throughout the world as a result of the increased interconnectedness of the global economy. Financial innovation also played an important part in the financial crisis. Two new chapters deal with (1) financial crises, including an overview of the causes and consequences of the 2007–2009 financial crisis as well as the more recent sovereign and banking crisis in Europe, and (2) financial innovation, including the role of securitisation.

The chapters on financial markets and institutions are updated with new data. These extensive updates illustrate the impact of the financial crisis on the process of European financial integration. On the policy side, a new chapter on the monetary policy of the European Central Bank (ECB) has been added. A good understanding of the ECB's monetary policy is crucial to appreciate the working of the European financial system. The policy chapters of the first edition have been updated. New elements are the Basel 3 capital adequacy framework for banking supervision, the emergence of macroprudential supervision, and state aid control applied to banks.

How does this textbook compare with other books?

Different from other textbooks, *Financial Markets and Institutions: A European Perspective* has a wide coverage dealing with the various elements of the European financial system supported by recent data and examples. This wide coverage implies that we treat not only the functioning of financial markets where trading takes place but also the working of supporting infrastructures (clearing and settlement) where trades are executed. Turning to financial institutions, we cover the full range of financial intermediaries, from institutional investors to banks and insurance companies. Based on new data, we document the gradual shift of financial intermediation from banks towards institutional investors, such as pension funds, mutual funds, and hedge funds. In this process of re-intermediation, the assets of institutional investors have tripled over the last two decades. As to policy making, we cover the full range of financial regulation and supervision, financial stability, and competition. We deal with the challenges of European financial integration for nationally based financial supervision and stability policies. Competition is a new topic for a finance textbook.

The existing textbooks in the field of financial markets and institutions generally describe the relevant theories and subsequently relate these theories to the general characteristics of financial markets. An excellent example of a more in-depth textbook is *The Economics of Financial Markets* by Roy E. Bailey. The broad coverage of our book is comparable to the widely used textbook *Financial Markets and Institutions* by Frederic S. Mishkin and Stanley G. Eakins. Whereas our book focuses on the EU, Mishkin and Eakins analyse the US financial system. The early European textbooks (e.g. *The Economics of Money, Banking and Finance – A European Text*, by Peter Howells and Keith Bain) typically contain chapters on the UK, French, and German banking systems, but do not provide an overview of European banking. More advanced textbooks that do discuss the specifics of the European financial system mostly do this in the context of monetary policy making.

Finally, the excellent *Handbook of European Financial Markets and Institutions*, edited by Xavier Freixas, Philipp Hartmann, and Colin Mayer, has a broad coverage of the European financial system, but deals with topics on a stand-alone basis in separate chapters and is not constructed as an integrated textbook. Nevertheless, this handbook contains very useful material for further study of a particular aspect of the European financial system.

How to use this book

Financial Markets and Institutions: A European Perspective is an accessible textbook for both undergraduate and graduate students of Finance, Economics, and Business Administration. Each chapter first gives an overview and identifies learning objectives. Throughout the book we use boxes in which certain issues are explained in more detail, by referring to theory or practical examples. Furthermore, we make abundant use of graphs and tables to give students a comprehensive overview of the European financial system. At the end of each chapter we provide suggestions for further reading. Cambridge University Press provides a supporting website for this book. This website contains exercises (and their solutions) for each chapter. The website also provides regular updates of figures and tables used in the book, and identifies new policy issues.

A basic understanding of finance is needed to use this textbook, as we assume that students are familiar with the basic finance models, such as the standard Capital Asset Pricing Model (CAPM). The book can be used for third-year undergraduate courses as well as for graduate courses. More advanced material for graduate students is contained in special boxes marked by a star (*). Undergraduate students can skip these technical boxes.

Jakob de Haan
Sander Oosterloo
Dirk Schoenmaker

Part I

Setting the Stage

Functions of the Financial System

OVERVIEW

Having a well-functioning financial system in place that directs funds to their most productive uses is a crucial prerequisite for economic development. The financial system consists of all financial intermediaries and financial markets, and their relations with respect to the flow of funds to and from households, governments, business firms, and foreigners, as well as the financial infrastructure.

The main task of the financial system is to channel funds from sectors that have a surplus to sectors that have a shortage of funds. In doing so, the financial sector performs two main functions: (1) reducing information and transaction costs, and (2) facilitating the trading, diversification, and management of risk. These functions are discussed at length in this chapter.

The importance of financial markets and financial intermediaries differs across Member States of the European Union (EU). An important question is how differences in financial systems affect macroeconomic outcomes. Atomistic markets face a free-rider problem: when an investor acquires information about an investment project and behaves accordingly, he reveals this information to all investors, thereby dissuading other investors from devoting resources towards acquiring information. Financial intermediaries may be better able to deal with this problem than financial markets.

This chapter discusses these and other pros and cons of bank-based and market-based systems. A specific element in this debate is the role of corporate governance, i.e. the set of mechanisms arranging the relationship between stakeholders of a firm, notably holders of equity, and the management of the firm. Investors (the outsiders) cannot perfectly monitor managers acting on their behalf since managers (the insiders) have superior information about the performance of the company. So there is a need for certain mechanisms that prevent the insiders of a company using the profits of the firm for their own benefit rather than returning the money to the outside investors. This chapter outlines the various mechanisms in place.

While there is considerable evidence that financial development is good for economic growth, there is no clear evidence that one type of financial system is better for growth than another. However, various recent studies suggest that differences in financial systems may influence the type of activity in which a country specialises. The reason is that different forms of economic activity may be more easily provided by one financial system than another. Likewise, there is some evidence suggesting that in a market-based system households may be better able to smooth consumption in the face of income shocks. However, there is also evidence indicating that a bank-based system is better able to provide inter-temporal smoothing of investment.

In the years before the credit crisis, the banking system in industrial countries saw two major changes. First, the traditional banking model, in which the issuing banks hold loans until they are repaid, was increasingly replaced by the 'originate and distribute' banking model. In this model, banks pool loans (like mortgages) and then tranch and sell them via securitisation. Second, this securitisation led to a non-regulated shadow banking system. The shadow banking system refers to institutions that support bank-style maturity transformation – funding of long-term assets (primarily highly rated tranches of asset-backed securities) with short-term debt – outside banks and without access to a central bank liquidity backstop.

Finally, the chapter discusses the 'law and finance' view according to which legal system differences are key in explaining international differences in financial structure. According to this approach, distinguishing countries by the efficiency of national legal systems in supporting financial transactions is more useful than distinguishing countries by whether they have bank-based or market-based financial systems.

LEARNING OBJECTIVES

After you have studied this chapter, you should be able to:
- explain the main functions of a financial system
- differentiate between the roles of financial markets and financial intermediaries
- explain why financial development may stimulate economic growth
- explain why government regulation and supervision of the financial system is needed
- describe the advantages and disadvantages of bank-based and market-based financial systems
- explain the various corporate governance mechanisms
- describe recent changes in the banking system of several industrial countries
- explain the 'law and finance' view.

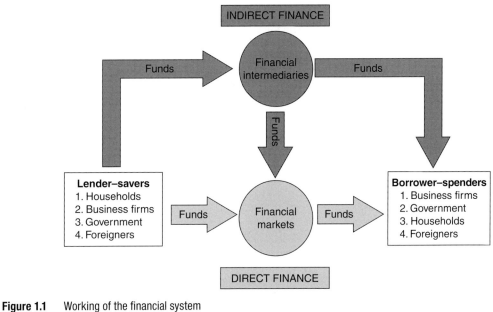

Figure 1.1   Working of the financial system
Source: Mishkin (2006)

1.1 Functions of a financial system

The financial system

This section explains why financial development matters for economic welfare. To understand the importance of financial development, the essentials of a country's *financial system* will first be outlined. The financial system encompasses all financial intermediaries and financial markets, and their relations with respect to the flow of funds to and from households, governments, business firms, and foreigners, as well as the financial infrastructure. *Financial infrastructure* is the set of institutions that enables effective operation of financial intermediaries and financial markets, including such elements as payment systems, credit information bureaus, and collateral registries.

The main task of the financial system is to channel funds from sectors that have a surplus to sectors that have a shortage of funds. Figure 1.1 offers a schematic diagram explaining the working of the financial system.

Sectors that have saved and are lending funds are on the left, and those that must borrow to finance their spending are on the right. *Direct finance* occurs if a sector in need of funds borrows from another sector via a financial market. A *financial market* is a market where participants issue and trade securities. This direct finance route is shown at the bottom of Figure 1.1. With *indirect finance*, a financial intermediary obtains funds from savers and uses these savings to make loans to a sector in need of finance. *Financial intermediaries* are coalitions of agents that combine to provide financial services, such as banks, insurance companies, finance companies, mutual funds, pension funds, etc. (Levine, 1997). This indirect finance route is shown at the top of Figure 1.1. In most countries, indirect finance is the main route for moving funds from lenders to borrowers. These countries have a *bank-based system*, while countries that rely more on financial markets have a *market-based system*.

Figure 1.2 shows the relative importance of credit finance, equity finance, and bond finance in the euro area, Japan, and the United States over the period 2005–2009. Clearly, in the euro area, banks are the most important source of finance, accounting for more than equity finance and bond finance put together. In the United States, bank credit accounts for less than 20 per cent of total finance, and private bond finance for almost 50 per cent. In Japan, credit finance and stock-market finance are more or less equally large (ECB, 2011).

The financial system transforms household savings into funds available for investment by firms. However, the importance of financial markets and financial intermediaries differs across Member States of the EU, as will be explained in some detail in this chapter. Also, the types of assets held by households differ among the various European countries. Despite all these differences, there is one feature that is common to all the financial systems in these countries and that is the importance of *internal finance*. Most investments by firms in industrial countries are financed through retained earnings, regardless of the relative importance of financial markets and intermediaries (Allen and Gale, 2000).

The past 30 years have seen revolutionary changes in the structure of the world's financial markets and institutions. Some financial markets have become obsolete, while new ones have emerged. Similarly, some financial institutions have gone bankrupt, while new entrants have emerged. However, the functions of the financial system have been more stable than the markets and institutions used to accomplish these functions (Merton, 1995). This first chapter of the book discusses at length the functions of the financial system. The later chapters discuss the changes in the financial markets and financial institutions in Europe.

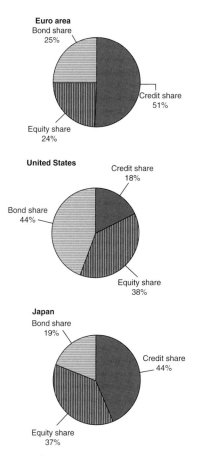

Figure 1.2   Relative shares of credit, equity, and bond finance in the euro area, US, and Japan, 2005–2009
Source: ECB (2011)

At times, major disruptions occur in the financial system which are characterised by sharp declines in asset prices and the failure of financial intermediaries. Such financial crises have been a feature of capitalist economies for hundreds of years. Often they are followed by severe economic downturns. Chapter 2 will discuss financial crises, zooming in on the most recent banking and debt crises which have hit the euro area since 2008.

Having a well-functioning financial system in place that directs funds to their most productive uses is a crucial prerequisite for economic development. If sectors with surplus funds cannot channel their money to sectors with good investment opportunities, many productive investments will never take place. Indeed, cross-country, case-study, industry- and firm-level analyses suggest that the functioning of financial systems is vitally linked to economic growth. Specifically, countries with larger banks and more active stock markets grow faster over subsequent decades, even after controlling for many other factors underlying economic growth (Levine, 2005). Box 1.1 discusses some studies coming to this conclusion.

Box 1.1   Financial development and economic growth

King and Levine (1993a, 1993b) were among the first to argue that financial development is related to economic development. King and Levine (1993b) suggest that current financial depth can predict economic growth over the consequent 10–30 years and conclude that 'better financial systems stimulate faster productivity growth and growth in per capita output by funnelling society's resources to promising productivity-enhancing endeavours' (King and Levine, 1993b, p. 540).

Rajan and Zingales (1998) argue that financial development should be most relevant to industries that depend on external finance and that these industries should grow fastest in countries with well-developed financial systems. They therefore focus on 36 individual industries in 41 countries and analyse the influence of the interaction between the external financial dependence of those industries and the financial development of the countries on the growth rates of those industries in the different countries over the period 1980 to 1990. Using various measures of financial development of a country (the ratio of market capitalisation to GDP, domestic credit to the private sector over GDP, and accounting standards), they report a strong relation between economic growth in different industries and countries and the interaction of financial development of countries and the financial dependence of industries. Rajan and Zingales (1998, p. 584) conclude that their results 'suggest that financial development has a substantial supportive influence on the rate of economic growth and this works, at least partly, by reducing the cost of external finance to financially dependent firms'.

Papaioannou (2008) points out that evidence based on cross-country cross-sectional regressions faces various problems in establishing causality. First, it is almost impossible to account for all possible factors that may foster growth. Second, the effect of financial development may be heterogeneous across countries. Third, there can be reverse causation: financial development can be both the cause and the consequence of economic growth. Finally, the indicators of financial development as generally used in these studies (such as private domestic credit to GDP and market capitalisation as a share of GDP) lack a sound theoretical basis.

Other important studies include Levine *et al.* (2000), who address the endogeneity problems inherent in finance and growth regressions, and the papers in Demirgüç-Kunt and Levine (2001) that use a number of different econometric techniques on datasets ranging from micro-level firm data to international comparative studies. All these studies, and many others, report evidence that financial development stimulates economic growth (Levine, 2005; Papaioannou, 2008).

However, some other studies voice concerns about this conclusion. For instance, Driffill (2003) questions the robustness of some well-known studies, arguing that a number of results hinge on the inclusion of outliers, while the inclusion of regional dummies, especially those for the Asian Tigers, also renders coefficients on financial development insignificant. Trew (2006) argues that most empirical evidence on the finance-growth nexus is disconnected from theories suggesting why financial development affects growth.

Main functions

Let us focus on the two main *functions of the financial system*, i.e. (1) reducing information and transaction costs, and (2) facilitating the trading, diversification, and management of risk, to explain why the financial sector may stimulate capital formation and/or technological innovation, two of the driving forces of economic growth.

Reducing information asymmetry and transaction costs

The financial system helps overcome an information asymmetry between borrowers and lenders. An information asymmetry can occur ex ante and ex post, i.e. before and after a financial contract has been agreed upon. The ex-ante information asymmetry arises because borrowers generally know more about their investment projects than lenders. Borrowers most eager to engage in a transaction are the most likely ones to produce an undesirable outcome for the lender (*adverse selection*). It is difficult and costly to evaluate potential borrowers. Individual savers may not have the time, capacity, or means to collect and process information on a wide array of potential borrowers. So high information costs may keep funds from flowing to their highest productive use. Financial intermediaries may reduce the costs of acquiring and processing information and thereby improve resource allocation (see Chapters 9, 10, and 11). Without intermediaries, each investor would face the large fixed cost associated with evaluating investment projects. Also, financial markets may reduce information costs (see Chapter 5). Economising on information-acquisition costs facilitates the gathering of information about investment opportunities and thereby improves resource allocation. Besides identifying the best investments, financial intermediaries may boost the rate of technological innovation by identifying those entrepreneurs with the best chances of successfully initiating new goods and production processes (Levine, 2005).

The information asymmetry problem occurs ex post when borrowers, but not investors, can observe actual behaviour. Once a loan has been granted, there is a risk that the borrower will engage in activities that are undesirable from the perspective of the lender (*moral hazard*). Financial markets and intermediaries also mitigate the information acquisition and enforcement costs of monitoring borrowers. For example, equity holders and banks will create financial arrangements that compel managers to manage the firm in their best interest (see section 1.2 for more details).

Furthermore, the financial system reduces the time and money spent in carrying out financial transactions (*transaction costs*). Financial intermediaries can reduce transaction costs as they have developed expertise and can take advantage of economies of scale and scope. A good example of how the financial system reduces transaction costs is *pooling*, i.e. the (costly) process of agglomerating capital from disparate savers for investment. By pooling the funds of various small savers, large investment projects can be financed. Without pooling, savers would have to buy and sell entire firms (Levine, 1997). Mobilising savings involves (1) overcoming the transaction costs associated with collecting savings from different individuals, and (2) overcoming the informational asymmetries associated with making savers feel comfortable in relinquishing control of their savings (Levine, 2005).

By reducing information and transaction costs, financial systems lower the cost of channelling funds between borrowers and lenders, which frees up resources for other uses, such as investment and innovation. In addition, financial intermediation affects capital accumulation by allocating funds to their most productive uses. However, higher returns on investment ambiguously affect saving rates, as the income and substitution effects work in opposite directions. A higher return makes saving more attractive (substitution effect), but fewer savings are needed to receive the same returns (income effect). Similarly, lower risk – to which we will turn below – also ambiguously affects savings rates. Thus, the improved resource allocation and lower risk brought about by the financial system may lower saving rates (Levine, 2005).

Trading, diversification, and management of risk

The second main service the financial sector provides is facilitating the trading, diversification, and management of risk. Financial systems may mitigate the risks associated with individual investment projects by providing opportunities for trading and diversifying risk which – in the end – may affect long-run economic growth. In general, high-return projects tend to be riskier than low-return projects. Thus, financial systems that make it easier for people to diversify risk by offering a broad range of high-risk (like equity) and low-risk (like government bonds) investment opportunities tend to induce a portfolio shift towards projects with higher expected returns. Likewise, the ability to hold a diversified portfolio of innovative projects reduces risk and promotes investment in growth-enhancing innovative activities (Levine, 2005).

One particular way in which financial intermediaries and markets reduce risk is by providing *liquidity*, i.e. the ease and speed with which agents can convert assets into purchasing power at agreed prices (Levine, 1997). Savers are generally unwilling to delegate control over their savings to investors for long periods, so less investment is likely to occur in high-return projects that require a long-term commitment of capital. However, the financial system creates the possibility for savers to hold liquid assets – like equity, bonds, or demand deposits – that they can sell quickly and easily if they seek access to their savings, simultaneously transforming these liquid financial instruments into long-term capital investments. Without a financial system, all investors would be locked into illiquid long-term investments that yield high payoffs only to those who consume at the end of the investment. Liquidity is created by financial intermediaries as well as financial markets. For instance, a bank transforms short-term liquid deposits into long-term illiquid loans, therefore making it possible for households to withdraw deposits without interrupting industrial production. Similarly, stock markets reduce liquidity risks by allowing stock holders to trade their shares, while firms still have access to long-term capital.

Risk measurement and management is a key function of financial intermediaries. The traditional role of banks in monitoring the credit risk of borrowers has evolved towards the use of advanced models by all types of financial intermediaries to measure and manage financial risks. Progress in information technology has facilitated the development of advanced risk-management models, which rely on statistical methods to process financial data (see Chapters 10 and 11 for more details).

Securitisation is an important means for the financial system to perform the function of trading, diversification, and management of risk. *Securitisation* is the packaging of particular assets and the redistribution of these packages by selling securities, backed by these assets, to investors (see also section 1.3). For instance, an intermediary may create a pool of mortgage loans (bundling) and then issue bonds backed by those mortgage loans (unbundling). Securitisation thereby converts illiquid assets into liquid assets. While residential mortgages were the first financial assets to be securitised, many other types of financial assets have undergone the same process. A recent example is so-called catastrophe bonds (also known as cat bonds). If insurers have built up a portfolio of risks by insuring properties in a region that may be hit by a catastrophe, they could create a special-purpose entity that would issue the cat bond (see Chapter 11 for more details). Investors who buy the bond make a healthy return on their investment, unless a catastrophe, like a hurricane or an earthquake, hits the region, because then the principal initially paid by the investors is forgiven and is used by the sponsors to pay their claims to policy holders.

Role of government

A well-functioning financial system requires particular government actions. First, government regulation is needed to protect *property rights* and to *enforce* contracts. Property rights refer to control of the use of the property, the right to any benefit from the property, the right to transfer or sell the property, and the right to exclude others from the property. Absence of secure property rights and enforcement of contracts severely restrict financial transactions and investment, thereby hampering financial development. If it is not clear who is entitled to perform a transaction, exchange will be unlikely. As the financial system allocates capital across time and space, contracts are needed to connect providers and users of funds. If one of the parties does not adhere to the content of a contract, an independent enforcement agency (for instance, a court) is needed; otherwise contracts would be useless.

Second, government regulation is needed to encourage proper information provision (*transparency*) so that providers of funds can take better decisions on how to allocate their money. Government regulation can reduce adverse selection and moral hazard problems in financial systems and enhance their efficiency by increasing the amount of information available to investors, for instance by setting and enforcing accounting standards. Although government regulation to increase transparency is crucial to reducing adverse selection and moral hazard problems, borrowers have strong incentives to cheat, so government regulation may not always be sufficient, as various corporate scandals, such as WorldCom, Parmalat, and Ahold, illustrate.

Third, in view of the importance of financial intermediaries, government should arrange for regulation and supervision of financial institutions in order to ensure their *soundness*. Savers are often unable to properly evaluate the financial soundness of a financial intermediary as that requires extensive effort and technical knowledge. Financial intermediaries have an incentive to take too many risks. This is because high-risk investments generally bring in more revenues that accrue to the intermediary, while if the intermediary fails a substantial part of the costs will be borne by the depositors. Government regulation may prevent financial intermediaries from taking too much risk. Depositors may also be protected by introducing some deposit-insurance system, but this may provide the intermediary with an even stronger incentive for risky behaviour. Finally, there is a risk that a sound financial intermediary may fail when another intermediary goes bankrupt due to taking too much risk (*contagion*). Since the public cannot distinguish between sound and unsound financial institutions, they may withdraw their money once a financial intermediary fails, thereby perhaps destroying a sound institution. Chapter 12 discusses *financial supervision* in the EU, while Chapter 13 deals with *financial stability* in the EU. The latter can be defined as a situation in which the financial system is capable of withstanding shocks and the unravelling of financial imbalances, thereby mitigating the likelihood of disruptions in the financial-intermediation process, which are severe enough to significantly impair the allocation of savings to profitable investment opportunities (ECB, 2006). An important prerequisite for financial stability is a well-functioning financial infrastructure, which is discussed in Chapter 7.

Finally, governments are responsible for *competition policy* to ensure competition. There are many ways that competition may be hampered. For instance, competitors may agree to sell the same product or service at the same price (*price fixing*), leading to profits for all the sellers. Another example is that banks may receive support from the government (*state aid*), leading to an unfair advantage over their competitors. In the EU, competition policy is based on the Treaty on the Functioning of the European Union, particularly Articles 101 (Restrictive practices), 102 (Abuse of dominant market power), and 107 (State aid control). The Treaty states: 'The following shall be prohibited …: (a) directly or indirectly fix purchase or selling prices … (b) limit or control production … (c) share markets or sources of supply.…' Chapter 14 provides further details on EU competition policy for the financial sector.

Foreign participants

Figure 1.1 assumes that foreigners also participate in the financial system and that domestic sectors can borrow from or lend to foreigners. What are the benefits if it becomes possible to lend or borrow in foreign financial markets and to do business with foreign financial intermediaries? Following Mishkin (2006), we may differentiate between the direct and indirect effects of (international) *financial liberalisation*, i.e. the opening up of domestic financial markets to foreign capital and foreign financial intermediaries.

Allowing foreign capital to freely enter domestic markets increases the availability of funds, stimulating investment and economic growth. Furthermore, competition in the financial system may be enhanced when foreign financial intermediaries enter a country, stimulating domestic financial intermediaries to become more efficient.[1] Finally, opening up to foreign capital and foreign financial institutions may lead to a constitution for institutional reforms that stimulate financial development (see also Box 1.2). For instance, when domestic financial intermediaries lose customers to foreign intermediaries, they may support institutional reforms, such as improved transparency regulation, helping them to compete better (Mishkin, 2006).

As will be explained in some detail in Chapter 3, the EU has gone beyond financial liberalisation and has taken various steps to promote the creation of a single market for financial services. Chapter 6 will analyse *financial market integration* in the EU. According to Baele *et al.* (2008), a market for a given set of financial instruments or services is fully integrated when all potential market participants in such a market (1) are subject to a single set of rules when they decide to deal with those financial instruments or services, (2) have equal access to this set of financial instruments or services, and (3) are treated equally when they operate in the market.

Box 1.2 The political economy of financial reform

Reform of the financial system may foster financial development, which, in turn, may stimulate economic growth. For instance, Bekeart *et al.* (2005) study countries that liberalised their equity markets in the period 1980–1997. They report that these policies resulted in an overall increase of the annual per-capita GDP growth of approximately 1 per cent. This finding is robust to controlling for other reforms, such as capital-account liberalisation.

Some countries have reformed earlier and also more extensively than others. What explains these policy differences? A small but highly relevant line of research has examined the forces driving financial reform. The basis of the analysis is that there are winners and losers in financial reform. The status quo will persist as long as the benefits of no reform outweigh the costs of no reform for those who determine the timing and pace of policies. Fernandez and Rodrik (1991) explain the tendency to retain the status quo on the basis of uncertainty faced by individuals with respect to the benefits of the reform. If it is not known ex ante who will benefit from reform, a majority may oppose the policy change even if they will benefit ex post from reform. So even if some of the existing financial institutions may prosper after the reform, uncertainty regarding the identities of the winners and losers may cause the sector as a whole to oppose the reform. Learning, made possible by the accumulation of new information, is particularly relevant in this context (Abiad and Mody, 2005). If the reform takes place in various stages, then early reform may help agents assess whether they will benefit or lose so that they may change their views. Consequently, some agents who initially opposed reforms may become advocates for further reforms.

Abiad and Mody (2005) use a newly constructed financial-reform index, covering 35 countries over the period 1973–1996, to examine the driving forces of financial reform. The index captures six dimensions of financial liberalisation, including the degree of controls on international financial transactions. On each dimension, a country is classified as being fully repressed, partially repressed, largely liberalised, or fully liberalised. When they relate their index to various explanatory variables, Abiad and Mody (2005) find that countries with highly repressed financial sectors tend to stay that way, but once reforms are initiated, the likelihood of additional reforms increases. This suggests that learning plays an important role. Also, the occurrence of crises plays a role. While balance-of-payments crises tend to increase the likelihood of financial reforms, banking crises tend to increase the likelihood of reversals of reform. According to Abiad and Mody (2005), left-wing and right-wing governments are seen to operate similarly in similar situations, and openness to trade does not, on average, increase the pace of reform.

1.2 Bank-based versus market-based financial systems

There are important differences among the financial systems of the Member States of the EU. For instance, the size of financial markets and the importance of bank and non-bank financial intermediaries (such as mutual funds, private pension funds, and insurance companies) differ substantially across countries. Figure 1.3 shows that banks play a major role in the EU followed by stock markets. Of course, the new Member States (NMS-12) differ significantly from the 'old' Member States (EU-15). Figure 1.3 illustrates that the financial system is more developed in the old Member States and that

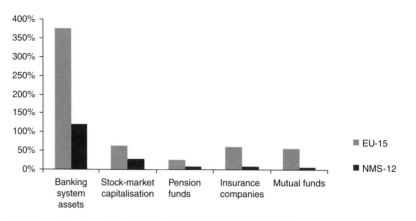

Figure 1.3   The financial system in the EU-15 and the NMS-12 (% GDP), 2009
Source: ECB, FESE

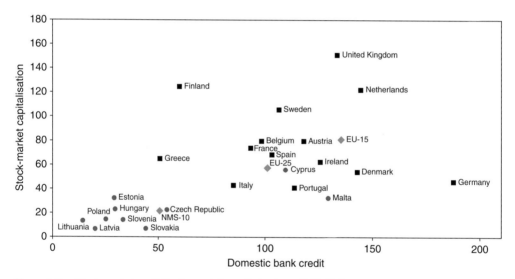

Figure 1.4   Stock-market capitalisation and domestic bank credit (% GDP), 1995–2004
Source: Allen *et al.* (2006)

non-bank financial intermediaries play almost no role in the new Member States. Financing is almost exclusively provided by banks and stock markets in the latter group of countries. However, also in the old Member States (EU-15) there are major differences, as illustrated by Figure 1.4. For instance, average stock-market capitalisation as a ratio to GDP during 1995–2004 was 150 per cent in the United Kingdom, while in Portugal stock-market capitalisation amounted to only 40 per cent. Similarly, over the same period,

German bank credit was 188 per cent of GDP, while in Greece this ratio was around only 51 per cent.

A key question is how these differences in financial systems affect macro-economic outcomes. For instance, do bank-based financial systems (like that of Germany) lead to higher rates of economic growth than market-based systems (like that of the UK)? The post-war high growth rates of Germany and Japan – where banks are dominant in the financial system – were often considered as 'evidence' that bank-based systems outperform market-based systems. However, more detailed empirical work, using micro-level data, has frequently failed to identify the superiority of bank-based systems. Also, the much better growth performance of Anglo-American countries during the 1990s raised scepticism about the acclaimed advantages of bank-based systems (Carlin and Mayer, 2000).

Providing financial functions

What are the theoretical reasons explaining differences in the growth performance of countries with bank-based or market-based systems? As Levine (2005) pointed out, the case for a bank-based system refers to the role of markets in providing financial functions. Atomistic markets face a *free-rider problem*: when an investor acquires information about an investment project and behaves accordingly, he reveals this information to all investors, thereby dissuading other investors from devoting resources towards acquiring information. So investors do not have strong incentives to properly acquire information as they cannot keep the benefits of this information. Consequently, innovative projects that foster growth may not be identified. Banks, however, may keep the information they acquire, often by having long-run relationships with firms, and use it in a profitable way. Since banks can make investments without revealing their decisions immediately in public markets, they have the right incentives to do research on investment projects. Furthermore, banks with close ties to firms may be more effective than atomistic markets at exerting pressure on firms to repay their loans. Often, firms obtain a variety of financial services from their bank and also maintain checking accounts with it, thereby increasing the bank's information about the borrower. For example, the bank can learn about the firm's sales by monitoring the cash flowing through its checking account or by factoring the firm's accounts receivables. Firms may profit from these long-term relationships in the form of access to credit at lower prices.[2]

The problem of free riding that occurs due to diffuse shareholders may be less in the case of large, concentrated ownership. In some countries,

Table 1.1 The median size of largest voting blocks, 1999

Country	Number of companies	Median largest voting block (%)
Austria	50	52.0
Belgium	121	50.6
France	40	20.0
Germany	374	52.1
Italy	216	54.5
Netherlands	137	43.5
Spain	193	34.2
United Kingdom	250	9.9
United States	4,140	<5

Source: Becht and Roëll (1999)

ownership of firms is very concentrated. Table 1.1 shows the median of the largest voting block of listed companies in 1999. It is clear that there are no meaningful voting blocks in the UK and the US due to dispersed ownership. By contrast, in continental Europe there are large voting blocks, sometimes even a majority block of over 50 per cent.[3] In these countries, mostly with a bank-based system, shareholders can control the company directly.

However, concentrated owners may maximise the private benefits of control at the expense of minority shareholders. Furthermore, large equity owners may stimulate the firm to undertake higher-risk activities since shareholders benefit on the upside, while debt holders share the costs of failure. Finally, concentrated control of corporate assets produces market power that may distort public policies (Levine, 2005). Empirical evidence does not suggest that international differences in concentrated ownership are associated with disciplining firms' management (Carlin and Mayer, 2000).

Corporate governance

A second element in the debate on the pros and cons of bank-based vs. market-based systems refers to *corporate governance*, i.e. the set of mechanisms arranging the relationship between stakeholders of a firm, notably holders of equity, and the management of the firm. Principal-agent theory predicts that the managers, the agents, may not always act in the best interest of the owners, the principal (Jensen and Meckling, 1976). Investors (the outsiders) cannot perfectly monitor managers acting on their behalf since managers (the insiders) have superior information about the performance of the company. So there is a need for certain mechanisms that prevent the insiders of a company using the profits of the firm for their own benefit rather than returning the money to the outside investors. Corporate governance systems differ across the EU Member States (see Box 1.3).

Box 1.3 Corporate governance in EU Member States

Governance Metrics International (GMI) publishes ratings of the corporate governance of firms on a scale of 1.0 (lowest) to 10.0 (highest). Each GMI rating report includes a summary of the company's overall governance profile and commentary on each of the six research categories employed by GMI: board accountability, financial disclosure and internal controls, shareholder rights, executive compensation, market for control and ownership base, and corporate-behaviour and corporate-social-responsibility issues. All company ratings are calculated relative to the 3,400+ companies rated by GMI worldwide ('global rating'). A GMI rating of 9.0 or higher is considered to be well above average. A rating of 7.5–8.5 is considered to be above average, 6.0–7.0 is considered average, 3.5–5.5 is considered to be below average, and 3.0 or less is considered well below average.

The number of firms with a GMI rating differs across countries – ranging from 14 for Poland to 394 for the UK. Figure 1.5 shows the average GMI score for various EU Member States. The figure shows that the corporate governance regimes differ substantially. While the average score for Spain (14 firms) is only 3.97, in the UK it amounts to 7.60.

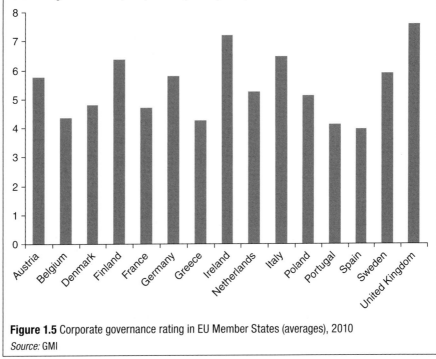

Figure 1.5 Corporate governance rating in EU Member States (averages), 2010
Source: GMI

Investors can use several tools to ensure that the management of a firm acts in their interest. The most important of these are the appointment of the board of directors, executive compensation, the market for corporate control, concentrated holdings, and monitoring by financial intermediaries (Allen and Gale, 2000).

By appointing the board of directors,[4] shareholders have an instrument to control managers and ensure that the firm is run in their interest. The way that boards are chosen differs across countries. In many countries, the management of the firm effectively determines who is nominated for the board, so that an incestuous relationship may blossom between boards of directors and management (Jensen, 1993). Boards may, for instance, approve various protection mechanisms that reduce the attractiveness of a takeover, one of the mechanisms in the market for corporate control (see below).

A second method of ensuring that managers pursue the interests of shareholders is to structure executive compensation appropriately. By making managers' compensation depend on the firm's performance, shareholders can provide incentives for the management of the firm. Examples include direct ownership of shares, stock options, and bonuses dependent on the share price. However, contingent compensation may also have a less desirable effect. If the managers' compensation is sensitive to the performance of the firm, they will have an incentive to take excessive risks as they benefit greatly from good performance, while the penalties for poor performance are limited (Allen and Gale, 2000).

Probably the most important mechanism to control firm management is the market for corporate control that can operate in three ways: proxy contests, friendly mergers and takeovers, and hostile takeovers. In *proxy contests*, a shareholder tries to persuade other shareholders to act in concert with him and force the management of the firm to change course or even to unseat the board of directors. Whether proxy contests work depends, among other things, on the dispersion of shareholding. *Friendly mergers and takeovers* occur when the management of both firms agree that combining the firms would create additional value. The transaction can occur in various ways, such as an exchange of stock or a tender offer by one firm for the other firm's stock (Allen and Gale, 2000).

The potentially most important device in the market for corporate control forcing managers to behave in accordance with the interests of stock holders is a hostile takeover. A *takeover bid* is an attempt by a potential acquirer to obtain a controlling block of shares in a target firm, and thereby gain control of the board and, through it, the firm's management. If a firm does not exploit all of its growth potential, some outsiders may consider the firm an attractive takeover target. After a takeover, they will try to improve the performance of the firm by replacing the current management. This threat gives managers the right incentives to behave in the interest of current stock holders. However, a takeover threat may not be effective for various reasons. First, a takeover threat may not work well due to the information asymmetry between insiders and outsiders: ill-informed outsiders will outbid relatively well-informed insiders for control of firms only when they pay too much. Second, there may again be a free-rider problem. If an outsider spends resources obtaining information, other market participants will observe the results of this research when the outsider bids for shares of the firm. Third, firms often take various actions that deter takeovers and thereby weaken the market as a disciplining device. For instance, a firm may issue rights to existing shareholders to acquire a large number of new securities.

Since the market for corporate control may not always ensure that managers behave in accordance with the interest of shareholders, proponents of a bank-based system argue that monitoring by financial institutions may be more effective in this regard. The agency problem is solved by financial institutions acting as the outside monitor for firms (Allen and Gale, 2000). The main characteristics of this system are a long-term relationship between banks – but potentially also other financial intermediaries like institutional investors (see Chapter 9) – and firms, the holding of both equity and debt by the financial intermediary, and the active intervention by the financial intermediary should the firm become financially distressed.

The case for a market-based system focuses on the problems created by powerful banks. While firms with close ties to a 'main bank' have greater access to capital and are less cash constrained than firms without such a bank, the dependence on an influential bank may have various negative effects. Bankers act in their own best interests, not necessarily in the best interests of all stakeholders. For instance, banks with power can extract part of the expected future profits from potentially profitable investments, which may reduce the firm's effort to undertake innovative investments. Influential banks may also prevent outsiders from removing inefficient managers if these managers are particularly generous to the bankers. Bank managers may also be more reluctant to bankrupt firms with which they have had long-term ties (Levine, 2005).

Furthermore, there may be difficulties in governing banks themselves. The information asymmetries between bank insiders and outsiders may be larger than with non-financial corporations. Therefore, banks are even more likely than non-financial firms to have a large, controlling owner.

Finally, proponents of market-based financial systems claim that markets provide a richer set of instruments to manage risks. While bank-based systems may provide inexpensive, basic risk-management services for standardised situations, market-based systems provide greater flexibility to tailor make products.

Types of activity

While there is considerable evidence that financial development is good for economic growth, there is no clear evidence that one kind of financial system is better for growth than another. For instance, Levine (2002) finds that the quality of the financial services produced by the entire financial system (intermediaries and markets) matters for economic growth. However, various recent studies suggest that differences in financial systems may influence the type of activity in which a country specialises. The reason is that different forms of economic activity may be more easily provided by one financial system than the other. Box 1.4 summarises a study providing support for this view.

Box 1.4 Does the financial system matter after all?

To pursue the hypothesis that different financial systems might favour industries with different kinds of characteristics, Carlin and Mayer (2003) examine the interrelation between types of systems, the nature of different industries, and the levels of activity in those industries in different countries. They evaluate whether there is a relationship between the growth rates of industries in different countries and the interaction between country structures (e.g. the degree of market and bank orientation of their financial systems) and industry characteristics (the dependence of industries on external equity or bank-debt sources of finance and inputs of skilled labour). The sample comprises 14 OECD countries and 27 industries over the period from 1970 to 1995. The financial structure of different countries is measured by the size of their stock markets, accounting standards, the ratio of bank credit to GDP, and the degree of bank ownership of corporate equity. The structure of corporate systems is captured by the degree of concentration of ownership and by the extent of pyramid ownership. The characteristics of legal systems are measured by indicators of legal protection of investors or creditors and by the common- or civil-law origin of the legal system as indicated by its source in English, German, Scandinavian, or French law (see below). Carlin and Mayer report strong evidence of a relation between industry growth rates in different countries and the interaction of country financial structures with industry characteristics. Market-oriented financial systems are associated with high growth of external equity-financed and skill-intensive industries. The effect comes through investment in R&D rather than fixed capital expenditures.

Economies of scale in monitoring make banks more efficient monitors than individual market participants. However, securities markets have the advantage of aggregating diverse views of a large number of market participants and are therefore more likely to support activities where there is a high degree of uncertainty in production, while banks are more likely to support activities in which uncertainty is low but gestation periods are long (Carlin and Mayer, 2000). Banks may be effective at eliminating duplication of information gathering and processing, but may not be effective gatherers and processors of information in new, uncertain situations involving innovative products and processes, in which case securities markets work better. Similarly, Dewatripont and Maskin (1995) argue that banks will find it difficult to credibly commit not to renegotiate contracts in the case of long-run contacts with firms. The credible imposition of tight budget constraints may be necessary for the funding of newer, higher-risk firms.

Other differences

In practice, financial systems are always a mixture of financial markets and financial intermediaries. The IMF (2006) classifies financial systems using the degree to which financial transactions are conducted on the basis of a direct (and generally longer-term) relationship between two entities, usually a bank and a customer, or are conducted at 'arm's-length', where parties concerned typically do not have any special knowledge about each other that is not available publicly. The IMF has constructed a Financial Index, ranging between 0 and 1, with a higher value representing a greater 'arm's-length' content in the financial system (i.e. it is more market-based).[5] Figure 1.6 shows the IMF Financial Index.

The Financial Index suggests that despite an increase in the arm's-length content of financial systems across advanced economies, important differences remain. Indeed, the increase in the index has generally been larger for those countries with relatively high values already in 1995. Thus, there is little evidence of convergence. This variation in the Financial Index across countries is indicative of important differences in the way financial systems perform their intermediation function. In countries with more arm's-length content, a larger share of household and firm financing takes place through financial markets.

According to the IMF (2006), the degree of arm's-length transactions in a financial system may affect household behaviour. A large body of empirical evidence shows that private consumption is sensitive to changes in current income, contrary to the implications of the permanent income hypothesis.

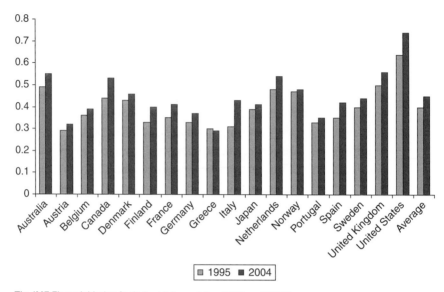

Figure 1.6   The IMF Financial Index for industrial countries, 1995 and 2004
Source: IMF (2006)

This finding of 'excess sensitivity' of consumption to current income has most often been attributed to borrowing constraints faced by households, implying that as borrowing constraints ease, consumption can be expected to become less sensitive to current income. In a more arm's-length financial system, households may be better able to smooth consumption in the face of income shocks. In such systems, investors can price collateral more effectively in a liquid market and acquire financial claims on a diversified pool of borrowers. The IMF (2006) provides some evidence that countries with more arm's-length systems tend to exhibit a lower correlation between consumption and current income growth, suggesting a greater degree of consumption smoothing. Figure 1.7 is reproduced here from the IMF study. The figure shows the correlation between consumption and current income growth and the Financial Index. There is a negative relationship that is significant. This finding is consistent with the notion that consumers in countries with a more arm's-length financial system are better able to smooth consumption in the face of changes in their income.

The IMF (2006) also presents evidence that the degree of arm's-length transactions in a financial system may affect investment behaviour. During normal business-cycle downturns, financial systems with a lower degree of arm's-length transactions (and a higher degree of relationship-based lending)

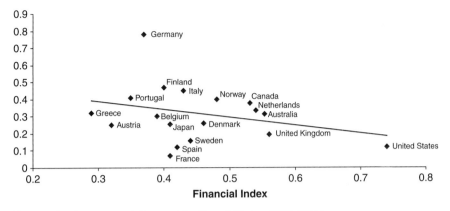

Figure 1.7   Consumption-income correlations and the Financial Index, 1985–2005
Source: IMF (2006)

could be expected to give greater weight to the long-term gains from maintaining an existing relationship with a borrower by providing short-term assurance that financing will be available in the event of a temporary disruption in cash flow, particularly as the lender's own balance sheet is on average more exposed to the borrower. Providing financing to ride out such temporary downturns may not be in the interest of the borrower only but also of the lender. The capital buffer of the bank (as lender) then absorbs part of the losses caused by the downturn. Allen and Gale (2000) also argue that a bank-based system is better able to provide inter-temporal smoothing of investment (and thereby the wider economy) than a market-based system. This is illustrated in Figure 1.8, also taken from the IMF (2006) study. The response of the business investment to business cycles is smoother for countries in the lower half of the Financial Index (more relationship-based).

Complements

Some authors argue that financial markets and financial intermediaries may provide complementary growth-enhancing financial services to the economy. Intermediaries may be necessary for the successful functioning of markets. A historical perspective shows that financial markets did not develop spontaneously. The earliest financial transactions involving loans were handled by financial intermediaries. It was not until the Amsterdam Bourse was founded at the start of the seventeenth century that anything like a formal financial market existed (Allen and Gale, 2000). Stock markets

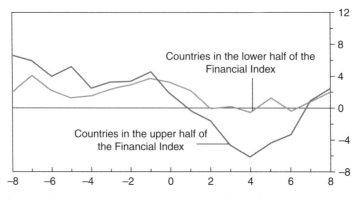

Figure 1.8   Business investment response to business cycles (per cent change year-on-year; constant prices),
1985–2005
Source: IMF (2006)

may complement banks by spurring competition for corporate control and
by offering alternative means of financing investment, thereby reducing the
potentially harmful effects of excessive bank power. Indeed, banks have
increasingly moved away from their traditional deposit-taking and lending
role into fee-generating activities, such as the securitisation of loans and the
sale of risk-management products (see section 1.3). Financial markets, of
course, also compete with banks. Consumers can invest directly in securities
(government and private bonds, and stocks) rather than leaving their money
in savings accounts, while borrowers can go to the capital markets rather
than to banks. This is often called *dis-intermediation*.

Allen and Santomero (1997) forcefully argue that financial intermediaries reduce what they call *participation costs*, i.e. the costs of learning about
effectively using financial markets as well as participating in them on a day-
to-day basis. As financial markets have become increasingly complex over
time, financial intermediaries offer various services to the uninformed investors, such as providing information, investing on their behalf, or offering a
fixed-income claim against the intermediary's balance sheet. Investors get
access to financial markets through the intermediary's services, which add
value to the transaction by reducing the (perceived) participation costs of
uninformed investors. Allen and Santomero argue that the increase in the
breadth and depth of financial markets has been the result of greater use
of these instruments by financial intermediaries and firms. The increased
size of financial markets has coincided with a dramatic shift away from direct participation by individuals in financial markets towards participation

through various kinds of intermediaries. The importance of different types of intermediary has also undergone a significant change. While the share of assets held by banks has fallen, that of institutional investors has dramatically increased in size (see Chapter 9 for a further analysis). Also, in countries with a bank-dominated financial system, like France and Italy, the role of institutional investors has increased. As a consequence, institutional investors have also become more dominant in corporate governance issues.

Legal systems

Finally, some recent research suggests that legal system differences are key in explaining international differences in financial structure. In this approach, the financial system is a set of contracts that is defined and made more or less effective by legal rights and enforcement mechanisms. A well-functioning legal system facilitates the operation of both financial markets and intermediaries. According to this literature, distinguishing countries by the efficiency of national legal systems in supporting financial transactions is more useful than distinguishing countries by whether they have bank-based or market-based financial systems. La Porta *et al.* (1997) argue that financial systems offer different levels of creditor and shareholder protection depending on the origin of the legal rules in place, i.e. English, French, German, or Scandinavian origin. Common-law countries of the English tradition protect both shareholders and creditors the most, French civil-law countries the least, and German and Scandinavian civil-law countries somewhere in the middle. La Porta *et al.* (1997, p. 1149) find that 'civil law, and particularly French civil law, countries, have both the weakest investor protections and the least developed capital markets, especially as compared to common law countries'.

Table 1.2 summarises some of the measures as developed by La Porta *et al.* (1997) and extended and updated by Djankov *et al.* (2006; 2007) for the EU Member States. Column (2) shows the legal family to which the country belongs. The rationale of the other measures is as follows. Those who control a firm, whether they are managers, controlling shareholders, or both, can use their power to deliver firm wealth to themselves, without sharing it with the other investors. The measures quantify the extent to which various investors are protected. Column (3) presents a creditor rights index that measures powers of secured lenders in bankruptcy (Djankov *et al.*, 2007). The creditor rights index varies between 0 (poor creditor rights) and 4 (strong creditor rights). For their full sample, Djankov *et al.* report that the index of

Table 1.2 Indicators of investor and creditor protection, 2003

(1)	(2)	(3)	(4)	(5)
Country	Law family	Creditor rights	Shareholder rights	Anti-self dealing index
Austria	German	3	2.5	0.21
Belgium	French	2	2	0.54
Bulgaria	German	n.a.	4	0.66
Czech Republic	German	3	4	0.34
Denmark	Scandinavian	3	4	0.47
Finland	Scandinavian	1	3.5	0.46
France	French	0	3	0.38
Germany	German	3	2.5	0.28
Greece	French	1	2	0.23
Hungary	German	1	2	0.20
Ireland	English	1	4	0.79
Italy	French	2	2.5	0.39
Latvia	German	3	3	0.35
Lithuania	French	2	4	0.38
Luxembourg	French	n.a.	1	0.25
Netherlands	French	3	3	0.21
Portugal	French	1	2.5	0.49
Slovakia	German	2	3	0.29
Slovenia	German	3	n.a.	n.a.
Spain	French	2	5	0.37
Sweden	Scandinavian	1	3.5	0.34
United Kingdom	English	4	5	0.93
Average German		2.57	3.00	0.33
Average French		1.63	2.78	0.36
Average English		2.50	4.50	0.55
Average Scandinavian		1.67	3.67	0.42

Note: n.a. means not available
Source: La Porta *et al.* (1997), Djankov *et al.* (2006, 2007)

creditor rights for 2003 is lowest in French legal-origin countries and highest in German legal-origin ones.

Column (4) shows an index reflecting shareholder rights. The original index, reported in La Porta *et al.* (1997), has been criticised by a number of scholars for its ad hoc nature, for mistakes in its coding, and for conceptual ambiguity in the definitions of some of its components. Therefore, Djankov *et al.* (2006) came up with a revised and extended index that is shown in column (4) of Table 1.2. This index is available for 72 countries and is based on laws and regulations applicable to publicly traded firms in May 2003. The index summarises the protection of minority shareholders in the corporate decision-making process, including the right to vote. This index varies between 0 (poor shareholder rights) and 6 (strong shareholder rights). For their full sample, Djankov *et al.* report that the index of shareholder rights is lowest in French legal-origin countries and highest in English legal-origin ones.

A recent alternative measure of shareholder protection quantifies their rights against expropriation by corporate insiders through self-dealing (see Djankov *et al.*, 2006). Various forms of such self-dealing include executive perquisites to excessive compensation, transfer pricing, self-serving financial transactions such as directed equity issuance or personal loans to insiders, and outright theft of corporate assets. This index ranges between 0 (poor protection) and 1 (high protection) and is shown in column (5) of Table 1.2. For their full sample, Djankov *et al.* report that the index is lowest in French legal-origin countries and highest in English legal-origin ones.

Various conclusions can be drawn from Table 1.2. First, the EU Member States clearly have different legal traditions. So, if the finance and law view is correct (see Box 1.5 for some discussion), financial differences in the EU are likely to remain in place, despite attempts to create one single financial market (see Chapter 3 for further details on the various policy initiatives to create such a single market). Second, the various indicators vary widely across EU Member States, suggesting that the degree that investors are protected differs substantially across these countries. For instance, the creditor rights index ranges between 0 (France) and 4 (the UK), while the shareholder index ranges between 1 (Luxembourg) and 5 (Spain and the UK).

1.3 Recent changes

In the years before the financial crisis (which will be discussed in Chapter 2), the banking system in industrial countries saw two major changes. First, the traditional banking model, in which the issuing banks hold loans until they are repaid, was increasingly replaced by the *'originate and distribute'* banking model. As will be explained in more detail below, in this model banks pool loans (like mortgages) and then tranch and sell them via securitisation. Starting with mortgages, securitisation gradually grew to encompass trade

---

Box 1.5 Legal origin or political institutions?

According to the law and finance literature, the financial development of countries can be traced back to their legal origins (La Porta *et al.*, 1997). There is some evidence in support of this view. Beck *et al.* (2001) investigate the relative effects of political arrangements, legal origin, and different historical factors on financial development. They conclude that legal origin offers a substantially stronger explanation of financial development than political conditions. However, Keefer (2007) challenges this conclusion. He uses total credit extended to the private sector by banks and other financial institutions as a measure of financial-sector development. This is the preferred way of Beck *et al.* (2001) to measure financial development. Keefer reports that various political variables, including his measure of political checks and balances (i.e. how many political actors can block proposed legislation, therefore tracking whether formal institutions exist that potentially impose constraints on arbitrary behaviour by the executive branch) and newspaper circulation (a proxy for the extent of voter information), have a significant influence on financial-sector development. More importantly, these variables remain significant determinants of financial-sector development, even controlling for legal origin. In fact, the legal-origin variables often become insignificant once political variables are included in the regression model.

---

receivables, credit card receivables, lease payments, and even future royalty payments.

Second, this securitisation led to a non-regulated *shadow banking system*. The shadow banking system refers to institutions that support bank-style maturity transformation – funding of long-term assets (primarily highly rated tranches of asset-backed securities) with short-term debt – outside banks and without access to a central bank liquidity backstop. It includes hedge funds, investment banks, and other non-depository financial firms. To facilitate securitisation, banks set up off-balance sheet vehicles, like conduits and special purpose vehicles (SPVs). These are shell companies holding financial assets such as securitised mortgages. They generally have no employees or headquarters. Their management is outsourced to an administrator, typically a commercial bank that sets up the conduit in the first place. The administrator manages the asset portfolio according to pre-specified investment guidelines and issues asset-backed commercial paper to finance the conduit's assets. Banks often provided liquidity enhancement and credit enhancement to these off-balance sheet vehicles. So if the quality of their assets deteriorated, the investors in these off-balance sheet vehicles often had recourse to banks. The economic rationale for setting up these vehicles was to reduce capital requirements imposed by bank regulation. Banks were not required to hold up equity capital for these vehicles' assets but instead needed to hold equity against liquidity and credit enhancement provided to them. And these requirements were lower (Acharya and Schnabl, 2009).

Under the 'originate and distribute' model, banks pool and repackage loans and then pass them on to other financial investors (including conduits created for this purpose). Banks create 'structured' products often referred to as *collateralised debt obligations* (CDOs). The first step is to form diversified portfolios of mortgages and other types of loans. The next step is to slice these portfolios into different tranches. These tranches are then sold to investors. The safest tranche – known as the 'super senior tranche' – offers investors a (relatively) low interest rate, but it is the first to be paid out of the cash flows of the portfolio. In contrast, the most junior tranche – referred to as the 'equity tranche', 'toxic waste', or 'stub' – will be paid only after all other tranches have been paid. The mezzanine tranches are between these extremes. In terms of loss absorption, the most junior security, or stub, absorbs the first loss; once this class of security is wiped out, the mezzanine securities bear loss; then the senior securities, and then finally the super-senior securities.

The exact cutoffs between the tranches are typically chosen to ensure a specific rating for each tranche. These ratings are provided by credit rating agencies (see Chapter 8 for further details). For example, the top tranches are constructed to receive the highest rating. The more senior tranches are then sold to various investors, while the issuing bank usually (but not always) holds the toxic waste (see Figure 1.9).

The increasing complexity of securitised credit required that credit rating techniques were applied to new varieties of structured security, where no historic record existed. These ratings proved highly imperfect predictors of risk and were subject to rapid rating downgrades once the crisis broke (see Chapter 2).

Buyers of securitised instruments can protect themselves by purchasing *credit default swaps* (CDSs), which are contracts insuring default. The buyer of these contracts pays a periodic fixed fee in exchange for a contingent payment in the event of credit default. Anyone who purchased a tranche of a collateralised debt obligation with the highest rating combined with a credit default swap had reason to believe that the investment had low risk because the probability of the CDS counterparty defaulting was considered to be small (Brunnermeier, 2009). However, the financial crisis showed them to be wrong (see Chapter 2).

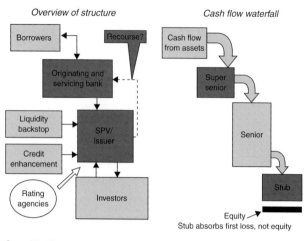

Overview of structure   Cash flow waterfall

Figure 1.9   Securitisation
Source: Huertas (2010)

It was not only via SPVs and conduits that a growing proportion of aggregate maturity transformation has been occurring outside regulated banks with central bank access. Investment banks increasingly funded holdings of long-term to maturity assets with much shorter-term liabilities. In addition, particularly in the US, mutual funds increasingly performed a bank-like form of maturity transformation. They have held long-term credit assets against liabilities to investors which promise immediate redemption (Turner, 2009).

As pointed out by Adrian and Shin (2010), these changes in the financial system of some countries, notably the US, have changed the mode of financial intermediation as well. A characteristic feature of financial intermediation that operates through the capital market is the long chain of financial intermediaries involved in channelling funds from the ultimate creditors to the ultimate borrowers. Figure 1.10, taken from Adrian and Shin (2010), illustrates this by showing one possible chain of lending relationships in a market-based financial system.

In this illustration, banks issue mortgages that are then pooled. These pooled mortgages are then packaged to form mortgage-backed securities (MBSs), which are liabilities issued against the mortgage assets. The MBS might then be owned by an SPV which pools and tranches them into another layer of claims, such as collateralised debt obligations. A securities firm (e.g. an investment bank) might hold collateralised debt obligations on its own books for their yield but will finance such assets by collateralised borrowing through repurchase agreements (i.e. repos) with a larger commercial bank.

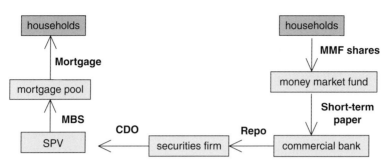

Figure 1.10   Long intermediation chain
Source: Adrian and Shin (2010)

(In a repo, the borrower sells a security today for below the current market price on the understanding that it will buy it back in the future at a pre-agreed price. The difference between the current market price of the security and the price at which it is sold is called the haircut in the repo.) In turn, the commercial bank would fund its lending to the securities firm by issuing short-term liabilities. Money market mutual funds would be natural buyers of such short-term paper, and, ultimately, the money market fund would complete the circle, as household savers would own shares of these funds.

1.4 Conclusions

The financial system encompasses all financial intermediaries and financial markets, and their relations with respect to the flow of funds to and from households, governments, business firms, and foreigners (including the financial infrastructure). The main task of the financial system is to channel funds from sectors that have a surplus to sectors that have a shortage of funds. The importance of financial markets and financial intermediaries differs across Member States of the European Union. However, most investments by firms in the EU are financed through retained earnings, regardless of the relative importance of financial markets and intermediaries.

The financial system helps overcome an information asymmetry between borrowers and lenders. An information asymmetry can occur ex ante and ex post, i.e. before and after a financial contract has been agreed upon. The ex-ante information asymmetry arises because borrowers generally know more about their investment projects than lenders. The ex-post information asymmetry arises because borrowers, but not investors, can observe actual behaviour. Furthermore, the financial system reduces the time and money spent in carrying out financial transactions.

A well-functioning financial system requires particular government actions. First, government regulation is needed to protect property rights and to enforce contracts. Second, government regulation is needed to encourage proper information provision so that providers of funds can take better decisions on how to allocate their money. Third, government should arrange for regulation and supervision of financial institutions in order to ensure their soundness. Finally, governments are responsible for competition policy to ensure competition.

An important question is how differences in financial systems affect macroeconomic outcomes. Atomistic markets face a free-rider problem: when an investor acquires information about an investment project and behaves accordingly, he reveals this information to all investors, thereby dissuading other investors from devoting resources towards acquiring information. Financial intermediaries may be better able to deal with this problem than financial markets.

Another element in the debate on the pros and cons of bank-based vs. market-based systems refers to corporate governance, i.e. the set of mechanisms arranging the relationship between stakeholders of a firm, notably holders of equity, and the management of the firm. Investors (the outsiders) cannot perfectly monitor managers acting on their behalf since managers (the insiders) have superior information about the performance of the company. So there is a need for certain mechanisms that prevent the insiders of a company using the profits of the firm for their own benefit rather than returning the money to the outside investors.

While there is considerable evidence that financial development is good for economic growth, there is no clear evidence that one kind of financial system is better for growth than another. However, various recent studies suggest that differences in financial systems may influence the type of activity in which a country specialises. The reason is that different forms of economic activity may be more easily provided by one financial system than the other. Likewise, there is some evidence suggesting that in financial systems characterised by a greater degree of arm's-length transactions, households seem to be able to smooth consumption more effectively in the face of unanticipated changes in their income, although they may be more sensitive to changes in asset prices. By contrast, financial systems characterised by a greater degree of relationship-based lending are able to smooth business investment more effectively in the face of changes in the business cycle. Table 1.3 summarises these issues.

Some authors argue that financial markets and financial intermediaries provide complementary growth-enhancing financial services to the economy.

Table 1.3 Bank-based vs. market-based financial systems

	Bank-based	Market-based
Economic growth	++	++
High-uncertainty investment	− −	++
Low-uncertainty investment	++	− −
Consumption smoothing	−	+
Investment smoothing	+	−

Intermediaries are necessary for the successful functioning of markets. Due to several recent changes, market-based financial intermediaries have become very important in some countries, notably the US, making the chain of intermediation much longer.

Finally, according to the 'law and finance' view, legal system differences are key in explaining international differences in financial structure. Therefore, distinguishing countries by the efficiency of national legal systems in supporting financial transactions is more useful than distinguishing countries by whether they have bank-based or market-based financial systems.

NOTES

1 Whether competition increases depends on the entry strategy of foreign intermediaries. For instance, if a foreign intermediary acquires various domestic intermediaries and merges them, competition may decrease.

2 Various studies examine this issue. A good example is Petersen and Rajan (1994) who, on the basis of a large-scale sample of US firms with less than 500 employees, found evidence that relationships increase the availability and reduce the price of credit to firms. The empirical results suggest that the availability of finance increases as the firm spends more time in a relationship, as it increases ties to a lender by expanding the number of financial services it buys from it, and as it concentrates its borrowing with the lender.

3 While the median is over 50 per cent for the overall group of 374 companies in Germany, the median for the 30 large companies in the DAX30 is only 11 per cent. Similarly, the relatively low median reported for France relates only to the 40 large companies in the CAC40 (Becht and Roëll, 1999).

4 There are two main types of board of directors. The UK and the US have a so-called one-tier board, which consists of a mix of outside (non-executive) directors and inside (executive) directors, who are the top executives of the firm. The role of management is to implement the business policies that the board has determined. Continental European countries apply the two-tier board system with a supervisory board and a management board. The supervisory board is the controlling body and elected by the shareholders (and

sometimes also by the employees). The management board is appointed by the supervisory board.

5   The interested reader is referred to Appendix 4.1 of IMF (2006) for further details.

SUGGESTED READING

Allen, F. and D. Gale (2000), *Comparing Financial Systems*, MIT Press, Cambridge (MA).

Carlin, W. and C. P. Mayer (2003), Finance, Investment and Growth, *Journal of Financial Economics*, 69(1), 191–226.

Papaioannou, E. (2008), Finance and Growth. A Macroeconomic Assessment of the Evidence from a European Angle, in: X. Freixas, P. Hartmann, and C. Mayer (eds.), *Handbook of European Financial Markets and Institutions*, Oxford University Press, 68–98.

REFERENCES

Abiad, A. and A. Mody (2005), Financial Reform: What Shakes It? What Shapes It?, *American Economic Review*, 95(1), 66–88.

Acharya, V. V. and P. Schnabl (2009), How Banks Played the Leverage Game, in: V. V. Acharya and M. Richardson, *Restoring Financial Stability*, Wiley, Hoboken (NJ), 83–100.

Adrian, T. and H. S. Shin (2010), The Changing Nature of Financial Intermediation and the Financial Crisis of 2007–09, Federal Reserve Bank of New York Staff Reports 439.

Allen, F. and D. Gale (2000), *Comparing Financial Systems*, MIT Press, Cambridge (MA).

Allen, F. and A. M. Santomero (1997), The Theory of Financial Intermediation, *Journal of Banking and Finance*, 21, 1461–1485.

Allen, F., L. Bartiloro, and O. Kowalewski (2006), The Financial System of EU 25, in: K. Liebscher, J. Christl, P. Mooslechner, and D. Ritzberger-Grünwald (eds.), *Financial Development, Integration and Stability in Central, Eastern and South-Eastern Europe*, Edward Elgar, Cheltenham, 80–104.

Baele, L., A. Ferrando, P. Hördahl, E. Krylova, and C. Monnet (2008), Measuring European Financial Integration, in: X. Freixas, P. Hartmann, and C. Mayer (eds.), *Handbook of European Financial Markets and Institutions*, Oxford University Press, 165–194.

Becht, M. and A. Roëll (1999), Blockholdings in Europe: An International Comparison, *European Economic Review*, 43, 1049–1056.

Beck, T., A. Demirgüç-Kunt, and R. Levine (2001), Law, Politics and Finance, World Bank, Policy Research Working Paper 2585.

Bekeart, G., C. R. Harvey, and C. Lundblad (2005), Does Financial Liberalization Spur Growth? *Journal of Financial Economics*, 77, 3–55.

Brunnermeier, M. K. (2009), Deciphering the Liquidity and Credit Crunch 2007–2008, *Journal of Economic Perspectives*, 23(1), 77–100.

Carlin, W. and C. P. Mayer (2000), How Do Financial Systems Affect Economic Performance?, in: X. Vives (ed.), *Corporate Governance: Theoretical and Empirical Perspectives*, Cambridge University Press, 137–168.

(2003), Finance, Investment and Growth, *Journal of Financial Economics*, 69(1), 191–226.

Demirgüç-Kunt, A. and Levine, R. (eds.) (2001), *Financial Structure and Economic Growth: A Cross-Country Comparison of Banks, Markets and Development*, MIT Press, Cambridge (MA).

Dewatripont, M. and E. Maskin (1995), Credit Efficiency in Centralized and Decentralized Economies, *Review of Economic Studies*, 62, 541–555.

Djankov, S., R. La Porta, F. Lopez-de Silanes, and A. Shleifer (2006), The Law and Economics of Self-dealing, working paper.

Djankov, S., C. McLiesh, and A. Shleifer (2007), Private Credit in 129 Countries, *Journal of Financial Economics*, 84, 299–329.

Driffill, J. (2003), Growth and Finance, *The Manchester School*, 71, 363–380.

European Central Bank (2006), *Financial Stability Review* (December), ECB, Frankfurt am Main.

(2011), *Financial Integration in Europe* (May), ECB, Frankfurt am Main.

Fernandez, R. and D. Rodrik (1991), Resistance to Reform: Status Quo Bias in the Presence of Individual-specific Uncertainty, *American Economic Review*, 81, 1146–1155.

Governance Metrics International (2006), *Ratings on 3800 Global Companies*, GMI, New York.

Huertas, T. F. (2010), *Crisis: Cause, Containment and Cure*, Palgrave MacMillan, Houndsmills.

International Monetary Fund (2006), *World Economic Outlook*, Chapter 4, IMF, Washington DC.

Jensen, M. (1993), The Modern Industrial Revolution, Exit, and the Failure of Internal Control Systems, *Journal of Finance*, 48, 831–880.

Jensen, M. and W. Meckling (1976), Theory of the Firm: Managerial Behavior, Agency Costs, and Capital Structure, *Journal of Financial Economics*, 3, 287–322.

Keefer, P. (2007), Beyond Legal Origin and Checks and Balances: Political Credibility, Citizen Information and Financial Sector Development, World Bank Policy Research Working Paper 4154.

King, R. G. and R. Levine (1993a), Finance and Growth: Schumpeter Might Be Right, *Quarterly Journal of Economics*, 108, 717–737.

(1993b), Finance, Entrepreneurship, and Growth: Theory and Evidence, *Journal of Monetary Economics*, 32, 513–542.

La Porta, R., F. Lopez-de-Silanes, A. Shleifer, and R. Vishny (1997), Legal Determinants of External Finance, *Journal of Finance*, 52, 1131–1150.

Levine, R. (1997), Financial Development and Economic Growth: Views and Agenda, *Journal of Economic Literature*, 35, 688–726.

(2002), Bank-Based or Market-Based Financial Systems: Which is Better?, *Journal of Financial Intermediation*, 11, 398–428.

(2005), Finance and Growth: Theory, Mechanisms and Evidence, in: P. Aghion and S. N. Durlauf (eds.), *Handbook of Economic Growth*, Elsevier, Amsterdam, 865–923.

Levine, R., N. Loayza, and T. Beck (2000), Financial Intermediation and Growth: Causality and Causes, *Journal of Monetary Economics*, 46, 31–77.

Merton, R. C. (1995), Financial Innovation and the Management and Regulation of Financial Institutions, *Journal of Banking and Finance*, 19, 461–481.

Mishkin, F. S. (2006), *The Next Great Globalization*, Princeton University Press.

Papaioannou, E. (2008), Finance and Growth. A Macroeconomic Assessment of the Evidence from a European Angle, in: X. Freixas, P. Hartmann, and C. Mayer (eds.), *Handbook of European Financial Markets and Institutions*, Oxford University Press, 68–98.

Petersen, M. A. and R. G. Rajan (1994), The Benefits of Lending Relationships: Evidence from Small Business Data, *The Journal of Finance*, 49(1), 3–37.

Rajan, R. and L. Zingales (1998), Financial Dependence and Growth, *American Economic Review*, 88, 559–586.

Trew, A. (2006), Finance and Growth: A Critical Survey, *The Economic Record*, 82, 481–490.

Turner, A. (2009), *The Turner Review: A Regulatory Response to the Global Banking Crisis*, Financial Services Authority, London.

Financial Crises

OVERVIEW

Financial crises have been pervasive phenomena throughout history. This chapter starts by exploring the different types of crises: banking crises, sovereign debt crises, and currency crises. In a banking crisis a significant part of a country's banking sector has become insolvent after heavy investment losses, banking panics, or both. A sovereign default occurs when a government fails to meet interest or principal payments on its debt obligations. Finally, in a currency crisis the value of a country's currency falls precipitously.

This chapter first provides facts and figures about financial crises, after which some theoretical models are discussed. A first set of models is related to the liability side of banks. As banks finance long-term loans with short-term deposits, they are vulnerable to massive withdrawals cumulating in a banking run. A second set of models looks at the asset side of banks. Banking problems arise from deteriorating asset quality. This decline in assets is closely related to the business cycle, resulting from shocks to fundamentals.

In 2007–2009, the world's financial system went through its greatest crisis for at least a century. What made this crisis unique was that severe financial problems emerged simultaneously in many different countries, and its economic impact was felt throughout the world as a result of the increased interconnectedness of the global economy. The second part of this chapter offers an overview of the causes and consequences of this crisis. This crisis was followed by a sovereign and banking crisis in Europe which is discussed in the final part of this chapter.

LEARNING OBJECTIVES

After you have studied this chapter, you should be able to:
- explain the characteristics of different types of financial crises
- understand the link between sovereign and banking crises
- explain the main theoretical models of banking crises
- understand the pro-cyclicality of the financial system

- explain the main drivers and contagion mechanisms of the 2007–2009 financial crisis
- explain the recent sovereign debt and banking crisis in Europe.

2.1 Introduction

Financial crises have been around since the development of money and financial markets. They come in different forms: banking crises, sovereign debt crises, and currency crises.

In a *banking crisis* a significant part of a country's banking sector has become insolvent after heavy investment losses, banking panics, or both. Often a distinction is made between systemic and non-systemic banking crises. Following Laeven and Valencia (2008), we may define a *systemic banking crisis* as follows: In a systemic banking crisis, a country's corporate and financial sectors experience a large number of defaults and financial firms face great difficulties repaying contracts on time. As a result, non-performing loans increase sharply and all or most of the aggregate banking system capital is exhausted.

A *sovereign debt crisis* involves outright default on payment of debt obligations, i.e. repudiation or the restructuring of debt into terms less favourable to the lender than in the original. A sovereign default occurs when a government fails to meet interest or principal payments on its debt obligations. A distinction can be made here between external and domestic debt obligations. External debt consists of loans issued under another country's jurisdiction and is often denominated in a foreign currency and held by foreign creditors. Domestic debt is issued under a country's own jurisdiction and is typically denominated in the local currency and held by domestic creditors. In a default sometimes countries repudiate their debt, but it is more common that a government restructures debt on terms less favourable to the lender than those in the original contract (like a longer maturity and a lower interest rate). Although debt crises are often believed to occur mainly in emerging countries, only a few industrial countries (like Denmark and the US) have managed to avoid default on their government debt (Reinhart and Rogoff, 2009).

Finally, in a *currency crisis* the value of a country's currency falls precipitously. Countries maintaining an (almost) fixed exchange rate regime are vulnerable to sudden crises of confidence, leading to speculative attacks that can blow up seemingly stable regimes overnight. Although currency crises are often believed to be a phenomenon of emerging countries, they also occurred in the European Union (EU). Before the start of the Economic and

Monetary Union (EMU) in 1999 (see Chapter 4), several European countries tried to stabilise their exchange rates through the so-called Exchange Rate Mechanism (ERM). However, the track record of this system is mixed at best; in 1992–1993 several participating currencies plummeted vis-à-vis the German mark, the anchor of the system (see Box 2.1).

Box 2.1 The EMS crisis

The European Monetary System (EMS) started in March 1979. The cornerstone of the EMS was the *Exchange Rate Mechanism* (ERM). Within the ERM each currency was kept within a band defined by a grid of central rates for the various pairs of currencies. For most countries, this band was defined as plus and minus 2.25 per cent of the central parity. These parities could be changed by mutual consent. Whenever an exchange rate reached the edge of the band, the central banks of both countries concerned were supposed to intervene on the foreign exchange market. The ERM went through a number of phases that can be clearly distinguished:

- a turbulent start, 1979–1983
- a calmer intermediate phase, 1983–1987
- no realignments, 1987–1992
- crises, 1992–1993
- tranquillity restored, 1993–1998.

Initially, there were frequent and substantial realignments. For instance, already in September 1979 a number of currencies were devaluated vis-à-vis the German mark. This was a pattern to be repeated many times. Although some devaluations occurred in the second phase, both their frequency and magnitude were substantially lower than in the previous phase. In the period 1987–1992 the sequence of devaluations came to a halt. The parities and the bands of the ERM were considered to be very credible. This third phase of the ERM was also marked by new entries: the Spanish peseta in June 1989, the British pound in October 1990, and the Portuguese escudo in April 1992. During this period it looked as if exchange rates were almost fixed. However, this turned out to be illusionary. The fourth phase of the ERM was very turbulent. There was a severe currency crisis. In August 1992 the British pound fell close to the ERM floor and the Italian lira even fell below it. Eventually, the two currencies left the system. Except for the Dutch guilder, all currencies came under attack between September 1992 and August 1993. Only after the fluctuation margins were increased to 15 per cent did the foreign exchange markets become more tranquil. During the fifth phase, ERM membership broadened again as participation in the exchange rate system was one of the convergence criteria for participation in the EMU (see Chapter 3).

Source: Eijffinger and de Haan (2000)

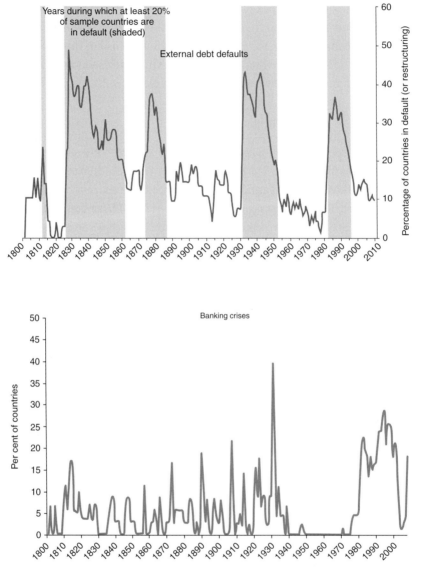

Figure 2.1   Incidence of financial crises, 1800–2009
Source: Reinhart and Rogoff (2010) and Qian *et al.* (2010)

The remainder of this section will focus on debt and banking crises. Figure 2.1 plots the incidence of government external debt defaults and banking crises according to the data of Reinhart and Rogoff (2010). These data are for a large sample of countries, accounting for about 90 per cent of world income. The graphs show the percentage of all independent countries that experienced a crisis in any given year from 1800 through 2008–2009.

The first graph identifies five episodes with many external debt defaults. The first is during the Napoleonic War, while the second runs from the 1820s through the late 1840s, when nearly half the countries in the world were in default. The third episode begins in the early 1870s and lasts for two decades, while the fourth episode begins in the Great Depression of the 1930s and extends through the 1950s, when almost 50 per cent of all countries stood in default. The most recent default episode encompasses the emerging market debt crises of the 1980s and 1990s. The median duration of default spells after the Second World War is three years (Reinhart and Rogoff, 2010).

The second graph shows that the highest incidence of banking crises occurred during the Great Depression of the 1930s. The share of countries with banking difficulties began to expand in the 1970s, while in the early 1980s there were severe banking crises in emerging economies, notably in Latin America. During the early 1990s, the Nordic countries as well as Japan experienced some of the worst banking crises. In the second half of the 1990s, crises in Mexico and Argentina (in 1994–1995) were followed by the Asian crisis of 1997–1998. A brief tranquil period came to an abrupt halt in the summer of 2007 when the subprime crisis in the United States began (see section 2.3 for further details). Although the frequency of banking crises drops off markedly in the advanced economies, all except Portugal experienced at least one post-War crisis prior to the current episode.

Reinhart and Rogoff (2009) report that systemic banking crises are typically preceded by *credit booms* (growth of credit above the trend of GDP growth) and *asset price bubbles* (a rise of asset prices above their fundamental economic value). As will be explained in section 2.3, the crisis that started in 2007–2008 is no exception. In addition, they find that crises result, on average, in a 35 per cent real drop in housing prices spread over a period of six years, while equity prices decline by 55 per cent over three-and-a-half years.

Many financial crises, especially those in countries with fixed exchange rates, are so-called *twin crises* with currency depreciation exacerbating banking sector problems through foreign currency exposures of borrowers or banks themselves. Banking crises often precede or accompany sovereign debt crises. The aftermath of a systemic banking crisis often involves protracted and pronounced contraction in economic activity and puts important strains on the government's financial position. The government often has to bail out financial institutions in a crisis. However, the most important driver of the worsening fiscal position after a systemic banking crisis is the economic downturn following the crisis. The data provided by Reinhart and Rogoff (2009) suggest that after a banking crisis output falls by 9 per cent over two years, while unemployment rises 7 per cent over a period of four years. The indirect fiscal consequences of a banking crisis are thus much larger than the costs of bank bailouts. Government debt, on average, increases by 86 per cent in the three years following a systemic banking crisis. The experience of Finland and Sweden stand out in this regard. Both countries experienced a systemic banking crisis at the beginning of the 1990s (see Box 2.2). In Sweden the government's budget balance increased from a surplus of 3.8 per cent of GDP before the crisis to a deficit of 11.6 per cent at the peak of the crisis, i.e. a deterioration of 15.4 per cent. Likewise, in Finland the fiscal position worsened by almost 12 per cent (Reinhart and Rogoff, 2009).

Box 2.2 The banking crisis in Sweden

The financial system in Sweden was liberalised in the 1980s. At the time, the financial system was dominated by a few, large commercial banks offering wide-ranging financial services leading to predominance of debt financing of the non-financial sector. The financial deregulation and liberalisation of capital flows led to a credit-financed surge in investment. The credit surge also contributed to a jump in asset prices, especially real-estate prices. Before the liberalisation, banks relied almost exclusively on deposits for funding but, in the course of time, they relied increasingly on (more expensive) money market and foreign funding. As monetary policy was not able to stem the credit boom due to its focus on maintaining the stability of the exchange rate, losses from defaulted bank loans began to mount rapidly in the early 1990s after asset prices collapsed and a severe recession set in. While losses on real estate loans represented a significant part of the problem, other sectors also experienced financial distress when economic growth slowed down. The major Swedish banks were hit by massive credit losses totalling around 7 per cent of GDP in 1992. These losses threatened to quickly put all but one of the seven major Swedish banks, controlling most of the Swedish market, below the capital requirement of 8 per cent. Consequently, the government had to intervene heavily to preserve financial stability. Initially, the crisis was dealt with in an ad hoc manner but in September 1992 the conservative Swedish government decided to guarantee the debt of the banks. The guarantee did not cover equity capital; in case of financial support by the government, owners generally lost their equity stakes. The guarantee was formulated in an explicit and transparent way and received wide support in the parliament; also the social-democratic opposition supported the measures. A new agency under the finance ministry, the Bank Support Authority, was created in 1993 to implement the program.

The banking crisis in Sweden started with the largest savings bank, Första Sparbanken. The Swedish government provided a lending guarantee to the bank but this was later converted into a loan. Eventually, the bank was merged into the Savings Bank of Sweden together with several other savings banks. The second problem bank was Nordbanken, the third largest commercial bank at the time, which was largely owned by the government. The government guaranteed a new share issue and the bank was restructured. An asset management company, Securum, took over the bad assets, while Nordbanken received in return a capital injection of 1 per cent of GDP. Also Gota Bank, the fourth largest commercial bank, got into difficulties. The government decided to meet all the commitments of Gota Bank but not those of the parent company, which was declared bankrupt. Again, as part of restructuring, non-performing assets, largely in the form of commercial real estate, were put in a separate asset management company (Retriva, which merged with Securum in December 1995). In 1993, Gota Bank was merged with Nordbanken, retaining the name Nordbanken.

Nordbanken became part of the pan-Nordic bank, Nordea.

Source: De Haan *et al.* (2009)

Now let's zoom in on crises in Europe. Drawing on the seminal work by Reinhart and Rogoff (2009), Table 2.1 presents four crisis indicators for European countries: the share of years a country was in default since 1800 or the year in which it became independent, the share of years with a banking crisis, and the number of banking crises since 1800 and 1945. Four conclusions can be drawn from this table. First, the share of years in default varies considerably among European countries. Second, whereas several countries have been able to avoid a debt crisis, all countries have spent some time in a banking crisis since 1800. Third, the average length of time a country spends in a state of average default exceeds the average amount of time spent in banking crisis. Finally, the number of banking crises has dropped off markedly after the Second World War. Nevertheless, except for Portugal, all countries included in Table 2.1 experienced at least one banking crisis since 1945.[1] One such crisis is described in more detail in Box 2.2.

2.2 Theory

Broadly speaking, theoretical models either focus on the asset or the liability side of the bank balance sheet to explain banking crises. We first describe

Table 2.1 Debt and banking crises in European countries

Country	Share of years in default since independence or 1800 (in %)	Share of years in banking crisis since independence or 1800 (in %)	Number of banking crises since independence or 1800	Number of banking crises since independence or 1945
Austria	17.4	1.9	3	1
Belgium	0	7.3	10	1
Denmark	0	7.2	10	1
Finland	0	8.7	5	1
France	0	11.5	15	1
Germany	13.0	6.2	8	2
Greece	50.6	4.4	2	1
Hungary	37.1	6.6	2	2
Italy	3.4	8.7	11	1
Netherlands	6.3	1.9	4	1
Norway	0.0	15.7	6	1
Poland	32.6	5.6	1	1
Portugal	10.6	2.4	5	0
Romania	23.3	7.8	1	1
Spain	23.7	8.1	8	2
Sweden	0	4.8	5	1
United Kingdom	0	9.2	12	4

Source: Reinhart and Rogoff (2009)

how problems at the liability side may cause a banking crisis, after which we discuss some theories focusing on the asset side.

As explained in Chapter 1, banks transform short-term deposit funding into long-term loans. They borrow in the form of short-term savings and demand deposits which can be withdrawn at short notice. At the same time, they lend at longer maturities in the form of loans to firms and households. This makes them vulnerable. In normal times, banks hold more than sufficient reserves to handle withdrawals of deposits. However, during a run, depositors lose confidence in the bank and withdraw their deposits en masse. As withdrawals increase, the bank is forced to liquidate assets, typically against 'fire sale' prices, especially if the assets are illiquid. As banks often hold broadly similar portfolios of assets the market can dry up completely if all banks try to sell at once. This typically happens during a systemic banking crisis. Assets that are liquid during normal times can suddenly become highly illiquid at the time that banks need them most. So even a bank that would be solvent in the absence of a bank run may see its balance sheet destroyed, so that the bank run becomes self-fulfilling.

If everyone expects a problem and acts as if one is about to occur, then the run becomes a self-fulfilling prophecy. Conversely, if no one expects a bank to be in crisis, this expectation is also self-fulfilling and no run occurs (Reinhart and Rogoff, 2009).

As has been explained in Chapter 1, modern banking systems have increased in complexity over the last two decades. Despite running off-balance sheet vehicles or using various financial instruments to transfer credit risk, banks remained sensitive to panics and runs. In the summer of 2007 holders of short-term liabilities refused to fund US banks, expecting losses on subprime and subprime-related securities. So there were runs on banks. The difference is that modern runs typically involve the drying up of liquidity in the short-term markets (a wholesale run) instead of retail depositor withdrawals (Allen *et al.*, 2009). Still, in modern times classical bank runs may occur, as the example of Northern Rock as described in Box 2.3 illustrates.

From a theoretical perspective, events as described above imply that there are *multiple equilibria*. A confidence shock can cause a jump from the good equilibrium to the bad equilibrium. According to the Diamond and Dybvig (1983) model, bank runs are self-fulfilling prophecies. In this model, agents have uncertain needs for consumption in an environment in which long-term investments are costly to liquidate. If depositors believe that other depositors will withdraw then they all find it rational to redeem their claims and a panic occurs. Another equilibrium exists where everybody believes no panic will occur and depositors withdraw funds according to their consumption needs. In this case, their demand can be met without costly liquidation of assets (Allen *et al.*, 2009). While this model explains how panics may occur, it does not explain which of the two equilibria will be selected. Depositors' beliefs are self-fulfilling and are coordinated by so-called 'sunspots'.

In the second line of argument, banking problems do not arise from the liability side, but from a protracted deterioration in asset quality due to poor fundamentals arising from the business cycle, like a collapse in real estate prices or increased bankruptcies in the non-financial sector. Some authors consider crises as an intrinsic part of the business cycle, resulting from shocks to economic fundamentals. When the economy goes into a recession, borrowers will have difficulty repaying loans. So, an economic downturn will reduce the value of bank assets, raising the possibility that banks are unable to meet their commitments. If depositors anticipate financial difficulties in the banking sector they will try to withdraw their bank deposits. The result is the same as in the panic story, but the cause is different. According to this interpretation, crises are not random events but a response of depositors to the arrival of some negative news on economic circumstances (Allen *et al.*,

---

Box 2.3 The run on the Rock

Northern Rock was formerly a building society in the UK, but it demutualised on 1 October 1997. At the end of 1997, Northern Rock had assets on a consolidated basis of £15.8 billion, but by the end of 2006 its consolidated balance sheet had grown to £101.0 billion. It comprised mainly secured lending on residential properties. Wholesale markets became an important source of funding, making up some 25 per cent of total funding, of which half had a duration of less than one year. Northern Rock had not foreseen all its funding markets closing simultaneously, as happened after 9 August 2007. It also had insufficient insurance and standby facilities to cover this risk. It soon became evident that Northern Rock would face severe problems if the markets stayed frozen for long. Initially, the Bank of England refused to provide support to financial institutions, including Northern Rock. In a letter of 12 September 2007, the Governor of the Bank of England (BoE) pointed to the risk of 'moral hazard': should the central bank provide extra liquidity against weaker collateral, markets would take it as a signal that the central bank would always rescue them. And such a signal would lead to ever more risk taking by banks.

At 8.30 p.m. on the evening of Thursday 13 September 2007, the BBC leaked that Northern Rock had asked for and received emergency financial support from the Bank of England. The next day, long queues began to form outside some of Northern Rock's branches; later, its website collapsed and its phone lines were reported to be jammed. The first bank run in the United Kingdom since Victorian times was underway. The momentum of the run on Northern Rock deposits once it had begun was caused by two factors. First, depositors were becoming aware that, were the run to continue, Northern Rock would eventually cease to be a going concern. Second, public awareness increased that deposits above £2,000 were not guaranteed in full. Only after four days did the BoE announce that it would guarantee all the existing deposits in Northern Rock. On 9 October, the BoE announced that 'additional facilities' would be available to Northern Rock and, on 18 December, the government granted a further extension of the earlier guarantee arrangements. Eventually, on 22 February 2008 Northern Rock was taken into state ownership as a result of two unsuccessful private sector bids to take over the bank.

Source: Treasury Committee (2008)

2009). Allen and Gale (1998) develop a model in which they assume that depositors can observe a leading economic indicator that provides public information about future bank asset returns. If returns are high, depositors will want to keep their funds in the bank. However, if returns are low, depositors will withdraw their money in anticipation of low returns and there is a crisis. Box 2.4 presents the Allen–Gale model.

One particular theory linking the business cycle to financial crises is Minsky's 'financial-instability' hypothesis (see Minsky, 1986). While his views were initially often regarded as radical, if not crackpot, the credit crisis of 2007–2009 (see section 2.3) has revived interest in his theory. In the

---

Box 2.4 Bank runs and the business cycle*

Allen and Gale (1998) developed a model to show how cyclical fluctuations in asset values can produce bank runs. Time is divided in three periods: $t = 0, 1, 2$. There are early consumers c_1 at date 1 and late consumers c_2 at date 2, each with probability half. The consumer's utility function is as follows:

$$U(c_1, c_2) = \begin{cases} u(c_1) \text{ with probability } 1/2 \\ u(c_2) \text{ with probability } 1/2 \end{cases} \tag{2.1}$$

where c_t denotes consumption at date $t = 1, 2$. Consumers want to maximise consumption. Their objective function is given by:

$$\max \quad E[u(c_1(R)) + u(c_2(R))] \tag{2.2}$$

where $c_1(R)$ and $c_2(R)$ give the consumption of the early and late consumers conditional on the return to the risky asset R (see below). Let E denote the consumer's total endowment of the consumption good at date 0. The role of banks is to make investments on behalf of consumers. Banks have two assets: a safe asset L and a risky asset X. The total amount invested must be less or equal to the amount deposited:

$$L + X \leq E \tag{2.3}$$

The return r on the safe asset is zero and that is why $r = 1$. The return R on the risky asset X is stochastic, where R is a non-negative random variable. The risky asset is more productive than the safe asset L but cannot be liquidated at date 1. The expected return is thus larger than zero: $E[R] > 1$. At date 1, depositors receive a signal about R, which can be thought of as a leading economic indicator representing the state of the business cycle. The signal is realised at date 2. The holding of the safe asset must be sufficient to provide for consumption of the early consumers:

$$c_1(R) \leq L \tag{2.4}$$

The consumption of the late consumers cannot exceed the total value of the risky asset plus the amount of the safe asset left over after the early consumers are paid off. Together with the previous constraint in equation 2.4, this condition gives:

$$c_1(R) + c_2(R) \leq L + RX \tag{2.5}$$

The deposit contract needs to be incentive compatible. For each value of R, the late consumers must be at least as well off as the early consumers. Since late consumers are paid off at date 2, an early consumer cannot imitate a late consumer. But a late consumer can imitate an early consumer, obtain $c_1(R)$ at date 1, and consume that at date 2. It will be optimal to do so unless:

$$c_1(R) \leq c_2(R) \tag{2.6}$$

Until now, the deposit contract is assumed to be contingent on the return on the risky asset R. But a standard deposit contract is non-contingent. Allen and Gale (1998) take a standard deposit contract that promises a fixed amount at each date. In the event that the bank does not have enough liquid assets to make the promised payment, the bank pays out all available liquid assets, divided equally among those withdrawing. Let $\bar{c}$ denote the fixed payment promised to the early consumers. The amount promised to the late consumers can be ignored, since they are always paid what is available at the last date.

Next, the equilibrium conditions of the standard contract and the possibility of bank runs are analysed. Let c_{21} and c_{22} denote the equilibrium consumption of late consumers who withdraw from the bank at dates 1 and 2. Let $\alpha(R)$ denote the fraction of late consumers who decide to withdraw early, conditional on the risky return R. So, a bank run is dependent on the signal about R and thus related to the business cycle.

If a run does not occur, the feasibility conditions in equations 2.4 and 2.5 still apply as before. If there is a run, then the early consumers and the early-withdrawing late consumers share the liquid assets available at date 1:

$$c_1(R) + \alpha(R)c_{21}(R = L \tag{2.7}$$

And the late-withdrawing late consumers get the returns to the risky asset at date 2:

$$(1 - \alpha(R))\, c_{22}(R) = R\, X \tag{2.8}$$

Since early consumers and early-withdrawing late consumers are treated the same in a run and all late consumers must have the same utility in equilibrium:

$$c_1(R) = c_{21}(R) = c_{22}(R) \tag{2.9}$$

The final condition comes from the standard deposit contract, which promises the early consumers $c_1(R) = \bar{c}$ or, if that is infeasible, an equal share of the liquid assets L, where it has to be borne in mind that some of the late consumers may want to withdraw early as well. In the latter case $c_1(R) < \bar{c}$, the early withdrawers (including the early-withdrawing late consumers) exhaust the liquid assets of the bank:

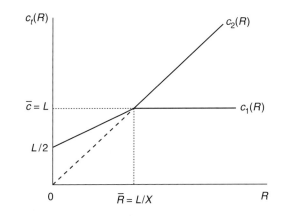

Figure 2.2 The standard deposit contract with bank runs
Source: Allen and Gale (1998)

$$\begin{cases} c_1(R) = \bar{c} & \text{no bank run} \\ c_1(R) < \bar{c} \implies c_1(R) + \alpha(R) \cdot c_{21}(R) = L & \text{bank run} \end{cases} \qquad (2.10)$$

The optimal deposit contract is solved for $\bar{c} = L$. In that case, the bank holds exactly sufficient liquid assets to pay the early consumers. The remainder is invested in risky assets with a positive expected return. Figure 2.2 illustrates the optimal deposit contract. The figure plots consumption $c_1(R)$ and $c_2(R)$ against the return on the risky asset R. Remember that R can be observed at date 1 but not at date 0. When $R = 0$ the only consumption available is from the safe asset. To maximise expected utility at t=0, this safe asset is split equally between the two groups so $c_1(0)=c_2(0)=L/2$. As R increases both groups can consume more. At $\bar{R} = L/X$, L is consumed by the early consumers and $\bar{R}X$ is consumed by the late consumers. Note that at $\bar{R} = L/X$, the consumption of the early and late consumers is still equal. As R increases above $\bar{R}$, it is not possible for the early consumers to have more than L since this is the only consumption available at date 1. At date 2, the late consumers are able to consume $RX > L$.

Minsky model the events leading up to the crisis start with a 'displacement'– some exogenous, outside shock to the macroeconomic system – an invention or an abrupt change of economic policy about which investors get excited. Subsequently there are five stages to the boom and eventual bust:
1. credit expansion, characterised by rising assets prices;
2. euphoria, characterised by overtrading;
3. distress, characterised by unexpected failures;
4. discredit, characterised by liquidation; and
5. panic, characterised by the desire for cash.

The displacement sets in a boom fuelled by credit. As a boom leads to euphoria, banks extend credit to ever more dubious borrowers, often creating new financial instruments to do the job. Then, at the top of the market, some smart traders start to cash in their profits. The onset of panic is usually heralded by a dramatic event, such as a bank not being able to meet its obligations. Losses on loans begin to mount, and the drop in the value of the loans falls relative to liabilities, driving down the capital of financial institutions. With less capital, financial institutions cut back on their lending (*deleveraging*).

Minsky's financial-instability hypothesis highlights the *pro-cyclicality* of the financial system. Several factors contribute to this pro-cyclicality. First, the role of risk assessment is important. While risk tends to be underestimated in good times (euphoria with 'low risk'), it is overestimated in bad times (distress with 'high risk'). Moreover, risk can be endogenous. For example, when financial institutions sell a particular asset to reduce risk, the price of that asset may fall further. Second, the amount of debt (leverage) is a key factor explaining the depth of the financial crisis. The more debt is built up in the upswing, the more severe is the deleveraging in the downswing. Third and last, capital requirements play a role. Banks have to keep minimum capital against new loans (see Chapter 12). In good times, retained earnings boost capital, which enables banks to increase lending. In bad times, capital shrinks through losses, which may hamper the granting of new credit. Figure 2.3 illustrates how the financial cycle (measured by credit) can amplify the business cycle (measured by GDP). This is a stylised figure, as the financial cycle and business cycle do not necessarily move synchronously.

Finally, some recent theories on financial instability focus on information problems. For example, Mishkin (1992) argues that a financial crisis is a disruption to financial markets in which adverse selection and moral hazard problems become much worse, so that financial markets are unable to efficiently channel funds to those who have the most productive investment opportunities. Uncertainty about the future (e.g. business prospects of firms) increases in a financial crisis, which widens the information asymmetry between contracting parties (e.g. information on the repayment capacity of a counterparty or information on the behaviour of a counterparty) and worsens the incentives of parties. *Adverse selection* occurs when investments that are most likely to produce an undesirable outcome are the most likely to be selected. *Moral hazard* arises when a borrower has the incentive to invest in high-risk projects, in which the borrower does well if the project succeeds but the lender bears a substantial loss if the project fails.

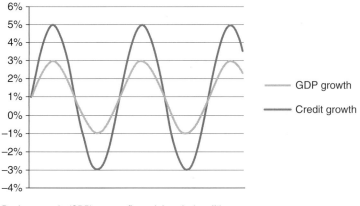

Figure 2.3   Business cycle (GDP) versus financial cycle (credit)

2.3 The credit crisis of 2007–2009

The credit crisis of 2007–2009 started with the bursting of the housing market bubble in the US forcing banks to write down several hundred billion dollars in bad loans caused by mortgage delinquencies, especially in the subprime part of the market. *Subprime mortgages* are housing loans to high-risk borrowers with a weak or a bad credit history who do not qualify for a conventional mortgage. Although these loans are relatively risky, subprime mortgages represented about 20 per cent of all newly issued mortgages in the US in 2005–2006. The mortgages were initially sold at bargain rates, but would be reset after some time (i.e. these contracts had a low or zero starting interest rate, which would rise significantly after a year or two). Due to the housing boom in the US – which began around 2001 – these mortgages could be refinanced before the interest rates were reset at market rates (thereby averting the high interest costs). However, when housing prices started to fall in 2006, many subprime owners could not refinance their mortgage and a significant number of them were unable to continue payments. This resulted in many defaults among subprime borrowers.

Why did financial institutions provide these mortgages? In the years before the crisis, interest rates in the US were very low. Low interest rates were caused by both large capital inflows from abroad, especially from Asian countries, and the policies of the Federal Reserve, the central bank of the US. Several Asian countries, including Japan and China, accumulated large current account surpluses prior to the crisis. As China and several other surplus countries were committed to (more or less) fixed exchange rates, the rising claims on other countries due to their current account surpluses took the form of central bank reserves. These are typically invested not in a wide array of equity, property, or fixed income assets, but almost exclusively in risk-free government securities (Turner, 2009). The loose policies by the Federal Reserve were caused by fears of deflation after the bursting of the Internet bubble. Between October 2007, when the stock market reached an all-time high, and October 2008 $8 trillion of US stock-market wealth was lost (Brunnermeier, 2009). As inflation was also low, real interest rates in the US were at a historically low level. Low interest rates in turn led to a rapid growth of credit extension, particularly for residential mortgages, which fuelled the property price boom. For banks (and other providers), subprime loans were interesting as a relatively high interest rate could be charged while (at that time) the default rate was very low because of the housing boom.

As of 2004, the Federal Reserve began to raise interest rates gradually from 1 per cent to 5.25 per cent in order to cool down the economy and keep inflation under control. As a result, it became more expensive to buy a house as mortgage rates increased substantially. This led to a slowdown in the housing market and eventually a housing-price crash. As the subprime mortgages were sold under the (false) assumption that housing prices would continue to increase, many subprime mortgage holders defaulted as they were unable to refinance their loans. This created a domino effect, as a result of which problems spread through the financial system. Summing up, the US banking crisis followed Minsky's model, starting with cheap credit ('low risk') and rising house prices, euphoria with overextension, distress with defaults, forced liquidations and fire sales, and finally panic with a freezing of short-term funding markets ('high risk').

But how did problems in the US housing market lead to a global financial crisis? Even though banks initially faced serious losses, they were small compared to the wealth losses of the dotcom bubble which did not lead to a serious recession. There is one particular aspect of the subprime crisis that makes this crisis different from previous financial crises (Brunnermeier, 2009). As discussed in Chapter 1, banks traditionally finance their mortgage loans through the deposits received from depositors and keep the mortgage loans (as well as the associated risks) on their balance sheet. In return, banks receive an upfront fee as well as interest income. However, in this case the providers of subprime loans bundled the mortgage loans and sold them to investors via collateralised debt obligations (CDOs). As mortgage providers were merely interested in receiving the upfront fee, they tried to sell as many mortgages as possible and there was no incentive to perform a proper credit check as the risks were transferred to third parties. The process of pooling, packaging, and reselling the loans as securities is referred to as *securitisation*.[2] The securitised instruments were in high demand by investors searching for as much as possible spread above the risk-free rate, to offset at least partially the declining risk-free rate (Turner, 2009).

Before the securitised instruments were sold, they were rated by credit rating agencies (CRAs). The agencies reviewed the proposed transactions prior to their coming to market, and placed their seal of approval on the deals in the form of a rating on the various tranches (see Chapter 8 for a discussion of CRAs). The most critical rating was the one for the senior tranche, which was almost invariably AAA, i.e. the highest possible rating. Indeed, deals were constructed so as to be sure that the senior tranches would get this rating. Although the ratings for securitisation issues were not directly comparable with ratings on sovereign or corporate bonds, the use of the same rating scale for securitisation issues as for sovereign and corporate bonds created exactly the opposite impression. Consequently, AAA-rated securitisation issues would pass the same investment and regulatory screens as AAA-rated corporate bonds, thereby opening the door to selling securitisation issues to investors (Huertas, 2010). However, during the crisis it became clear that the CRAs had not adequately assessed the risks related to the subprime mortgages. Moreover, there was poor investor due diligence as investors relied excessively on credit ratings. The poor credit assessment by CRAs and over-reliance on credit ratings by investors clearly contributed to the build-up of the crisis.

As pointed out by Turner (2009), securitisation led to a remarkable growth in the relative size of wholesale financial services within the overall economy, with activities internal to the banking system growing far more rapidly than end services to the real economy. This growth of the relative size of the financial sector, and in particular of securitised credit activities, increased the potential impact of financial system instability on the real economy. This growing size of the financial sector was accompanied by an increase in total system *leverage*, which played an important role in driving the boom and in creating vulnerabilities that have arguably increased the severity of the crisis (see Figure 2.4). Moreover, there was a maturity transformation, as the SPVs and conduits through which the securities were distributed (see Chapter 1) were often funded with (short-term) asset-backed commercial paper. By contrast, the dotcom bubble was predominantly financed by equity.

Not only the volume of securitised instruments increased; also the volume of credit derivatives grew extremely fast. During the 1990s and the first years of the twenty-first century they increased to over $45 trillion in notional value by

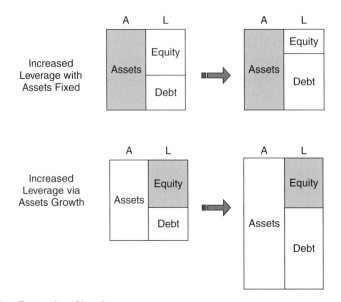

Figure 2.4 Two modes of levering up
Source: Hahm *et al.* (2011)

mid-2007. Credit derivatives (like Credit Default Swaps, see Chapter 1) allow an investor to take a position with respect to the possibility that the so-called reference entity will default. The investor can either buy protection, in which case he or she will receive a payment if the reference entity defaults, or the investor can sell protection, in which case he or she will make a payment if the reference entity defaults. In return for providing this protection, the seller of protection receives a premium from the buyer of protection (Huertas, 2010).

Financial guarantee insurance performed a similar function to credit derivatives. In exchange for a premium, financial guarantee insurance companies (generally they only wrote this type of insurance and they were therefore known as *monolines*) provided protection against the possibility that an issuer would not be able to make timely payments of interest and/or principal on its securities.

When the crisis broke, it became apparent that diversification of risk holding that securitisation was supposed to deliver had not been achieved. Instead in the books of end investors intending to hold the assets to maturity, many instruments were on the books of banks and bank-like institutions. Instruments were not simply sold through to an end investor, but bought by the propriety trading desk of another bank, or sold by the first bank but with part of the risk retained via the use of credit derivatives, or 'resecuritised' into

---

Box 2.5 Off-balance sheet vehicles

As explained in Chapter 1, banks used off-balance sheet vehicles like conduits in the securitisation process. These conduits were funded with some equity and the rest in roll-over finance in the form of asset-backed commercial paper (ACP). They had recourse to bank balance sheets. Recourse is the institutional arrangement through which risks of the conduit get transferred back to the commercial bank setting up the conduit. This recourse could consist of liquidity enhancement and credit enhancement. Liquidity enhancement provides a backup credit line or commitment to repurchase non-defaulted assets in case a conduit cannot roll over maturing commercial paper. Credit enhancement covers credit losses on a conduit's assets.

Acharya and Schnabl (2009) distinguish three types of off-balance sheet vehicles:

Fully supported conduits, which have liquidity enhancement that covers the entire amount of commercial paper outstanding and credit enhancement that covers all assets in the conduit.

Partially supported conduits, which have liquidity enhancement and partial credit enhancement.

Structured investment vehicles (SIVs), which have only partial liquidity and credit enhancement. The extent of liquidity and credit enhancement varies depending on the underlying assets.

Table 2.2 shows the ten largest conduit administrators.

---

increasingly complex and opaque instruments (Turner, 2009). According to Acharya and Schnabl (2009), in the US about 30 per cent of all AAA asset-backed securities remained within the banking system, and if conduits (see Box 2.5) are included as part of the banking system, then this fraction rises to 50 per cent. Consequently, most of the risk was still somewhere on the balance sheets of banks (be it directly or indirectly via guarantees of insurances) but not in a transparent fashion.

The uncertainty as to who was exposed to these risks disturbed the functioning of many financial markets, including the interbank money market. Problems started to occur in the money market due to the damage done to two hedge funds affiliated with the US investment bank, Bear Stearns. Increasingly, banks started to be reluctant to lend to each other (which resulted in a liquidity crisis). Apart from this so-called *funding liquidity*, also *market liquidity* became a problem. A wide range of institutions – both banks and near banks – developed an increasing reliance on 'liquidity through marketability', believing that it would be safe to hold long-term assets funded

Table 2.2 Ten largest conduit administrators by size (January 2007)

	Conduits		Administrator			
	Number	CP (in $ bn)	Assets	Equity	CP/Asset	CP/Equity
Citibank	23	93	1,884	120	4.9%	77.5%
ABN AMRO	9	69	1,300	34	5.3%	202.9%
Bank of America	12	46	1,464	136	3.1%	33.8%
HBOS	2	44	1,160	42	3.8%	104.8%
JPMorgan Chase	9	42	1,352	116	3.1%	36.2%
HSBC	6	39	1,861	123	2.1%	31.7%
Société Générale	7	39	1,260	44	3.1%	88.6%
Deutsche Bank	14	38	1,483	44	2.6%	86.4%
Barclays	3	33	1,957	54	1.7%	61.1%
WestLB	8	30	376	9	8.0%	333.3%

Source: Acharya and Schnabl (2009)

by short-term liabilities as these assets could be sold rapidly in liquid markets if needed. This assumption was valid at the level of firms individually in non-crisis conditions, but became rapidly invalid in mid-2007, as many firms attempted simultaneously to liquidate their positions. So often they had to sell assets at fire sale prices. In 2007 several hundred non-bank mortgage lenders collapsed, while others were merged into larger banking institutions.

Increased *risk aversion* and *deleveraging* amplified the initial shock. Central banks were forced to inject liquidity into the financial system to ensure that banks were not exposed to long periods of tight liquidity. Banks reported substantial losses as they had invested directly in structured securities or had contracts requiring them to support conduits. Many firms were, however, unable to rapidly assess their exposures as their assets had become illiquid (since the underlying market had imploded). This resulted in a loss spiral for the financial system, as illustrated in Figure 2.5. When banks mark their balance sheet to market, changes in prices lead to losses for all banks holding these assets. Losses worsen funding liquidity for many banks forcing them to shed even more assets which further depresses prices and increases losses. The loss spiral can thus lead to sharp asset price movements (Brunnermeier *et al.*, 2009).

In 2008, problems worsened and the US authorities were forced to bail out Bear Stearns, the fifth largest investment bank in the US. It was highly leveraged and exposed significantly to the subprime mortgage market. The US government helped engineer JPMorgan Chase's purchase of the bank by guaranteeing $29 billion of subprime-backed securities. Later, the mortgage

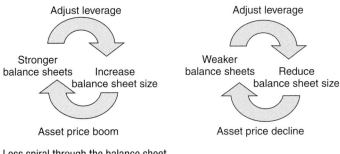

Figure 2.5 Loss spiral through the balance sheet
Source: Brunnermeier *et al.* (2009)

agencies Fannie Mae and Freddie Mac, accounting for nearly half of the outstanding mortgages in the US, were nationalised. When problems occurred at the fourth largest investment bank, Lehman Brothers, the authorities tried persuading rival institutions to take over the troubled firm. In the absence of a buyer, the government felt that an example had to be set to combat 'moral hazard', and decided to allow Lehman Brothers to fail in September 2008. The subsequent fears over counterparty risk turned into panic (if Lehman Brothers was not too big to fail, other investment banks might fail as well). In addition, several institutions had an exposure on Lehman that became virtually worthless. For instance, the Reserve Primary Fund, one of the largest money market funds, owned $700 million of Lehman Brothers' short-term paper and came into serious financial difficulties due to Lehman's collapse. This, in turn, led to uncertainty about all money market funds. As money market funds are the primary source for funding repos and commercial paper in the US, money markets came close to a breakdown (Richardson, 2009). Central banks in the US and elsewhere had to step in and eventually became vital suppliers in the money market.

Both in the EU and the US, authorities were eventually forced to rescue financial institutions to prevent a systemic meltdown. The world's largest insurance company, American International Group (AIG), received an emergency loan in return for an 80 per cent public stake in the firm. The landscape of American finance was changed radically. The investment bank Merrill Lynch was bought by Bank of America. Two investment banks, Goldman Sachs and Morgan Stanley, converted themselves into commercial banks. In a rescue deal backed by US authorities, Washington Mutual and Wachovia were sold to JPMorgan Chase and Citigroup respectively. Moving to Europe, Box 2.6 highlights the concerted crisis management of the governments. Benelux authorities had to bail out Fortis. Eventually the Dutch activities of

Box 2.6 Financial crisis management in Europe

In a historical summit of the euro-area leaders in October 2008, Sarkozy (then president of the EU) presented an impressive concerted European action plan of the euro-area countries to face the challenges of the financial crisis. The declaration of this euro-area summit introduced an action plan with three main measures:

1. Ensuring appropriate liquidity conditions for banks. The ECB provides ample liquidity to banks against adequate collateral.
2. Facilitating the funding of banks. National governments provide a guarantee for medium-term funding of banks. These government guarantees cover medium-term bank debt issuance with a maturity ranging from three months up to three to five years.
3. Recapitalising banks. Governments provide capital injections to restore Tier 1 capital at an appropriate level. Furthermore, governments may allow for an efficient recapitalisation of distressed banks, including nationalisation as an ultimate remedy.

Between end-September and end-October 2008, several EU countries announced bank rescue schemes which complemented the exceptional liquidity support provided by the ECB (see Chapter 4 on the liquidity support). In order to ensure respect of the EU state aid rules the European Commission provided guidance on how to design these measures (see also Chapter 14). In particular, the measures under (2) and (3) should avoid any discrimination against financial institutions based in other Member States and should ensure that beneficiary banks do not unfairly attract new additional business solely as a result of the government support. Although individual governments provided the funding guarantees under (2), the ECB managed to broker a common fee across the EU. The market for bank funding is integrated and a common fee ensures a level playing field. For maturities up to one year, there was a flat fee of 50 basis points. The fee for maturities from one year up to three to five years was based on the credit default swap spread of the involved bank plus 50 basis points.

Initially, public support targeted the liabilities side of banks' balance sheets. In early 2009, public support to the banking sector began to target the assets side of banks' balance sheets, with the aim of providing relief for impaired bank assets. This support complemented existing measures and was mainly motivated by the persisting uncertainty regarding asset valuations and the risk that new asset write-downs could impair banks' balance sheets, thus undermining confidence in the banking sector. Asset relief schemes include: (1) asset removal schemes, which aim at removing impaired assets from a bank's balance sheet either via direct government purchases or by transferring them to independent asset management companies (which are sometimes referred to as 'bad banks'); and (2) asset insurance schemes, which keep the assets on the banks' balance sheets but insure them against tail risk.

Source: Van Riet (2010)

Fortis were nationalised by the Dutch government, while the other activities were sold to the French banking group, BNP Paribas. The French, Belgian, and Luxembourg authorities also had to recapitalise the financial conglomerate, Dexia. In the UK, the authorities were forced to take over the mortgages and loans of Bradford & Bingley, while its savings operations and branches were sold to the Spanish banking group, Santander. The UK authorities also took a major equity stake in two large banks: RBS and Lloyds-HBOS. Germany's Hypo Real Estate, a large commercial property lender, received a €50 billion secured-credit facility by a consortium of German banks and the government. The Icelandic authorities had to nationalise their entire banking system, leading to a near bankruptcy of the country itself.

2.4 The recent euro crisis

At the time of writing, the euro zone faces a serious financial crisis. This crisis is a joint sovereign debt and banking crisis, as several European banks are heavily exposed to sovereign debt. Default of several countries could only be avoided as other countries, the International Monetary Fund (IMF), and the ECB provided financial support. This section describes the events that led to the crisis and the policy response so far.

Already before the start of the Economic and Monetary Union (EMU) in 1999, long-term interest rates in the participating countries converged (see Chapter 5). Interest differentials were very small. This changed in the aftermath of the 2007–2009 crisis. The public finances in most countries deteriorated very quickly (see Table 2.3), causing serious doubts about their sustainability in financial markets. Spreads between ten-year government bonds of some euro-area countries relative to German bonds started to increase. The concerns about fiscal sustainability were such that some secondary markets dried up.

The problems started in Greece. Market confidence took a severe blow when it emerged that the budget deficit in Greece was twice as high as previously thought. This news fed through to some other countries, including Portugal, Ireland, and – albeit to a lesser extent – Spain.

In mid-February, the European authorities attempted to allay concerns about Greece by promising support to that country. However, the absence of a concrete aid programme and continuing uncertainty about the Greek government's fiscal problems caused mounting tensions in the financial markets. The Greek government announced several austerity measures, which

Table 2.3 Government debt in euro-area countries (% GDP), 2006–2010

	2006	2007	2008	2009	2010
Austria	62.8	60.7	63.8	69.6	72.3
Belgium	88.1	84.2	89.6	96.2	96.8
Cyprus	64.6	58.3	48.3	58.0	60.8
Estonia	4.4	3.7	4.6	7.2	6.6
Finland	39.7	35.2	35.1	43.8	48.4
France	64.0	63.9	67.7	78.3	81.7
Germany	67.6	64.9	66.3	73.5	83.2
Greece	106.4	105.4	110.7	127.1	142.8
Ireland	24.8	25.0	44.4	65.6	96.2
Italy	106.6	103.6	106.3	116.1	119.0
Luxembourg	6.7	6.7	13.6	14.6	18.4
Malta	64.2	62.0	61.5	67.6	68.0
Netherlands	47.4	45.3	58.2	60.8	62.7
Portugal	69.5	68.3	71.6	83.0	93.0
Slovakia	30.5	29.6	27.8	35.4	41.0
Slovenia	26.4	23.1	21.9	35.2	38.0
Spain	39.6	36.1	39.8	53.3	60.1

Source: ECB

met strong resistance among the population. For instance, on 11 March 2010 flights were grounded and trains suspended amid a nationwide general strike. On 2 May 2010, the euro countries agreed to provide bilateral loans for a total amount of €80 billion to be disbursed over the period May 2010 through June 2013, with the International Monetary Fund (IMF) financing an additional €30 billion under a stand-by arrangement (SBA). The European Commission has been entrusted with the coordination and administration of the pooled bilateral loans, including their disbursement to Greece. The loans are subject to strict conditionalities aimed at consolidating Greek public finances and restoring competitiveness. However, the proposed policy measures led to continuing protests by the Greek population, raising doubts about their legitimacy and sustainability.

Why was Greece rescued? Several economists argued that Greece and other countries facing insolvency should default as quickly as possible, to allow for a substantial debt restructuring (haircut) aimed at restoring sustainable debt levels and stabilising financial markets. Delaying such a decision – according to this logic – would make things even worse. European policy makers did not follow this advice, as they were worried that a Greek default would have serious consequences. First, a Greek default was considered to easily spread to other countries (contagion). A worsening of the Greek crisis could further aggravate the situation in Portugal and Ireland – two other countries facing severe financial problems at the time – also pushing them into default and the crisis might spread even to Spain or Italy, pushing them to ask for a rescue. This would overburden the abilities and willingness of the other EU countries to come to the rescue. A major default would also activate CDSs, with unforeseeable consequences not only for European but also for global financial markets.

Second, many banks and other financial institutions had a large exposure on Greece. It was feared that a sovereign default would lead to another banking crisis as many banks were just recovering from the 2007–2009 crisis and would not be able to absorb the substantial losses that a Greek default would imply. More generally, financial institutions have extensive exposures to European governments (see Table 2.4) and to each other. In turn, owing to their efforts to contain the banking crisis, governments hold considerable participations in banks or stand guarantee for large amounts. The governments' involvement is essential to preserve market confidence in vulnerable institutions. At the same time, this involvement could give rise to doubt about the sustainability of fiscal policy, especially if there are other factors that knock public finances off course, like poor economic growth rates. If this happens, risk premiums rise and downgrades occur, jeopardising the (re)financing of debt (DNB, 2011).

But the support to Greece proved insufficient to stabilise the markets and prevent contagion between countries. Tensions in financial markets continued to mount; the euro tumbled to a 14-month low against the US dollar. In view of these mounting instabilities, in May 2011 the euro-area countries agreed to establish two facilities to provide financial support to EU countries experiencing severe economic or financial disturbances. First, the European Financial Stabilisation Mechanism (EFSM) was set up, which allows the European Commission to raise up to €60 billion on behalf of the EU for providing financial assistance to EU Member States experiencing serious financial difficulties. Second, the euro countries established the European Financial Stability Facility (EFSF). The EFSF was set up as a limited liability company authorised to issue debt securities, guaranteed up to a total of €440 billion by euro-area countries on a pro rata basis, for lending to euro-area countries.[3] The IMF committed itself to adding half of the funding provided by Europe. Moreover, the IMF is closely involved in designing adjustment programmes for a country (*conditionality*) that seeks recourse to the safety net.

Also, the ECB announced far-reaching measures. On 10 May 2010, it announced the launch of the Securities Markets Programme (SMP). Under

Table 2.4 Exposure of euro-area banks on euro-area countries ($ million), March 2011

	Greece	Ireland	Italy	Portugal	Spain
Austria	104	3,193	105,097	187	5,288
Belgium	240	4,689	4,173	465	4,441
Cyprus	11,351	–	1,729	82	92
Estonia	3	–	399	–	12
Finland	2	–	1,271	59	3,014
France	1,675	15,955	41,153	7,411	28,790
Germany	5,246	62,664	266,138	3,910	58,840
Greece	–	773	4,694	10,158	1,265
Ireland	544	–	14,324	22,250	11,052
Italy	537	13,182	–	2,998	35,190
Luxembourg	7,687	3,088	28,598	2,613	8,325
Malta	382	–	890	848	166
Netherlands	4,502	5,986	25,908	13,111	19,892
Portugal	92	2,475	4,331	–	89,932
Slovakia	–	–	19,711	86	167
Slovenia	2	–	8,778	43	110
Spain	361	13,737	31,764	25,616	–

Source: BIS

the SMP, the ECB makes purchases in secondary public and private bond markets in order to enhance depth and liquidity in dysfunctional markets. This improves the monetary transmission in the euro area. In line with the provisions of the Treaty on the Functioning of the European Union, ECB purchases of government bonds are strictly limited to secondary markets. To ensure that liquidity conditions will not be affected, all purchases are fully sterilised by conducting liquidity-absorbing operations (see Chapter 4). In May and June 2010, ECB interventions amounted to €64.5 billion. At end-2010, purchases under the SMP ran up to a total of €73.5 billion (DNB, 2011).

The announcement of this safety net for governments broke the negative spiral in a number of sub-markets. Following the statements by euro-area governments and by the ECB, tensions in financial markets abated for a short period of time. Market sentiment improved in the summer. New debt issues by European governments were successful. This revival was short-lived, however. The country risk premiums in notably Greece, Ireland, and Portugal expanded substantially relative to countries with a stronger economic recovery and healthier financial positions, such as Germany and the Netherlands.

On 21 November 2010, Ireland requested financial assistance. The problems in Ireland are completely different, although no less serious than those in Greece. For many years, Ireland had high growth rates, climbing up among the top ten richest countries in the world. However, the tide began to turn in 2007. Up until that year, there were sharp rises in the prices of real estate, which in turn resulted in substantial investments in the construction sector. As abundant credit was available to accommodate this process, a bubble arose, which began to deflate when the subprime crisis broke out. Since then, house prices have fallen by close on 40 per cent and the prices of commercial real estate by even more than 50 per cent. This caused an exceptionally deep recession during which unemployment doubled. The Irish banking sector had to absorb unprecedented losses on mortgage lending and was confronted with extensive withdrawals from the international liabilities, so that state support was unavoidable. Serious concerns arose about the sustainability of Irish public finances in particular when the extent of the Irish government's support to the banking sector became clear, forcing Ireland to ask for European support. The EU, the EFSF, the IMF, and some non-euro-area EU countries (UK, Denmark, and Sweden) promised Ireland financial support amounting to €67.5 billion. In return for aid, Ireland had to commit itself to an ambitious programme aiming to restructure the financial sector and restoring public finances (DNB, 2011).

In October 2010, European politicians decided to create a permanent crisis mechanism, the European Stability Mechanism (ESM). The ESM will be a permanent last-resort rescue mechanism set up among euro-area countries and able to issue AAA bonds to provide assistance to euro countries in difficulty, on the basis of strict conditionality. The ESM will have an effective lending capacity of €500 billion. In line with the current EFSF, the ESM will seek to supplement its lending capacity through the participation of the IMF and non-euro EU countries. The ESM will only provide financial assistance if this is deemed indispensable to safeguard the stability of the euro as a whole. The decision to activate the ESM and the terms under which assistance will be made available will be taken by its Board of Governors, which will be made up of the finance ministers of the euro-area countries. ESM assistance will predominantly take the form of loans that will be conditional on agreement to and compliance with a strict macroeconomic adjustment programme. The interest rate on the loans will be the sum of the funding cost to the ESM and a charge of 200 basis points.

The ESM will be an intergovernmental institution established under public international law by a treaty signed by the euro-area countries. The EFSF, by contrast, is a private company incorporated under Luxembourg law (ECB, 2011). Figure 2.6 shows all the support mechanisms in place and compares it

	Euro area intergovernmental loans to Greece	European Financial Stabilisation Mechanism	European Financial Stability Facility	European Stability Mechanism
Legal/ institutional form	Intergovernmental agreement	EU mechanism	Private company owned by euro area countries	Intergovernmental organisation
Capital structure	None, bilateral loans pooled by the European Commission	Guaranteed by EU budget (i.e. all EU Member States)	Guarantees and over-guarantees from euro area countries	€80 billion paid-in capital and €620 billion callable capital (payment of initial shares by euro area countries to be made in five annual instalments of 20% of the total amount)
Lending capacity EU/euro area limit	€80 billion	€60 billion	€440 billion[1]	€500 billion
Commitments	€80 billion	€22.5 billion for Ireland	€17.7 billion for Ireland (plus €4.8 billion in bilateral loans)	N/A
		€26 billion for Portugal	€26 billion for Portugal	N/A
Instruments	Loans	Loans, credit lines	Loans, bond purchase on the primary market[1]	Loans, bond purchases on the primary market
Duration	Loans to be repaid seven and a half years after disbursement date in 22 equal quarterly payments	Until the end of June 2013	Until the end of June 2013. Will also remain operational thereafter until all outstanding liabilities are repaid	Permanent mechanism from the beginning of July 2013 onwards
ECB involvement	Involved in programme design and monitoring, and as paying agent	Involved in programme design and monitoring, and as paying agent	Involved in programme design and monitoring, and as paying agent	Involved in conducting debt sustainability analysis, programme design and monitoring, and as paying agent
Main decision-making bodies	Eurogroup	Ecofin, acting by qualified majority voting on proposal from European Commission	Eurogroup/EFSF Board of Directors	Eurogroup/ESM Board of Governors and ESM Board of Directors
Legal basis Financing	Intergovernmental decision and Treaty Article 136	Treaty Article 122 (a Member State facing 'exceptional occurrences beyond its control')	Intergovernmental decision	Intergovernmental treaty linked to amended Treaty Article 136
Conditionality	Treaty Articles 126 and 136	EU Council Decision on basis of EFSM Regulation	EFSF Framework Agreement by cross-reference with Memorandum of Understanding and EU Council Decision	EU Council Decision on basis of regulation under Treaty Article 136 (forthcoming)

1) After adoption of the amended EFSF Framework Agreement.

Figure 2.6   Financial assistance facilities to euro-area countries
Source: ECB (2011)

with the ESM. The ESM is scheduled to become operational on 1 July 2012. It will supersede both the EFSF and the EFSM. The EFSF and the ESM will operate in parallel until the active EFSF programmes are completed. The EFSF will not launch any new programmes but will continue to ensure the financing of ongoing programmes as needed.

In 2011 the problems continued. First, Portugal had to seek international financial assistance in April. Portugal had not performed well since its accession to EMU: it had sluggish growth, pronounced credit expansion, seriously eroding competitiveness, and excessive government and current account deficits. Following the Portuguese request, the terms and conditions of the financial assistance package were agreed upon by the EU's Council of Economics and Finance Ministers on 17 May 2011. The financial package will cover Portugal's financing needs of up to €78 billion. The EFSM and the EFSF will each provide up to €26 billion to be disbursed over three years. Further support will be made available through the IMF for up to €26 billion, as approved by the IMF Executive Board on 20 May.

Second, in the course of 2011 it became obvious that Greece would require a second major rescue package because it would not be able to return to financial markets in 2012 when the first assistance package runs out. At their summit in July 2011, the Heads of State or Government of the euro-area countries announced several measures to alleviate the Greek debt crisis and ensure the financial stability of the euro area as a whole. The summit in Brussels saw agreement on a new financial support programme for Greece worth some €109 billion, a voluntary contribution from the private sector estimated at a net effect of €37 billion, the extension of maturities, and lowering of lending rates (Emmanouilidis, 2011).

The most contentious part of the plan was the involvement of the private sector. Germany, strongly supported by the Netherlands and Finland, insisted that private investors should be involved in any new package. The ECB warned of the destabilising effects of involving private investors, which could lead credit rating agencies to consider the deal as a 'credit event', potentially triggering a request for payment by the holders of credit default swaps (CDSs). At a bilateral meeting in Berlin in the week before the summit, German Chancellor, Angela Merkel, and French President, Nicolas Sarkozy, reached a compromise over the involvement of private bondholders, with Berlin agreeing that private investors should be involved on a purely voluntary basis, which arguably should not be classified as a default and thus avoid a credit event (Emmanouilidis, 2011).

Again, the agreement did not have a lasting effect on financial market volatility. This time, interest rates on Italian and Spanish government bonds started to rise, without a clear change in the underlying fundamentals. In response, in August 2011 a majority of the Governing Council of the ECB decided to purchase government bonds again under the SMP after the Spanish and Italian governments had agreed to additional fiscal consolidation measures. In the week thereafter, the ECB purchased €22 billion of government bonds.

The Belgian-French Dexia bank was the first large bank which had to be rescued in this phase of the crisis due to its heavy exposure on sovereign debt. In October 2011, a bailout was arranged in which the Belgian government assumed control of 100 per cent of the company's Belgian operations. Some units of the bank were put up for sale, while the remaining troubled assets would remain in a 'bad bank' that received funding guarantees of up to €90 billion provided by the governments of Belgium (60.5 per cent), France (36.5 per cent), and Luxembourg (3 per cent). In the beginning of 2012, financial markets calmed down. No doubt, the measures taken by the ECB (notably the LTROs as discussed in Chapter 4) and governments (notably the agreement on the fiscal compact as discussed in Chapter 3) contributed to this development. Still, at the time of writing the crisis is not over. Several countries in the euro area faced a recession, making the necessary fiscal adjustments and structural reforms more difficult. Likewise, many financial institutions are still very vulnerable.

Although unsustainable fiscal policies play a major role in the recent crisis in the euro area, also lack of competitiveness is important. Before EMU the current euro area countries followed different economic strategies. Between 1970 and 1999, unit labour costs in southern European countries increased much more than in other countries in the euro area. By regularly devaluing their currencies (see Box 2.1), southern European countries were able to restore competitiveness. But after the launch of EMU, this policy option was no longer available. After the start of EMU, unit labour costs in southern European countries went up at a much higher pace than those in other euro area countries. This proved unsustainable. The countries that ran into troubles when the sovereign debt tensions started in 2009 – that is Greece, Spain, Ireland, Portugal and Italy – all had serious competitiveness problems.

2.5 Conclusions

Crises are a permanent feature of the financial system. While a good functioning financial system can contribute to economic growth as discussed in Chapter 1, crises may temporarily hamper economic growth. From a welfare perspective, the growth benefits exceed the costs of the temporary setbacks.

In a systemic banking crisis, a significant part of a country's banking system becomes insolvent after heavy investment losses and/or banking panics. Theory suggests that such banking crises are often rooted in the business cycle. In the upswing credit is expanded, while credit is reduced in the downswing ('credit crunch'). The financial system can thus amplify the business cycle. Banking crises can have a large impact on the economy. While problem banks may need to be refinanced by the government, the real cost of a banking crisis is the loss of economic growth.

The credit crisis of 2007–2009 was a banking crisis, which started with the bursting of the housing market bubble in the US. A particular feature of the credit crisis was the role of securitised credit. In the process of securitisation, subprime mortgages (i.e. housing loans to high risk borrowers) were repackaged by originating banks and sold to other financial institutions across the world. In that way, the credit crisis spread very fast and also became very deep.

In a sovereign crisis, governments default on their debt obligations. While countries sometimes repudiate their debt in a default, it is more common that a government restructures debt on less favourable terms to the lender. Debt crises are a common feature of emerging countries, but can also happen in industrial countries. A banking crisis can turn into a sovereign debt crisis, as highlighted by Reinhart and Rogoff (2009). In the euro zone, the extra government debt generated in the 2007–2009 banking crisis and the output loss it created cumulated in a full-blown euro crisis.

NOTES

1 Only Austria, Belgium, the Netherlands, and Portugal managed to escape banking crises from 1945 to 2007. Except for Portugal, even these countries had massive bailouts in 2008.
2 As Turner (2009, p. 14) points out, securitised credit has existed for almost as long as modern banking. But from the mid-1990s the scale of securitisation increased rapidly. In addition, there was 'an explosion in the complexity of the securities sold, with the growth of the alphabet soup of structured credit products'. See also Chapter 8.
3 In practice, however, the capacity of the EFSF is only around half of the €440 billion announced, primarily because only a limited part of the governments' guarantees may actually be used to raise funding.

SUGGESTED READING

Allen, F. and D. Gale (1998), Optimal Financial Crises, *Journal of Finance*, 53, 1245–1284.

Brunnermeier, M. K. (2009), Deciphering the Liquidity and Credit Crunch 2007–2008, *Journal of Economic Perspectives*, 23(1), 77–100.

Reinhart, C. M. and K. S. Rogoff (2009), *This Time Is Different: Eight Centuries of Financial Folly*, Princeton University Press.

REFERENCES

Acharya, V. V. and P. Schnabl (2009), How Banks Played the Leverage Game, in: V. V. Acharya and M. Richardson, *Restoring Financial Stability*, Wiley, Hoboken (NJ).

Allen, F. and D. Gale (1998), Optimal Financial Crises, *Journal of Finance*, 53, 1245–1284.

Allen, F., A. Babus, and E. Carletti (2009), Financial Crises: Theory and Evidence, *Annual Review of Financial Economics*, 1, 97–116.

Brunnermeier, M. K. (2009), Deciphering the Liquidity and Credit Crunch 2007–2008, *Journal of Economic Perspectives*, 23(1), 77–100.

Brunnermeier, M., A. Crockett, C. Goodhart, A. Persaud, and H. Shin (2009), *The Fundamental Principles of Financial Regulation*, Geneva Report on the World Economy 11, ICBM, Geneva, and CEPR, London.

De Haan, J., J.-E. Sturm, and E. Zandberg (2009), The Impact of Financial and Economic Crises on Economic Freedom, in: *Economic Freedom of the World Report 2009*, Fraser Institute, Vancouver.

De Nederlandsche Bank (2011), *Annual Report 2010*, DNB, Amsterdam.

Diamond, D. and P. H. Dybvig (1983), Bank Runs, Deposit Insurance, and Liquidity, *Journal of Political Economy*, 91(3), 401–419.

Eijffinger, S. C. W. and J. de Haan (2000), *European Monetary and Fiscal Policy*, Oxford University Press.

Emmanouilidis, J. A. (2011), All Eyes on Greece – the EU in Crisis Mode, Again!, European Policy Center, 27–06–2011.

European Central Bank (2011), *Monthly Bulletin*, July 2011, ECB, Frankfurt.

Hahm, J., H. S. Shin, and K. Shin (2011), Non-Core Bank Liabilities and Financial Vulnerability, paper presented at Federal Reserve Board conference, Regulation of Systemic Risk, Washington, 15–16 September, 2011.

Huertas, T. F. (2010), *Crisis: Cause, Containment and Cure*, Palgrave MacMillan, Houndsmills.

Laeven, L. and F. Valencia (2008), Systemic Banking Crises: A New Database, IMF Working Paper 08/224.

Minsky, H. P. (1986), *Stabilizing An Unstable Economy*, Yale University Press.

Mishkin, F. S. (1992), Anatomy of a Financial Crisis, *Journal of Evolutionary Economics*, 2(2), 115–130.

Reinhart, C. M. and K. S. Rogoff (2009), *This Time Is Different: Eight Centuries of Financial Folly*, Princeton University Press.

(2010), From Financial Crash to Debt Crisis, NBER Working Paper 15795.

Richardson, M. (2009), Causes of the Financial Crisis, in: V. V. Acharya and M. Richardson, *Restoring Financial Stability*, Wiley, Hoboken (NJ).

Qian, R., C. M. Reinhart, and K. S. Rogoff (2010), On Graduation from Default, Inflation and Banking Crisis: Elusive or Illusion? NBER Working Paper 16168.

Treasury Committee of the House of Commons (2008), The Run on the Rock, Fifth Report of Session 2007–08, Volume I.

Turner, A. (2009), *The Turner Review: A Regulatory Response to the Global Banking Crisis*, Financial Services Authority, London.

Van Riet, A. (2010), Euro Area Fiscal Policies and the Crisis, ECB Occasional Paper 109.

3

European Financial Integration: Origins and History

OVERVIEW

The European Union (EU) consists of 27 Member States at the time of writing and has supranational and intergovernmental forms of cooperation. The EU has its origins in the European Coal and Steel Community (ECSC) formed by six European countries in 1951. Since then, it has grown in size through the accession of new Member States, while it has also increased its powers by the addition of new policy areas to its remit.

This chapter describes the major steps towards monetary and financial integration in the European Union. In addition, it explains the most important EU institutions (European Commission, Council of the EU, European Council, the European Parliament, and the European Court of Justice) and legal instruments (like directives and regulations).

A major step in the history of European integration was the publication of the report of the Committee for the Study of Economic and Monetary Union in 1989. In this so-called Delors Report, named after the chairman of this committee, a three-phase transition towards monetary unification was proposed. The main conclusions of the Delors Committee were incorporated in the 1992 Treaty on European Union and finally led to the introduction of the single currency as well as the European Central Bank (ECB). To protect monetary policy, the Stability and Growth Pact restricts fiscal policy of the Member States in the currency union.

An important milestone for financial integration was the launch of the Financial Services Action Plan (FSAP) by the European Commission in May 1999. The purpose of the FSAP was to remove regulatory and market barriers that limit the cross-border provision of financial services and the free flow of capital within the EU, and to create a level playing field among market participants. Since the financial crisis, the Commission has proposed several financial reform measures.

After you have studied this chapter, you should be able to:
- outline the various steps in the process of European monetary and financial integration
- explain the Stability and Growth Pact
- describe the fundamental principles underlying the financial integration process
- explain the functioning of the most important EU institutions and their responsibilities
- describe the various EU legal instruments.

3.1 European integration: introduction

Although the idea of economic integration of European countries was pro-posed earlier, it was put into practice only after the Second World War. The major impetus was the Schuman plan of May 1950 that foresaw the establish-ment of the so-called European Coal and Steel Community (ECSC). It was very much inspired by political considerations as the ECSC was seen as the basis for Franco–German reconciliation. To ensure that reconstruction in the western part of Germany would not endanger peace, the ECSC intended to integrate the coal and steel sectors, which were at the time considered to be of central importance for the defence industry. The main objective of the ECSC was the elimination of barriers and the encouragement of competition in these sectors.

The ECSC that started in 1951 was in many ways characteristic for the European integration process of the years to come. First, its membership was limited. Only Belgium, Germany, France, Italy, Luxembourg, and the Netherlands were members. The United Kingdom and various other European countries remained outside the organisation. It was only in 1973 that Denmark, Ireland, and the UK joined what was then called the European Communities, to be followed by Greece (1981) and Spain and Portugal (1986). Austria, Finland, and Sweden became members in 1995. After the collapse of communism at the end of the 1980s, various Eastern- and Central-European countries became candidate members of what was by then called the European Union. In 2004, Cyprus, the Czech Republic, Estonia, Hungary, Latvia, Lithuania, Malta, Poland, Slovakia, and Slovenia acceded to the EU, followed in 2007 by Bulgaria and Romania. Croatia is set to become the 28th Member State of the EU in 2013.

Second, much of the organisational structure of the EU as we know it today (see section 3.2) is very similar to that of the ECSC. For instance, the High

---

Box 3.1 The role of treaties

Treaties form the basis of the European integration process. The basic treaty is the *Treaty of Rome* (1957) establishing the European Economic Community. The Treaty of Rome contains the legal basis for most decisions taken by the institutions of the European Union (see section 3.2) and is still the main source of communitary legislation. The original Treaty of Rome has been amended by subsequent treaties.

A first major amendment is the *Single European Act* (1986) completing the internal market. The chief objective of the Single European Act was to add new momentum to the process of European integration. An important innovation was that it moved away from the principle of unanimity for the harmonisation of legislation. Another major treaty is the *Maastricht Treaty on European Union (TEU)* (1992) launching Economic and Monetary Union. The Maastricht Treaty also created the European Union.

Next, the *Treaty of Amsterdam* (1997) puts a greater emphasis on security and justice matters and contains the beginning of a common foreign and security policy. A further amendment is the *Treaty of Nice* (2001). This Treaty deals with reforming the institutions so that the EU could continue to function effectively after its enlargement to 25 Member States in 2004 and subsequently to 27 Member States in 2007. The Treaty of Nice also changed the number of votes, as specified in Table 3.1.

The final change is the *Treaty of Lisbon* (2007), which entered into force on 1 December 2009. This Treaty further streamlines the institutions of the EU and upgrades the powers of the European Parliament (see Box 3.2). The Treaty of Lisbon amends the EU's two core treaties: the Treaty on European Union (TEU) and the Treaty establishing the European Community (also known as the Maastricht Treaty and the Treaty of Rome, respectively). The latter is renamed the Treaty on the Functioning of the European Union (TFEU). The Treaty of Lisbon was drafted as a replacement for the Constitutional Treaty which was rejected by French and Dutch voters in 2005.

Authority, the ECSC's supranational executive organ, was the predecessor of the European Commission. The first president of this High Authority was Jean Monnet. Other institutions of the ECSC were the Council of Ministers (representing member governments), the Assembly (composed of 68 delegates from the national parliaments, later transformed into the European Parliament), and the European Court of Justice.

With the entering into force of the Treaty of Rome in 1958 (see Box 3.1), the European Economic Community (EEC) and the European Atomic Energy Community (Euratom) came into being. Of the three communities (i.e. the ECSC, the EEC, and Euratom), the EEC was by far the most important in terms of scope and instruments.[1] The Treaty paved the way for the creation of a common market where goods, services, labour, and capital could move freely. It directed Europe towards a single financial market, but it was not until the 1980s that major steps were taken in this direction.

In 1985, the European Commission published a White Paper on the Completion of the Internal Market, which provided for the free circulation of persons, goods, services, and capital in the European Union. Economies of scale and scope would result from decreased border controls, unified technical standards, reduced distribution and marketing costs, and standardised rules and regulations in the manufacturing and services sectors. To provide an economic underpinning of the Internal Market Project, the Cecchini Report (1988) calculated the costs of nationally fragmented markets, i.e. the costs of 'non-Europe', and estimated the benefits of the internal market at approximately 4–7 per cent of GDP. The White Paper led to the adoption of the so-called Single European Act (SEA) in 1986 that aimed at completing the internal market by 1992.

Another major step in the history of European integration was the publication of the report of the Committee for the Study of Economic and Monetary Union in 1989. In the *Delors Report* – named after the chairman of this committee and then-president of the European Commission, Jacques Delors – a three-phase transition towards monetary unification was proposed. The main conclusions of the Delors Committee were incorporated in the 1992 Treaty on European Union, better known as the Maastricht Treaty, named after the Dutch city where the final negotiations took place. As a consequence, the Economic and Monetary Union (EMU) started on 1 January 1999 with the irrevocable fixing of the exchange rates of the then 11 participating countries and the start of the common monetary policy by the ECB. Euro notes and coins were introduced in January 2002.

In May 1999, the European Commission launched the Financial Services Action Plan (FSAP). The purpose of the FSAP was to remove regulatory and market barriers that limit the cross-border provision of financial services and the free flow of capital within the EU, and to create a level playing field among market participants.

This chapter outlines the most important steps taken towards European financial integration. The next section goes on to explain the most important European institutions and the legal instruments used to shape integration. As full financial integration requires monetary integration, section 3.3 describes first how monetary integration has evolved. Section 3.4 discusses coordination of fiscal policy. Section 3.5 sets out the major steps towards financial integration.

3.2 European institutions and instruments

There are two basic approaches towards integration. In the *supranational approach*, an international institution that is independent from national governments is responsible for policy making, while in the *intergovernmental approach* an international institution basically fulfils a secretariat role for the governments and has no real power. The key difference in the two approaches is the transfer of sovereignty from the Member States to that institution. Whereas in the intergovernmental approach no sovereignty is transferred, in the supranational approach Member States lose their power to enact legislation. Interestingly, in the EU both types of integration exist (Craig and De Burca, 2007).

Institutions

The *European Commission* is the EU institution that is most independent from the Member States. Its most important task is to initiate legislation. Only the Commission can come up with formal proposals for legislation (the so-called right of initiative). The Council and Parliament, to be explained below, are only able to request legislation. The formal legislative process starts with the presentation of a proposal by the European Commission to the European Parliament and the European Council, after which the process of negotiation between the latter parties starts. Currently, the Commission consists of 27 Commissioners, one from each Member State, who are appointed for a five-year term (see Box 3.2 for the changes due to the Lisbon Treaty). Commissioners are expected to detach themselves from national interests. The President of the Commission and the other Commissioners are first nominated by the European Council and are officially approved by the European Parliament. The Commission has its own staff, sometimes referred to as 'the Brussels bureaucracy'. Although this name suggests otherwise, the size of the Commission staff is relatively small – in 2008 the Commission employed just over 24,000 officials. Each Commissioner is responsible for a particular policy area, and politically responsible for a Directorate General (DG).[2] The most important DGs for financial services are DG Internal Market and Services, DG Economic and Financial Affairs, and DG Competition.

The *Council* of the European Union consists of representatives of each Member State at the ministerial level. When the Council meetings comprise ministers of economics and finance, it is known as *Ecofin*. Decision making in the Council is on the basis of unanimity, simple majority, or qualified

Table 3.1 Number of votes of EU Member States

Austria	10	Latvia	4
Belgium	12	Lithuania	7
Bulgaria	10	Luxembourg	4
Cyprus	4	Malta	3
Czech Republic	12	Netherlands	13
Denmark	7	Poland	27
Estonia	4	Portugal	12
Finland	7	Romania	14
France	29	Slovakia	7
Germany	29	Slovenia	4
Greece	12	Spain	27
Hungary	12	Sweden	10
Ireland	7	United Kingdom	29
Italy	29		
		Total	345
		Qualified majority	255

majority. In most cases, the Council votes on issues by qualified majority, meaning that there must be a minimum of 255 votes out of 345 and a majority of Member States. Table 3.1 indicates that the number of votes of the Member States reflects their size and ranges between 29 (for Germany, France, Italy, and the UK) and 3 (for Malta). Decisions on financial services policy are mainly taken by qualified majority.

The *European Council* has become a very powerful body. Comprised of the heads of government or state, and the President of the European Commission, it 'shall provide the Union with the necessary impetus for its development' (Article 15 TEU). Essentially, it defines the Union's policy agenda. Major policy initiatives, such as the Internal Market Programme, the Maastricht Treaty, and the Financial Services Action Plan, were adopted by the European Council. The European Council also comes into play when the ministers are caught in stalemate. When the Council cannot reach a decision, the issue concerned is typically transferred to the European Council.

The role of the *European Parliament* (EP), which since 1979 is elected by the people of the EU Member States in direct elections every five years (coinciding with the term of the Commissioners of the European Commission), is more limited than that of national parliaments. Still, over time, the influence of the EP has increased. Currently, it has 736 members. The EP has veto power over the appointment of the Commission. It can also dismiss the

Box 3.2 The Lisbon Treaty

After the French and Dutch electorate had rejected a proposal for a 'European Constitution' in Spring 2005, it took until October 2007 before the Heads of State and Government agreed in the Portuguese capital on the text of the Lisbon Treaty that amends the existing Treaties. The Treaty of Lisbon amends the EU's two core treaties, the Treaty on European Union (TEU) and the Treaty establishing the European Community. The latter is renamed the Treaty on the Functioning of the European Union (TFEU) and implies the following changes with respect to the institutions of the EU as outlined above.

The Lisbon Treaty originally intended to reduce the size of the European Commission to 18 Commissioners. However, negotiations following Ireland's rejection of the Treaty in 2008 led to an agreement that all Member States will keep their Commissioner unless national governments decide otherwise unanimously.

Like the European Parliament and the Commission, the European Council has become an EU institution with its own full-time president who will not be able to assume a national mandate. The president is elected by qualified majority by the European Council for two and a half years; this term can be renewed once. The president of the European Council represents the EU in the international arena and chairs and coordinates the European Council's work. The Lisbon Treaty also provides for a so-called 'High Representative of the Union for Foreign Affairs and Security Policy' who will be responsible in the Council for the EU's common foreign and defence policies.

There will be new decision-making rules within the Council. A decision will be adopted within the Council if it wins the approval of 55 per cent of the EU Member States (i.e. 15 Member States in an EU comprising 27 Member States) representing at least 65 per cent of the EU's population. Furthermore, a blocking minority has to include at least 4 Member States. The new double-majority voting rule that emerged with the Lisbon Treaty will come into force in October 2014 with a transitional period until March 2017. During this period it will be possible for the Members of the Council to ask that decisions that need to be adopted by qualified majority be adopted according to qualified majority as stipulated in the Treaty of Nice. It will also be possible to suspend decisions using the so-called 'Ioannina mechanism', a mechanism which was included during negotiations in order to win over Poland. If Member States that are against a text are significant in number but still insufficient to block the decision (one-third of the Member States or 25 per cent of the population), all of the Member States commit to seeking a solution to rally opponents while reserving the option to vote at any time. The efficiency of the decision-making process will also be enhanced by the extension of the qualified majority vote to new areas. The qualified majority replaces unanimity in several areas, such as the adoption of measures relating to external border control, asylum, and immigration.

Finally, the powers of the European Parliament have been extended. In the legislative domain, the co-decision procedure will be applied in nearly 50 new areas, including the internal market. As to the budget, the European Parliament has been given the same right to decision as the Council, notably with regard to the adoption of the entire annual budget (whilst today the Council has the last word on the so-called 'compulsory' expenditures, which represent a major part of the European budget, notably agricultural expenditures).

Commission. The EP also has the right to reject the EU Budget. It plays an important role in legislation, which may go through different procedures. Under the *consultation procedure*, the EP only gives its opinion. Under the *cooperation procedure* it has the right to amend or even reject legislation, but these decisions may be overruled by the Council. Under the *co-decision procedure*, acceptance by the EP is necessary. The Commission presents a proposal to Parliament and the Council, then the EP sends amendments to the Council, which can either adopt the text with those amendments or send back a 'common position'. That proposal may be approved or further amendments may be tabled by the EP. If the Council does not approve those, a 'Conciliation Committee' is formed that seeks agreement. Finally, under the *assent procedure* the Council is required to obtain the European Parliament's assent before certain important decisions are taken. The assent principle is based on a single reading. The EP may accept or reject a proposal but cannot amend it. If the EP does not give its assent, the act in question cannot be adopted. The assent procedure applies mainly to the accession of new Member States, association agreements, and other fundamental agreements with third countries. It is, among others, also required with regard to the specific tasks of the ECB and amendments to the Statutes of the European System of Central Banks (ESCB) and the ECB. Parliament's assent is given by a majority of votes cast, but a majority of Members is also required in case of the accession of a new Member State and the electoral procedure.

The *European Court of Justice* (ECJ) consists of 27 judges (one judge per Member State) and 8 advocates-general. Judgments of the ECJ on matters relating to the interpretation and application of European law have been of great importance for the development of the EU. As the supreme court of the EU, the ECJ gives a coherent and uniform interpretation of Community law and ensures compliance by the Member States. The ECJ has rejected protectionism in many judgments and thus contributed significantly to the realisation of the internal market.

Legal instruments

Legislative measures in the EU are proposed by the European Commission and – in the case of nearly all the measures under the Financial Services Action Plan (see section 3.5) – are adopted by co-decision under which the Council and the European Parliament consider, amend, and agree on the final content of each legislative measure. These measures are published in the *Official Journal of the European Union* and can take the form of:

- *regulations* – a regulation is binding in its entirety and directly applicable in all Member States, and does not require transposition into the respective national laws (although there may be changes required in Member States' laws to achieve the full effect of the regulation);
- *directives* – a directive is binding upon each Member State to which it is addressed, but gives national authorities the choice of form and methods. In other words, directives must be incorporated in the national law of each Member State, generally by introducing or amending national laws, within a deadline of usually 18 or 24 months after publication.

In addition to regulations and directives, the Commission or the Council can take *decisions* which are binding upon those to whom they are addressed. The Commission and the Council can also formulate *recommendations* or deliver *opinions*. These are not legally binding, although politically they can be important. The various instruments have a different impact on integration (see also Box 3.3). A regulation fosters full integration, because of its direct application. Basically, the rules are uniform and overrule national legislation, to the extent that the latter is not consistent with the regulation. By contrast, a directive needs to be implemented by the Member States, leaving scope for minor or major differences. The rules are then harmonised and are generally not uniform.

The adoption or implementation of legal instruments is only the first element of the legislative framework. The second element is the putting in place of the relevant administrative arrangements to ensure that the new rules are observed. The third element, sometimes referred to as enforcement, is ensuring that the new rules work effectively and are complied with across the EU.

3.3 Monetary integration

During the initial phase of European integration, the emphasis was on integration of goods markets. As far as monetary issues were concerned, the

---

Box 3.3 Dynamics of integration

The combination of the choice of the decision-making procedure (supranational or inter-governmental) and the choice of legal instrument (regulation or directive) determines to a large extent the degree of integration. In the area of competition policy and monetary policy, the EU has chosen for regulations to ensure uniformity across the EU. A good example is the Regulation on the Introduction of the Euro (EC/974/98), according to which the national currencies participating in the euro could only be converted into the euro in a uniform way. If the euro denomination of the German D-Mark, for example, were calculated differently across countries, there would be scope for arbitrage. A supranational institution (the European Central Bank) is responsible for policy making.

In the area of financial services policy, the EU has often opted for directives. These directives are mostly implemented in a different way by each Member State. An example is the definition of 'capital' under the Banking Directive (2006/48/EC). This directive determines how much capital banks must maintain in view of the risks that a bank faces. All 27 Member States use their own definition of capital. Moreover, banking supervision is executed by national supervisory authorities. Banking groups that have cross-border operations in the EU sometimes complain about the differences in rules and approach taken by national supervisors.

Rome Treaty described exchange rate policies as a matter of 'common concern', but did not offer substantive contents as to its meaning. It was only at the summit in 1969 in The Hague that the European governments agreed on monetary union. Pierre Werner, prime minister of Luxembourg at the time, was appointed to chair a committee that was to draw up a plan. The Werner Report was completed in 1970. It called for the completion of a monetary union by 1980. The Werner Committee proposed a three-stage approach towards monetary union, leading eventually to fixed exchange rates and a common monetary policy.

Although the Council adopted the plan, the turmoil in the currency markets at the time made it falter. The mid-1970s can be characterised as a low point in European monetary integration. However, at the end of the 1970s the then French president, Valéry Giscard d'Estaing, and German chancellor, Helmut Schmidt, took the initiative for the European Monetary System (EMS). The aim of the EMS was to create a 'zone of monetary stability' in Europe. The core was the so-called Exchange Rate Mechanism (ERM). Currencies participating in the ERM were supposed to fluctuate vis-à-vis one another within a band of plus and minus 2.25 per cent around agreed-upon central rates. These central rates could be adjusted. Although this system brought some stability for the participating currencies, there were, at times, frequent adjustments of the central rates. Within the system, the German D-Mark functioned as the anchor. Countries that pegged their currency to the German one had little room for manoeuvre in monetary policy making. If the German monetary authorities decided to change their interest rates, the other countries had to follow if they wanted to maintain their peg. Various countries, notably France, felt that the German-dominated ERM did not always serve their interests as the German monetary authorities, in deciding on interest rates, took into account only the economic situation in Germany. A monetary union was considered the proper answer to this problem.

During the 1980s, the discussion therefore focused again on monetary integration. There is no doubt that the signing of the Single European Act (SEA) in 1986 and the commitment to complete the internal market by 1992 were important in furthering monetary union. Initially regarded as rather modest in nature, the SEA succeeded in developing renewed momentum for European integration, not least by establishing a clear deadline for completion of the internal market. It was argued that in order to reap the full gains from the internal market, exchange-rate risks and transaction costs were to be banished by introducing a common currency. This view is apparent from the title of an important study by the European Commission: 'One Market, One Money' (Emerson *et al.*, 1992). Although many economists do not subscribe to the view that fixed exchange rates are needed to fully capture the gains from the Single Market, the argument gained popularity under policy makers.

At the Hannover summit in June 1988, the European Council decided to establish a committee that should propose concrete stages leading to Economic and Monetary Union (EMU). The committee was chaired by Jacques Delors. A year later the committee presented its report. Although it did not offer a specified timetable, the committee proposed a gradual process towards EMU, eventually leading to monetary union, but stressed that the timing of each stage required a political decision. In the final stage, there would be a single currency under a new central bank's authority. Although not strictly necessary for the creation of monetary union, the Delors Committee argued in favour of a single currency, as this would demonstrate the irreversibility of the union. The countries participating were not only supposed to have a common currency but would also coordinate their economic policies, notably fiscal policy. That is why the system is called Economic and Monetary Union.[3]

Subsequent negotiations eventually led to the adoption of the 1992 Treaty on European Union, signed in Maastricht, where the leaders of the EU

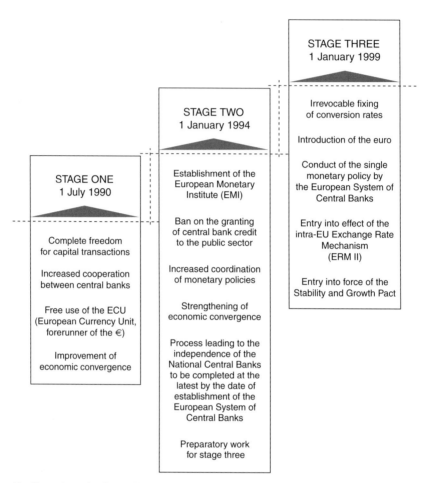

Figure 3.1   The three stages leading to EMU
Source: ECB

countries met to take a decision on EMU. The negotiations were difficult as the United Kingdom had strong reservations about moving towards an EU-wide currency union. The compromise that was reached was to give the UK a so-called 'opt-out clause', i.e. even if the UK meets the convergence criteria for entering the euro area as stipulated in the Maastricht Treaty, it is up to the UK government to decide about entry.

Many of the suggestions of the Delors Committee found their way into the Treaty, including a three-stage approach (see Figure 3.1). As suggested in the Delors Report, the first stage of EMU started on 1 July 1990 with the liberalisation of capital controls (see section 3.5 for further details).

However, ratification of the Treaty turned out to be difficult. Denmark rejected the Maastricht Treaty at a referendum in June 1992.[4] The rejection, with a slight majority, came as a huge shock. In France, where the Maastricht Treaty was put to a referendum after the Danes initially had said no, the majority in favour was a wafer-thin 51 per cent. Ratification was tortuous and contentious in some other countries too.

Perspectives for EMU became dim when serious currency crises occurred in 1992–1993 that forced governments to broaden the ERM fluctuation band to plus and minus 15 per cent. Many sceptics asked what hope there could be for a monetary union among countries unable to keep national currencies aligned. Sometimes EMU was perceived as an ambitious project that would never fly, just like the emu, the large Australian bird. For instance, the then prime minister of the UK, John Major, wrote in *The Economist* that continuing 'to recite the mantra of full economic and monetary union … will have all the quaintness of a rain dance and about the same potency'. Although the currency crises for some time led to lingering doubts, with the start of the second stage of EMU on 1 January 1994 it became clear that EMU was becoming more and more likely.

At the beginning of 1998, the European Council decided that 11 of the then 15 EU Member States could join the currency union. This decision was based on the so-called convergence criteria as outlined in the Maastricht Treaty that refer to inflation, long-term interest rates, exchange rate stability, and the public deficit and debt-to-GDP ratios (see Table 3.2).

On 1 January 1999 Europe entered a new era with the adoption of a single currency – the euro – by 11 Member States of the EU. Greece joined the euro area in 2001 and Slovenia in 2007, while Cyprus and Malta introduced the euro in 2008 and Slovakia in 2009. Estonia joined the euro area in 2011. It was the first time that countries of anything like this number, size, or global economic weight had gathered together on a voluntary basis to share a currency and to pool their monetary sovereignty.

With the start of EMU, participating countries no longer had their own monetary sovereignty. As of 1 January 1999, monetary policy in the euro area was delegated to the European Central Bank (ECB). The *Governing Council of the ECB* is responsible for taking monetary policy decisions. This Council consists of the Executive Board of the ECB – made up of the president, the vice-president, and four other members – and the Central Bank governors from the countries in the euro area. Together with National Central Banks (NCBs), the ECB is part of the European System of Central Banks (ESCB). While the ECB is responsible for policy decisions, NCBs play a role in

Table 3.2 Convergence criteria

Inflation	Member State has a price performance that is sustainable and an average rate of inflation, observed over a period of one year before the examination, that does not exceed by more than 1½ percentage points that of, at most, the three best-performing Member States in terms of price stability.
Interest rate	Member State has had an average nominal long-term interest rate that does not exceed by more than 2 percentage points that of, at most, the three best-performing Member States in terms of price stability.
Exchange rate	Member State has observed the normal fluctuation margins provided for by the ERM for at least two years, without devaluing against the currency of any other Member State on its own initiative.
Budget deficit	Member State's planned or actual government deficit to GDP ratio must not exceed 3 per cent unless: - either the ratio has declined substantially and continuously and reached a level that comes close to the reference value; or, alternatively, - the excess over the reference value is only exceptional and temporary and the ratio remains close to the reference value.
Debt	Member State's government debt to GDP ratio must not exceed 60 per cent, unless the ratio is sufficiently diminishing and approaching the reference value at a satisfactory pace.

implementing monetary policy. The central banks of the EU Member States that do not participate in the euro area are members of the ESCB but they do not take part in the decision making on the single monetary policy for the euro area and the implementation of such decisions.

The ECB's primary objective as laid down in the Treaty on the Functioning of the EU (TFEU), is price stability. The ECB has announced its interpretation of price stability (maintaining inflation in the euro area below but close to 2 per cent in the medium term) and has developed a monetary policy strategy to accomplish this objective (see Chapter 4 for further details). Although the primary objective is to maintain price stability, there are explicit references in the Treaty to financial regulation and supervision. For instance, the Treaty states that the ESCB has to promote the smooth operations of payment systems. According to Article 127(5) TFEU, the ESCB shall contribute to the smooth conduct of policies pursued by the competent authorities relating to the prudential supervision of credit institutions and the stability of the financial system. Similarly, Article 127(6) TFEU states that the Council may confer upon the ECB specific tasks concerning policies relating to the prudential supervision of credit institutions and other financial institutions with the exception of insurance undertakings. However, the Treaty is explicit on the principle of decentralisation and allocation of regulatory and supervisory powers to National Central Banks. Only in very special circumstances, and with unanimity in the European Council, will the ECB be allowed to regulate and supervise financial institutions.

3.4 Coordination of fiscal policy

Stability and Growth Pact

Whereas monetary policy in EMU is conducted at the supranational level, fiscal policy has remained largely the competence of national governments. According to ECB (2011), a well-functioning monetary union requires the maintenance of fiscal discipline among its member countries. High deficits can give rise to demand and inflationary pressures that may force the ECB to keep short-term interest rates at a higher level than would otherwise be necessary. Furthermore, fiscal policies may undermine confidence in the ECB's monetary policy if markets come to expect that excessive government borrowing will ultimately be financed through money creation, and thus adjust their inflation expectations accordingly.

Therefore, the Maastricht Treaty contains provisions for the monitoring and coordination of EU Member States' fiscal policies which were further specified in the Stability and Growth Pact (SGP) that was adopted in 1997. It contains a preventive and a corrective arm. The preventive arm prescribes the path for sound fiscal policies, while the corrective arm is intended to prevent 'gross policy errors' by deterring excessive deficits and requiring their prompt correction should they occur.

Under the preventive arm of the SGP, Member States submit stability or convergence programmes in which they detail their medium-term budgetary plans. Under the original SGP, Member States were required to pursue the medium-term objective of budgetary positions that were 'close to balance or in surplus'.

The corrective arm of the SGP specifies the Excessive Deficit Procedure (EDP). When the Ecofin decides that an excessive deficit exists in a Member State, the procedure provides for a sequence of steps to be taken that should intensify the pressure on the Member State concerned to take effective action to correct its excessive deficit. For each step, the Ecofin has to take decisions on the basis of recommendations by the Commission. If a Member State does not take (sufficient) action to redress an excessive deficit, sanctions may be imposed. Sanctions include the requirement for the Member State concerned to make a non-interest-bearing deposit, which, if non-compliance persists, is eventually turned into a fine.

Critics of the SGP pointed to a major weakness of the rules in place: the Ecofin will not automatically impose sanctions, as each step requires a discretionary decision by the Council, thus following an intergovernmental approach. And the same ministers who are responsible for drafting national budgets also have to decide whether one of their colleagues breaches the rules. There are no strong incentives for Member States to prevent other Member States from deviating from the objective to strive for a balanced budget in the medium term. Furthermore, the Member States have no other means than peer pressure in the multilateral surveillance part of the SGP. No wonder, therefore, that various Member States did not adhere to this medium-term objective. Large countries, in particular, did not bring down their deficit sufficiently. As a consequence, they exceeded the 3 per cent deficit threshold once the economic downturn set in during 2000–2001. It then became clear that the enforcement mechanism in the excessive deficit procedure is also weak. Its major shortcoming is the lack of an impartial enforcement mechanism, as the Ecofin is responsible for enforcing the rules.

In 2005 the SGP was amended and this introduced more discretion and flexibility into the surveillance procedures, but made the corrective arm slightly more stringent. Each Member State will present its own country-specific medium-term objective (MTO) in its stability programme. These country-specific MTOs will be differentiated and may diverge from the close to balance or in surplus requirement depending on the current debt ratio and potential growth. The adjustment effort should be greater in good times and could be more limited in bad times. As a benchmark, the Member States should pursue an annual adjustment in cyclically adjusted terms, net of one-off and temporary measures, of 0.5 per cent of GDP. Under the amended SGP more emphasis is also put on the government debt ratio. This was important, as in implementing the SGP until then the Ecofin had only focused on the government budget deficit. However, the reform has not introduced any fundamental institutional changes.

Recent changes

In response to the debt crisis, the European Commission has proposed several changes to the SGP. The amended proposals have been adopted by the European Parliament and the Council.

Preventive arm

Progress towards the MTO will be assessed also on the basis of expenditure developments. Expenditure growth should be linked to the mid-term GDP growth rate, so that any extra expenditure is financed by either expenditure cuts or an increase in revenue. If a Member State does not respect the agreed principles it may receive a warning from the Commission, followed by a recommendation to the Member State to take corrective action. The recommendation will be adopted by the Council by qualified majority voting. If the Member State does not take appropriate action within the deadline specified in this Council recommendation, the Commission will immediately recommend to the Council to adopt a decision establishing that no effective action has been taken. If the Council does not adopt the decision and the Member State concerned does not take appropriate action, one month later the decision will be considered again and will be adopted unless a simple majority of Member States vote against it (the so-called *reverse simple majority voting* procedure). For euro-area Member States, the recommendation will be backed by an enforcement mechanism in the form of an interest-bearing deposit amounting to 0.2 per cent of GDP. Euro-area Member States which misrepresent deficit and debt data relevant to the SGP may face an additional fine of up to 0.2 per cent of GDP. At the same time, the professional independence of national statistical authorities is reinforced.

Corrective arm

It will be possible to open an EDP on the basis of the debt criterion. Member States with government debt ratios in excess of 60 per cent of GDP should reduce this ratio in line with a numerical benchmark, which implies a decline of the amount by which their debt exceeds the threshold at a rate in the order of 1/20th per year over three years. If they do not, they could be placed in EDP. In addition, a non-interest-bearing deposit of 0.2 per cent of GDP may be requested from a euro-area country that is placed in EDP. On a recommendation by the Commission, a decision to impose this sanction will be adopted by the Council by reverse qualified majority voting procedure. In case of non-compliance with the initial recommendation for corrective action, this non-interest-bearing deposit will be converted into a fine. The fine will be increased in case of repeated non-respect of the recommendations.

Fiscal compact

As European policymakers came to the conclusion that insufficient fiscal discipline was one of the causes of the recent crisis in the euro area (see Chapter 2), they discussed ways to enhance the Stability and Growth Pact. On 30 January 2012 after several weeks of negotiations, all EU leaders except those from the United Kingdom and the Czech Republic endorsed a new Treaty, the Treaty on Stability, Coordination and Governance. The fiscal part of the Treaty is referred to as fiscal compact. The new treaty will come into force once it has been ratified by at least 12 countries that use the euro. It will only apply to those contracting parties whose currency is the euro, while the others will be bound by its provisions once they adopt the euro.

The fiscal compact aims to strengthen fiscal discipline through the introduction of more automatic adjustments and stricter surveillance, and in particular through the balanced budget rule. The new Treaty requires national budgets to be in balance or in surplus. This objective will be achieved if the annual cyclically adjusted government deficit does not exceed 0.5 per cent of GDP but countries with government debt levels significantly below 60 per cent are allowed to have a structural deficit of at most 1.0 per cent of GDP. This rule will be introduced in Member States' national legal systems at the constitutional level. The EU's highest court will be able to fine a country that does not adopt the rule in its constitution - with a penalty equivalent to up to 0.1 per cent of GDP. The rule will contain an automatic correction mechanism that shall be triggered in the event of deviation from the country-specific medium-term objective as defined in the SGP.

As soon as a Member State's deficit exceeds the 3 per cent ceiling, the Commission submits a proposal of counter-measures, concerning in particular the nature, the size and the timeframe of the corrective action to be undertaken. Only a qualified majority of Member States may reject these proposals.

3.5 Financial integration

The Treaty of Rome of 1957 identified the 'creation of a unified economic area with a common market' as a task of the Community. As for the creation of a single market for financial services, policy primarily focused on the banking system in the first decades. The first step towards harmonisation of prudential standards for supervision of banks was set with the First Banking Directive (77/780/EEC). This directive required full harmonisation of relevant banking standards, such as solvency, liquidity, and internal controls. But the national approaches to basic prudential standards, including capital requirements, continued to diverge. Major subsequent steps were taken under the Internal Market Programme and the Financial Services Action Plan.

The Internal Market Programme

As pointed out in section 3.1, in the second half of the 1980s completion of the internal market was high on the agenda of European policy makers. In the context of banking, the European Commission called for a single banking licence and home-country control. Accordingly, the Second Banking Directive (89/646/EEC) determines that a credit institution that is authorised in any EU Member State is allowed to establish branches or supply cross-border financial services in the other EU Member States. Such a *single banking licence* is necessary and sufficient for cross-border provision of banking services and the establishment of branches in other Member States. The single banking licence has therefore significantly contributed to stimulating cross-border banking in Europe. However, the main limitation of the Second Banking Directive is that the single licence does not extend to subsidiaries in host Member States. This is unfortunate, as the process of cross-border European banking more often takes place via subsidiaries, especially when the cross-border operations involve major banking operations (see Chapter 10).

Importantly, the Second Banking Directive also introduced the principle of *home-country control* in supervision of branches with some exceptions, notably the supervision of branch liquidity. The authorities in the home country are responsible for supervision on solvency that extends to the bank itself, its foreign and national subsidiaries, which have to be consolidated for supervisory purposes, and its foreign branches. The authorities in the host state retain the right to regulate a foreign bank's activities in that state only to the extent that such regulation is necessary for the protection of 'public interest'. Also, in emergency situations, the host-country supervisor may take precautionary measures necessary to protect depositors, investors, and others to whom services are provided (Dermine, 2006).

The European legal framework incorporates the international banking standards of the Basel Committee on Banking Supervision (see Box 3.4). An important element in banking supervision is the so-called *capital adequacy requirements*, i.e. regulations on the minimum amount of capital that banks have to provide for. The Solvency and Own Funds Directives (89/647/EEC and 89/299/EEC) that laid down the solvency rules for banks were based on the 1988 Basel Capital Accord. Likewise, Basel III forms the basis for new EU regulation.

Box 3.4 Basel Committee on Banking Supervision

The Basel Committee on Banking Supervision provides a forum for regular cooperation on banking supervisory matters. Its objective is to enhance understanding of key supervisory issues and improve the quality of banking supervision worldwide. It seeks to do so by exchanging information on national supervisory issues, approaches, and techniques, with a view to promoting common understanding. At times, the Committee develops guidelines and supervisory standards in areas where they are considered desirable. Examples include Standards on Capital Adequacy (Basel I, Basel II, and Basel III; see below), the Core Principles for Effective Banking Supervision, and the Concordat on cross-border banking supervision.

The Committee's members come from Argentina, Australia, Belgium, Brazil, Canada, China, France, Germany, Hong Kong SAR, India, Indonesia, Italy, Japan, Korea, Luxembourg, Mexico, the Netherlands, Russia, Saudi Arabia, Singapore, South Africa, Spain, Sweden, Switzerland, Turkey, the United Kingdom, and the United States. Countries are represented by their central bank and also by the authority with formal responsibility for the prudential supervision of banking business where this is not the central bank. The Committee's Secretariat is located at the Bank for International Settlements in Basel, Switzerland.

One of the issues that the Committee frequently discusses is minimum capital requirements for banks. In 2004, an agreement was reached, generally referred to as the *Basel II Accord*. It uses a three-pillars concept: (1) minimum capital requirements, (2) supervisory review, and (3) market discipline. Its predecessor, the *Basel I Accord* of 1988, dealt with only parts of each of these pillars. Basel II seeks to improve on the existing rules by aligning regulatory capital requirements more closely to the underlying risks that banks face. In response to the financial crisis, the Committee proposed several changes in 2010, generally referred to as *Basel III* (see Chapter 12 for further details).

An important principle underlying European financial integration is *minimum harmonisation*. Instead of fully harmonising rules, a common minimum is defined that Member States have to implement. However, they are free to move beyond this minimum. A good example of this approach is the Directive on Deposit Guarantee Schemes (94/19/EEC) that was accepted by the Council in 1994. This directive provides for mandatory coverage per depositor with a minimum of €20,000. The directive does not deal with funding, so that the financing has to be arranged at the national level (e.g. ex-ante or ex-post funding). Deposits of a branch are covered by the deposit-insurance system of the home country. All EU countries adopted an explicit deposit-insurance scheme with compulsory participation. Practical arrangements with respect to coverage limits, funding, and co-insurance differed substantially across EU Member States. During the crisis, the EU rules were changed. Directive 2009/14/EC of 11 March 2009 determines that Member States are required to increase the coverage level to eventually €100,000. According to the European Commission, the new level would cover an estimated 90 per cent of deposits. Another important change is that the time allowed for the deposit guarantee system to pay depositors in the event that a bank fails is reduced to three days.

So far, this section has discussed banking integration under the Internal Market Programme. Similar developments have taken place in the fields of insurance and securities. The Third Insurance Directives (92/49/EEC and 92/96/EEC) and the Investment Services Directive (93/22/EEC) also adopted the principles of a single licence, home-country control, and minimum harmonisation of standards.

Another important milestone for European financial integration was the Directive on Liberalisation of Capital Flows (88/361/EEC). Starting from 1 July 1990 – i.e. the start of the first phase of EMU – capital controls were, as a rule, no longer allowed. Only in the case of large, speculative movements could the European Commission authorise capital controls.

The Financial Services Action Plan

The European Council of Cardiff in 1998 underlined the importance of financial market integration as a political priority. In reaction, the European Commission published a Communication entitled 'Financial Services: Building a Framework for Action' which set out a series of measures to strengthen integration. This document recognised the crucial role of financial services in the EU's economy, and aimed to complement the introduction of the euro by creating the right conditions for the financial sector to strengthen integration. The overall objective was to create deeper and more liquid capital markets and remove remaining barriers to cross-border provision of financial services. Financial integration was not perceived as a goal in itself but rather as a means to deliver economic growth. The Communication was discussed at the European Council meeting in 1998 in Vienna, whereupon the Council called for a 'concrete and urgent working programme'. This resulted in May 1999 in the launch of the *Financial Services Action Plan (FSAP)* by the European Commission. The purpose of the FSAP, endorsed by the European Council in March 2000, is to remove regulatory and market barriers that limit the cross-border provision of financial services and the free flow of capital within the EU, and to create a level playing field among market participants. It consists of a set of 42 measures to fill gaps and remove

The Financial Services Action Plan has four objectives:

- single EU wholesale market
- open and secure retail markets
- state-of-the-art prudential rules and supervision
- optimal single financial market.

Figure 3.2   Objectives of FSAP

remaining barriers to provide a legal and regulatory environment that supports the integration of financial markets across the EU.

The FSAP has four objectives (see Figure 3.2). The first objective is a single EU wholesale market. The Markets in Financial Instruments Directive (MiFID, 2004/39/EC) is, to a large extent, the cornerstone of the FSAP. This directive provides securities firms with an updated EU passport, allowing them to offer a range of financial services across Member States on a 'home-country control' basis (Haas, 2005). Under the passport principle, a firm licensed to provide financial services in its home country has the right to provide these same services throughout the EU, without the need for an additional licence. MiFID applies the passport to a broader range of financial instruments and significantly extends the list of financial services that can be 'passported' across European countries. A major innovation is the introduction of new trading venues. While the Investment Services Directive (ISD) restricted securities trading to regulated markets (i.e. stock exchanges), MiFID also allows trading on multilateral trading facilities (MTFs), i.e. systems that bring together multiple parties (e.g. retail investors or other investment firms) that are interested in buying and selling financial instruments and enable them to do so. MiFID also facilitates in-house matching (i.e. matching a buyer and a seller within the same firm). Under certain conditions regarding pre-trade transparency and best execution, banks are allowed to 'match' customer trades internally. MTFs and in-house matching are expected to be major competitors of the more traditional exchanges.

The objective of MiFID is to foster the emergence of a single, more competitive, cross-border securities market across the EU. The directive promotes, and often prescribes through detailed rules, European-wide legislative harmonisation for key components of the provision of financial services along the following central principles (Haas, 2007): increased competition, a level playing field, increased market efficiency, and better investor protection.

The second objective of the FSAP is open and secure retail markets. The Commission acknowledged that certain barriers prevented consumers and suppliers from reaping the single-market benefits of increased choice and competitive terms. In order to develop open and secure markets for retail financial services, the Commission therefore aimed to:

- promote enhanced information, transparency, and security for cross-border provision of retail financial services;
- expedite speedy resolution of consumer disputes through effective extra-judicial procedures; and
- balance application of local consumer-protection rules.

Examples of FSAP directives in the domain of retail financial services include the Distance Selling Directive and the Insurance Mediation Directive. The Distance Marketing Directive (2002/65/EC) aims to protect retail customers who deal with a financial services firm or acquire a financial product through the exclusive use of distance means such as telephone, Internet, fax, or post. It ensures that retail customers are given minimum specified information about financial services or products before contracting and have the right to cancel some types of contracts after entering into them. The Insurance Mediation Directive (2002/92/EC) aims to improve choice and reinforce protection for customers while helping insurance intermediaries (like insurance brokers and banks) to market their services cross-border in the EU. The directive sets common minimum standards across the EU for the regulation of the sale and administration of insurance. It provides rights for an insurance intermediary established in one Member State to operate in another Member State.

The third objective of the FSAP is state-of-the-art prudential rules and supervision. The Capital Requirements Directive (CRD), comprising Directive 2006/48/EC and Directive 2006/49/EC, lay down these new capital adequacy rules for banks and is based on the 2004 Basel II Capital Accord. Under these directives investment firms and credit institutions are allowed to use internal models for risk management to calculate their capital requirement.

Capital requirement rules stipulate the minimum amounts of own financial resources that credit institutions and investment firms must have in order to cover the risks to which they are exposed. The aim is to ensure the financial soundness of these institutions – in particular to ensure that they can weather difficult periods, thereby protecting depositors and clients, and fostering the stability of the financial system. Under the CRD, capital requirements are more comprehensive than in the past. In particular they cover the so-called 'operational risk', which is the risk of loss from inadequate or failed internal processes, people, or systems, or from external events. The CRD introduces capital requirements to ensure that institutions are resilient to such risks.

Similarly, the Solvency II Directive (2009/138/EC) introduces risk-based capital requirements for insurance companies (see Chapter 12).

The final objective of the FSAP is related to wider conditions for an optimal single financial market, e.g. addressing disparities in tax treatment and creating an efficient and transparent legal system for corporate governance. An example is the Savings Directive (2003/48/EC) that aims to enable interest on savings received in one Member State, by individuals who are resident for tax purposes in another Member State, to be made subject to effective taxation in accordance with the laws of the latter Member State. It establishes automatic exchange of information as the way of combating cross-border tax evasion on savings income.

In 2004, the European Commission concluded that the Financial Services Action Plan was delivered on time, with 40 out of 42 measures being adopted before the 2005 deadline.

After the crisis

In its Communication of 2 June 2010, 'Regulating financial services for sustainable growth', the European Commission announced an extensive list of reform proposals, reflecting the lessons learned during the 2007–2009 financial crisis. According to the Commission, efficient and integrated financial markets play a decisive role in order to stimulate economic recovery in Europe.

One of the crucial elements of the package is the creation of a new architecture for financial supervision in Europe, consisting of three new European Supervisory Authorities for the banking, securities markets, and insurance and occupational pensions sectors, together with a European Systemic Risk Board (ESRB). This new financial supervision architecture that started in 2011 will be discussed in more detail in Chapters 12 and 13.

The list of other envisaged measures include the following (European Commission, 2011):

1. A revision of the CRD in order to implement the Basel III agreement of the Basel committee of banking supervisors, which significantly increases the levels of capital which banks and investment firms must hold to cover their risk-weighted assets (see Chapter 12).
2. For the insurance sector, the 'Solvency II' Directive, which will enter into force at the beginning of 2013. It makes capital rules for insurance companies more detailed, stringent, and risk-sensitive (see Chapter 12).
3. The recently introduced Regulation on Credit Rating Agencies (CRAs), which introduces strict authorisation requirements and supervision for CRAs, will be further revised (see Chapter 8).

4. The Markets in Financial Instruments Directive (MiFID) will be adjusted to improve transparency, efficiency, and integrity of securities markets in several ways. For example, the scope of MiFID will be extended to new types of trading platform and financial products.
5. The Market Abuse Directive (MAD) will also be revised to provide for a more effective prevention, detection, and sanctioning of market abuses.
6. A Regulation has been proposed on over-the-counter (OTC) derivatives markets. The draft Regulation contains a new requirement for standardised OTC derivative transactions to be cleared via central counterparties. Furthermore, OTC derivatives have to be registered in trade repositories, with access for supervisors in the EU, which will provide a better overview of who owes what and to whom and to detect any potential problems, such as accumulation of risk, early on (see Chapter 7).
7. A proposed Regulation regarding short selling and credit default swaps (CDSs) will increase transparency enabling supervisors to detect when such transactions are reaching dangerous levels and consider intervention on markets.

All these measures intend to enhance the stability of the financial sector. But since there is no guarantee that a crisis will not happen again, the European Commission launched at the end of 2010 a consultation for the establishment of a crisis management framework in the EU. This will enlarge the toolkit of supervisors to deal with financial institutions in difficulty, including a requirement for banks to prepare 'Living Wills' providing for their own dissolution in case of failure, and the power of supervisors to replace the Board, organise the sale of a financial institution or attempt to organise 'bail-ins' of banks, by which its own shareholders contribute to the funding requirements of a failing institution (see Chapter 13).

3.6 Conclusions

The EU has its origins in the European Coal and Steel Community, formed by six European countries in 1951. Since then, the EU has grown in size through the accession of new Member States, while it has also increased its powers by the addition of new policy areas to its remit. At the time of writing, the European Union consists of 27 Member States and has supranational and intergovernmental forms of cooperation.

Legislation has been the main mechanism for fostering economic integration. Treaties are the milestones in the integration process. An example is the Maastricht Treaty establishing the European Central Bank (ECB). Within the broader framework of these treaties, legislative measures are proposed by the European Commission and adopted by the Council and the European Parliament. These legislative measures include regulations, which apply directly in each Member State, and directives, which need to be incorporated in the national law of each Member State. While regulations ensure a uniform regulatory framework throughout the EU, the implementation of directives by Member States leaves scope for differences.

Monetary integration is characterised by two major steps. In 1979, the European Monetary System (EMS) was introduced. A key element of the EMS was the Exchange Rate Mechanism, within which the currencies of participating countries were supposed to fluctuate within a band of plus and minus 2.25 per cent. In the early 1990s, the EMS was strained by the differing economic policies and conditions of its members and the band of fluctuation was subsequently widened to plus and minus 15 per cent. In 1999, the European Central Bank took over responsibility for monetary policy making, and a common currency, the euro, was introduced in 11 of the 15 EU Member States.

Whereas monetary policy has been delegated to the supranational ECB, fiscal policy has remained largely the competence of national governments. In order to protect monetary policy, the Stability and Growth Pact has introduced restrictions on national fiscal policy of the countries in the monetary union.

While monetary integration in Europe took place with some major steps, financial integration is a more gradual process. In 1992, the EU created an internal market by a system of laws which apply in all Member States, guaranteeing the freedom of movement of people, goods, services, and capital. In the area of financial services, the internal market introduced a single licence and home-country control for financial institutions. With a licence from the home country, financial institutions can expand throughout the EU. To strengthen financial integration further, the Commission launched the Financial Services Action Plan (FSAP) in 1999 with the purpose of removing any remaining barriers that limit the cross-border provision of financial services. The FSAP measures are complemented by a system of supervisory committees to enhance convergence of supervisory standards and practices across the EU. Financial supervision is the responsibility of national supervisory agencies. It is important not only to have common rules but also to apply these rules in a similar way to achieve financial integration. Only then can a level playing field between countries be achieved.

NOTES

1 The three communities were merged in 1967. Since then, one often referred to the European Communities, later to be changed to European Community. Since the Maastricht Treaty one generally refers to the European Union.
2 Sometimes a Commissioner is responsible for more than one DG.
3 So EMU does not mean European Monetary Union. Unfortunately, this is how the abbreviation is often explained, sometimes in academic publications.
4 After Denmark attained a similar position to the UK, the Danes voted again about the Treaty in a second referendum in 1993, in which 57 per cent of the voters favoured ratification.

SUGGESTED READING

Decressin, J., H. Faruqee, and W. Fonteyne (eds.) (2007), *Integrating Europe's Financial Markets*, IMF, Washington DC.

Dermine, J. (2006), European Banking Integration: Don't Put the Cart before the Horse, *Financial Markets, Institutions & Instruments*, 15(2), 57–106.

REFERENCES

Cecchini, P. (1988), *The European Challenge, 1992: The Benefits of a Single Market*, Gower, Aldershot.

Craig, P. and G. de Burca (2007), *EU Law: Text, Cases, and Materials*, 4th edition, Oxford University Press.

Dermine, J. (2006), European Banking Integration: Don't Put the Cart before the Horse, *Financial Markets, Institutions & Instruments*, 15(2), 57–106.

Emerson, M., D. Gros, A. Italianer, J. Pisani-Ferry, and H. Reichenbach (1992), *One Market, One Money: An Evaluation of the Potential Benefits and Costs of Forming an Economic and Monetary Union*, Oxford University Press.

European Central Bank (2011), The Reform of Economic Governance in the Euro Area – Essential Elements, *ECB Monthly Bulletin*, March 2011, 99–119.

European Commission (2011), *Regulating Financial Services for Sustainable Growth. A Progress Report*, February 2011, EC, Brussels.

Haas, F. (2005), The Integration of European Financial Markets, in: *Euro Area Policies: Selected Issues*, IMF Country Report 05/266, IMF, Washington DC.

(2007), Current State of Play, in: J. Decressin, H. Faruqee, and W. Fonteyne (eds.), *Integrating Europe's Financial Markets*, IMF, Washington DC.

Monetary Policy of the European Central Bank

OVERVIEW

This chapter describes the monetary policy of the European Central Bank (ECB). Since the start of the monetary union in 1999, the ECB has been responsible for monetary policy making in the euro area. The ECB and the National Central Banks (NCBs) of the EU Member States whose currency is the euro make up the Eurosystem. Under the Maastricht Treaty, the primary objective of the ECB is 'price stability'. The ECB specifies this objective as inflation 'below but close to' 2 per cent in the euro area in the medium term. The ECB has an array of instruments available of which interest rate decisions generally attract most attention. Policy decisions are the outcome of the monetary policy strategy. The ECB has a 'two-pillar' strategy that explicitly pairs the discussion of monetary factors ('monetary analysis') with a broad-based non-monetary analysis of the risks to price stability in the short to medium run ('economic analysis').

During the financial crisis the ECB adopted a number of temporary non-standard measures, subsequently referred to as Enhanced Credit Support. This chapter discusses the ECB's communication policy. Nowadays, central bank communication is widely believed to enhance the effectiveness of monetary policy. The ECB has always regarded its communication policies as an integral part of its monetary policy.

LEARNING OBJECTIVES

After you have studied this chapter, you should be able to:
- explain the functioning of the ECB
- describe the monetary policy strategy of the ECB
- explain the monetary policy instruments of the ECB

- describe the unconventional policy measures of the ECB taken in response to the crisis
- describe the ECB's communication policies.

4.1 The European Central Bank

On 1 January 1999 a new currency – the euro – was created and the European Central Bank (ECB) became responsible for monetary policy in the euro area – the second largest economic area in the world after the United States. At the time of writing, the euro is the official currency of 17 EU Member States with more than 330 million citizens. It is also used in five small European countries outside the EU.

The ECB and the National Central Banks (NCBs) of the EU Member States whose currency is the euro make up the Eurosystem. While the ECB is responsible for monetary policy decisions, the NCBs of the countries in the euro area play a role in implementing monetary policy through open market operations (see section 4.3 for further details). In addition to the definition and implementation of the monetary policy of the euro area, the Eurosystem is responsible for:

- the conduct of foreign exchange operations;
- the holding and management of the official foreign reserves of the EU Member States;
- the promotion of the smooth operation of payment systems.

Structure

The three decision-making bodies of the ECB are the Governing Council, the Executive Board, and the General Council (see Figure 4.1).

The *Governing Council* of the ECB is the most important decision-making body of the ECB. It consists of the six members of the Executive Board and the governors of the euro-area NCBs (17 governors in 2011), who have been appointed by their respective governments. However, when taking monetary policy decisions, the members of the Governing Council of the ECB should not act as national representatives, but in a fully independent personal capacity. In other words, when taking policy decisions they are supposed to focus on the euro area as a whole and not on their own country. The Governing Council is responsible for formulating monetary policy, including decisions about interest rates. The Council decides, in principle, by simple majority on the basis of the principle of 'one person, one vote'. However, if the

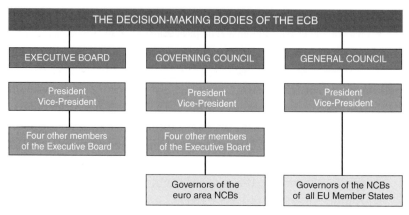

Figure 4.1   Structure of the ECB
Source: ECB (2011)

number of countries in the euro area increases above 18, a rotation system will be introduced (see Box 4.1). Compared to other central banks, the ECB's Governing Council's size and the proportion of outsiders appear rather large (see Table 4.1), especially if one takes into account that 7 out of the 12 Federal Reserve Presidents do not vote as a result of the rotation system in place at the Federal Open Market Committee (FOMC).

The *Executive Board* of the ECB consists of the President, the Vice-President, and up to four other members. Its members are appointed by the European Council, acting by a qualified majority, on a recommendation from the Council of the European Union. Their term in office is eight years and is not renewable. The Executive Board prepares the meetings of the Governing Council and implements monetary policy decisions taken by the Governing Council. In doing so, it may give instructions to National Central Banks. Both the Governing Council and the Executive Board are chaired by the President of the ECB or, in his or her absence, by the Vice-President (ECB, 2011).

As long as not all EU Member States use the euro as their currency, the *General Council* will also play a role. It consists of the President and Vice-President of the ECB and the governors of the National Central Banks of all EU member countries. As the central banks of the EU countries that have not (yet) adopted the euro continue to pursue national monetary policies, they do not participate in decisions related to the single monetary policy for the euro area. In the General Council, however, they have the opportunity to discuss monetary policy issues and their exchange rate relations with the euro.

Box 4.1 Decision making within the ECB Governing Council

Under the Maastricht Treaty, the ECB Governing Council takes monetary policy decisions by a simple majority of the votes cast by the members who are present in person. In practice, monetary policy decisions have generally been supported by a 'consensus' among members of the Governing Council (ECB, 2011). Each member of the Governing Council has one vote. The principle of 'one member, one vote' reflects that all the members, including the governors of the NCBs, are appointed in their personal capacity and not as representatives of their Member States. At some point in time, the new EU Member States will join the euro area. Furthermore, three 'old' EU Member States that are currently not members of the euro area – the United Kingdom, Sweden, and Denmark – could decide to adopt the euro.[1] So membership in the Eurosystem might increase to 27. The size of the ECB Governing Council could therefore increase to 33, making it by far the largest monetary policy-making institution among OECD countries. Due to this increase in membership, discussion and voting procedures would likely become more time-consuming and complicated.

In 2003, new voting rules were agreed upon. Under the new rules, there is a limit of 15 NCB governors exercising a voting right, although all members of the Governing Council (with and without voting rights) may participate in the policy meetings.

If the euro area increases to more than 18 countries, there will be 2 groups with rotating voting rights. Governors will rotate in and out of voting rights every month. The first group will consist of the 5 governors of the largest Member States, who share four voting rights. The second group will consist of all other governors, who will share 11 voting rights.

Once there are 22 euro-area members, there will be 3 groups with rotation. The first group with 4 votes consists of the 'big 5'. The second group, with 8 voting rights, will consist of half of all National Central Bank governors selected from the subsequent positions in a ranking primarily determined by size of the economy. The third group will be composed of the remaining governors. They will share 3 voting rights.

The new decision-making rules have met considerable criticism from academic observers. Apart from critique on the size of the Governing Council, Gros (2003) argues that the new rules give up the principle of equality of Member States, thus potentially undermining the idea that all members of the Governing Council should forget the particular interests of their home country and act only in the interest of the entire euro area.

Objectives

The Maastricht Treaty made price stability the ECB's primary objective, but left it to the ECB to give a precise meaning to this objective. Moreover, and

Table 4.1 Main characteristics of selected Monetary Policy Committees

Country	MPC size	Number of outsiders	De jure decision rule	Non-voting MPC members
Euro area	23	17	Simple majority	0
United States	19	12	Simple majority	7
Japan	9	6	Simple majority	0
United Kingdom	9	4	Simple majority	0

Note: 'Outsider' means committee member without full-time managerial position within the central bank.
Source: Stella and Vandenbussche (2010)

'without prejudice to the objective of price stability', the ECB shall 'support the general economic policies in the Community with a view to contributing to the achievement of the objectives of the Community', which include a 'high level of employment', and 'sustainable and non-inflationary growth'. The primary objective, first specified by the ECB as inflation less than 2 per cent in the euro area, was made more precise in 2003 following an internal evaluation of the ECB's monetary policy strategy. Today, the ECB aims for maintaining inflation below but close to 2 per cent in the euro area in the medium term. The ECB has developed a monetary-policy strategy to accomplish this objective (see section 4.2 for further details).

Inflation is measured by the Harmonised Index of Consumer Prices (HICP) for the euro area. The HICP is a comprehensive measure for prices of consumption goods. The aim of an inflation rate 'below but close to' 2 per cent clearly delineates the maximum rate of inflation deemed to be consistent with price stability. Price decreases – deflation – are also not consistent with price stability. Price stability is to be maintained over the medium term. This implies that price levels may be temporarily distorted by short-term factors. Euro-area-wide developments, instead of specific national or regional factors, are the only determinants of decisions regarding the single monetary policy. A year-on-year increase of the HICP for the euro area as a whole below 2 per cent represents price stability, even if increases in national price indices are above 2 per cent per year. Box 4.2 discusses why price stability is deemed so important.

Although the primary objective of the ECB is to maintain price stability, there are explicit references in the Treaty to financial regulation and supervision. For instance, the Treaty refers to promoting the smooth operations of payment systems. Still, the Treaty is explicit on the principle of

---

Box 4.2 Price stability

Not all central banks have price stability as their primary objective. For instance, the Federal Reserve's mandate is 'to promote effectively the goals of maximum employment, stable prices, and moderate long-term interest rates'. Because long-term interest rates can remain low only in a stable macroeconomic environment, these goals are often referred to as the *dual mandate*; that is, the Federal Reserve seeks to promote maximum employment and price stability. Why is price stability the primary objective of the ECB's policies? The ECB (2011) provides several reasons.

First, price stability makes it easier for people to disentangle changes in relative prices (i.e. movements in prices of any individual good or service) from changes in the general price level. This allows markets to allocate resources efficiently. Second, with price stability creditors can be sure that prices will remain stable in the future and they will therefore not demand an inflation risk premium to compensate them for the risks associated with holding nominal assets over the longer term. Third, price stability makes it less likely that individuals and firms will divert resources from productive uses in order to hedge against inflation. For example, high inflation provides an incentive to stockpile real goods since they retain their value better in such circumstances than money or certain financial assets. Fourth, as tax and welfare systems are not fully indexed, inflation (or deflation) exacerbates the perverse incentives of these systems which distort economic behaviour. For instance, a nominal increase of income to compensate for inflation may cause someone to move to a higher marginal tax rate which, in turn, may affect this person's labour supply. Fifth, inflation acts as a tax on holdings of cash because households have an incentive not to use cash as often in order to reduce transaction costs. These so-called shoe-leather costs arise because individuals have to visit the bank (or cash machine) more frequently to withdraw banknotes.

Sixth, unexpected inflation causes considerable and arbitrary redistribution of wealth and income (e.g. redistribution effects from creditors to debtors). Typically, the weakest groups of society often suffer the most from inflation, as they have only limited possibilities for hedging against it. Finally, inflation leads to sudden revaluations of financial assets which may undermine the soundness of the banking sector's balance sheets and decrease households' and firms' wealth, leading to financial instability.

According to the ECB (2011), the previous discussion suggests that a central bank that maintains price stability makes a substantial contribution to the achievement of broader economic goals, such as high levels of economic activity and better employment prospects. Indeed, several empirical studies suggest the existence of a negative relationship between inflation and economic growth. However, this relationship is less clear at low rates of inflation. One may therefore wonder why the ECB has defined price stability as inflation below but close to 2 per cent. Several arguments have been put forward in support of the view that a maximum inflation rate of 2 per cent (even if it refers to the medium term) may be too low (De Haan *et al.*, 2005).

In the first place, there may be an upward measurement bias in inflation. It has long been recognised that due to *measurement bias*, measured inflation may overstate actual inflation. There are several reasons for this. For instance, improvements in the quality of goods may cause price changes to be overestimated. The quality of goods typically increases over time, and this, for example, makes computers bought at two different points in time not directly comparable. Ignoring this quality change will induce a measurement error in the price index. Likewise, prices of new goods often fall rapidly in the first years after their introduction. It may be several years before goods are included in the basket of goods used to calculate the price index, and thus the fall in their prices may be missed. According to the Governing Council of the ECB, the quality of the HICP makes it possible to set a precise definition of price stability in the euro area (Issing, 2001).

In the second place, even if an inflation objective of 'below but close to 2 per cent' seems high enough to forego deflation in the euro area as a whole, it is possible that deflation occurs in an individual country, depending on how large inflation differentials are in the monetary union. Deflation shares many of the costs of inflation. However, Sibert (2003) argues that the redistribution due to unexpected deflation may be more costly than the redistribution resulting from unanticipated inflation. Defaults may occur and the resulting bankruptcies and restructurings destroy real wealth. The deterioration in debtors' balance sheets brought about by unexpected deflation may thus lower both consumption and investment demand. Persistent deflation may turn into a deflationary spiral of falling prices, output, profits, and employment. Aggregate demand-induced deflation can reduce employment when nominal wages are rigid downwards. With sticky wages, price declines cause real wages to rise, profit margins to fall, and employment to be cut back. This may set off a deflationary cycle. So how large are inflation differentials in the euro area? Before the start of EMU, the inflation dispersion in the founding countries of EMU decreased over time, especially during the second half of the 1990s. The non-weighted standard deviation declined from around 4 percentage points at the beginning of the 1990s to about 1 percentage point at the start of the monetary union. Since then the standard deviation initially declined, but more recently inflation dispersion slightly increased. Although some countries in the euro area have experienced deflation, this turned out not to be persistent.

In the third place, it has been argued that since nominal interest rates cannot fall below zero, *monetary policy faces a trade-off between a very low level of inflation and stabilising the economy*. If the economy is faced with a recession when inflation is zero, the monetary authority is constrained in its ability to engineer a negative short-term real interest rate to counter the output loss. This constraint reflects the fact that the nominal short-term interest rate cannot be lowered below zero, the so-called zero interest rate bound. Japan is often mentioned as an example of a country where this problem has occurred. However, even if the zero bound is hit, this may not imply that monetary policy is impotent as there may be other mechanisms through which monetary policy may influence the real economy. As will be discussed in more detail in section 4.4, central banks have other instruments at their disposal when short-term interest rates are close to zero.

Finally, Akerlof *et al.* (2000) argue that *a moderate level of inflation provides 'grease' to the price and wage setting process*. The economic adjustment of relative prices to shocks can become sluggish in the presence of downward nominal rigidities in wages and prices. For instance, with a zero inflation rate, individual firms facing an adverse firm-specific shock will not be able to secure real wage reductions in the presence of downward nominal wage rigidity and will, instead, lay off workers. Likewise, at low levels of inflation, a significant part of the price and wage setters probably ignore or underweight anticipated inflation in setting future prices. A moderate level of inflation provides for some real wage flexibility, which reduces the natural, or long run, rate of unemployment. According to the ECB (2003), however, the empirical evidence on the importance of downward nominal rigidities for the euro area is not conclusive. Evidence based on the distribution of changes in the euro-area price indices indicates that nominal price cuts are not as uncommon as often believed. According to micro-based studies a substantial proportion of wage earners have experienced wage cuts. However, even if downward nominal rigidities were pervasive, one may wonder whether 'accommodating' them with a higher inflation rate makes this undesirable structural feature of some economies not even more 'entrenched' (ECB, 2003).

decentralisation and allocation of regulatory and supervisory powers to national supervisors. Only in very special circumstances, and with unanimity in the European Council, will the ECB be allowed to regulate and supervise financial institutions.

However, the ECB plays an important role in the European Systemic Risk Board (ESRB), an independent EU body, responsible for the macroprudential oversight of the financial system within the EU. The responsibilities of the ESRB will be discussed in detail in Chapter 13. The ECB provides the Secretariat function for the ESRB, and is also in charge of providing analytical, statistical, administrative, and logistical support to the ESRB. All

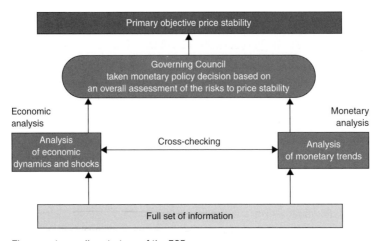

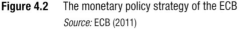

Figure 4.2   The monetary policy strategy of the ECB
Source: ECB (2011)

members of the ECB's General Council are voting members of the General Board of the ESRB. The President of the ECB is the first Chair of the ESRB for a term of five years. The first Vice-Chair (currently Mervyn King, the Governor of the Bank of England) is a member of the General Council of the ECB and is also appointed for a term of five years. The Steering Committee of the ESRB includes the President of the ECB, the Vice-President of the ECB, and four other members of the General Council.

4.2 Monetary policy strategy

The ECB's monetary policy is based on a 'two-pillar' strategy that explicitly pairs the discussion of monetary factors ('monetary analysis') with a broad-based non-monetary analysis of the risks to price stability in the short to medium run ('economic analysis'). Figure 4.2 provides a schematic overview. According to the ECB (2011, p. 69), 'the two-pillar approach is designed to ensure that no relevant information is lost in the assessment of the risks to price stability and that appropriate attention is paid to different perspectives and the cross-checking of information in order to reach an overall judgement on the risks to price stability'. The two-pillar approach provides a cross-check of the indications that stem from the shorter-term economic analysis with those from the longer-term-oriented monetary analysis, which, according to the ECB, ensures that monetary policy does not overlook important information relevant for assessing future inflation trends. By taking policy decisions and evaluating their consequences not only on the basis of the short-term indications stemming from the analysis of economic and financial conditions but also on the basis of money and liquidity considerations, the ECB arguably will not be tempted to take an overly activist course in determining the monetary policy stance (ECB, 2011).

The 'economic analysis' focuses on the assessment of current economic and financial developments and the implied short- to medium-term risks to price stability. The economic and financial variables that are the subject of this analysis include, for example: developments in overall output; aggregate demand and its components; fiscal policy; capital and labour market conditions; a broad range of price and cost indicators; developments in the exchange rate, the global economy, and the balance of payments; financial markets and the balance sheet positions of euro-area sectors (ECB, 2011). Moreover, macroeconomic staff projections play an important role in the economic analysis, although their role is different from that of inflation forecasts in an inflation-targeting strategy (see Box 4.3). The ECB publishes these projections for the euro area four times a year in its *Monthly Bulletin*. The Governing Council uses them with many other pieces of information to assess the risks to price stability, but it neither assumes responsibility for the projections nor does it use the staff projections as its only tool for organising and communicating its assessment as done under inflation targeting.

In the economic analysis, due attention is paid to the need to identify the nature of shocks hitting the economy, their effects on cost and pricing behaviour, and the short- to medium-term prospects for their propagation in the economy. For example, the appropriate monetary policy response to a temporary rise in the international price of oil might be different from the appropriate response to wage increases that are not in line with productivity growth. The former results in a transient and short-lived increase in inflation which quickly reverses, whereas the latter entails the risk of a self-sustaining spiral of higher costs, higher prices, and higher wage demands. The ECB also carries out several surveys that provide further input into the economic analysis. Also, asset prices and financial yields are analysed to derive information about the expectations of the financial markets, including expected future price developments. Likewise, developments in the exchange rate are closely assessed for their implications for price stability as exchange rate movements have a direct effect on price developments through their impact on import prices (ECB, 2011).

Box 4.3 Inflation targeting

Inflation targeting has become a very popular monetary policy strategy. By the end of 2009, 31 countries had adopted inflation targeting. According to Mishkin and Savastano (2001), *inflation targeting* involves the public announcement of numerical targets for inflation, a strong commitment of the central bank to price stability as a final monetary policy objective, and a high degree of transparency and accountability. The distinctive feature of this strategy is a forward-looking decision-making process known as 'inflation-forecast targeting'. It means that the central bank sets its policy instruments in such a way that its inflation forecast (after some time) equals the inflation target. Although in practice, different forms of inflation targeting exist, they all have in common a published numerical inflation target and a predefined policy horizon. Central banks using this approach communicate monetary policy decisions in terms of a reaction to deviations in a forecast for a particular measure of inflation from the inflation target at a particular horizon. The central bank's forecast for inflation is therefore centrepiece both when it comes to decision making and in communicating to the public. Several central banks of European countries outside the euro area use inflation targeting as their monetary policy strategy. For instance, both the Bank of England and the Riksbank (the central bank of Sweden) apply this strategy.

The ECB (2011) provides several arguments against using this approach. First, focusing entirely on a forecast inflation figure does not provide a comprehensive and reliable framework for identifying the nature of threats to price stability. Second, various aspects of the textbook inflation targeting approach – such as the fixed horizon of the forecast from which monetary policy decisions feed back – are somewhat arbitrary and in many circumstances do not appear to be optimal. Third, it is difficult to integrate the information contained in monetary aggregates into inflation forecasts that are based on conventional macroeconomic models. Finally, the ECB takes the view that relying on a single forecast would not be appropriate, given the considerable uncertainty relating to the structure of the euro-area economy. It is considered preferable to adopt a diversified approach to the analysis of economic data based on a variety of analytical methodologies.

The so-called 'monetary analysis' focuses on a medium- to long-term horizon. When the ECB's monetary policy strategy was introduced in 1998, the ECB Governing Council announced a quantitative 'reference value' for the annual growth rate of a broad monetary aggregate (M3). This focus on money growth was motivated by the view that inflation in the long run is considered to be a mostly monetary phenomenon. The choice for M3 growth was justified by its perceived favourable empirical properties, especially a relatively stable money demand relationship. Furthermore, M3 growth was shown to exhibit leading indicator properties for future inflation. However, the ECB has always stressed that monetary policy does not react mechanically to deviations of M3 growth from the reference value. Such deviations, however, trigger increased efforts to identify and assess the underlying driving forces. Nowadays, the monetary analysis entails a comprehensive analysis of the liquidity situation, going well beyond M3 growth. For instance, the composition of M3 growth (i.e. the components and sectoral contributions) is extensively analysed.

In December 2002 the ECB Governing Council decided to evaluate this strategy in the light of the experience, taking into account the public debate and the outcomes of research undertaken by ECB and NCB staff. The results of this evaluation were published in May 2003. Although many observers had expected that the ECB would abandon the monetary pillar, the Governing Council made it clear that the ECB would continue to include monetary analysis in its policy strategy, although it needed some 'clarification'. As the Governing Council explained, the monetary analysis was to mainly serve as a means of 'cross-checking', from a medium- to long-term perspective, the short- to medium-term indications from the economic analysis. To underscore the longer-term nature of the reference value for monetary growth, the Governing Council decided to discontinue the practice of an annual review of the reference value for M3 growth.

According to the ECB (2011), its policies have contributed to keeping longer-term inflation expectations in the euro area firmly anchored at levels consistent with the ECB's definition of price stability (see Figure 4.3).

4.3 Monetary policy instruments

The ECB has several instruments at its disposal. By using these instruments, the ECB is able to affect inflation and output (see Box 4.4 for a further discussion of how monetary policy affects the economy). This section discusses the ECB's policy instruments, starting with a description of the ECB policy rates which signal the ECB's monetary policy stance. Then we turn to open market operations and minimum reserve requirements.

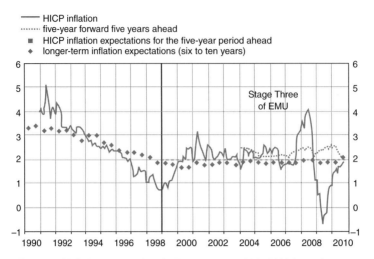

HICP inflation
five-year forward five years ahead
■ HICP inflation expectations for the five-year period ahead
◆ longer-term inflation expectations (six to ten years)

Figure 4.3   Inflation and inflation expectations in the euro area, 1990–2010 (annual percentage changes)
Source: ECB (2011)

Policy rates

To understand ECB interest rate decisions, it is important that we first explain the so-called standing facilities, i.e. the marginal lending facility and the deposit facility. Banks can use these facilities if they need liquidity or if they want to stall liquidity. Both facilities have an overnight maturity and are available to banks on their own initiative. The deposit facility is used for mopping up liquidity from the banks at rates which normally are substantially below market rates. The marginal lending facility provides liquidity to the banks at rates that are usually substantially above market rates.

As the interest rates on the standing facilities are normally substantially higher (for borrowing) or lower (for depositing) than the corresponding money market rate, banks normally only use the standing facilities in the absence of other alternatives. As there are no limits on access to these facilities (except for the collateral requirements of the marginal lending facility), the rate on the marginal lending facility and the rate on the deposit facility normally provide a ceiling and a floor, respectively, for the overnight rate in the interbank money market. The standing facilities thus constitute a corridor for the interbank money market rate. By setting the rates on the standing facilities, the ECB effectively determines the corridor within which the overnight money market rate can fluctuate.

Box 4.4 Monetary policy transmission

Monetary policy decisions affect the real economy and inflation through various channels. Changes in money market rates due to ECB policy measures in turn affect other short-term interest rates (*interest channel*). For example, changes in money market rates have an impact on the interest rates set by banks on short-term loans and deposits.

Furthermore, changes in central bank interest rates may also affect the supply of credit (*credit channel*). The credit channel has three mechanisms: the bank lending channel, the balance sheet channel, and the risk-taking channel.

Following an increase in interest rates, the risk that some borrowers cannot safely pay back their loans may increase to a level such that the bank will not grant a loan to these borrowers (the *bank lending channel*). As a consequence, such borrowers are forced to postpone their consumption or investment plans. Interest rate changes also affect firms' balance sheets.

An increase in interest rates leads to a lower net worth of assets which means a lower collateral value and thus a reduced ability to borrow (the *balance sheet channel*).

Whereas the bank-lending channel focuses on the quantity of loans supplied, the *risk-taking channel* zooms in on banks' incentive to bear risk related to the provision of loans. The risk-taking channel is thought to operate mainly via two mechanisms. First, low interest rates boost asset and collateral values. This, in conjunction with the belief that the increase in asset values is sustainable, leads both borrowers and banks to accept higher risks. Second, low interest rates make riskier assets more attractive, as agents search for higher yields. In the case of banks, these two effects usually translate into a softening of credit standards, which can lead to an excessive increase in loan supply.

Interest rate changes may also affect the exchange rate which, in turn, will normally affect inflation in three ways (*exchange rate channel*). First, exchange rate movements may directly affect the domestic price of imported goods. If the exchange rate appreciates, the price of imported goods tends to fall, thus helping to reduce inflation directly, insofar as these products are directly used in consumption. Second, if these imports are used as inputs into the production process, lower prices for inputs might, over time, feed through into lower prices for final goods. Third, an appreciation in the exchange rate may make domestically produced goods less competitive in terms of their price on world markets; this tends to constrain external demand and thus reduce overall demand pressure in the economy. All other things being equal, an appreciation of the exchange rate would thus tend to reduce inflationary pressures. The strength of exchange rate effects depends on how open the economy is to international trade. Exchange rate effects are in general less important for large economies than for small open economies. Furthermore, financial asset prices like the exchange rate depend on many other factors in addition to monetary policy.

The *expectations channel* mainly works by influencing the private sector's longer-term expectations. It has gained particular relevance for the conduct of monetary policy over past decades. Its effectiveness crucially depends on the credibility of central bank communication (see section 4.5). For instance, if a central bank enjoys a high degree of credibility in pursuing its objective, monetary policy can exert a powerful direct influence on price developments by guiding economic agents' expectations of future inflation and thereby influencing their wage- and price-setting behaviour. The credibility of a central bank to maintain price stability in a lasting manner is crucial in this respect. If economic agents believe in the central bank's ability and commitment to maintain price stability, inflation expectations will remain firmly anchored to price stability. This, in turn, will influence wage- and price-setting, as wage- and price-setters will not have to adjust their prices upwards for fear of higher inflation in the future.

According to the ECB (2011), monetary policy transmission in the euro area has several characteristics. First, long and uncertain lags exist in the transmission of monetary impulses to the domestic price level. Second, in normal times, monetary policy works mainly through the interest rate channel: a tightening of monetary policy leads to a transitory decrease in output, which is estimated to reach its maximum between one and two years after the interest rate increase. Prices tend to decline more gradually, and respond more sluggishly, to the tightening of monetary policy than output. Third, interest rate changes also affect economic activity via their impact on firms' cash flows and the supply of bank loans, hence confirming the relevance of the credit channel of monetary policy.

Source: ECB (2011)

Figure 4.4 shows the development of key ECB interest rates since January 1999 and illustrates how the interest rates on the standing facilities have provided a ceiling and a floor for the overnight interbank market interest rate, measured by EONIA (euro overnight index average). EONIA represents the average rate on unsecured overnight euro lending transactions in the interbank market. It is the (weighted) average rate on transactions reported to the ECB on that day by a representative panel of banks, known as the EONIA Panel.

Figure 4.4 shows that in the past EONIA generally remained close to the rate on the main refinancing operations, one of the ECB's open market operations explained below. This changed in October 2008, when the ECB adopted non-standard measures to counter the negative effects of the financial crisis (see section 4.4).

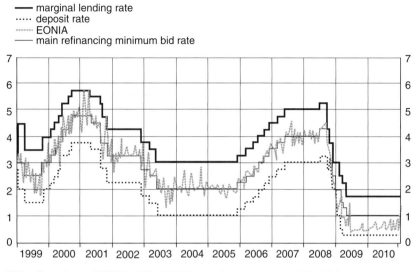

— marginal lending rate
····· deposit rate
······ EONIA
— main refinancing minimum bid rate

Figure 4.4   ECB policy rates and EONIA, 1999–2010 (percentage per annum; daily data)
Source: ECB (2011)

Open market operations

The Eurosystem affects money market interest rates by providing more (or less) liquidity to banks if it wants to decrease (increase) interest rates. It allocates an amount of liquidity that allows banks to fulfil their liquidity needs at a price that is in line with the ECB policy intentions. To manage liquidity in the money market and steer short-term interest rates, it uses *open market operations*, i.e. it buys (or sells) financial assets. If assets are bought from (sold to) a bank, the reserves of that bank at the central bank increase (decrease).

The Eurosystem's open market operations can be divided into the following four categories (ECB, 2011): main refinancing operations (MROs), longer-term refinancing operations (LTROs), fine tune operations (FTOs), and structural operations (see Table 4.2). Lending through open market operations normally takes place in the form of reverse transactions. In these reverse transactions, the central bank buys assets from a bank under a repurchase agreement (i.e. the bank buys the asset back) or grants a loan against assets pledged as collateral. Reverse transactions are therefore temporary open market operations which provide funds for a limited, pre-specified period only. The Eurosystem accepts instruments issued by both private and public debtors as collateral.

Table 4.2 Monetary policy instruments

Monetary policy operations	Liquidity provision	Liquidity absorption	Maturity	Frequency
Open market operations				
Main refinancing operations	Reverse transactions	–	One week	Weekly
Longer-term refinancing operations	Reverse transactions	–	Three months	Monthly
Fine tune operations	Reverse transactions	Reverse transactions Several fixed-term deposits	Non-standardised	Non-regular
	Foreign exchange swaps	Foreign exchange swaps		
Structural operations	Reverse transactions	Issuance of ECB debt certificates	Standardised/Non-standardised	Regular and non-regular
	Outright purchases	Outright sales	–	Non-regular
Standing facilities				
Marginal lending facility	Reverse transactions	–	Overnight	Access at discretion of counterparties
Deposit facility	–	Deposits	Overnight	Access at discretion of counterparties

Source: ECB (2011)

In addition to the weekly MROs, the Eurosystem also executes regular monthly LTROs with various maturities (e.g. 6 months or 12 months). These operations are aimed at providing longer-term liquidity to the banking system. After October 2008, when the ECB took several measures to combat the financial crisis (see section 4.4), the weight of the refinancing operations shifted towards LTROs (see Figure 4.5).

The Eurosystem may also carry out open market operations on an ad hoc basis, the so-called fine tune operations (FTOs). The frequency and maturity of such operations are not standardised. FTOs are aimed at managing the liquidity situation in the money market and steering interest rates, in particular in order to smooth the effects on interest rates of unexpected liquidity fluctuations in the market. Finally, the Eurosystem may issue debt certificates and carry out reverse or outright transactions whenever it wishes to adjust the structural position of the Eurosystem vis-à-vis the financial sector (ECB, 2011).

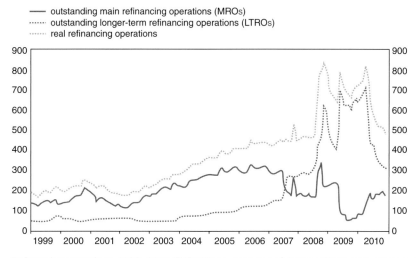

— outstanding main refinancing operations (MROs)
······ outstanding longer-term refinancing operations (LTROs)
······ real refinancing operations

Figure 4.5   Refinancing operations, 1999–2010 (EUR billions, averages of daily positions over maintenance period)
Source: ECB (2011)

Minimum reserve requirements

The final instrument that we discuss is the *minimum reserve requirements* imposed on banks. Under the minimum reserve system banks are required to hold compulsory deposits with NCBs. The amount of the required reserves is determined by the size and composition of the liabilities on the balance sheet of the bank concerned. For most liabilities included in the reserve base the reserve ratio used to be 2 per cent. The minimum reserve system serves two main purposes: (1) to create sufficient structural demand for central bank credit, and (2) to contribute to the stabilisation of money market interest rates.

The minimum reserve system enlarges the structural liquidity shortage of the banking system. The need for banks to hold reserves with the NCBs contributes to increasing the demand for central bank credit which, in turn, makes it easier for the ECB to steer money market rates through regular liquidity-providing operations.

Interest rates are stabilised by allowing banks to use averaging provisions, i.e. to comply with reserve requirements on the basis of average daily reserve holdings over the maintenance period. This allows banks to smooth out daily liquidity fluctuations, since transitory reserve imbalances can be offset by opposite reserve imbalances generated within the same maintenance period. The averaging provision implies that banks can profit from lending in the market and run a reserve deficit whenever the money market rates are above those expected to prevail for the remainder of the maintenance period. In the opposite scenario, they can borrow in the market and run a reserve surplus. Since March 2004, the timing of the reserve maintenance period has been such that it will always start on the settlement day of the main refinancing operation following the Governing Council meeting at which a monetary decision is taken. Furthermore, as a rule, the implementation of changes to the standing facility rates will be aligned with the start of the new reserve maintenance period. The averaging provision works very smoothly during the maintenance period. However, at the end of the period, the reserve requirement becomes binding and banks can no longer transfer a liquidity surplus or deficit into the future. This explains the spikes in the EONIA towards the end of each maintenance period, which can be seen in Figure 4.4. It also explains why the use of the standing facilities is most extensive towards the end of the maintenance period.

4.4 Unconventional monetary policy during the crisis

At the beginning of the financial crisis, the ECB, like other major central banks, reduced its key interest rates to historically low levels. The main refinancing rate was cut by a total of 325 basis points to 1 per cent between October 2008 and May 2009. In addition, the Governing Council adopted a number of temporary non-standard measures, subsequently referred to as Enhanced Credit Support. This focuses primarily on banks. Due to uncertainty about the creditworthiness of other banks, the interbank market did not function properly. After the failure of Lehman Brothers in September 2008 the interbank market effectively shut down. Amid significantly impaired markets and elevated counterparty credit concerns, demand for liquidity rose sharply while interbank lending declined rapidly.

There are five main building blocks of the Enhanced Credit Support:
(1) unlimited provision of liquidity through 'fixed rate tenders with full allotment';
(2) extension of the (already long) list of collateral assets, so that the share of private sector assets increased to 56 per cent of the nominal value of securities on the list;

(3) extension of the maturity of long-term refinancing operations, initially to 6 months, and then, in late June 2009, to 12 months, aiming to decrease uncertainty in commercial banks' liquidity planning;

(4) liquidity provision in foreign currencies, particularly US dollars, through swap lines with the Federal Reserve; and

(5) outright purchases of covered bonds in order to revive that market, which is important for banks' funding.

Fixed rate full allotment

A fixed rate full allotment tender procedure was adopted for all refinancing operations during the financial crisis. Thus, contrary to normal practice, banks had unlimited access to central bank liquidity at the main refinancing rate, subject to adequate collateral.

Collateral requirements

The list of eligible collateral accepted in Eurosystem refinancing operations was extended, allowing banks to use a larger range and proportion of their assets to obtain central bank liquidity. The ability to refinance illiquid assets through the central bank provides an effective remedy to liquidity shortages caused by a sudden halt in interbank lending. This includes, for instance, asset-backed securities, which became illiquid when the market collapsed after the default of Lehman Brothers.

Extension of the maturity of liquidity provision

The Eurosystem had already increased the amount of liquidity provided in longer-term refinancing operations (LTROs) after the ECB's decision to introduce supplementary refinancing operations with maturities of 3 and 6 months during the period of financial turmoil. After the collapse of Lehman Brothers, the maximum maturity of the LTROs was temporarily extended to 12 months. This increased the Eurosystem's intermediation role aimed at easing refinancing concerns of the euro-area banking system. Reduced uncertainty and a longer liquidity planning horizon was expected to encourage banks to continue providing credit to the economy. Moreover, the measures were expected to contribute to keeping money market interest rates at low levels.

Currency swap agreements

The Eurosystem also temporarily provided liquidity in foreign currencies during the financial crisis, most notably in US dollars, at various maturities. It used reciprocal currency arrangements with the Federal Reserve System to provide funding in US dollars against Eurosystem eligible collateral at various maturities at fixed interest rates with full allotment. This measure supported banks which otherwise faced a massive shortfall in US dollar funding during the period of financial crisis.

Covered bond purchase programme

The Eurosystem purchased euro-denominated covered bonds issued in the euro area at a value of €60 billion over the period between May 2009 and June 2010. The covered bonds market (see Chapter 5) had virtually dried up in terms of liquidity, issuance, and spreads. The aim of the programme was to revive the covered bond market, which is a very important financial market in Europe and a primary source of financing for banks.

In October 2011, the ECB announced a new covered bond purchase programme (CBPP2). The purchases will be for an intended amount of €40 billion. They will be conducted in the primary and secondary markets between November 2011 and October 2012.

As a result of the non-standard measures taken during the financial crisis, the relationship between the main refinancing rate and money market rates temporarily changed. Whereas in normal circumstances the EONIA rate closely follows movements in the main refinancing rate, the high demand from banks for central bank liquidity in refinancing operations with full allotment has resulted in the deposit rate playing a greater role in steering the EONIA, as can be seen in Figure 4.4.

Securities Markets Programme

In addition to the Enhanced Credit Support, the ECB introduced the *Securities Markets Programme* in response to tensions in the euro-area sovereign bond markets in May 2010 (see Chapter 2). The spreads between the yields on ten-year bonds of some euro-area governments (notably Greece, Ireland, and Portugal) and the German Bund yield increased sharply. Under the programme, Eurosystem interventions can be carried out in the euro-area public and private debt securities markets to ensure depth and liquidity in dysfunctional market segments and to restore the proper functioning of the monetary policy transmission mechanism. Purchases of government bonds are strictly limited to secondary markets. To ensure that liquidity conditions are not affected, all purchases are fully neutralised through liquidity-absorbing operations.

LTROs

In November and December 2011, the ECB Governing Council reduced interest rates by 25 basis points. The refinancing interest rate came down from 1.50 to 1.00 per cent. These rate cuts were deemed necessary in view of the worsened economic forecasts which indicated increased recession risk. The ECB in addition introduced liquidity-enhancing measures in order to strengthen the liquidity position of European banks. The interest rate cuts were expected by the market, but the liquidity-enhancing measures were not. The ECB introduced two longer-term refinancing operations (LTROs) with a maturity of 36 months and the option of early repayment after one year. In December 2011, the ECB lent almost €490 billion to banks. In February 2012, the ECB lent almost €530 billion. Whereas the number of banks participating in the first LTRO was 523, in the second LTRO 800 banks asked for and received three-years loans. Banks considered three-years central bank funding at favourable rates as a very attractive way of funding current and new business. In addition to introducing these LTROs, the Governing Council in its December 2011 meeting decided to extend the list of eligible collateral and to temporary reduce the reserve ratio from 2 to 1 per cent.

4.5 ECB communication policies

Theory

Since its inception, the ECB has regarded communication as an integral part of its monetary policy. It has communicated frequently to the public on various issues, such as its objective, its policy decisions, and the economic outlook. In doing so, the ECB has used various communication channels. For instance, the ECB extensively uses press conferences to inform the public on its decisions almost on a real-time basis. In addition, the ECB employs other communication channels, like the *Monthly Bulletin*, its website, as well as speeches by and interviews with ECB policy makers.

This emphasis on communication is not unique to the ECB. Over the past two decades, a true revolution in thinking and practice has occurred with respect to central bank openness. For a number of reasons – including the greater independence from the political process and the related increased need for accountability – central banks have shed their previous shrouds of mystery. Most importantly, communication has become important because it has the potential to affect private sector expectations. As such, it offers central banks an additional instrument to achieve their monetary policy objectives. By now, communication has developed into a key instrument in the toolbox of many central bankers (Blinder *et al.*, 2008).

Central bank communication has two main objectives. First, it contributes to the accountability of the central bank and, second, it helps the central bank in managing expectations. Here we leave the first objective aside and focus upon the second objective of central bank communication (see De Haan *et al.*, 2005 for a further discussion on the accountability of the ECB).

Why are expectations relevant? Nowadays, it is widely accepted that the central bank's ability to affect the economy critically depends upon the degree to which it can influence market expectations regarding the *future path* of overnight interest rates. The reason is simple: few, if any, economic decisions hinge on the overnight bank rate, which is the only market interest rate that is effectively controlled by the central bank. Long-term interest rates, reflecting expected future short-term interest rates, affect saving and investment decisions by households and firms. Therefore, the public's perception of future policy rates is critical for the effectiveness of monetary policy.

Still, from a theoretical point of view, it is not obvious that communication may help the central bank to realise its ultimate objective(s), like price stability and stable economic growth. For instance, communication has little value added if the central bank credibly commits to a policy rule. Assuming that the public has rational expectations, any systematic pattern in the way that policy is conducted should be correctly inferred from the central bank's observed behaviour (Woodford, 2005). Thus, when it comes to predicting future interest rates, the public merely has to interpret (forecasts of) economic data in view of the central bank's policy rule; there is no role for central bank communication. A central bank can be fully transparent without any communication.

This reasoning is highly stylised. Still, it points out three conditions under which central bank communication may matter: non-rational expectations, absence of commitment to unchanging policy rules, and asymmetric information.

First, the assumption that the public will understand monetary policy perfectly regardless of the efforts that are made to explain it may be unrealistic. As a correct understanding of the central bank's policy commitments does not occur automatically, it is clearly desirable for the central bank to explain the rule that it follows (Woodford, 2005). By communicating to the public, the central bank may help anchor inflation expectations.

Second, it is unlikely that the central bank would stick to an unchanged policy rule for long. Former ECB President Trichet has repeatedly emphasised that the ECB takes its decisions one step at a time, rather than following a rule.

Third, financial market participants generally do not have as much information as monetary policy makers on a number of key inputs to policy making, including the weights policy makers assign to possible objectives, or their assessment of the economic situation. If there is *asymmetric information*, so that the public and the central bank dispose of different information, it may be perfectly rational for the public to adjust their expectations if the central bank provides new information. Here it is important that we distinguish between the types of information on which asymmetries may exist.

In the first place, the central bank may provide *information about its reaction function*. This should lead, *ceteris paribus*, to an increase in the private sector's ability to forecast the central bank's policy decisions. One possibility is that the central bank provides information about its long-run inflation target. Likewise, central banks could also provide information on the relative weights that the central bank places on its objectives if it has more than one objective.

By publicly announcing its monetary policy strategy and communicating its regular assessment of economic developments, the central bank provides guidance to the markets so that expectations can be formed more efficiently and accurately. This helps markets to understand the systematic response pattern of monetary policy to economic developments and shocks and thus to anticipate the broad direction of monetary policy over the medium term.

Furthermore, the central bank may have better information on the economic outlook. Several studies find that financial markets not only react to macroeconomic news, but also to *information on the economic outlook* provided by the central bank. Apparently investors update their own views in response to the information conveyed by the central bank. Private agents may lend special credence to the economic pronouncements of the central bank, particularly if the central bank has established credibility as an effective forecaster of the economy.

Even though there are good reasons why communication may be beneficial, it is by no means clear what constitutes an optimal communication strategy. The literature on central bank transparency has shown that full disclosure of all available information is often not optimal. Unfortunately, the theoretical literature has not come up with clear-cut conclusions regarding the optimal level of transparency.

ECB communications policy

Most central banks nowadays inform the public about their monetary policy decisions on the day they are taken. Many central banks do so by releasing short press statements. The ECB has been rather unique in detailing the motives behind a particular policy decision at elaborate press conferences after policy meetings. So far, it has refrained from releasing minutes of the policy meeting. Press conferences may provide less detail than minutes, but they are timelier and more flexible, especially if the media are allowed to ask questions.

Policy meetings of the ECB Governing Council typically take place on the first Thursday of each month. Following these meetings, the ECB announces the monetary policy decisions at 13:45 CET. Some 45 minutes later, the ECB President and Vice-President hold a press conference that comprises two elements: a prepared introductory statement containing the background considerations for the monetary policy decision, and a Questions & Answers (Q&A) part during which the President and the Vice-President are available to answer questions by the attending journalists. The introductory statement is understood to reflect the position and views of the Council, agreed upon on a word-by-word basis by its members. While providing background information on the rationale for its decision, the ECB press conference is generally less detailed than the minutes of the Bank of England or the Federal Reserve (Blinder *et al.*, 2008). In particular, it does not provide information on voting. However, the press conference avoids the substantial time delay of the minutes. Furthermore, the Q&A session allows the press to ask follow-up questions and thus can help clarify open issues.

A second important communication device for the ECB is its *Monthly Bulletin*, which is usually published one week after the meeting of the Governing Council and contains the information that the Governing Council possessed when it took its policy decisions. The *Monthly Bulletin* provides the general public and the financial markets with a detailed and comprehensive analysis of the economic environment. It also contains articles which provide insights into long-term developments, general topics, or into the analytical tools used by the Eurosystem within the framework of the monetary policy strategy.

The testimonies of the ECB President to the European Parliament (EP) offer a third opportunity to communicate. Four times a year, the President appears before the EP's Committee on Economic and Monetary Affairs and explains the ECB's policy decisions and its economic outlook. Subsequently, he answers questions posed by Committee members. These testimonies are open to the public and the transcripts of the presentations are published on the websites of both the EP and the ECB.

Finally, ECB officials often give speeches or interviews on monetary policy. Communications by individual central bankers offer greater flexibility in timing than pre-scheduled events. Speeches and interviews by individual committee members between meetings offer a way to communicate changes in views rapidly, if so desired (Blinder *et al.*, 2008).

One perceived benefit of central bank transparency is that it will contribute to predictability of monetary policy. Such predictability is important for the conduct of monetary policy: while central banks only directly control very short-term interest rates, the expected path of these rates over longer horizons and the premia for uncertainty are significant for the transmission of monetary policy to the economy. If agents can broadly anticipate policy responses, this allows a rapid incorporation of any (expected) changes in monetary policy into financial variables. This in turn can shorten the process by which monetary policy is transmitted into investment and consumption decisions and accelerate any necessary economic adjustments, thus potentially enhancing the effectiveness of monetary policy (ECB, 2011). Indeed, empirical evidence points out that ECB monetary policy generally has been quite predictable. Also, predictability of ECB policy decisions has increased over time (see Blattner *et al.* 2008 for an overview).

An important line of research focuses on the impact of central bank communications on financial markets. The basic idea is that if communications steer expectations, asset prices should react. There is a broad consensus that ECB communication affects financial markets. There is substantive evidence that various forms of ECB communication affect volatility, which implies that expectations changed. This holds true for short-term interest rates, the bond market, the stock market, and the swap markets. The strongest effects are generally found for the President's introductory statements at the ECB press conference following the Governing Council's meeting. There is also substantive evidence that financial markets also moved in the intended direction (Blinder *et al.*, 2008).

4.6 Conclusions

Since 1999, the ECB has been responsible for monetary policy making in the euro area. The Governing Council takes monetary policy decisions. The Governing Council consists of the six members of the ECB's Executive Board and the governors of the central banks of the EU Member States in the euro area. Under the Maastricht Treaty, the primary objective of the ECB is 'price stability', which the ECB specifies as inflation 'below but close to' 2 per cent in the euro area in the medium term. The ECB has been quite successful in keeping inflation and inflation expectation in the euro area in line with this target. The ECB's monetary policy is based on a 'two-pillar' strategy that explicitly pairs the discussion of monetary factors ('monetary analysis') with a broad-based non-monetary analysis of the risks to price stability in the short to medium run ('economic analysis'). The ECB's policy instruments are (1) policy rates which signal the ECB's monetary policy stance; (2) open market operations to steer liquidity and thereby money market rates; and (3) minimum reserve requirements. In the beginning of the financial crisis, the ECB reduced its policy interest rates to historically low levels. In addition, the ECB introduced several temporary non-standard measures, subsequently referred to as Enhanced Credit Support, as the interbank money market does not function properly in times of financial distress. Another instrument of modern central banking is central bank communication. The ECB has a very active communication strategy. The most important communication instrument is the press conference following the policy meeting of the ECB's Governing Council.

NOTES

1   As explained in Chapter 3, Denmark and the UK may decide to remain outside the euro area even if they meet the convergence criteria. Sweden does not meet all the convergence criteria, notably the exchange rate criterion.

SUGGESTED READING

De Haan, J. and H. Berger (eds.) (2010), *The European Central Bank at Ten*, Heidelberg, Springer.

European Central Bank (2011), *The Monetary Policy of the ECB*, ECB, Frankfurt.

REFERENCES

Akerlof, G. A., W. T. Dickens, and G. L. Perry (2000), Near-rational Wage and Price Setting and the Long-Run Phillips Curve, *Brookings Papers on Economic Activity*, 2000–1, 1–44.

Blattner, T., M. Catenaro, M. Ehrmann, R. Strauch, and J. Turunen (2008), The Predictability of Monetary Policy, European Central Bank Occasional Paper No. 83.

Blinder, A. S., M. Ehrmann, M. Fratzscher, J. de Haan, and D. Jansen (2008), Central Bank Communication and Monetary Policy: A Survey of Theory and Evidence, *Journal of Economic Literature*, 46(4), 910–945.

De Haan, J. and H. Berger (eds.) (2010), *The European Central Bank at Ten*, Heidelberg, Springer.

De Haan, J., S. C. W. Eijffinger, and S. Waller (2005), *The European Central Bank Credibility, Transparency, and Centralization*, MIT Press, Cambridge (MA)..

European Central Bank (2003), *Background Studies for the ECB's Evaluation of its Monetary Policy Strategy*, ECB, Frankfurt.

(2011), *The Monetary Policy of the ECB*, ECB, Frankfurt.

Gros, D. (2003), Reforming the Composition of the ECB Governing Council in View of Enlargement: How Not to Do It!, Briefing paper for the Monetary Committee of the European Parliament, February.

Issing, O. (2001), Why Price Stability?, in: A. Garcia Herrero, V. Gaspar, L. H. Hoogduin, J. Morgan, and B. Winkler (eds.), *Why Price Stability?*, ECB, Frankfurt.

Mishkin, F. S. and M. Savastano (2001), Monetary Policy Strategies for Latin America, *Journal of Development Economics*, 66, 415–444.

Sibert, A. (2003), The New Monetary Policy Strategy of the ECB, Briefing paper for the Committee on Economic and Monetary Affairs of the European Parliament, May 2003.

Stella, P. and J. Vandenbussche (2010), Governance and Monetary Policy Decision-making at the ECB, in: J. de Haan and H. Berger (eds.), *The European Central Bank at Ten*, Springer, Heidelberg, 143–170.

Woodford, M. (2005), Central-bank Communication and Policy Effectiveness, in: *The Greenspan Era: Lessons for the Future*, Federal Reserve Bank of Kansas City, 399–474.

Part II

Financial Markets

European Financial Markets

OVERVIEW

This chapter starts off by reviewing the functions that financial markets perform. First, financial markets release information to aid the price discovery process. Second, markets provide a platform to trade. The main trading mechanisms, i.e. quote-driven and order-driven markets, are discussed. Finally, markets provide an infrastructure to settle trades. The remainder of the chapter describes the main financial markets in the EU (the money, bond, equity, derivatives, and foreign exchange markets).

The euro money market is the market for euro-denominated short-term funds and related derivative instruments. It consists of various segments, including unsecured deposit contracts with various maturities, ranging from overnight to one year, and repurchase agreements (so-called repos, i.e. reverse transactions secured by securities) also ranging from overnight to one year. Banks account for the largest share of the euro money market. The ECB has a major influence on the money market via its use of various monetary policy instruments (reserve requirements, standing facilities, and open market operations). There are three main market interest rates for the money market: EONIA (euro overnight index average), EURIBOR (euro interbank offered rate), and EUREPO (the repo market reference rate for the euro).

The bulk of euro-denominated bonds (i.e. debt securities with a maturity of more than one year) is issued by euro-area issuers. Although the share of private-sector securities (corporate bonds) in all euro-denominated debt securities outstanding has risen, securities issued by public authorities (government bonds) still form the most important market segment. The introduction of the euro in 1999 created a pan-European capital market, making government-debt managers small to medium-sized players in a larger European market, instead of being the dominant player in the national market. Before the financial crisis, long-term interest rates were very similar in the euro area. Especially after the crisis differentials vis-à-vis the German yield vary considerably across countries, while for each country the yield differential varies considerably over time.

The importance of equity finance in the EU is growing, although there are large differences across exchanges. The market capitalisations of Euronext and the London Stock Exchange (LSE) are much higher than those of other exchanges in the EU. Despite the increase in equity finance, public equity markets play a limited role as a source of new funds as firms generally raise external financing via bank loans and, to a lesser extent, debt securities.

Next, the chapter discusses derivatives, i.e. financial instruments whose value is derived from the value of the underlying financial instruments. They can be based on different types of assets (such as equities or commodities), prices (such as interest rates or exchange rates), or indexes (such as a stock market index). They are traded on organised exchanges or over-the-counter (OTC). Derivatives can provide a source of income but are also important risk-management tools. The most important derivatives are futures, forwards, options, and swaps.

Finally, the foreign exchange market is discussed.

LEARNING OBJECTIVES

After you have studied this chapter, you should be able to:
- explain the purpose and structure of financial markets
- describe the essentials of the euro money market, including its functions and main interest rates
- explain how the monetary policy of the ECB affects the money market
- discuss the most important developments in the money market since the start of the monetary union
- discuss the most important developments in the bond markets since the start of the monetary union
- discuss the most important developments in the equity markets since the start of the monetary union
- describe the essentials of the derivatives market
- describe the foreign exchange market.

5.1 Financial markets: functions and structure

Functions

A *financial market* is a market where individuals issue and trade securities and derivatives. *Securities* are fungible, negotiable instruments representing financial value, and are broadly categorised in debt securities and equity securities. In financial markets, funds are channelled from those with a surplus, who buy securities, to those with a shortage, who issue new securities or sell existing securities (see Chapter 1). A financial market can be seen as a set of arrangements that allows trading among its participants. The following functions are performed by a financial market depending on the phase of trading (Bailey, 2005):

- Price discovery: the market facilitates the dissemination of information. This enables participants who want to buy or sell to find out the prices at which trades can be agreed upon (pre-trading phase).
- Trading mechanism: the market provides a mechanism to facilitate the making of agreements. There must be a means by which those who want to sell can communicate with those who want to buy (trading phase).
- Clearing and settlement arrangements: the agreements are executed. The market must ensure that the terms of each agreement are honoured (post-trading phase).

Price discovery involves the incorporation of new information into asset prices (O'Hara, 2003). Securities represent a promise of future payments. The value of a security depends on expectations of the size and the risk of these future payments. New information can affect these expectations. In an efficient market, prices reflect all (publicly) available information.[1] Markets also provide liquidity. Market liquidity refers to the matching of buyers and sellers (O'Hara, 2003). Liquidity is inter-temporal in nature as buyers and sellers may enter the market at different points in time. The trading mechanism is the means of matching those buyers to sellers. Below we discuss the main trading mechanisms in more detail. Finally, clearing and settlement arrangements include: (1) confirmation of the terms of the transactions; (2) clearing of the trades to establish the obligations of buyers and sellers; (3) settlement of the accounts to finalise the delivery of securities against payment of money. These post-trading arrangements are discussed in Chapter 7.

The participants in financial markets can be classified into various groups, according to their motive for trading:

1. *Public investors*, who ultimately own the securities and who are motivated by the returns from holding the securities. Public investors include private individuals and institutional investors, such as pension funds and mutual funds.
2. *Brokers*, who act as agents for public investors and who are motivated by the remuneration received (typically in the form of commission fees) for

the services they provide. Brokers thus trade for others and not on their own account.

3. *Dealers*, who do trade on their own account but whose primary motive is to profit from trading rather than from holding securities. Typically, dealers obtain their return from the differences between the prices at which they buy and sell the security over short intervals of time.

In practice the three groups are not mutually exclusive. Some public investors may occasionally act on behalf of others; brokers may act as dealers and hold securities on their own, while dealers often hold securities in excess of the inventories needed to facilitate their trading activities. The role of these three groups differs according to the trading mechanism adopted by a financial market.

Another important group of firms are the credit rating agencies (CRAs) that assess the credit risk of borrowers (see Chapter 8).

Trading mechanisms

Financial markets use a trading mechanism for matching buyers to sellers. As the trading mechanism is a defining characteristic, financial markets are often classified by their trading mechanism (Harris, 2003). The two main types are quote-driven markets and order-driven markets, while hybrid markets use some combination of the two.

Quote-driven markets

In *quote-driven markets* (also known as dealer markets), dealers quote *bid* and ask prices at which they are prepared to buy or sell, respectively, specified amounts of the security (Bailey, 2005). Quote-driven markets require little formal organisation, but need mechanisms for publishing the dealers' price quotations and for regulating the conduct of dealers. Stock exchanges normally grant dealers (or market makers) privileged access to certain administrative procedures or market information. In return for these privileges, dealers have particular obligations, most importantly to quote 'firm' bid and ask prices at which they guarantee to make trades of up to specified volumes. Anyone who wants to trade in a quote-driven market must trade with a dealer. Either the investors negotiate with the dealers themselves or their brokers negotiate with the dealers.

When a security is traded, the buyer pays the ask price, p_a, and the seller receives the bid price, p_b. The difference is the *bid-ask spread*: $s = p_a - p_b$ received by the dealer. The dealer typically holds an inventory of securities during the day to be able to sell (and buy) immediately. From his return (i.e. the bid-ask spread), the dealer has to cover the costs of holding his inventory (e.g. interest costs of financing the securities inventory) and the risks (e.g. prices may move while the securities are in the inventory). While bid and ask prices are published, dealers may negotiate special prices for large transactions. The spread could be broader for particularly large transactions (i.e. block trades) to cover the price risk of such block trades before the dealer can sell on (or buy) the bought (sold) securities to (from) other dealers in the market.

Order-driven markets

In *order-driven markets* (also known as auction markets), participants issue orders to buy or sell at stated prices, which can be modelled as 'double auctions'. Participants issue instructions that specific actions should be taken in response to the arrival of publicly verifiable price observations. The price is then adjusted by an 'auctioneer' until the total orders to buy equal the total orders to sell (Bailey, 2005). There are different forms of order-driven markets. In call markets, the price is determined at a limited number of specified times. In that way, orders can be collected and the auction takes place at the specified time. This type of auction is widely used for new issues of government debt (see section 5.3) and initial public offerings of equity (see section 5.4). The call-market mechanism has disappeared in secondary markets for bonds and equity and has been replaced by continuous trading systems.

In continuous auction markets, public investors send their instructions ('orders') to buy or sell to brokers. There are different sorts of order. The most well-known are the *limit order*, which specifies purchase or sale at maximum buying prices or minimum selling prices, respectively, and the *market order*, which specifies purchase or sale at the best available price. The outstanding limit orders are generally listed in a limit order book. The existence of a limit order book implies automatic trade matching, though in practice some element of discretion remains (e.g. in setting the priority of orders). Order-driven markets are highly formalised as the auction rules for matching trades have to be specified in great detail to ensure an orderly and fair trading process.

Hybrid markets

Trading mechanisms are often compared with respect to transparency and liquidity (Bailey, 2005). In terms of fundamental principles, quote-driven markets and order-driven markets should result in the same market prices if all trades are made public. But in practice quote-driven markets tend to be more fragmented. Dealers quote different bid and ask prices, and deals that have been executed are not necessarily public information or may be published with some delay (to allow dealers some time to off-load large trades in the market). Thus, order-driven markets tend to be more transparent than quote-driven markets.

Liquidity does not depend only on the trading mechanism. In a call market, investors must wait until the next price fixing takes place. By contrast, they can trade immediately in continuous order-driven markets. The price, however, depends on the availability of sufficient orders on the other side of the market. Investors may therefore sometimes prefer the opportunity to negotiate individual agreements with dealers in quote-driven markets. Also, quote-driven markets may allow a delay of publication so that deals can be kept secret, if only for a limited time.

In practice, we observe *hybrid markets*, which combine characteristics of quote-driven and order-driven markets. Advances in IT have spurred the development of order-driven markets, in particular for equity trading. The combination of smart trading rules (software) with fast computers (hardware) allows an almost instantaneous matching of orders. Euronext, for example, applies an order-driven trading mechanism with a centralised electronic order book. Nevertheless, Euronext also enables small and medium-sized listed companies to hire a designated market maker to act as 'liquidity provider' in their stock. Similarly, the London Stock Exchange's premier electronic trading system (SETS) combines electronic order-driven trading with liquidity provision by market makers. While stock exchanges are becoming more order-driven, bond markets tend to be more quote-driven (making use of dealers). Sections 5.3 and 5.4 discuss the main bond markets and stock exchanges in more detail.

Overview of financial markets

Generally, a distinction can be made between primary and secondary markets. At a *primary market* new issues of a security are sold to investors. At a *secondary market* securities that have been previously issued are traded. Secondary markets can be organised in exchanges, where buyers and sellers meet in one central location to conduct trade, or over-the-counter (OTC) markets in which dealers at different locations stand ready to sell and buy securities 'over-the-counter'.

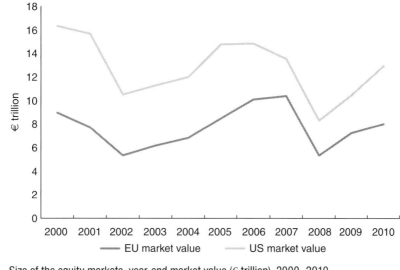

Figure 5.1   Size of the equity markets, year-end market value (€ trillion), 2000–2010
Source: World Federation of Exchanges

The principal financial markets that we discuss in the remainder of the chapter are:

- the money market – this is the market for short-term funds up to one year. In particular, banks use the money market for the management of their short-term liquidity positions;
- the bond markets – these are the most important segment of the market for debt securities with a maturity of more than one year. Governments and firms issue bonds to raise medium- and long-term debt against a fixed or flexible interest rate;
- the equity markets – firms may raise funds by issuing equity that grants the investor a residual claim on the company's income;
- the derivatives market – derivatives are financial instruments whose value is derived from the value of the underlying financial instruments. Derivatives are important risk-management tools;
- the foreign exchange market, where the relative values of currencies are determined.

Figures 5.1 and 5.2 compare the size of the main funding markets, the equity and bond markets, in the EU and the US. These figures demonstrate the fundamental difference between the financial systems of the EU and the US (see also Chapter 1). The US financial system is primarily market-based. Nevertheless, the importance of equity finance is growing in the EU and

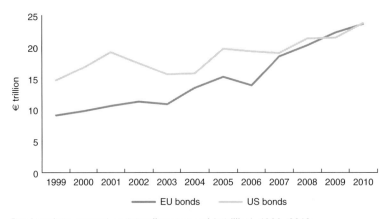

Figure 5.2   Bond markets, amounts outstanding year-end (€ trillion), 1999–2010
Source: Bank for International Settlements, Quarterly Reviews

slowly catching up with the US. The equity market capitalisation was €8 trillion in 2010. The large fluctuations in market capitalisation reflect the dot-com bubble in 2000–2001 and the 2007–2009 financial crisis.

At the time of the introduction of the euro, the EU bond market amounted to €9 trillion compared with €15 trillion in the US (see Figure 5.2). The EU bond market has experienced spectacular growth since then so that the EU and US bond markets have become similar in size, with the outstanding value of bonds equal to €24 trillion in 2010.

5.2 Money market

In a broad sense, the *money market* consists of the market for short-term funds, usually with maturity up to one year. The '*euro money market*' is the market for euro-denominated short-term funds and related derivative instruments (i.e. contracts, such as options and futures, whose value is derived from the value of the underlying instrument). Credit institutions (i.e. banks) account for the largest share of the euro money market. As will be explained below, these institutions rely on the euro money market for the management of their short-term liquidity positions and for the fulfilment of their minimum reserve requirements. Other important market participants are money market funds, other financial intermediaries (such as investment funds other than money market funds), insurance companies and pension funds, as well as large non-financial corporations.

The most important money-market segments are the unsecured deposit markets (with various maturities, ranging from overnight to one year) and the secured repo markets (often called repos) with maturities also ranging from overnight to one year.[2] A *repurchase agreement* is an arrangement whereby an asset is sold while the seller simultaneously obtains the right and obligation to repurchase it at a specific price on a future date or on demand (ECB, 2008b). The most important difference between the secured and the unsecured segments is the amount of risk involved. When providing unsecured interbank deposits, a bank transfers funds to another bank for a specified period of time during which it assumes full counterparty credit risk. In the secured repo markets, this counterparty credit risk is mitigated as the bank that provides liquidity receives collateral (e.g. bonds) in return. In the event of a credit default, the liquidity-providing bank can utilise the collateral received to satisfy its claim against the defaulting bank. Because of this lower credit risk, secured repo rates are usually somewhat lower than unsecured deposit rates (ECB, 2008a).

Apart from transactions with the central bank, money market participants trade with each other to take positions in relation to their short-term interest rate expectations, to finance their securities trading portfolios (bonds, shares, etc.), to hedge their more long-term positions with more short-term contracts, and to square individual liquidity imbalances (Hartmann *et al.*, 2001).

As explained in Chapter 4, the euro money market is strongly influenced by the monetary policy of the ECB. In addition to decisions concerning interest rates, the ECB influences the euro money market through three monetary policy instruments:

- reserve requirements
- open market operations
- standing facilities.

The ECB requires banks to hold *required reserves*. Currently, banks established in the euro area have to keep 1 per cent of the total amount of overnight deposits, other deposits with maturity below two years, debt securities with maturity below two years, and money market paper (excluding interbank liabilities) at reserve accounts with their National Central Banks. Reserve requirements have to be fulfilled on average over a one-month maintenance period (averaging).

The minimum reserve system helps to stabilise money market interest rates by the *averaging provision*, i.e. banks' compliance with reserve requirements is judged on the basis of the average of the daily balances on their reserve accounts over a reserve maintenance period. As a consequence, banks can smooth out daily liquidity fluctuations since transitory reserve imbalances can be offset by opposite reserve imbalances within the same maintenance period. The averaging provision also implies that if institutions believe that money market rates are currently higher than in the remainder of the maintenance period, they can profit from lending in the market and run a reserve deficit. If they believe that money market rates will go up, they can borrow in the market and run a reserve surplus. This mechanism stabilises the overnight interest rate during the maintenance period.

Open market operations are the general instruments used to manage the liquidity situation and to steer interest rates. The *main refinancing operations* (MROs) are the most important instrument (see Chapter 4 for further details).

The *standing facilities* provide or absorb liquidity with an overnight maturity when unforeseen liquidity shocks occur. Therefore they provide a type of insurance mechanism for banks, but at penalty interest rates. The initiative in these transactions is on the side of the credit institution.

Apart from the ECB interest rates on the standing facilities and the MROs, there are three main market interest rates for the money market:

- EONIA (euro overnight index average). The *EONIA* is the effective overnight reference rate for the euro. It is computed daily as a volume-weighted average of unsecured euro overnight lending transactions in the interbank market, as reported by a representative panel of large banks.[3]
- EURIBOR (euro interbank offered rate). The *EURIBOR* is the benchmark rate of the large unsecured euro money market for maturities longer than overnight (one week to one year) that has emerged since 1999. It is based on information provided by the same panel of banks.
- EUREPO (the repo market reference rate for the euro) for different maturities. The *EUREPO* is the benchmark rate of the euro repo market and has been released since March 2002. It is the rate at which one prime bank offers funds in euros to another prime bank when the funds are secured by a repo transaction using general collateral.

Developments in money-market segments

Figure 5.3 shows the development of an index of daily turnover (turnover in 2002 is 100). The upper part of the figure refers to the unsecured segments, while the lower part shows the secured segments. After five years of continuous growth, total activity in the unsecured market began to shrink in 2008.

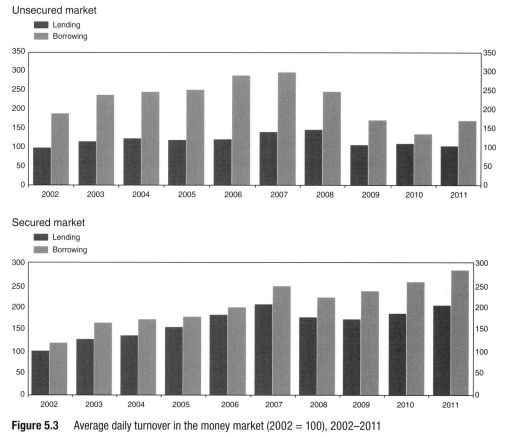

Figure 5.3 Average daily turnover in the money market (2002 = 100), 2002–2011
Source: ECB (2011b)

In 2009 and 2010 turnover declined much more on the borrowing side than on the lending side. In 2010, for example, the former declined by 22 per cent whereas the latter fell by only 11 per cent. As unsecured lending exposes the lender to the highest degree of counterparty default risk, this decline is not surprising since aversion to counterparty credit risk remained very high as a result of the crisis. As unsecured transactions declined, the secured segment of the money market strengthened its position as the largest segment of the market, representing 36 per cent of total turnover in 2010. An important reason is banks' desire to limit credit risk exposure (ECB, 2011b).

A breakdown by maturity shows that turnover is concentrated in short maturities. Most of the turnover in the unsecured market is concentrated in the overnight (O/N) maturity segment, both in lending and borrowing as O/N is the maturity which banks typically use to adjust their day-to-day cash imbalances. The average maturity of secured transactions is comparatively longer than that for unsecured transactions. Transactions in the maturity bucket 'tomorrow/next up to one month' increased to 76 per cent of the total in 2010.

5.3 Bond markets

A *bond* is a debt security that promises that payments will be made periodically for a specified time. The re-denomination of debt from former national currencies into euros at the beginning of the monetary union paved the way for a European debt securities market. The increased role of the euro as an international investment currency has made the market in euro-denominated issues attractive for both investors and issuers. The bulk of euro-denominated debt securities is issued by euro-area issuers. However, for issuers outside the euro area it has also become attractive to borrow in euros.

As Figure 5.4 shows, debt securities issued by public authorities still form the most important market segment, followed by bank bonds.

Bonds are the main instrument of governments (mainly central governments, but also regional and local government authorities, and social securities funds) within the euro area to finance their budget deficits. Furthermore, government bonds often serve as a benchmark for pricing other assets and they are also frequently used as collateral in various financial transactions.

The non-government bond market is dominated by bank debt securities. This segment encompasses numerous different types of bonds, including unsecured bank debt securities and covered bonds. *Covered bonds* are claims of the bond holders against the issuing bank that are secured by a pool of cover assets on the bank's balance sheet, such as mortgage loans or loans to the public sector.

Government bonds

Issuance

The introduction of the euro in 1999 had a major impact on the operations of government-debt managers as the disappearance of exchange-rate risks within the euro area created the conditions for a pan-European capital market. As a result, debt managers have become small to medium-sized players in a larger European market, instead of being the dominant player in

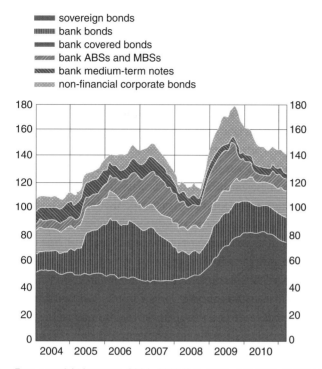

Figure 5.4   Euro-area debt issuance, 2004–2010 (Jan. 2004–Apr. 2011; € billions; 12-month moving average)
Source: ECB (2011a)

the national market. Investors now focus more on credit risk and liquidity, while bond portfolios have become increasingly internationally diversified, especially in the smaller euro-area countries. Consequently, competition among debt managers has increased, stimulating a more efficient primary market and a deeper, more liquid secondary market. Governments have put great effort into making their outstanding debt and new issues more attractive to international bond investors. To this end, they have adopted a number of supply-side innovations (see Box 5.1 for further details). These innovations were enabled by the rapid expansion of electronic trading systems. In addition to local systems, the European electronic platform for government securities, EuroMTS, was introduced in 1999, enabling quotation and trading of some European benchmark bonds (see Chapter 7 for further details).

Table 5.1 provides an overview of public-debt securities by country of issuer in the period 2000–2010.

Box 5.1 Government-debt management

The primary objective of debt-management agencies in the euro area is to ensure financing of the government's annual borrowing at the lowest possible (medium-term) cost with acceptable risks, although precise wordings and emphasis differ from country to country. The operational targets or guidelines for debt-management units differ more substantially. Often, these are based on asset-liability studies or cost-at-risk models, weighing interest costs against budgetary risks. Targets can take the form of a target (range) for the average maturity or the (modified) duration,[4] subject to certain restrictions such as quantitative limits on the use of interest rate swaps.

Debt-management units were generally given more independence in the 1990s. A stronger focus on 'narrow' debt-management goals allowed for delegation to separate units. In addition, higher product complexity and competition among debt managers require a higher degree of operational independence and professionalism, which is easier to accomplish in a non-government unit. Cost considerations sometimes also played a role in the decision to delegate tasks to more independent units (Wolswijk and de Haan, 2005).

The increased competition has led to increasing liquidity of government securities and larger volumes of outstanding issues. While issues of around €2 billion were standard in smaller countries before the start of EMU, the minimum is now €5 billion, with large countries in the euro area having bond issuances of over €20 billion.[5] Governments sometimes focus on 'niches' targeting particular investor needs. For instance, Spain and France have introduced constant-maturity bonds, while France (followed by Greece and Italy) has taken the lead in the issuance of index-linked bonds (Baele *et al.*, 2004). The return of an index-linked bond is depending on the development of a price index. In 2006, Germany issued an index-linked bond. Outside the euro area, the UK and the US are major issuers of index-linked bonds. In the segment of long-term debt securities, securities with a maturity of ten years or more play the major role. The 3-, 5-, and 30-year segments also remained attractive, with about half of the debt managers issuing at least one security in those segments. More recently, debt managers have selected a somewhat wider spectrum of maturities, including some reversion to issuing short-term securities (Wolswijk and de Haan, 2005). In the euro area, the share of securities with a residual maturity of up to one year in total outstanding government securities is slightly above 20 per cent. In 2010 the figure stood at 21.4 per cent (ECB, 2011a).

Debt managers have also made issuance activity more regular and predictable by introducing pre-announced auction calendars, which has improved market transparency. Increased competition in the primary and secondary government bond markets has also led to changes in distribution channels. Primary dealers and bank syndicates are now popular means to reach more non-domestic investors. Primary dealers mediate between the debt agency and buyers in both the primary and secondary markets. All euro-area countries (except Germany) now use primary dealers to distribute government bonds. Tasks for primary dealers usually include the obligation to bid at auctions or to buy a certain amount of newly issued bonds, promotion of government debt, and market making. In all countries concerned, many foreign financial institutions are included as primary dealers, reflecting the wish to spread ownership of government securities widely. Bank syndicates have also become increasingly popular as a way to distribute new government debt, particularly when approaching new market segments. Syndicate participants may select specific investors to whom the government security to be issued may be especially interesting. For smaller countries, a particular advantage is that a significant amount can be placed at once, thus immediately creating liquidity.

Eager to benefit from the improved diversification benefits and liquidity, investors have considerably increased their holdings of non-domestic bonds, leading to a reduction in the home bias of government bond markets in the euro area. In 2010 the share of euro-area total government debt held by non-residents (including those of other euro-area countries) stood at about 52 per cent (compared with 32 per cent in 1999). The share of public debt held by non-residents varies greatly across countries, roughly from 6 to 75 per cent (ECB, 2011a).

Government bond yields

Figure 5.5 shows the euro-area yield for AAA-rated government bonds for three different maturities and the term spread calculated, as the difference between the ten-year bond yield and the three-month T-bill rate. Yields of government bonds are influenced by expected short-term interest rates and the term premium. Risk-averse investors demand a risk premium (*term premium*) for investments in long-term bonds to compensate them for the risk of losses due to (unexpected) interest rate hikes; those losses increase with bond duration. The *term premium* leads to a positive *term spread*, i.e. the spread of yields for bonds with longer maturity over yields for bonds with shorter maturity, even when markets expect increasing and decreasing interest rates to be equally likely. The term spread in the euro area has been mostly positive since 1999, reflecting what is often called a 'normal' yield curve (ECB, 2007). However, the term spread has been changing over time, with peaks in

Table 5.1 Outstanding euro-denominated public-debt securities (€ billion), 2000–2010

	2000	2002	2004	2006	2008	2010	Increase between 2000–2010 (%)
Austria	101.3	109.8	114.9	128.9	138.7	165.2	63.1
Belgium	243.8	257.0	255.1	258.0	283.5	320.4	31.4
Cyprus	-	-	6.4	6.7	5.1	7.8	–
Germany	779.9	867.3	1,006.6	1,123.1	1,182.2	1,514.0	94.1
Finland	53.9	51.0	54.8	53.4	51.3	69.1	28.0
France	643.2	747.5	891.9	950.2	1,084.1	1,316.4	104.7
Greece	98.6	123.3	158.8	185.5	239.5	282.2	186.1
Ireland	21.8	22.3	31.3	31.2	41.9	96.3	341.9
Italy	1,064.9	1,094.9	1,144.3	1,232.8	1,341.5	1,507.2	41.5
Luxembourg	0.7	0.6	0.4	0.1	2.0	4.0	510.7
Malta	-	-	2.9	3.0	3.3	4.0	–
Netherlands	177.6	189.1	215.3	211.7	271.5	288.9	62.7
Portugal	47.2	58.9	71.2	89.5	101.2	137.1	190.6
Slovenia	3.4	6.2	6.6	7.5	7.6	12.6	265.0
Slovakia	4.9	8.2	11.3	12.7	16.6	25.1	413.4
Spain	303.0	319.0	330.9	336.9	382.8	585.8	93.4
Euro area	3,544.3	3,855.1	4,302.6	4,631.3	5,153.1	6,336.1	78.8
Rest of the world	100.7	102.0	114.4	122.3	120.9	138.7	37.8
Total	3,645.0	3,957.2	4,417.0	4,753.5	5,274.0	6,474.8	77.6

Source: ECB

mid-1999 and mid-2004, while it was low in 2000 and again towards the end of 2006.

Apart from interest rate expectations and the term premium, credit risk and liquidity also influence government bond yields. *Credit risk* is the risk of loss because of the failure of a counterparty to perform according to a contractual arrangement, for instance due to a default by a borrower. The spread between the yield of a particular bond and the yield of a bond with similar characteristics but without credit risk is the credit risk premium. Rating agencies – like Moody's, Standard & Poor's (S&P), and Fitch – indicate issuers' credit risk by assigning them a rating (see Chapter 8 for further details). Table 5.2 shows the ratings of EU Member States in September 2011.

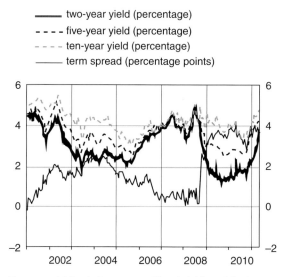

two-year yield (percentage)
five-year yield (percentage)
ten-year yield (percentage)
term spread (percentage points)

Figure 5.5   Euro-area AAA-rated government bond yields and the term spread (%), 2001–2011
(Jan. 2001–May 2011; weekly averages)
Source: ECB (2011a)

Liquidity is the ease with which an investor can sell or buy a bond immediately at a price close to the mid-quote (i.e. the average of the bid-ask spread,
as defined in section 5.1). The spread between the yield of a bond with
liquidity and a similar bond with less liquidity is referred to as the liquidity
premium.

Figure 5.6 shows the yield spreads of ten-year euro-area government
bonds over the euro overnight index swap rate. This rate is used rather than
the German government bond yield in order to account for the impact of
flight-to-safety flows into German government bonds that occurred during
the euro-area debt crisis. Figure 5.6 shows that yield differentials vary considerably across countries, while for each country the yield differential varies considerably over time. Pagano and Von Thadden (2008) discuss studies
that try to explain these yield differentials, arguing that they may arise from
(1) intrinsic differences in country-specific default risk or different sensitivities of bonds' future payoffs to common shocks, or (2) market frictions, like
trading costs, clearing and settlement fees, and taxes. As Pagano and Von
Thadden (2008) point out, these factors may also interact. For instance, if an
asset on which a transaction tax has to be paid becomes riskier, the effect on

Table 5.2 Ratings and outlook of government debt, September 2011

Country	Moody's	Fitch	S&P
Austria	Aaa (stable)	AAA (stable)	AAA (stable)
Belgium	Aa1 (stable)	AA+ (negative)	AA+ (negative)
Cyprus	Baa1 (negative)	A- (negative)	A- (negative)
Czech Republic	A1 (stable)	A+ (positive)	A (positive)
Denmark	Aaa (stable)	AAA (stable)	AAA (stable)
Estonia	A1 (stable)	A+ (stable)	A (stable)
Finland	Aaa (stable)	AAA (stable)	AAA (stable)
France	Aaa (stable)	AAA (stable)	AAA (stable)
Germany	Aaa (stable)	AAA (stable)	AAA (stable)
Greece	Ca (developing)	CCC	CC (negative)
Hungary	Baa3 (negative)	BBB- (negative)	BBB- (negative)
Ireland	Ba1 (negative)	BBB+ (negative)	BBB+ (stable)
Italy	Aa2 (under review)	AA- (stable)	A (negative)
Latvia	Baa3 (positive)	BBB- (positive)	BB+ (positive)
Lithuania	Baa1 (stable)	BBB (positive)	BBB (stable)
Luxembourg	Aaa (stable)	AAA (stable)	AAA (stable)
Malta	A1 (stable)	A+ (stable)	A (stable)
Netherlands	Aaa (stable)	AAA (stable)	AAA (stable)
Poland	A2 (stable)	A- (stable)	A- (stable)
Portugal	Ba2 (negative)	BBB- (negative)	BBB- (negative)
Romania	Baa3 (stable)	BBB- (stable)	BB+ (stable)
Slovakia	A1 (stable)	A+ (stable)	A+ (stable)
Slovenia	Aa2 (stable)	AA (stable)	AA (negative)
Spain	Aa2 (under review)	AA+ (negative)	AA (negative)
Sweden	Aaa (stable)	AAA (stable)	AAA (stable)
UK	Aaa (stable)	AAA (stable)	AAA (stable)

Source: Website of CRAs

the price will be smaller the larger the tax, since the initial after-tax price is correspondingly lower. Pagano and Von Thadden (2008) conclude that credit risk explains a considerable portion of cross-country yield differences but explains very little of their variation over time.

Corporate bonds

In recent years the European corporate bond market has grown rapidly and the market's structure has undergone some important changes. Before 1998, the market was dominated by debt issued by highly rated financial corporations, whereas since that date industrial corporations have increasingly found

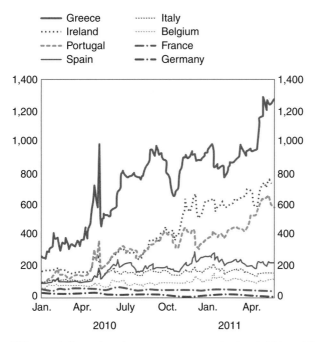

Figure 5.6   Difference between long-term euro-area sovereign bond yields and the overnight index swap rate in 2010 and 2011 (Jan. 2010–May 2011; ten-year bond yields and ten-year overnight index swap rate; basis points)
Source: ECB (2011a)

their way to the corporate bond market (Baele *et al.*, 2004). Nevertheless, financials are still more important than non-financial firms, being the second largest group of issuers of debt securities in the euro-area economy. In 2009 the issue of investment-grade bonds was high compared to other years in the period 2006–2011, both in terms of volume and number of deals (see Figure 5.7).

Spreads of corporate bond yields over AAA-rated government bond yields as shown in Figure 5.8 mainly reflect the perceived credit risk that results from an investment in corporate bonds. When the corporate outlook deteriorates, these spreads increase. For example, spreads were high during the years 2001 and 2002 when economic growth was low, but decreased significantly in 2003. Corporate bond spreads are higher for bonds of lower-rated issuers than for bonds of higher-rated issuers (see Figure 5.8). The ECB (2007) identifies two possible explanations for this. First, the default probabilities of lower-rated corporate issuers may be more closely linked to the business cycle than the default probabilities of higher-rated corporations. Second, bond spreads

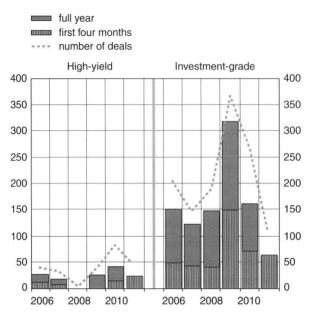

Figure 5.7 High-yield and investment-grade bond issuance in the euro area (Jan. 2006–Apr. 2011: issuance in € billions and the number of deals)
Source: ECB (2011a)

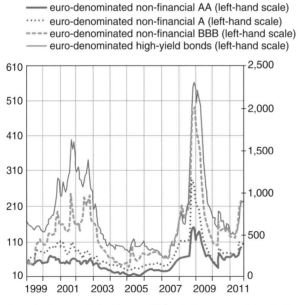

Figure 5.8 Spreads of corporate bonds over AAA-rated government bonds (basis points), 1999–2011
Source: ECB Monthly Bulletin (September 2011)

widen when bonds become less liquid. During recessions, lower-rated corporate bonds may suffer and might be traded less actively, thus reducing their liquidity, leading to higher liquidity premia. Spreads between non-financial corporate bond yields and AAA-rated government bond yields have widened continuously since May 2010 in the case of both higher-rated and lower-rated bonds. According to the ECB, these developments have been driven by disappointing economic data and increased uncertainty fuelled by the downgrading of US sovereign debt by one credit rating agency and by tensions related to the euro-area sovereign debt crisis (see Chapter 2), which continue to weaken market sentiment. More generally, there is a trade-off between liquidity and transparency in bond markets, which are quote-driven. Dealers quote prices at which they are prepared to trade bonds. To protect dealers with large positions, deals may be published with some delay. Box 5.2 discusses the optimal amount of trade transparency in bond markets.

An important type of debt securities are covered bonds, i.e. debt securities backed by cash flows from mortgages or public sector loans. Covered bonds provide investors with two layers of protection: recourse first to the underlying assets (mainly composed of good quality instruments) and second to the other unsecured assets of the issuing bank. By issuing covered bonds, banks retain the assets on their balance sheet or provide guarantees on dedicated structures to which the assets are transferred (ECB, 2011c). Covered bonds also form an important part of collateral used for Eurosystem operations. Germany is by far the most important euro-area country for covered bonds (so-called *Pfandbriefe*), followed by Spain and France (see Figure 5.9). Maturities of covered bonds typically range from 2–10 years. The majority of covered bonds are rated AAA.

Securitised instruments

Despite similarities, covered bonds are different to securitised products. The key difference between covered bonds and securitisation is that covered bonds do not involve credit risk transfer. The credit risk stays with the originator, which has to hold capital (against the risk of losses) but typically obtains cheaper funding through the covered bond issuance (ECB, 2007).

According to the ECB (2007), there are two objectives for the issuance of asset-backed securities, i.e. fund raising and credit risk transfer. Both objectives can be achieved through a 'true sale' securitisation or through a funded synthetic securitisation. In a *'true sale' securitisation*, the originator (typically a bank) transfers the ownership of a pool of assets to a special

■■■ self-funded covered bond issues (€ billions; left-hand scale)
▨▨▨ covered bonds issued (€ billions; left-hand scale)
--- percentage of self-funded revenues (right-hand scale)

Overall Europe

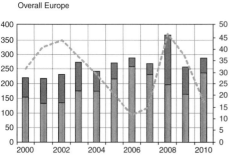

European countries other than Germany

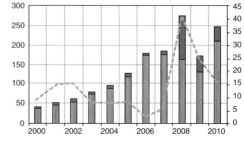

Figure 5.9   Covered bond issues, 2000–2010

Note: The figure distinguishes between market placements and issuance solely for the purpose of creating eligible collateral for Eurosystem credit operations (self-funded issuance).

Source: ECB (2011c)

purpose vehicle (SPV), which issues securities backed by the pool of assets and transfers the funds raised through selling these securities to the originator. In a *funded synthetic securitisation* process, the ownership of the asset pool is not transferred to the SPV but remains on the balance sheet of the originator.

Asset-backed securities (ABS) can be classified according to the type of underlying collateral. *Mortgage-backed securities* (MBS) are backed by mortgages loans, be it residential (RMBS) or commercial (CMBS). *Collateralised debt obligations* (CDOs) are backed by bonds or loans. All other securitisation products are called *asset-backed securities in a narrow sense*. These are typically backed by credit card receivables, leasing receivables, trade receivables, and others. As Figure 5.10 shows, in Europe RMBS represent by far the most prominent asset class. Between 2008 and 2010 the issuance ranges between 53 per cent (2009) and 76 per cent (2008) of total issuances. CMBS traditionally represent only a small part of total European issuance, which has decreased even further in the last three years. The lower aggregate volume of the ABS (consumer, cards, auto, leases) and CDO segments in 2010 is partly attributable to less benign macroeconomic conditions. Issuance in Europe is mainly concentrated in the United Kingdom, Spain, the Netherlands, and Italy. The Netherlands has become one of the main European markets for securitisation in 2010 (ECB, 2011c). Even though new issues have come down considerably in recent years, the amounts of ABS outstanding are still very high, as shown in Figure 5.11.

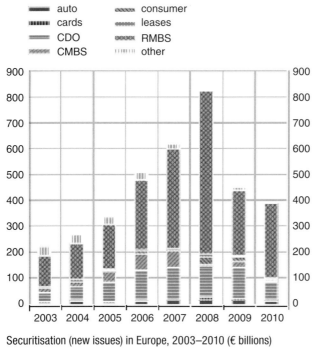

Figure 5.10   Securitisation (new issues) in Europe, 2003–2010 (€ billions)
Source: ECB (2011c)

5.4 Equity markets

Equities grant the investor a residual right to receive income from the company's earnings. Equity can be issued either privately (unquoted shares) or publicly via shares that are listed on a stock exchange (quoted shares). The importance of equity finance in the EU is lower than in the US, as reflected by the size of European equity markets as shown in Table 5.3 (see also Figure 5.1). Also within Europe, there are large differences. As Table 5.3 shows, the market capitalisations of Euronext and the LSE are much higher than those of other exchanges in the EU.

Consolidation

The EU stock market is highly concentrated. This high level of concentration may be explained by the fact that financial exchanges exhibit network externalities, as higher participation of traders on both sides of the market positively affects market liquidity and increases traders' utility.

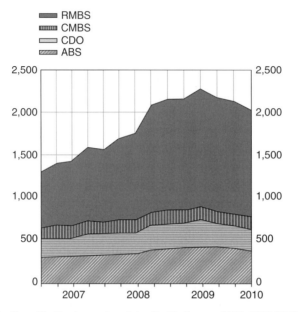

RMBS
CMBS
CDO
ABS

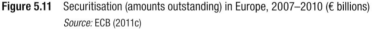

Figure 5.11   Securitisation (amounts outstanding) in Europe, 2007–2010 (€ billions)
Source: ECB (2011c)

Box 5.2 How much transparency is optimal?

Transparency refers to the absence or elimination of information asymmetries. In a fully transparent market, all relevant market information is common knowledge for all participants. The debate on bond market transparency is a difficult one. According to Dunne *et al.* (2006), the very existence of most financial markets depends on striking a balance between transparency, thought to promote competition, fairness, and investor protection, and opacity, in the interest of encouraging ongoing participation of both end-customers and liquidity providers. If market participants do not obtain adequate fairness, protection, and incentives, they will not participate in sufficient numbers and the market will not function properly.

This can be illustrated by the so-called Winner's Curse, according to which the highest bidder has probably bid too much. If the highest bidder wants to resell the product immediately after the auction, the best price he will obtain is the underbidder's price. Because of incomplete information or subjective factors, bidders will form a range of estimates of the item's 'intrinsic value'. As a result, the largest overestimation of an item's value ends up winning the auction. With perfect information and fully rational participants skilled in valuation, no overpayments should occur. A number of dealers submit quotes and the highest-bidding dealer secures the bonds. Typically, the successful dealer enters the inter-dealer market to hedge his risk. The underbidders are aware of this and can benefit by taking up contrarian positions in the market, thereby making it difficult for the successful bidder to share his position. The more transparent the inter-dealer market, the more difficult it is for the successful bidder to hedge his risk. Consequently, an increase in market transparency makes dealers more cautious about participating.

Yet there are powerful arguments in favour of enhancing transparency. Transparency can facilitate 'best execution', i.e. it allows investors to verify whether dealers and others indeed execute orders at the best price available. Goldstein *et al.* (2007) observe a decrease in transaction costs which is consistent with investors' ability to negotiate better terms of trade with dealers once investors have access to broader bond-pricing data. Costs may also be lower for bonds with transparent prices (see Edwards *et al.*, 2007). Greater price transparency can enhance investor protection as price movements signal default probabilities. Strengthening overall transparency may also create a level playing field between large institutional and smaller investors. Large institutional investors may already be able to obtain all relevant information, while smaller investors are not able to exert the same pressure on dealers.

Finally, transparency may improve liquidity. As for municipal bond trades, Harris and Piwowar (2006) argue that ongoing regulatory initiatives to increase transparency in the municipal bond market will lead to liquidity improvements. These improvements should have the greatest impact on retail investors. Next to this, Goldstein *et al.* (2007) find that adding transparency to corporate bond markets has either a neutral or a positive effect on liquidity. These findings seem contradictory to what has been argued by Dunne *et al.* (2006). However, Casey (2006) stresses that pre- and post-trade transparency may equally enhance or harm market liquidity and efficiency, depending on how they are applied, by whom, for what instruments, in which markets, and at which latency.

There has been an intensive regional cross-border consolidation. First, Euronext resulted from a merger of the Paris, Amsterdam, Brussels, and Lisbon stock exchanges during 2000–2002. Next, the stock exchanges of Copenhagen, Stockholm, Helsinki, Tallin, Riga, Vilnius, and Iceland merged between 2004 and 2006, creating the OMX Nordic Exchange. In 2006, the first trans-Atlantic stock exchange merger took place between Euronext and the New York Stock Exchange (NYSE), strengthening its position as the largest securities trading venue in the world. In 2008, a merger between NASDAQ and OMX was completed, while Italy's stock-exchange

Table 5.3 The world's largest equity exchanges, 2010

Exchange	Market capitalisation ($ billion)	Traded firms (number)	Turnover ($ billion)
NYSE Euronext (US)	13,394	2,238	17,796
NASDAQ OMX	3,889	2,778	12,659
Tokyo	3,828	2,293	3,793
LSE	3,613	2,966	2,749
NYSE Euronext (Europe)	2,930	1,135	2,022
Shanghai SE	2,716	894	4,486
Hong Kong Exchanges	2,711	1,413	1,496
TSX Group	2,170	3,741	1,366
Bombay SE	1,632	5,034	259
National Stock Exchange India	1,597	1,552	799
BM&FBOVESPA	1,546	381	867
Australian SE	1,454	1,999	1,062
Deutsche Börse	1,430	765	1,632
Shenzhen SE	1,311	1,169	3,564
SIX Swiss Exchange	1,229	296	790

Source: World Federation of Exchanges

operator Borsa Italiana accepted a takeover from the LSE. In February 2011, the London Stock Exchange Group announced that they had agreed to merge with the Toronto-based TMX Group, the owners of the Toronto Stock Exchange, while in the same month BATS Global Markets agreed to buy Chi-X Europe. Chi-X Europe is a London-based, order-driven pan-European equity exchange, while BATS (Better Alternative Trading System) is operator of the third largest stock exchange in the US. Also in February 2011, NYSE Euronext announced that it is in advanced merger talks with Frankfurt-based Deutsche Börse, which runs Germany's largest exchange. However, in February 2012 the European Commission prohibited the proposed merger between Deutsche Börse and NYSE Euronext. According to the Commission, the merger would have resulted in a quasi-monopoly in the area of European financial derivatives traded globally on exchanges. Eurex, operated by Deutsche Börse, and Liffe, operated by NYSE Euronext, are the two largest exchanges in the world for financial derivatives based on European underlying securities. Together, the two exchanges control more than 90 per cent of global trade in these products. With no effective competitive constraint left in the market, the Commission concluded that benefits of price competition would be taken away from customers. Although derivatives can also be traded over-the-counter (see below), the

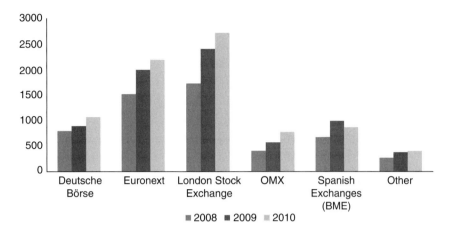

Figure 5.12 Market capitalisation of some exchanges in the EU, 2008–2010 (€ billion)
Source: World Federation of Exchanges

Commission concluded that customers generally do not consider exchange-traded derivatives and over-the-counter traded derivatives as substitutes, since they use them for different purposes and in different circumstances.

There is an advantage in consolidation. Bigger exchanges enjoy economies of scale that reduce trading costs, which in turn attracts more traders and listed companies (Wharton, 2006). The market capitalisation of Euronext and the LSE has grown faster than that of its smaller competitors (see Figure 5.12). While consolidation allows an exchange to exploit economies of scale, it may also reduce competition and thus lower an exchange's incentive for financial innovation (in the form of developing new, cheaper, trading mechanisms). The impact of competition is interesting in equity trading. Competition may reduce trading fees, but fragmentation of the order flow between exchanges may reduce the liquidity of equity trading. Examining the competition between Euronext and the LSE in the Dutch equity market, Foucault and Menkveld (2008) find evidence of reduced fees and improved liquidity. Liquidity is improved as some brokers automate the routing decision between the two exchanges to obtain the best execution price. In that way, the order flow at the two exchanges is indirectly combined.

There are still some challenges. First, the clearing and settlement infrastructure in Europe has remained fragmented so far. As documented in Chapter 7, post-trading costs per transaction in the EU are substantially higher than in the US. Next, cross-border exchanges like Euronext and OMX force national financial supervisors to cooperate. This challenge is discussed further in Chapter 12.

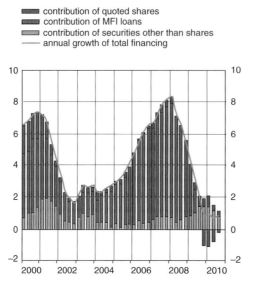

■ contribution of quoted shares
■ contribution of MFI loans
▥ contribution of securities other than shares
— annual growth of total financing

Figure 5.13   External sources of funding of non-financial firms in the euro area, 2000–2010 (annual percentage changes; percentage points)

Source: ECB Monthly Bulletin (January 2011)

Initial public offerings

In Europe, public equity markets play a limited role as a source of new funds for listed corporations. Figure 5.13 presents the different external sources of financing of non-financial corporations from 2000 to 2010. Figure 5.13 shows that debt financing via bank loans or bonds is far more important than financing via equity. This pattern is in line with the pecking-order theory (Myers and Majluf, 1984), which suggests that companies adopt a hierarchy of financial preferences. Due to asymmetric information, companies prefer internal financing (i.e. retained earnings) to external financing. If external financing is needed, companies first seek debt funding. Equity is issued only as a last resort.

When issuing public equity, a firm may obtain a listing on a stock exchange for the first time, the *initial public offering* (IPO). If a firm is already listed and issues additional shares, this is called *seasoned equity offering* (SEO) or *secondary public offering* (SPO). A firm issuing equity at a stock exchange may decide to substitute existing unquoted shares for quoted ones, or issue newly created shares. In the latter case, the funds raised accrue to the firm, while in the first case the proceeds are directed to the initial investors.

There are various motives for IPOs. One of the main reasons, of course, is to obtain funds to finance investment. Moreover, the listing of a firm's shares on a stock exchange also increases its financial autonomy, as the firm becomes less dependent on a single financial provider (like a bank). Further, by issuing equity the firm's owners can diversify their investment risk by selling stakes in the company in a liquid market. Another advantage of public issuance is increased recognition of the company name. In addition, from the time of the IPO investors receive better information due to improved transparency and the disclosure requirements that are part of the listing conditions. At the same time, the price of a company's stock acts as a measure of the company's value and as a disciplining mechanism for managers.

However, there are a number of disadvantages for a company inherent in listing its shares on a stock exchange. To start with, equity issuance is an expensive procedure, incurring costs such as underwriters' commission, legal fees, and other charges resulting primarily from the need to satisfy the additional disclosure requirements. From the perspective of investors, going public implies that the ownership of the company is likely to be shared more widely, resulting in a larger gap between external investors and managers. This separation of ownership and control could cause 'agency problems', where company insiders hold more accurate information on the prospects of the firm than external equity investors, resulting in a divergence of managers' and outside investors' interests. Lastly, by going public, a company exposes itself to scrutiny by shareholders, who may be excessively focused on short-term results.

The number of IPOs in 2010 amounted to 380, increasing from 126 transactions in 2009. The total offering amount rose almost fourfold from €7,112 million in 2009 to €26,286 million in 2010. London's market share by value jumped from 23 per cent in 2009 to 40 per cent in 2010 (PwC IPO Watch, 2011). As Figure 5.14 shows, the 2009 figure was extremely low compared to previous years.

While it is difficult to disentangle the different factors motivating a company's decision to issue public equity, the economic cycle is likely to play a significant role. This is mainly because equity is often used to finance capital formation, which fluctuates over the business cycle. Furthermore, significant increases in stock-market prices generally preceded increases in equity issuance. In the literature on behavioural finance (Shiller, 2003), a related factor explaining the timing of equity issuance is the effect of investor sentiment. Developments in investor optimism over time may have an impact on the cost of equity, thereby influencing the amount of equity issued. For example, excessive increases in risk aversion resulting in falling stock-market prices could raise the cost of equity, thereby dissuading companies from issuing equity. Although investor sentiment will inevitably change over time, it is

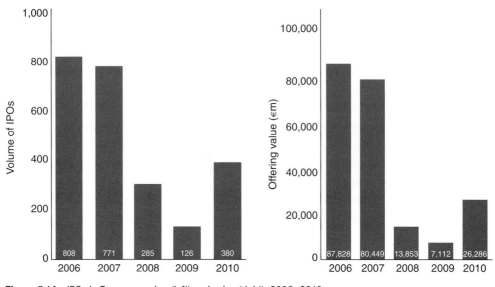

Figure 5.14   IPOs in Europe: number (left) and value (right), 2006–2010
Source: PwC (2011), IP. Watch Europe, Review 2010

difficult to measure risk aversion empirically, and/or investors' willingness to invest in the stock market. Companies also issue equity in order to finance the acquisition of other companies, either by using the cash proceeds of public offerings or by issuing shares, which are subsequently exchanged for the shares of a target company. Consequently, merger and acquisition (M&A) cycles can also be expected to correlate with equity issuance activity.

5.5 Derivatives

Derivatives are financial instruments whose value is derived from the value of the underlying financial instruments. They can be based on different types of assets (such as equities or commodities), prices (such as interest rates or exchange rates), or indexes (such as a stock market index). Derivatives can be used as a source of revenue but are also important risk-management tools (see Batten *et al.*, 2004). As for the latter, the BIS (1994) stresses that derivatives allow parties to identify, isolate, and manage the market risk in financial instruments and commodities, i.e. changes in market prices of financial instruments and changes in interest and exchange rates. When used properly, derivatives can reduce risks through hedging. This is done by transferring

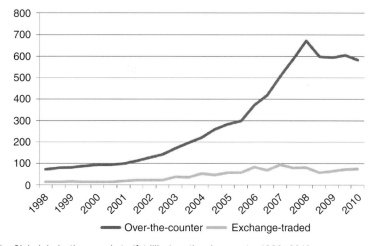

Figure 5.15   Global derivatives markets ($ trillion), notional amounts, 1998–2010
Source: TheCityUK (2010)

the cost of bearing the risk from one party to the other; the former wants to reduce the exposure to risk, whereas the latter is willing to assume that exposure in the expectation of making a profit (Reilly, 2005). Financial innovation and increased market demand led to a rapid growth of derivatives trading in the last decade (see Figure 5.15).

The use of derivatives has a major impact on asset management and risk management. A portfolio manager can, for example, change its risk profile through derivative transactions at a very low cost. Without derivatives, the portfolio manager would have to conduct transactions in the underlying cash markets (i.e. money, bond, or equity markets) at a higher cost, including the costly transfer of securities. Derivatives are thus a low-cost tool for risk management. Moreover, derivatives can be tailor-made in the over-the-counter market (see below). The spectacular growth of hedge funds can also be explained by the rise of low-cost derivatives markets. Hedge funds typically exploit small price differences of similar financial products, as explained in Chapter 9. Only when the transaction cost is smaller than the price differential will hedge funds take a position.

There are two broad types of derivatives: forwards and options. A *forward contract* gives the holder the obligation to buy or sell a certain underlying instrument (like a bond) at a certain date in the future (i.e. the delivery or final settlement date), at a specified price (i.e. the settlement price). Two examples are futures and swaps. *Futures contracts* are forward contracts traded on organised exchanges. *Swaps* are forward contracts in which counterparties agree to exchange streams of cash flows according to prede-termined rules. For example, an *interest rate swap* is a derivative in which one party exchanges a stream of interest payments for another party's stream of cash flows. The most important difference with options is that *options* give the holder the right (but not the obligation) to buy or sell a certain underlying instrument at a certain date in the future at a specified price.

Derivatives are traded on *organised exchanges* or *over-the-counter*. The old-est official derivatives market in Europe is the European Options Exchange (EOE) in Amsterdam, which started to trade options on stocks in 1978. EOE became part of the Amsterdam Exchanges and subsequently of Euronext. Next, the London International Financial Futures and Options Exchange (LIFFE) began its operations in 1982. LIFFE used a system of open-outcry floor trading. Later on, derivatives exchanges were opened in continental Europe. While some of these also adopted open-outcry floor trading, others (like the DTB, i.e. Deutsche Terminbörse) introduced electronic trading. DTB was founded in 1991. It introduced trading of futures on the Bund, i.e. German government bonds, in direct competition with a contract already trading at LIFFE. By 1998, the DTB had competed the Bund contract away from LIFFE (Anderson and McKay, 2008). Also, LIFFE moved to electronic trading.

EUREX is a serious competitor to LIFFE in the area of bond and short-term interest rate futures and options trading in Europe. This German–Swiss joint venture came about through the merger of the DTB and SOFFEX, the Swiss Options and Financial Futures Exchange, in 1998. Today, it trades a wide range of bond and money market derivative products. Access to the market is available in a number of major cities, including Chicago, New York, London, and Tokyo (Batten *et al.*, 2004).

OTC contracts are traded (and privately negotiated) directly between two parties. All contract terms, such as delivery quality, quantity, location, date, and price, are negotiable (Anderson and McKay, 2008). As Figure 5.15 shows, trade in OTC derivatives dwarfs trade in derivatives via exchanges. The United Kingdom is the leading OTC derivative market in the world. Derivatives such as swaps and forward rate agreements are generally traded on OTC markets. Derivative contracts (such as futures contracts and options) that are transacted on an organised futures exchange are standardised. However, Anderson and McKay (2008) point out that the traditional distinc-tion between exchange-based and OTC derivatives has become less clear. For instance, the International Swaps and Derivatives Association (ISDA) has provided a contract with standard pre-conditions. This standardisation has

Table 5.4 Amounts of outstanding OTC derivatives ($ trillion), 2003–2010

	2003	2005	2007	2008	2009	2010
Interest rate derivatives	142	212	393	433	450	452
Foreign exchange derivatives	24	31	56	50	49	53
Credit default swaps	—	14	58	42	33	30
Equity-linked derivatives	4	6	8	6	6	6
Commodities	1	5	8	4	3	3
Other	26	31	61	63	63	38
Total contracts	197	299	586	598	604	583

Source: TheCityUK (2010)

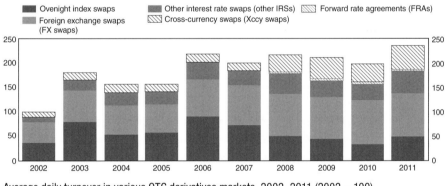

Figure 5.16 Average daily turnover in various OTC derivatives markets, 2002–2011 (2002 = 100)
Source: ECB

made it easier for more participants to access the OTC markets. Furthermore, OTC trades are increasingly being cleared through clearinghouses in much the same way as exchange-based contracts.

Table 5.4 shows the outstanding amounts of the different types of OTC derivatives. Interest rate derivatives dominate the market, followed by foreign exchange derivatives. Financial institutions, corporates, and government agencies use these derivatives to manage their interest rate and foreign exchange risks. Credit default swaps are a more recent phenomenon and will be discussed below.

Figure 5.16 shows that the average daily turnover in the various OTC derivatives markets increased rapidly at the beginning of the 2000s. In addition to the forward rate agreement (FRA) market and interest rate swap (IRS) market – comprising overnight interest rate swaps (OISs, also referred to as EONIA swaps) and other IRSs – the figure shows the share of OTC derivatives linked to the foreign exchange market, comprising FX swaps and cross-currency swaps (Xccy swaps). The figure shows that measured by volume, the OIS and FX swap markets are by far the most important OTC derivatives market segments, followed by other IRSs.

Credit derivatives

As can be seen in Table 5.4, an important development in the OTC derivatives markets has been the emergence of credit derivatives. The essence of a *credit derivative* is a contract in which a credit-protection seller promises a payment to a credit-protection buyer contingent upon the occurrence of a credit event (Anderson and McKay, 2008). The various types of contracts differ according to the terms and conditions that govern the promised payment, such as the definition of the 'credit event'. Various definitions are used, including formal bankruptcy and default. Increasingly diverse and complex products have appeared, but the most popular type of credit derivatives is the single-name *credit default swap* (CDS). Under this contract, the protection seller promises to buy at par from the protection buyer a specified bond (Anderson and McKay, 2008). A CDS requires fixed and regular premium payments from the protection buyer to the protection seller until a credit event occurs or the CDS matures. The premium is calculated as a percentage (called *credit spread*) of the nominal value of the reference obligation (the *notional amount*). Apart from single-name CDSs, the contract may refer to more reference entities (i.e. the underlying names on which credit risk is exchanged). A CDS resembles an insurance contract, in that it protects the 'protection buyer' against predefined credit events, in particular the risk of default in return for a periodic fee paid to the protection seller. Following a credit event, contracts settle either physically (i.e. through the delivery to the protection buyer of defaulting bonds and/or loans for an amount equivalent to the notional value of the swap) or in cash, with the net amount owed by the protection seller determined after the credit event. CDSs are an attractive instrument for risk management. Protection buyers can transfer credit risks without transferring credit claims or debt securities, while protection sellers can assume credit risks without granting credit or buying debt securities. So, both sides can optimise credit risk portfolios relatively efficiently (ECB, 2007).

Table 5.5 Notional amounts of CDSs outstanding ($ trillion), 2003–2010

	June 2003	June 2004	June 2005	June 2006	June 2007	June 2008	June 2009	June 2010
BIS	n.a.	n.a.	10.2	20.4	42.6	57.4	36.0	30.3
ISDA	2.7	5.4	12.4	26.0	45.5	54.6	31.2	26.3

Source: BIS, ISDA

Data on notional amounts of CDSs on euro-denominated reference obligations are not available. Table 5.5 describes the development in notional CDS amounts outstanding worldwide from two different sources, i.e. the ISDA and the BIS. The data from the two sources differ substantially. Nevertheless, they all indicate average annual growth rates in the CDS markets of 100 per cent or more. However, after 2008, the market shrank very quickly.

The most common maturities of CDSs are three, five, seven, and ten years, with the five-year maturity serving as a benchmark. The most active market participants in CDS markets, both as protection buyers and sellers, have been banks, hedge funds, and insurance companies. The majority of reference obligations are bonds or loans that are rated A or better (ECB, 2007).

5.6 Foreign exchange market

Funds transferred from one country to another have to be converted if the countries do not share the same currency. This takes place at the foreign exchange market which is an over-the-counter market, where most trading is done by banks. If countries have a floating exchange rate regime, transactions at the foreign exchange market determine the rate at which currencies are exchanged. These transactions consist of the buying and selling of different currencies. There are two types of transactions: *spot* and *forward transactions*. Spot transactions involve the immediate exchange of currency, while forward transactions involve the exchange of currency at some specified future date.

When a country's currency appreciates, i.e. rises in value vis-à-vis other currencies, the country's goods become more expensive in other countries, while foreign goods become cheaper. Likewise, a depreciation makes foreign goods more expensive. In other words, the exchange rate affects the rate of inflation. That is why central banks keep a close eye on the exchange rate.

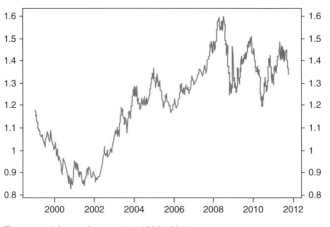

Figure 5.17   The euro-dollar exchange rate, 1999–2011
Source: ECB

Box 5.3 The role of the euro-dollar exchange rate in the ECB's policies

The euro-dollar exchange rate is one of the indicators of future inflationary developments in the monetary policy strategy of the ECB. The ECB has at various occasions made it clear that it closely monitors the euro-dollar exchange rate. Several studies have examined the so-called *exchange rate pass-through* (ERPT), i.e. the degree to which exchange rate changes are passed through in (domestic) prices. ERPT is defined as the percentage change of import prices (in local currency) resulting from a one per cent change in the exchange rate between the exporting and importing countries. Firms may choose to pass exchange rate alterations fully into their selling prices (*complete* ERPT). At the other extreme, firms may decide to absorb the shock by reducing their profit margins, so the selling prices will be unchanged (*no* ERPT). The relationship between exchange rates and prices is given by the following equation:

$$p_t = \alpha + \delta X + \gamma E_t + \psi Z_t + \varepsilon_t \tag{5.1}$$

In equation (5.1), *p* is the local currency import price; *X* is a measure of the export costs. Z may include import demand-shifting factors, such as competing prices or income, and *E* is the exchange rate (importer's currency per unit of exporter currency). Taking the logarithm of both sides yields the elasticity of ERPT with which γ is referred to as the *pass-through coefficient*. Campa and Goldberg (2005) report that in the long run ERPT is higher than in the short run, but for all European countries in their sample the ERPT is less than one both in the short and long run. They also find huge differences across the countries of the euro area.

Box 5.3 discusses the role of the euro-dollar exchange rate in the monetary policy of the ECB.

Figure 5.17 shows the euro-dollar exchange rate between 1999 and 2011. Since 1999, the euro initially depreciated against the dollar, but since 2002 it appreciated. However, during the recent financial crises the euro strongly fluctuated, reflecting changing market perceptions of the financial problems in the US and the euro area.

Not all countries have a floating exchange rate regime. Until 1971 most countries pegged their currency against the dollar. Also, after the demise of the Bretton Woods system several countries decided to peg their currency to another currency, like the euro. Other countries have a 'floating' or 'crawling' peg whereby they adjust the value of the peg periodically.

The *real exchange rate* is the rate at which domestic goods can be exchanged for foreign goods, i.e. the price of domestic goods relative to the price of foreign goods denominated in the domestic currency. So, the real exchange rate (r) can be defined as the nominal exchange rate (e) that is adjusted by the ratio of the foreign price level (P_f) to the domestic price level (P):

$$r = e^* P_f / P \tag{5.2}$$

5.7 Conclusions

Financial markets release information to aid the price discovery process, they provide a platform to trade, and they provide an infrastructure to settle trades. The main trading mechanisms are quote-driven and order-driven markets.

The euro money market is the market for euro-denominated short-term funds and related derivative instruments. It consists of various segments, including unsecured deposit contracts with various maturities, ranging from overnight to one year, and repurchase agreements (repos, i.e. reverse transactions secured by securities) also ranging from overnight to one year. Credit institutions account for the largest share of the euro money market. The ECB has a major influence on the money market via its use of various monetary policy instruments (reserve requirements, standing facilities, and open market operations). There are three main market interest rates for the money market: EONIA (euro overnight index average), EURIBOR (euro interbank offered rate), and EUREPO (the repo market reference rate for the euro).

The EU bond market has experienced spectacular growth since the introduction of the euro and is now matching the US bond market in size. The bulk of euro-denominated bonds (i.e. debt securities with a maturity of more than one year) is issued by euro-area issuers. Although the share of corporate bonds in all euro-denominated bonds outstanding has risen, government bonds still form the most important market segment. Also, since the introduction of the euro, yield differentials vary considerably across countries, while for each country the yield differential varies considerably over time. The issuance of asset-backed securities has increased rapidly during the last decade.

The importance of equity finance in the EU is growing, although there are large differences across exchanges. The market capitalisation of Euronext and the London Stock Exchange, which are the biggest exchanges in terms of turnover, are much higher than those of other exchanges in the EU. Despite the increase in equity finance, public equity markets play a limited role as a source of new funds for corporations that raise external financing generally via bank loans or debt securities.

Derivatives are financial instruments whose value is derived from the value of underlying financial instruments. They are traded on organised exchanges or over-the-counter. Derivatives can provide for a source of income but are also important risk-management tools. The most important derivatives are futures, forwards, options, and swaps. During recent years credit derivatives have become important. These are contracts in which a credit-protection seller promises a payment to a credit-protection buyer contingent upon the occurrence of a credit event.

If countries have a floating exchange rate regime, transactions at the foreign exchange market determine the rate at which currencies are exchanged. As changes in the exchange rate affect the rate of inflation, central banks keep a close eye on the exchange rate.

NOTES

1 Insiders of a company may have more information than outsiders. Regulation typically forbids insider trading (see Chapter 12).
2 In addition, the derivatives market has become increasingly important over recent years. The derivative money-market segments can be grouped into exchange-traded instruments, such as short-term interest rate futures and options, and instruments that are typically traded over-the-counter. This section will focus on the unsecured deposit markets and the secured repo markets.

3 See www.euribor-ebf.eu/euriborg-org/panelbanks.html for an overview of the banks in the panel.

4 The modified duration measures the change in the current value of the debt portfolio when the yield of the portfolio changes by 1 basis point.

5 The lower limit for government securities to be eligible for trading on EuroMTS is €5 billion.

SUGGESTED READING

Harris, L. E. (2003), *Trading and Exchanges: Market Microstructure for Practitioners, An Introductory Textbook to the Economics of Market Microstructure*, Oxford University Press.

Hull, J. C. (2005), *Options, Futures, and Other Derivatives*, 6th edition, Prentice Hall, Upper Saddle River (NJ).

Pagano, M. and E. Von Thadden (2008), The European Bond Markets under EMU, in: X. Freixas, P. Hartmann, and C. Mayer (eds.), *Handbook of European Financial Markets and Institutions*, Oxford University Press, 488–518.

REFERENCES

Anderson, R. W. and K. McKay (2008), Derivatives Markets, in: X. Freixas, P. Hartmann, and C. Mayer (eds.), *Handbook of European Financial Markets and Institutions*, Oxford University Press, 568–596.

Baele, L., A. Ferrando, P. Hördahl, E. Krylova, and C. Monnet (2004), Measuring Financial Integration in the Euro Area, ECB Occasional Paper 14.

Bailey, R. E. (2005), *The Economics of Financial Markets*, Cambridge University Press.

Bank for International Settlements (1994), Risk Management Guidelines for Derivatives, BIS, Basel.

Batten, J., T. Fetherson, and P. G. Szilagi (2004), *European Fixed Income Markets: Money, Bonds, and Interest Rate Derivatives*, John Wiley & Sons Ltd, Chichester.

Bearing Point (2007), The Electronic Bond Market – New Perspectives for Electronic Fixed Income Trading, May.

Campa, J. M. and L. S. Goldberg (2005), Exchange Rate Pass-Through into Import Prices, *The Review of Economics and Statistics*, 87(4), 679–690.

Casey, J. P. (2006), Bond Market Transparency: To Regulate or not to Regulate …, ECMI Policy Brief, Brussels.

Committee of European Securities Regulators (2008), The Role of Credit-Rating Agencies in Structured Finance, CESR, Paris.

Dunne, P., M. Moore, and R. Portes (2006), *European Government Bond Markets: Transparency, Liquidity, Efficiency*, CEPR, London.

Edwards, A. K., L. E. Harris, and M. S. Piwowar (2007), Corporate Bond Market Transaction Costs and Transparency, *Journal of Finance*, 62(3), 1421–1454.

European Central Bank (2007), *The Euro Bonds and Derivatives Markets*, ECB, Frankfurt am Main.

(2008a), The Analysis of the Euro Money Market from a Monetary Policy Perspective, *ECB Monthly Bulletin*, February.

(2008b), *Bond Markets and Long-term Interest Rates in Non-euro Area Member States of the European Union – Statistical Tables*, ECB, Frankfurt am Main.

(2010), *Euro Money Market Study December 2010*, ECB, Frankfurt am Main.

(2011a), *Financial Stability Review June 2010*, ECB, Frankfurt am Main.

(2011b), *Euro Money Market Study September 2011*, ECB, Frankfurt am Main.

(2011c), *Recent Developments in Securitisation*, ECB, Frankfurt am Main.

Financial Stability Forum (2008), *Report on Enhancing Market and Institutional Resilience*, FSF, Basel.

Foucault, T. and A. J. Menkveld (2008), Competition for Order Flow and Smart Order Routing Systems, *Journal of Finance*, 63, 119–158.

Goldstein, M. A., E. Hotchkiss, and E. Sirri (2007), Transparency and Liquidity: A Controlled Experiment on Corporate Bonds, *Review of Financial Studies*, 20(2), 235–273.

Harris, L. E. (2003), *Trading and Exchanges: Market Microstructure for Practitioners*, Oxford University Press.

Harris L. E. and M. S. Piwowar (2006), Secondary Trading Costs in the Municipal Bond Market, *Journal of Finance*, 61(3), 1361–1397.

Hartmann, P., M. Manna, and A. Manzanares (2001), The Microstructure of the Euro Money Market, ECB Working Paper 80.

Kyle, A. S. (1985), Continuous Auctions and Insider Trading, *Econometrica*, 53, 1315–1336.

Myers, S. and N. Majluf (1984), Corporate Financing and Investment Decisions when Firms Have Information that Investors Do Not Have, *Journal of Financial Economics*, 13, 187–221.

O'Hara, M. (2003), Presidential Address: Liquidity and Price Discovery, *Journal of Finance*, 58, 1335–1353.

Pagano, M. and E. Von Thadden (2008), The European Bond Markets under EMU, in: X. Freixas, P. Hartmann, and C. Mayer (eds.), *Handbook of European Financial Markets and Institutions*, Oxford University Press, 488–518.

PWC (2011), IPO Watch Europe, Review 2010; available at: www.pwc.com/sk/en/publikacie/assets/2012/IPOWatchEurope2011.pdf.

Reilly, A. (2005), Over-the-Counter Derivatives Markets in Ireland – An Overview, *CBFSAI Quarterly Bulletin*, Dublin, July.

Shiller, R. J. (2003), From Efficient Markets to Behavioral Finance, *Journal of Economic Perspectives*, 17, 83–104.

TheCityUK (2010), *Derivatives 2010*, London.

Wharton (2006), LSE, NYSE, OMX, Nasdaq, Euronext … Why Stock Exchanges Are Scrambling to Consolidate, Knowledge@Wharton, Wharton School, University of Pennsylvania.

Wolswijk, G. and J. de Haan (2005), Government Debt Management in the Euro Area: Recent Theoretical Developments and Changes in Practices, ECB Occasional Paper 25.

6

The Economics of Financial Integration

OVERVIEW

This chapter begins by defining financial integration and identifying its drivers. Financial integration may be defined as a situation without frictions that discriminate between economic agents in their access to – and their investment of – capital, particularly on the basis of their location. Not only market forces but also collective action and public action are shown to be driving financial integration.

The second part of the chapter deals with measuring financial integration. Three categories of measures have been used for this purpose. The first category consists of price-based indicators that measure discrepancies in prices or returns on assets caused by the geographic origin of the assets. The second category consists of news-based measures. The underlying idea is that in a financially integrated area, portfolios should be well diversified so that news (i.e. arrival of new economic information) of a regional character has little impact on prices, whereas common or global news is relatively more important. The third category of measures are quantity-based indicators that measure the effects of frictions faced by the demand for and supply of investment opportunities, like cross-border activities or listings, and statistics on the cross-border holdings of investors.

The third part of the chapter gives an overview of the extent to which various financial markets in the EU are integrated. An important reason why the European Union put the creation of a single financial market high on the policy agenda is that it widely believed that financial integration may stimulate economic growth. This growth effect and other consequences of financial integration are discussed at the end of the chapter.

LEARNING OBJECTIVES

After you have studied this chapter, you should be able to:
* define financial integration

- explain what drives financial integration
- describe the various ways of measuring financial integration, their shortcomings, and the reasoning underlying these various approaches
- assess the extent to which various financial markets in the EU are integrated
- discuss the consequences of financial integration.

6.1 Financial integration: definition and drivers

Definition of financial integration

While free capital mobility has been a reality in the EU since the late 1980s (see Chapter 3), financial market segmentation due to exchange-rate risk persisted until the start of the monetary union in 1999. The introduction of the euro was a powerful catalyst for the creation of integrated financial markets by removing one of the most important obstacles to the cross-border provision of financial services. At the same time, it became clear that there are other impediments to truly integrated financial markets, such as different regulations and institutions across the Member States of the EU.

Following Baele *et al.* (2008), the following definition of an *integrated financial market* is adopted: the market for a given set of financial instruments and/or services is fully integrated if all potential market participants with the same relevant characteristics:

(1) face a single set of rules when they decide to deal with those financial instruments and/or services;
(2) have equal access to the above-mentioned set of financial instruments and/or services; and
(3) are treated equally when they are active in the market.

Full integration requires the same access to banks or trading, clearing, and settlement platforms for both borrowers and lenders, regardless of their country of origin. In addition, full integration requires that there is no discrimination among comparable market participants based solely on their location of origin (Baele *et al.*, 2004).

This definition of financial integration is closely linked to the law of one price, which most empirical studies on financial integration take as the definition of financial integration (see section 6.2). According to the law of one price, assets with identical risks should be priced identically regardless of where they are transacted. As Baele *et al.* (2004) point out, the law of one price is very attractive since it allows for quantitative measures of financial integration, but it can be tested only on instruments that are listed or quoted. Hence, the analysis based on the law of one price cannot serve as a basis for measuring integration among unlisted instruments.

Drivers of financial integration

What drives financial integration? Following the ECB (2003), a differentiation can be made between (1) market forces, (2) collective action, and (3) public action.

Market forces

The first driver of financial integration is market forces. Firms benefit from the lower cost of capital that enhanced competition brings about, allowing a better allocation of capital. More productive investment opportunities will become available, and a reallocation of funds to the most productive investment opportunities will take place. Investors also benefit from access to a broader range of financial instruments and more opportunities to diversify their portfolios. The complete elimination of barriers to trading, clearing, and settlement platforms will allow firms to choose the most efficient trading, clearing, and/or settlement platforms. Also, financial intermediaries may profit by exploiting the potential economies of scale and scope that a larger market offers. But financial intermediaries may also face pressure on their profit margins.

Figure 6.1 illustrates the impact of enhanced competition with an example. The starting position is a market rate of 4 per cent. In a segmented market with low competition, a bank lends to firms at 6 per cent and offers depositors a return of 2 per cent. The bank earns a margin of 4 per cent. As markets integrate, increased competition forces the bank to reduce its lending rate to 5 per cent and to increase its deposit rate to 3 per cent. The lending firms experience a lower cost of capital, while depositors receive a higher return. The margin for the bank is reduced to 2 per cent. The bank can (partly) offset the reduction of its profit margin by increasing its business in an integrated market.

Since investors and financial intermediaries may benefit from financial integration, market forces could lead to the elimination of market segmentation. For instance, issuance practices of government bond issuers converged towards what was perceived as 'best' practice because they had to compete to attract investors (Wolswijk and De Haan, 2005). Likewise, mergers of stock exchanges, clearinghouses, and securities settlement systems are often

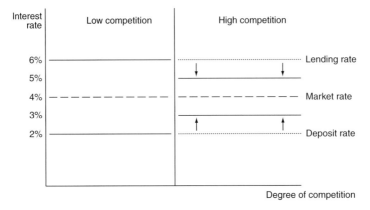

Figure 6.1   Impact of enhanced competition

motivated by efforts to exploit the economies of scale and scope potentially available within a broader market. Of course, market forces can foster integration only if there are no legislative or regulatory obstacles standing in the way.

Collective action

Sometimes market forces alone are not sufficient to remove obstacles to integration. This may happen, for instance, due to network externalities in the financial system. The more participants use a particular market, the more benefits it generally brings to its users. These benefits include greater depth and liquidity, reduced transaction costs, as well as easier and more effective opportunities for risk management (ECB, 2003). Individual market participants will not take these externalities into account. Through collective action, market participants can, for instance, agree on standard technical features of financial instruments, the definition of common practices and conventions, or the establishment of reference indices. However, the existence of powerful network externalities may also hamper integration as strong network effects are often associated with high switching costs, i.e. the cost of switching from one set of organisation, practices, conventions, rules, and infrastructure to another. A switch to a pan-European market entails costs – at least in the short term – for participants in national markets (ECB, 2003).

In 1998 a series of market conventions sponsored by several market organisations stimulated financial integration. A good example is the rules applicable to the basic market interest reference rate, the EURIBOR (the rate at which euro interbank term deposits are offered by one prime bank to another at 11 am CET). A similar initiative permitted the establishment of the other basic interest reference rate for overnight unsecured interbank deposits, the EONIA. In 2002, another market convention added a new reference index, the EUREPO, i.e. the rate at which one prime bank offers funds in euros to another prime bank if in exchange the former receives eligible assets as collateral from the latter (see Chapter 5 for further details).

Another good example of collective action is the creation of the Single Euro Payments Area (SEPA) that will allow customers to make non-cash euro payments to any beneficiary located anywhere in the euro area using a single bank account and a single set of payment instruments. In other words, there will no longer be any differentiation between national and cross-border retail payments within the euro area. This is a major step towards integration. Despite the introduction of the euro in 1999 and the development of TARGET (the EU-wide large-value payment system operated by the ESCB; see Chapter 7), retail payments continued to be processed differently throughout the euro area. However, in 2002, the banking industry took the initiative to create the European Payments Council (EPC), which defined the new rules and procedures for euro payments. The goal of SEPA is an integrated, competitive, and innovative retail payments market for all non-cash euro payments which, in time, will be conducted entirely electronically.

Public action

While financial integration benefits first and foremost the market community, its effects are much more widespread (see section 6.4). The pervasive effects of financial integration on the whole economy justify the involvement of public authorities to support its development towards an optimal outcome, e.g. in situations where a public good cannot be supplied privately or where a market or coordination failure occurs (ECB, 2003). In both cases, neither market forces alone nor collective action within the private sector is sufficient to deliver the desirable level of integration. In this context, action by public authorities may come in many forms. It can be a catalyst or facilitator of collective action to help overcome coordination problems (for instance, the neutral role of the ECB in the fixing of the EONIA rate as a service to the banking sector). It can also extend to direct intervention, as in the case of the development of TARGET. An essential responsibility of public action is the establishment of an appropriate legislative and regulatory framework. The European Commission's FSAP, described in Chapter 3, aimed to create a single wholesale market and an open and secure retail market.

A good example of 'FSAP in action' is the regulation on cross-border euro payments (No. 2560/2001) that gives EU consumers a guarantee that when they make a payment in euros to an account in another EU Member State, it will cost the same as it would to make a payment within their own Member State. As of 1 January 2006, the regulation applies to payments of up to €50,000. According to the European Commission (2006), prior to this regulation charges for cross-border euro payments were often excessive, with a €100 transfer costing the consumer on average €24. According to the Commission, charges for cross-border euro payments have reduced significantly since the introduction of the regulation, with a €100 transfer now costing on average less than €2.50.

6.2 Measuring financial integration

Following Baele *et al.* (2004, 2008), integration of financial markets can be assessed using three categories of measures. The first broad category consists of *price-based indicators*, which measure discrepancies in prices or returns on assets caused by the geographic origin of the assets. Most empirical research on financial market integration in Europe compares rates of return on assets. To properly test for integration, one should compare the prices of assets that have identical cash flows and risk characteristics but that are traded in different countries. The risk of an asset's return is composed of a systematic part and an idiosyncratic part; the latter can be diversified away, the former cannot. While this type of risk may be considered negligible in some cases, for example in the money market before the crisis, it is crucial to control for it in the corporate bond and equity markets (Baele *et al.*, 2004).

The second category of measures consists of *news-based indicators*. The underlying idea is that in a financially integrated area, portfolios should be well diversified so that news (i.e. arrival of new economic information) of a regional character has little impact on prices, whereas common or global news is relatively more important. This presumes that the degree of systematic risk is identical across assets in different countries.

The third category consists of *quantity-based indicators*, which quantify the effects of frictions faced by the demand for and supply of investment opportunities. Examples are statistics giving information on the ease of market access, such as cross-border activities or listings, and cross-border holdings of securities. However, cross-border activity is an imperfect measure of integration. Increased cross-border traffic typically indicates an increase in integration. But there is no need for cross-border activity in a fully integrated market, as prices are the same everywhere.

The remainder of this section will provide further details on these measures of financial integration.

Price-based measures

The construction of price-based integration measures for the money and government bond markets is facilitated by the fact that relatively homogeneous assets are available across countries. A widely used measure in research on integration of government bond markets is the *difference between local yields and some benchmark*, which is often the German yield. In the market for ten-year government bonds, for instance, market participants consider German bonds to be the reference bond. Consequently, it seems reasonable to measure integration in this segment of the bond market by calculating the spread between the yield on a local asset and the German benchmark asset. In perfectly integrated markets the spread should be equal to zero. The time variation in the size of the spread serves as a good indicator of how integration is proceeding in a particular country and market.[1] However, under stressed market conditions price-based measures may be problematic, because they may not adequately control for underlying risk characteristics, and therefore do not clearly distinguish effects stemming from changes in the credit standing of the issuers from the effects of financial integration (ECB, 2011).

A second price-based indicator of financial integration, proposed by Adam *et al.* (2002), is the *beta-convergence* measure. This concept has been developed in the economic growth literature but can be adapted for measuring financial market integration. It measures the speed of adjustment of deviations of countries to the long-run benchmark value. It involves running the following panel regression:

$$\Delta R_{i,t} = \alpha_i + \beta R_{i,t} + \sum_{l=1}^{L} \gamma_l \Delta R_{i,t-l} + \varepsilon_{i,t} \tag{6.1}$$

where $R_{i,t}$ represents the yield spread on a ten-year government bond in country i at time t, relative to the German benchmark rate, Δ is the difference operator, and α_i is a country dummy. β is the coefficient with respect to the yield spread, and γ_l is the coefficient with respect to lagged yield differences. The error term on the right-hand side of the equation $\varepsilon_{i,t}$ denotes exogenous shocks that force interest rate differentials between the considered countries.

A negative β coefficient signals convergence (if $\beta = 0$ there is no convergence). In the case of a negative β, yields in countries with relatively high yield spreads decrease more rapidly towards the benchmark rate than yields in countries with relatively low yield spreads. Moreover, β is a direct measure of the speed of convergence in the overall market.

While beta-convergence measures the speed of convergence, it does not indicate to what extent markets are already integrated. Therefore, Adam *et al.* (2002) also use *the cross-sectional dispersion in yields* as a measure of the degree of integration, which they refer to as 'sigma convergence'.[2] Also this third price-based measure of financial integration is borrowed from the empirical growth literature, where sigma convergence is said to occur if the cross-sectional distribution of a variable (in the economic growth literature this is typically income per capita) decreases over time. This indicator can be calculated at each point in time by taking the standard deviation of yields across countries. If the cross-sectional standard deviation $sd(i)_t$ is zero, the law of one price applies fully. The degree of financial integration increases when the cross-sectional standard deviation has a downward trend (moves towards zero). This measure is obtained from a regression of the cross-sectional dispersion on a time trend. It is also possible to differentiate between time periods. Adam *et al.* (2002) estimate, for instance, the following regression to check whether there is a systematic difference in convergence before and after the introduction of the euro:

$$sd(i)_t = \left(\alpha^{pre} + \sigma^{pre} trend\right) D^{pre} + \left(\alpha^{post} + \sigma^{post} trend\right) D^{post} + \varepsilon_t \tag{6.2}$$

where $sd(i)_t$ is the cross-sectional standard deviation in period t and D^{pre} and D^{post} are dummy variables that take value 1 before and after January 1999, respectively (and zero otherwise). Perfect convergence is achieved when the slope (σ) and the intercept (α) coefficients are both zero. By comparing the intercepts and the slopes before and after the start of the currency union, it becomes possible to assess convergence before and after the adoption of the euro.

News-based measures

To make news-based measures operational, one needs to provide a proxy for common news. Baele *et al.* (2004) argue that yield changes in the benchmark asset could be used to proxy all relevant common news. They suggest running the following regression:

$$\Delta R_{i,t} = \alpha_{i,t} + \beta_{i,t} \Delta R_{b,t} + \varepsilon_{i,t} \tag{6.3}$$

where $\Delta R_{i,t}$ is the change in the yield on an asset in country i at time t, $\Delta R_{b,t}$ is the yield change on a comparable asset in the benchmark country b, $\alpha_{i,t}$ is a time-varying intercept, $\beta_{i,t}$ is the time-dependent beta with respect to the benchmark asset, and $\varepsilon_{i,t}$ denotes a country-specific shock. If financial integration increases:

(1) the intercept $\alpha_{i,t}$ will converge to zero, since in integrated markets yield changes in one country should not be systematically larger or smaller than those in the benchmark market;

(2) the coefficient $\beta_{i,t}$ will converge to one, so that *the average distance of the different country betas to unity* may serve as an integration measure for the overall market. The reason is that $\beta_{i,t}$ depends on both the correlation between local and benchmark yield changes and the ratio between local and benchmark yield volatilities. When integration increases, yield changes should increasingly be driven by common factors, and the correlation should increase towards one. For the same reason, the level of local volatility should converge towards that of the benchmark asset. As a result, increasing integration implies that $\beta_{i,t}$ should converge to one (Baele *et al.*, 2004);

(3) the proportion of the variance in $\Delta R_{i,t}$ explained by the common factor $\Delta R_{b,t}$ will increase towards one, so that *the proportion of local variance explained by the common factor* can be used as another measure of integration. The reason is that the country-specific error $\varepsilon_{i,t}$ in equation (6.3) should shrink as integration increases.

This method can be used to assess integration of the bond and credit markets. A variant of this approach can be used to assess integration of equity markets. The natural equivalent to the benchmarks for the equity market is to use returns on a euro-area-wide equity market portfolio. However, Baele *et al.* (2004) argue that available empirical evidence shows that equity returns are significantly affected by global factors, not just regional ones. Hence, for the purpose of examining integration in euro-area equity markets, they distinguish between global and euro-area-wide effects on equity returns in the euro area. To this end, Baele *et al.* use the return on US stock markets as a proxy for world news, while the return on a euro-area-wide stock market index, corrected for US news, is used as the euro factor. While returns for all countries share the same two factors, they are allowed to have different sensitivities to these common factors. The portion of local returns not explained by common factors is due to local news.

Quantity-based measures

Baele *et al.* (2004) classify these measures into two groups. The first group includes measures dealing with cross-border activities in a specific market, and the second group refers to measures dealing with home bias.

Cross-border activity measures can be applied to the credit market and the money market. One way to assess the progress made towards integration is to consider whether the existing barriers to entry imposed on foreign economic agents willing to invest in a specific region have been reduced over time. An increase in the volumes of cross-border loans to non-banks and inter-bank loans would suggest that it has become easier for foreigners to access a regional credit market. In Chapters 10 and 11 the cross-border activity of banks and insurers will be discussed.

For corporate and government bonds, Baele *et al.* (2004) regard an increase in the share of non-domestic bond holdings as a sign of further integration as it reflects that economic agents are able to access non-domestic financial products more easily. The extent of the *home bias*, i.e. the degree to which agents invest in domestic assets even though risk is shared more effectively if foreign assets are held, is a sign that financial integration is still not complete. In Chapter 9 the home bias of the portfolios of institutional investors will be discussed.

6.3 Integration of European financial markets

This section summarises the main findings of empirical research on European financial integration. The available evidence suggests that the degree of integration varies depending on the market segment and is correlated with the degree of integration of the underlying financial infrastructure (see Chapter 7 for further details). The financial turmoil of 2007 and 2008 affected various financial markets to different degrees, resulting in a temporary retrenchment of market activity within domestic borders (ECB, 2011). During the debt crisis, interest differentials in the euro area increased.

Money market

To assess the extent to which the various segments of the money market rate are integrated, Figure 6.2 shows one of the price-based indicators explained in section 6.2, namely the (unweighted) standard deviation of the average daily interest rates prevailing in each euro-area country.

Box 6.1 Euro-area vs. non-euro-area member countries*

The information shown in section 6.3 refers only to countries in the euro area as our main source of information, i.e. the ECB, provides information for the euro area only. In a somewhat older study, Adam *et al.* (2002) contrast samples consisting of euro-area countries and all (then) EU Member States. Table 6.1 is reproduced from this study. It shows estimates of equation (6.2) for both samples of countries. There is more evidence of convergence in the euro area than for the sample of EU countries, although convergence also occurred in the latter sample. In the interbank three-month rates the negative trend is more pronounced after 1999 for both groups of countries. The coefficients before and after 1999 are statistically different from each other, as indicated by the *F*-test. Across the euro area, perfect convergence is achieved after 1999. Most of the convergence in the ten-year government-bond market occurs before 1999 and among euro-area countries (also in this case the *F*-test rejects the hypothesis that the slope coefficients are equal).

Hardouvelis *et al.* (2006) have examined to what extent the integration of equity markets in the EU is related to monetary integration. They assess the evolution of the relative influence of EU-wide risk factors over country-specific risk factors on required rates of return. The authors find that in the second half of the 1990s, the degree of integration gradually increased to the point where individual euro-area country stock markets appear to be fully integrated into the EU market. An important factor that drove the increase in the

Table 6.1 Sigma convergence (estimates of equation 6.2)

	Interbank 3-month rates		Benchmark 10-year yields	
	Euro and non-euro area	Euro area	Euro and non-euro area	Euro area
$\sigma_{\text{pre-emu}}$	−0.0021 (0.0013)	−0.0182** (0.0019)	−0.0150** (0.0005)	−0.0185** (0.0006)
$\sigma_{\text{post-emu}}$	−0.0429** (0.0022)	Convergence achieved	−0.0012** (0.0009)	0.0005 (0.001)
$\alpha_{\text{pre-emu}}$	69.2651** (17.2878)	276.7812** (25.0592)	214.6554** (7.1433)	261.9454** (8.6341)
$\alpha_{\text{post-emu}}$	652.3706** (33.0800)	Convergence achieved	20.6913 (13.6687)	−5.3027 (16.5214)
Observations	81	81	81	81
R-squared	0.9895	0.9548	0.9812	0.9748
F-test H_{0A}	249.16 (0.00001)		166.49 (0.00001)	216.81 (0.00001)
F-test H_{0B}	125.46 (0.00001)		233.45 (0.00001)	18.20 (0.0001)

Source: Adam *et al.* (2002)

level of integration was the evolution of the probability of joining the single currency that is proxied by each country's forward interest rate differential with Germany. During the 1990s, this forward interest differential was widely used by market analysts as an indicator of the probability that an EU country would eventually manage to join the currency union. In contrast to the euro-area countries, the United Kingdom did not show any signs of increased stock-market integration. As pointed out in Chapter 3, the UK has always been ambivalent about joining the euro area, having a so-called 'opt-out' clause. According to Hardouvelis *et al.* (2006, p. 367), 'the United Kingdom is the exception that proves the rule, indicating that the forces behind the formation of the Eurozone had a special role in stock market integration'.

As the first panel of Figure 6.2 shows, the unsecured money market reached a stage of 'near-perfect' integration almost immediately after the introduction of the euro. The cross-sectional standard deviation of the EONIA lending rates and the 1-month and 12-month EURIBOR rates across euro-area countries fell sharply to close to zero following the introduction of the euro, and remained stable until the financial crisis.

The second panel of Figure 6.2 shows the standard deviation of the same interest rate, zooming in on the period after the start of the currency union. Although the euro-area money market was the financial market which achieved the fastest and most complete integration after the introduction of the euro, it was also the hardest hit during the crisis (ECB, 2011). The collapse of the subprime mortgage market in the United States in the summer of 2007 led to rising yields on a variety of money market instruments. The deepening of the crisis due to the bankruptcy of Lehman Brothers in September 2008 had a sharp negative impact on the measured integration of the euro-area money market. During 2009, the money market gradually reverted to more stable conditions. However, the debt crisis led again to rising tensions in the money market, as reflected in increases in the cross-country standard deviation of the EONIA.

Government bond market

After the introduction of the euro, differences in government bond yields among euro-area countries were never more than 50 basis points until the financial crisis. After August 2007, some sovereign bond markets benefited from a 'flight to safety', while other euro-area sovereign bond spreads rose

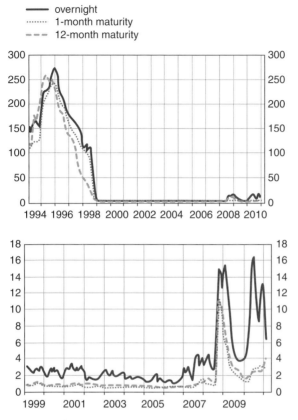

Figure 6.2   Integration of the money market: standard deviation of interest rates (61-day moving average; basis points), 1994–2010

Note: The second figure magnifies the data in the previous figure by changing the scaling of the years (x-axis) and the number of basis points (y-axis).

Source: ECB

sharply relative to the German benchmark (see Figure 5.6). The increase in yield spreads does not necessarily reflect a decline in bond market integration, as it is likely to incorporate a reassessment and repricing of risk for the respective sovereign issuers.

As explained in section 6.2, in fully integrated markets bond yields should react only to common news, since purely local risk factors can be diversified away. This is the underlying idea of equation (6.3). However, since divergence of yields may also represent differential pricing of underlying risks, the ECB (2011) estimates equation (6.3) controlling for sovereign risks. Perfect integration implies a value of 0 for the constant and 1 for the

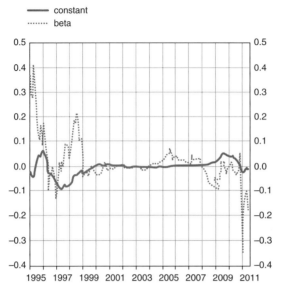

Figure 6.3   Average distance of intercepts/beta from the values implied by complete integration (ten-year bond yields), 1995–2011

Source: ECB

slope coefficient, assuming that no variables other than sovereign risk are affecting the change in yield. Figure 6.3 shows the estimation results, where the slope coefficient is normalised by subtracting 1. So deviations from zero for the constant and the slope coefficient indicate less than perfect integration. Figure 6.3 shows that even after accounting for differences in sovereign risks there are increasing signs of divergence from the theoretical benchmark values. Spreads in the government bond market remain even after controlling for country credit risk, and liquidity risk premiums are likely to be non-negligible.

Corporate bond market

In analysing corporate bond market integration, yield differentials relative to a benchmark cannot be used, as corporate bonds are generally not sufficiently homogeneous to allow for easy comparison. The yield on a corporate bond typically depends on a number of factors, such as the bond's credit rating, time-to-maturity, liquidity, and cash-flow structure. The ECB (2011) assesses progress in integration in the corporate bond market by measuring the relative importance of country components

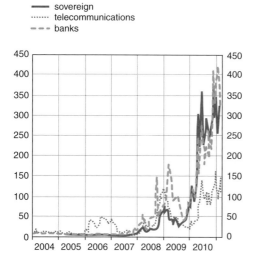

— sovereign
········ telecommunications
– – – banks

Figure 6.4   Dispersion in five-year CDS premia among leading telecommunications firms and large commercial banks in euro-area countries, 2004–2010 (daily data; basis points)
Source: ECB

versus common factors in explaining risk-adjusted yields. As integration advances, the proportion of the total yield spread variance explained by country effects should decrease. The within-country dispersion in CDS premia for two groups of firms producing relatively homogeneous products – the leading communications firms and the largest commercial banks in each country – are compared for the period 2004–2010. As Figure 6.4 shows, the country dispersion of CDS spreads for both commercial banks and telecommunications firms was close to zero before the financial crisis. But after August 2007 and especially after September 2008 it rose sharply. In the initial stages of the crisis, the increase in dispersion was most pronounced for commercial banks. In 2010 the dispersion in telecommunications firm CDSs also increased, but remained much lower than that of commercial banks.

Equity market

The cross-border integration of equity markets was less affected by the financial crisis than integration in other financial market segments. According to the ECB (2011), most available indicators suggest that the integration of equity markets strengthened in 2010.

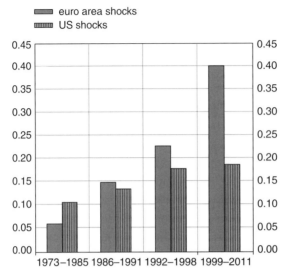

Figure 6.5   Proportion of variance in local equity returns explained by euro-area and US shocks, 1973–2011
Source: ECB

If the equity markets in the euro area were integrated, prices should be mainly driven by common euro-area factors rather than country-specific ones. Assuming that equity returns in euro-area countries react to both a local and a global factor – proxied respectively by shocks in aggregate euro-area and US equity markets – it is possible to measure the proportion of the total domestic equity volatility that can be explained by local and global factors, respectively. *Ceteris paribus*, a higher variance ratio associated with euro-area-wide changes is an indication of a more integrated euro-area equity market, signalling that national stock-market returns are increasingly driven by common news. Figure 6.5 shows that the variance ratios have increased over the past 30 years with respect to both euro-area-wide and US shocks (to 40 per cent for euro-area shocks and 18 per cent for US shocks). This suggests that regional euro-area integration has proceeded more quickly than worldwide integration. At the same time, the level of the variance explained by common factors reveals that local shocks are still important.

Also quantity-based measures of euro-area equity market integration indicate a rising degree of integration in the equity markets (see Figure 6.6). By 2009 almost 40 per cent of the equity holdings of euro-area residents were issued in other euro-area countries (as a share of their total holdings

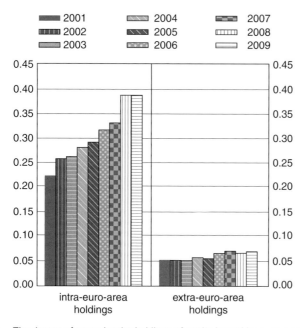

Figure 6.6   The degree of cross-border holdings of equity issued by euro-area residents (share), 2001–2009
Source: ECB

of shares), whereas the share of euro-area equity assets held outside the euro area remained at a much lower level and increased only slightly.

So far, we have discussed financial integration in the euro area. Box 6.2 reports on financial integration of the new EU Member States.

6.4 The consequences of financial integration

According to Baele *et al.* (2004), financial integration has three benefits: more opportunities for risk sharing and diversification, better allocation of capital, and the potential for higher growth. Financial integration may also have implications for financial stability and the structure of the EU financial system. These consequences of financial integration will be discussed in turn.

Financial integration will provide additional possibilities to diversify portfolios and share idiosyncratic risk across regions. When agents in an area fully share risk, the consumption of agents in one region co-moves with that of agents located in other regions of that area, while consumption does not

Box 6.2 Financial integration of the new EU Member States

The reports of the ECB on financial integration do not provide information regarding the new Member States of the EU (NMS). Cappiello *et al.* (2006) assess the degree of financial integration of Cyprus, the Czech Republic, Estonia, Hungary, Latvia, Poland, and Slovenia, amongst themselves and with the euro area. These authors examine integration between the NMS and the euro zone across two different periods: the pre-convergence and the convergence periods. They employ a factor model for market returns that distinguishes between common and local components. The intuition behind the model is similar to the news-based indicators discussed in section 6.2, i.e. the higher the amount of return variance explained by the common factor relative to the local components, the higher the degree of integration. The analysis is carried out on returns on equity market indices and ten-year government bonds.

The evidence suggests that the degree of integration of equity markets of the NMS with the euro zone has increased in their process towards EU accession. The three new EU Member States with the largest economies and most developed financial markets (i.e. the Czech Republic, Hungary, and Poland) exhibit stronger return co-movements both between themselves and with the euro area. However, Cappiello *et al.* (2006) find for the four smaller countries (i.e. Cyprus, Estonia, Latvia, and Slovenia) a very low degree of integration between themselves, although Estonia and, to a lesser extent, Cyprus show increased integration both with the euro zone and with the block of large accession economies. For the bond markets, Capiello *et al.* have reliable data for the largest countries only. They find that integration has increased only for the Czech Republic versus Germany (which is used as a benchmark for the euro area) and Poland.

In another study, Baltzer *et al.* (2008) apply various measures discussed in section 6.2 to the NMS. These authors find that financial markets in the NMS are significantly less integrated than those of the euro area. Nevertheless, Baltzer *et al.* conclude that there is strong evidence that the process of integration of the NMS has accelerated since their accession to the EU. This applies especially to money and banking markets that are becoming increasingly integrated both among themselves and vis-à-vis the euro area. Still, Baltzer *et al.* argue that the process of financial integration in the NMS is probably driven by different factors than those behind the financial integration in the euro area. The transition from planned to market economies has led to rapid financial developments, which has been further boosted by a strong foreign, mainly EU, banking presence. In line with the results of Capiello *et al.* (2006), Baltzer *et al.* report that only the government bond markets of the largest economies exhibit signs of integration. Indeed, Figure 6.7, which shows the spread between ten-year government bond yields of NMS and Germany, indicates that most NMS have been converging to the German benchmark. In particular, between the beginning of 2001 and mid-2003, government bond yields and yield spreads relative to the German

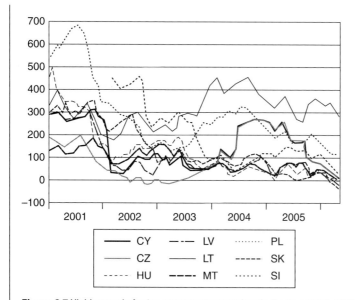

Figure 6.7 Yield spreads for ten-year government bonds (basis points), 2001–2006
Source: Baltzer *et al.* (2008)

benchmark declined substantially. However, afterwards spreads remained mostly stable or decreased even further, with the exception of those of Cyprus, Hungary, and Poland.

Finally, the evidence of Baltzer *et al.* for equities suggests a relatively low level of integration, although there is evidence that stock markets are increasingly affected by euro-area shocks, especially after the accession date (May 2004).

co-move with region-specific shocks. There is some evidence suggesting that in the euro area consumption in the various countries is still affected by country-specific shocks. For instance, Adjaouté and Danthine (2003) find that consumption growth rates in the euro area are less correlated than are GDP growth rates, suggesting that risk-sharing opportunities are far from fully exploited. Likewise, Adam *et al.* (2002) reject the hypothesis that consumption growth rates are unaffected by idiosyncratic changes in GDP growth rates.

Greater financial integration may also allow a better allocation of capital. Due to the elimination of barriers to trading, clearing, and settlement platforms, firms will be able to choose the most efficient trading, clearing, and/or settlement platforms. In addition, investors can invest their funds wherever they believe these funds will be allocated to the most productive uses (Baele *et al.*, 2004).

Financial integration may also affect economic growth, due to improved capital allocation and its contribution to financial development. As discussed in Chapter 1, recent studies show that financial development is associated with higher economic growth. Why would integration spur financial development?

Integration will stimulate local financial markets and foster internal competition, as well as open these markets to competitive pressure from foreign intermediaries. Guiso *et al.* (2004) argue that financial integration should increase the supply of funds in the less financially developed countries of the integrating area. This may occur for two reasons. First, integration facilitates the entry of more efficient intermediaries to firms in backward areas. Second, integration enables these firms to access more distant financial markets. In both cases, firms in less financially developed countries will face easier and cheaper access to external finance and this should spur capital accumulation and economic growth. Another reason why financial integration may affect financial development runs via improved regulation (Guiso *et al.*, 2004). A 'level playing field' in regulation is an essential prerequisite of an integrated market, and this convergence in regulatory standards is likely to result in an improvement in the regulatory standards of less developed financial markets. All of this will contribute to further financial development, which in turn may affect economic growth. Therefore, financial integration can have a 'growth dividend' in Europe (see also Box 6.3).

Guiso *et al.* (2004) provide an estimate of this growth dividend, based on the empirical relationship between financial market development and growth in the manufacturing industry. These authors examine a scenario where EU countries raise their regulatory standards to the highest current EU standard. They estimate that the effect of achieving full financial integration on the growth of European manufacturing industry is around 0.7 percentage points per year. As EU manufacturing accounts for about one-fourth of EU total value added, this estimate translates into 0.2 percentage points of GDP growth. This overall growth effect results from markedly different country and sector effects, reflecting the heterogeneity of the EU in terms of sector composition and level of financial development. Especially smaller businesses are the main beneficiaries of integration as they get access to a larger and more developed financial market than that within their national borders. There is also some evidence that financial integration has benefited the new EU Member States.

Box 6.3 Financial integration and economic growth[3]

Theoretically, the economic growth effects of international financial integration are ambiguous. On the one hand, integration facilitates risk sharing and thereby enhances production specialisation, capital allocation, and economic growth. It also eases the flow of capital to capital-scarce countries with positive output effects. Finally, financial integration may enhance the functioning of domestic financial systems, through the intensification of competition and the importation of financial services, with positive growth effects. On the other hand, in the presence of pre-existing distortions, integration can actually retard growth. For instance, in countries with weak institutions – like weak financial and legal systems – integration may induce a capital outflow from capital-scarce countries to capital-abundant countries with better institutions. This line of reasoning suggests that financial integration will promote growth only in countries with sound institutions.

Empirical research on the impact of integration on growth is complicated by the difficulty in measuring integration across a wide array of countries that may impose a complex array of price and quantity controls on a broad assortment of financial transactions. Researchers have used (1) proxies for government restrictions on capital flows, (2) measures of actual international capital flows, or (3) the accumulated stock of foreign assets and/or liabilities.

The IMF's restriction measure is the most commonly used proxy of government restrictions on international financial transactions. It classifies countries on an annual basis by the presence or absence of restrictions, i.e. it is a dummy variable. The advantage of this variable is that it proxies directly for government impediments. Its disadvantage stems from the difficulty in accurately gauging the magnitude and effectiveness of government restrictions (Edison *et al.*, 2002).

Measures of actual international capital flows are also employed to proxy for international financial openness. These measures are based on the assumption that more capital flows indicate more integration. The advantage of these measures is that they are widely available and they are not subjective measures of capital restrictions, but a disadvantage is that many factors influence capital flows, including economic growth (Edison *et al.*, 2002).

Lane and Milesi-Ferretti (2001) have computed the accumulated stock of foreign assets and liabilities for an extensive sample of countries. These stock measures are less sensitive to short-run fluctuations in capital flows associated with factors that are unrelated to integration.

Empirical evidence yields conflicting conclusions about the growth effects of financial integration. While, for instance, Quinn (1997) finds that his measure of capital account openness is positively linked with growth, others report that this relationship is not robust (see Edison *et al.*, 2002 for a more detailed review). Edison *et al.* (2002) examine the growth impact of international financial integration, which they define as the degree to which an economy does not restrict cross-border transactions, using new data and new econometric techniques. The authors want not only to investigate the impact of international financial integration on economic growth but also to assess whether this relationship depends on the level of economic development, financial development, legal system development, government corruption, and macroeconomic policies. They use a wide array of measures of international financial integration for 57 countries, including (variants of) the IMF-restriction measure, various measures of capital flows (FDI, portfolio, and total capital flows), and the accumulated stock of liabilities (as a share of GDP) and the accumulated stock of liabilities and assets (as a share of GDP). Interestingly, the authors find that international financial integration does not accelerate economic growth even when controlling for particular economic, financial, institutional, and policy characteristics. However, Abiad *et al.* (2007) present some recent research on the impact of financial integration in the NMS that comes to more optimistic conclusions. The authors find that financial integration raises growth in the new EU Member States and thus contributes to speeding up the convergence process.

Financial integration may also have an impact on financial stability, although its direction is not clear. On the one hand, a larger and more diversified financial system will be better able to absorb economic shocks than financial systems in individual countries. Highly integrated financial markets also allow a more efficient sharing of financial risk that ultimately enhances the stability of the financial system itself. On the other hand, financial integration may also increase the risk of cross-border contagion as the recent crisis has shown (ECB, 2011). Economic shocks will spread more easily and rapidly in an integrated financial system.

Financial integration may also affect the structure of the financial system, which in turn may have implications for financial stability. Although financial integration will bring about an improvement in the supply of finance in the less financially developed markets and an increase in the size of local financial markets, financial integration does not imply that the financial structures of the countries concerned will converge. As pointed out by Guiso *et al.* (2004), it is possible that the most financially developed countries will share the services provided by their financial system with the other integrating countries. The economies of scale and scope may fuel the expansion of the established intermediaries and markets of the more developed markets. For instance, banks of more developed countries may provide cross-border loans to the firms of less advanced countries, so that the additional provision of credit will not show up in the private domestic credit of the latter countries. Likewise, firms of less financially developed countries can decide to get their shares listed on foreign stock exchanges. Pagano *et al.* (2001) identify a variety of reasons for doing so: overcoming equity rationing in the domestic market, reducing their cost of capital by accessing a more liquid market, and signalling their quality by accepting the scrutiny of more informed investors or the rules of a better corporate governance system. Cross-border bank lending and listing at foreign stock exchanges implies that quantitative indicators of the financial structure remain different.

This discussion implies that the size of the financial market of a given country may no longer be a good indicator of its degree of financial development (Guiso *et al.*, 2004). Distance and geographical segmentation become less important in financially integrated markets. In fact, in a fully integrated market, only the total size of the financial market of the integrating area matters as firms of a given country may have equal access to financial services of all other countries even if their domestic financial sector (scaled by GDP) differs from that in other countries. So differences in the size of local financial markets cannot be exploited to identify the link between financial development and economic growth if countries are perfectly financially integrated (Guiso *et al.*, 2004).

6.5 Conclusions

This chapter defines financial integration as a situation without frictions that discriminate between economic agents in their access to – and their investment of – capital on the basis of their country. Market forces are an important driver of financial integration. Competition can initiate the elimination of segmentation between national markets, resulting in lower prices. Collective action by trade associations is also driving integration. The setting of reference rates, such as the overnight rate (EONIA) and the interbank rate (EURIBOR), is an example of collective action. Finally, public authorities can foster integration. The establishment of an integrated large-value payment system (TARGET) by the ECB was crucial to create a single money market. Likewise, the European Commission's Financial Services Action Plan contributed to completing the internal market for financial services.

There are different categories of financial integration measures. Price-based measures are widely used to identify differences in returns caused by the geographic origin of the assets. While price-based indicators are the most direct measure of financial integration, they can be applied only to relatively homogeneous assets. Financial assets tend to differ in credit risk (corporate bonds) or business risk (equities). News-based measures assume that in an integrated market, only common or global news will move prices. Local news has little impact on a geographically diversified portfolio. Quantity-based measures examine cross-border activities. More cross-border business is an indicator of increased integration.

Examining the integration of Europe's financial markets, it is found that the money market and the government bond market were fully integrated before the financial crisis. The corporate bond market also appears to be quite well integrated: country effects explain only a minor part of the differences in corporate bond yield spreads. Equity market integration is more difficult to assess. The empirical evidence suggests a rising degree of integration of equity markets. Due to the financial crisis, the integration of financial markets seems to have reached a standstill and has in some cases, such as money and sovereign bond markets, been reversed.

Finally, financial integration enables better risk sharing and better allocation of capital. The result is a more efficient and competitive financial system that promotes economic growth. There is also a downside to financial integration. While a well-diversified financial system can better absorb economic shocks, these shocks can also spread more easily in an integrated financial system. It is therefore important that financial stability policies stay in tune with advances in financial integration (see Chapter 13).

NOTES

1 In analysing other segments of the bond market, like the corporate bond market, one cannot directly analyse yield differentials relative to a benchmark to assess integration. Corporate bonds are generally not homogeneous enough to allow easy comparison as they differ in their cash-flow structure, liquidity, sector, and, most importantly, credit rating. See Baele *et al.* (2004, 2008) for various price-based measures to assess the integration of the corporate bond market.

2 As Adam *et al.* point out, beta- and sigma-convergence indicators have different informational contents. The reason is that mean reversion (β convergence) does not imply that the cross-sectional variance (σ convergence) decreases over time.

3 This box heavily draws on Edison *et al.* (2002).

SUGGESTED READING

Baele, L., A. Ferrando, P. Hördahl, E. Krylova, and C. Monnet (2008), Measuring European Financial Integration, in: X. Freixas, P. Hartmann, and C. Mayer (eds.), *Handbook of European Financial Markets and Institutions*, Oxford University Press, 165–194.

Edison, H. J., R. Levine, L. Ricci, and T. Sløk (2002), International Financial Integration and Economic Growth, *Journal of International Money and Finance*, 21(6), 749–776.

Guiso, L., T. Jappelli, M. Padula, and M. Pagano (2004), Financial Market Integration and Economic Growth in the EU, *Economic Policy*, 524–577.

REFERENCES

Abiad, A., D. Leigh and A. Mody (2007), International Finance and Income Convergence: Europe is Different, IMF Working Paper 07/64.

Adam, K., T. Jappelli, A. M. Menichini, M. Padula, and M. Pagano (2002), Analyse, Compare, and Apply Alternative Indicators and Monitoring Methodologies to Measure the Evolution of Capital Market Integration in the European Union, Report to the European Commission, EC, Brussels.

Adjaouté, K. and J.-P. Danthine (2003), European Financial Integration and Equity Returns: A Theory-Based Assessment, in: V. Gaspar *et al.* (eds.), *The Transformation of the European Financial System*, ECB, Frankfurt.

Baele, L., A. Ferrando, P. Hördahl, E. Krylova, and C. Monnet (2004), Measuring Financial Integration in the Euro Area, ECB Occasional Paper 14.

   (2008), Measuring European Financial Integration, in: X. Freixas, P. Hartmann, and C. Mayer (eds.), *Handbook of European Financial Markets and Institutions*, Oxford University Press, 165–194.

Baltzer, M., L. Cappiello, R. A. De Santis, and S. Manganelli (2008), Measuring Financial Integration in New EU Member States, ECB Occasional Paper 81.

Cappiello, L., B. Gérard, A. Kadareja, and S. Manganelli (2006), Financial Integration of New EU Member States, ECB Working Paper 683.

Edison, H. J., R. Levine, L. Ricci, and T. Sløk (2002), International Financial Integration and Economic Growth, *Journal of International Money and Finance*, 21(6), 749–776.

European Central Bank (2003), The Integration of Europe's Financial Markets, *Monthly Bulletin*, October, 53–56.

   (2011), *Financial Integration in Europe*, ECB, Frankfurt.

European Commission (2006), Commission Staff Working Document Addressed to the European Parliament and to the Council on the Impact of Regulation (EC) No. 2560/2001 on Bank Charges for National Payments, EC, Brussels.

Guiso, L., T. Jappelli, M. Padula, and M. Pagano (2004), Financial Market Integration and Economic Growth in the EU, *Economic Policy*, 524–577.

Hardouvelis, G. A., D. Malliaropulos, and R. Priestley (2006), EMU and European Stock Market Integration, *Journal of Business*, 79(1), 365–392.

Lane, P. R. and G. M. Milesi-Ferretti (2001), The External Wealth of Nations: Measures of Foreign Assets and Liabilities in Industrial and Developing Countries, *Journal of International Economics*, 55, 263–294.

Pagano, M., O. Randl, A. Roëll, and J. Zechne (2001). What Makes Stock Exchanges Succeed? Evidence from Cross-Listing Decisions, *European Economic Review*, 45, 770–782.

Quinn, D. (1997), The Correlates of Change in International Financial Regulation, *American Political Science Review*, 91, 531–551.

Wolswijk, G. and J. de Haan (2005), Government Debt Management in the Euro Area: Recent Theoretical Developments and Changes in Practices, ECB Occasional Paper 25.

7

Financial Infrastructures

OVERVIEW

This chapter discusses the payment and post-trading (i.e. securities clearing and settlement) systems in the EU. Over the past decade, the volume and value of transactions that are processed via these systems have grown tremendously. Stable and efficient payment and post-trading systems have become of great importance for the operation of financial markets and the economy in general. At present, these infrastructures are very fragmented and competition is limited.

This chapter starts by examining the different elements of payment and post-trading systems. A distinction is made between retail and wholesale payment systems. Given the growing importance of card-based retail payment systems, the main focus will be on the set-up of the existing card schemes. Furthermore, the different steps of the post-trading process, which arranges the transfer of ownership and the payment between buyers and sellers in security markets, will be discussed. Finally, the role of central banks in the regulation and oversight of payment and settlement systems will be clarified.

The second part of the chapter gives an overview of the economic features of payment and securities market infrastructures. These infrastructures are characterised by economies of scale and scope, and network externalities. Understanding these characteristics should enable the reader to better comprehend (future) developments within the EU payment and security market infrastructures.

The third part of this chapter describes: (1) the current situation in the payment and post-trading industry, (2) the barriers to cross-border payment and security settlement services, and (3) recent initiatives to promote further integration. Despite the Single Market and the common currency, the internal market for retail payments and post-trading services remains fragmented and could benefit from enhanced competition. Recent initiatives have the potential to take away some of the existing barriers for integration.

LEARNING OBJECTIVES

After you have studied this chapter, you should be able to:

- define what a payment system is
- explain the difference between wholesale and retail payment systems
- describe the various steps of the post-trading process
- understand the economic characteristics of payment and securities market infrastructures, and explain how these characteristics influence the EU market structure
- assess the extent to which the different elements of the EU financial infrastructure are integrated
- discuss the barriers that need to be removed in order to strengthen integration of financial infrastructures.

7.1 Payment systems and post-trading services

Payment systems

A *payment* is a transfer of money between economic actors. This transfer can take place, for example, between a consumer and a merchant to pay for delivered goods or services using cash and non-cash money. Cash payments require no systems for settlement between economic actors. Settlement is immediately final when bank notes or coins are handed over. This is different for non-cash payments, such as a transfer from a bank account. In order to settle a transaction, one bank account has to be debited and another has to be credited. Different systems are in place to make sure that the non-cash transfer is completed in a safe and efficient manner. If the transaction takes place between accounts held at the same bank, the bank's internal administrative system can settle the transaction. In general, however, economic agents hold accounts at different banks and therefore non-cash payments require cooperation between banks. A *payment system* can be defined as a combination of technical, legal, and commercial instruments, rules, and procedures that ensure the transfer of money between banks. A distinction can be made between (1) retail payment systems and (2) wholesale payment systems.

Retail payment systems

Retail payment systems are used for the transaction, clearing, and settlement of relatively low-value and non-time-critical payments initiated through payment instruments such as cheques, credit transfers, direct debits, and payment cards (BIS, 2001). Retail payments are generally made in large numbers (mass payments) by many economic actors and typically relate to the purchase of goods and services in both the consumer and business sectors (BIS, 2002a). Moreover, retail payments are made using a wide range of payment instruments and in varied contexts. Generally, private-sector systems are used for the transaction process and the clearing of retail payments.

Each retail payment system consists of:

- payment instruments used to initiate and direct the transfer of money between the accounts of the payer and the payee (see Box 7.1 for an overview of the main payment instruments available);
- payment infrastructures for transacting and clearing payment instruments, processing and communicating payment information, and transferring payment information between the paying and receiving institutions;
- financial institutions that provide payment accounts, instruments, and services to consumers, and organisations that operate payment transaction, clearing, and settlement service networks for those financial institutions;
- market arrangements (or payment schemes) such as conventions, regulations, and contracts for producing, pricing, delivering, and acquiring the various payment instruments and services in order to maintain a minimum level of efficiency and security between all payment service providers in a market. A *payment scheme* is the set of interbank rules, standards, and practices for the provision or operation of specific payment instruments. In a more practical sense, the scheme defines the characteristics of a specific payment instrument, e.g. the authorisation procedures, the fee structure, and the maximum time frame within which a payment is processed, thereby laying down the rules with which all participating payment service providers have to comply. These rules ensure predictability, security, and efficiency in the provision of the given payment instrument;
- laws, standards, rules, and procedures set by legislators, courts, and regulators that define and govern the mechanics of the payment process and the conduct of payment service markets in order to make payment service providers meet public policy goals (BIS, 2006).

A payment can start with a transaction initiated by the payer (*push transaction*) or initiated by the payee (*pull transaction*) and ends at the moment when the payee has received the agreed amount of money in good order. Depending on the actual payment instrument and the organisation of the banking sector, the payment instruction travels through one or more of the following: from an entry bank (paying/receiving bank or branch) to a

---

Box 7.1 Core payment instruments

Credit transfers: a payment initiated by the payer. The latter sends a payment instruction to his/her bank. The bank debits the payer's account and advises the receiver's bank to credit the beneficiary's account. This can happen through different channels and via intermediaries.

Direct debit: a payment initiated by the creditor, who sends the instructions to collect money via his/her bank or via a central processing entity (automated clearinghouse) to the debtor's bank(s). Direct debits are often used for recurring payments, like those for utilities. They require a pre-authorisation ('mandate') by the payer. Direct debits are also used for one-off payments in which case the payer authorises an individual payment.

Payment card: a differentiation can be made between three main types of card payment instruments: (1) *debit cards*, which allow the cardholder to charge purchases directly and individually to an account; (2) *credit cards*, which allow purchases within a certain credit limit. The balance is settled in full or partly by the end of a specified period. In the latter case the remaining balance is taken as extended credit on which the cardholder must pay interest; and (3) *stored value cards* (or prepaid cards) which allow users to pay merchants with funds transferred in advance to a prepaid account.

Cash: in the euro area, only the ECB has the right to authorise the issue of banknotes. The National Central Banks in the euro area bring bank notes into circulation by providing them to the banking sector. Banknotes are mainly distributed to the public via ATMs (automated teller machines).

Source: ECB

---

settlement bank (bank head office or correspondent bank) and then to a clearinghouse or processing centre (see Figure 7.1). The latter is a central processing mechanism through which financial institutions agree to exchange payment instructions. Settlement takes place at a designated time based on the rules and procedures of the clearinghouse (see also the next section on wholesale payment systems). In most cases the actual settlement of the payment takes place at the central bank (or in some cases a private entity) where the respective settlement banks have their accounts. The distribution of the payment to the payee completes the payment process. *Payment finality*, i.e. the guarantee of a payment to the payee, is critical in this respect.

The efficiency of retail payment systems has been enhanced over time by the transition from:

- bank branches towards ATMs in cash distribution;
- paper-based payments to electronic payment systems; and
- manual processing of payments to automated end-to-end processing. The latter is also referred to as straight-through processing (STP).

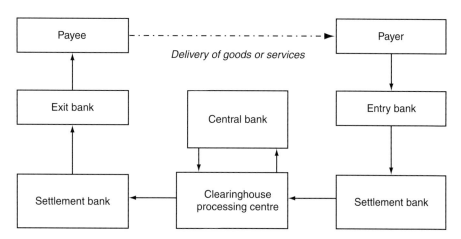

Figure 7.1 The process of initiating and receiving payments (push transaction)
Source: Khiaonarong (2003)

Strengthening the efficiency of these systems is essential as the costs of retail payments to society are substantial. Brits and Winder (2005) estimate that the costs of point-of-sale (POS) payment instruments in the Netherlands amount to €0.35 per transaction, making up 0.65 per cent of GDP. The authors find that e-purses or electronic wallets are most cost-efficient, irrespective of the size of a transaction. Cash is most economical for purchases below €11.63, while the debit card is to be preferred for larger purchases. Since this study has been published, this threshold has come down and is currently probably close to or even below 5 euro. In a similar study conducted for Sweden, Bergman *et al.* (2007) report that the overall cost of payments at a point of sale is approximately 0.4 per cent of GDP. Debit and credit cards are socially less costly than cash for payments above €8 and €18, respectively. The latter is interesting, as Brits and Winder (2005) argue that from a cost perspective credit cards should not be used at all. Notwithstanding these differences, it follows from both studies that a shift towards a more cashless society is likely to improve economic welfare.

Despite its relatively high costs, cash is still most frequently used by European citizens, as at least six out of seven payments are made in cash (Capgemini, 2010). However, non-cash payments (like cheques, credit transfers, direct debits, and payment cards) account for most of the value of payments in the EU, and the number of electronic payments (such as card transactions) has been growing rapidly (see Figure 7.2 and Figure 7.3). However, payment customs vary substantially across EU Member States. For example, in Greece, Italy, and Poland non-cash usage per inhabitant is still minimal (less than 60 transactions per year).

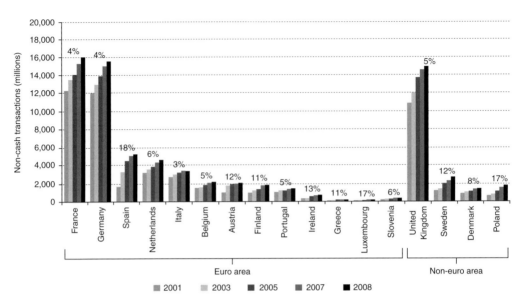

Figure 7.2 Number of non-cash transactions in Europe (millions), 2001–2008

Note: Figures shown are annual growth rates

Source: Capgemini (2010)

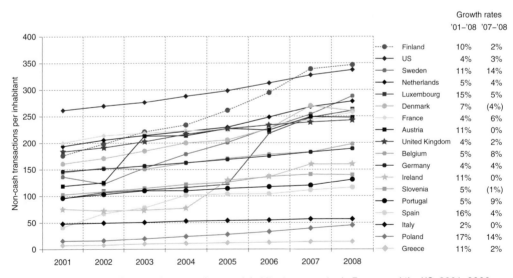

Figure 7.3 Evolution of non-cash transactions per inhabitant per country in Europe and the US, 2001–2008

Source: Capgemini (2010)

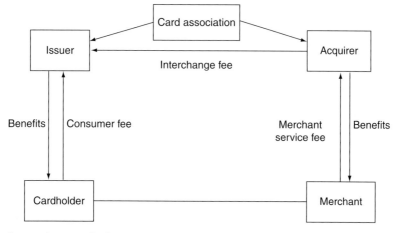

Figure 7.4 Four-party payment scheme
Source: Harper *et al.* (2006)

Card-based payment systems

Cards (credit and debit) remained the preferred means of non-cash payments globally, accounting for more than 40 per cent of non-cash volumes in most markets and above 58 per cent globally. Given the growing importance of card-based payment systems, this specific means of payment will be briefly explained. In principle, each debit or credit card payment involves the following four parties:

- the *cardholder*: the person who has received the payment card from the issuer and uses the card for payment of goods and services;
- the *issuer*: the payment service provider that issues the payment card to the cardholder;
- the *merchant*: the person accepting the card payment in return for goods or services; and
- the *acquirer*: the payment service provider that provides payment services to the merchant.

Moreover, interbank payment arrangements are in place for executing funds transfers between the two intermediaries. There are different arrangements to organise the processing of a card payment. Figure 7.4 depicts a *four-party payment scheme* (cardholder – issuer – acquirer – merchant). Such a scheme (such as Visa and Mastercard) is often referred to as 'open', as the issuer and acquirer can be any financial institution. A payment scheme where issuing and acquiring is performed by the same payment service provider (such as Diners Club or American Express) is referred to as a *three-party*

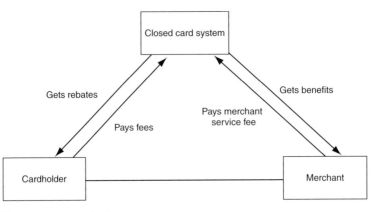

Figure 7.5   Three-party payment scheme
Source: Harper *et al.* (2006)

scheme (cardholder – payment service provider – merchant). This is shown in Figure 7.5. As in a three-party scheme the issuer and acquirer are the same payment service provider, it is also referred to as a 'closed' system.

Card schemes operate under a rather controversial construction, which is also the subject of several regulatory and antitrust investigations, i.e. the interchange and merchant service fees. The *interchange fee* is a fee paid by an acquiring institution to an issuing institution for each payment card transaction at the point of sale of a merchant. The *merchant service fee* is the fee paid for each transaction by a merchant to an acquirer who processes the merchant's transaction through the network and obtains the funds from the cardholder's bank (European Commission, 2007). In a four-party card scheme, the merchant finally receives the amount of the transaction, minus the merchant fee.

The usage of interchange or merchant service fees may raise several concerns. First, these fees may be seen as a collective agreement between competitors that distorts competition in the market for payment cards. Second, the non-transparent pricing of card payments (for example, as a result of the so-called 'no surcharge' rule[1]) creates hardly any incentive to make use of more efficient payment instruments. Third, as merchants adjust their prices for goods and services for these fees, cross-subsidisation occurs, i.e. consumers who make use of other (more efficient) means of payment subsidise the use of expensive (credit) cards.

Wholesale payment systems

Wholesale payment systems can be defined as those through which large-value and/or time-critical funds transfers are made between financial institutions within the system (for their own account or for their customers). Although no minimum value is set for these payments, the average value of payments passed through such systems is normally relatively high (BIS, 2001). In *real-time gross settlement (RTGS) systems*, each payment is immediately settled on a gross basis. The fact that each payment is processed on an individual basis at the time it is received (rather than at a later stage) enhances the stability of the system. TARGET (Trans-European Automated Real-Time Gross Settlement Express Transfer System) is the most important interbank payment system for real-time processing of cross-border transfers throughout the EU. It has been developed to: (1) provide a safe and reliable mechanism for the settlement of euro payments, (2) increase the efficiency of cross-border payments in euros, and (3) serve the needs of the monetary policy of the ECB and to promote the integration of the euro money market. The full integration of the large-value payment systems has been instrumental in achieving this result. TARGET included 16 national RTGS systems and the ECB payment mechanism (EPM).

In November 2007, the *Eurosystem*, i.e. the ECB and the National Central Banks of the countries in the euro area, launched the latest version of TARGET, which is referred to as TARGET2. In 2010, TARGET2 processed 88.6 million payments, with a total value of €593,194 billion. This translates into a daily average of 343,380 payments, with an average daily value of €2,299 billion. TARGET2 is the most important RTGS in the EU and one of the three largest wholesale payment systems in the world, alongside Fedwire in the United States and Continuous Linked Settlement (CLS), the international system for settling foreign exchange transactions (see Figure 7.6).

The largest *net settlement system* in Europe is EURO1, a multilateral, large-value payment system for euro payments established by the Euro Banking Association. This system processes credit transfers and direct debits throughout the day and balances are settled at close of business via a settlement account at the ECB.

Post-trading services

The smooth functioning of and confidence in securities markets depend, among other things, on the efficiency and reliability of their infrastructure. In particular, it is crucial that the transfer of ownership from the seller to the buyer in exchange for a payment takes place in a safe and efficient manner (Kazarian, 2006). In essence, the clearing and settlement or *post-trading*

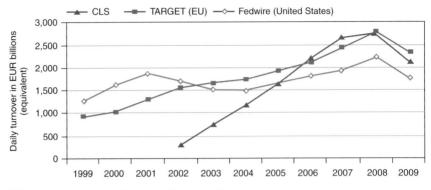

Figure 7.6   Major large-value payments systems in the world
Source: ECB (2010)

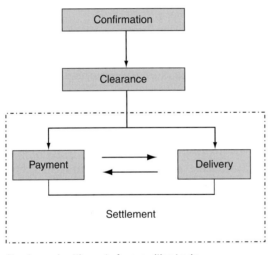

Figure 7.7   Clearing and settlement of a securities trade
Source: Giovannini Group (2001)

process provides for the transfer of ownership and payment between buyers and sellers in a security market.

The post-trading process begins when the actual securities trade has been executed. The subsequent securities settlement process encompasses a number of complementary steps and actions. Figure 7.7 shows that the post-trading process can be described in terms of four main activities (Giovannini Group, 2001):

- confirmation of terms of the trade as agreed by the buyer and the seller;

- clearance, by which the respective obligations of the buyer and seller are established;
- delivery, requiring the transfer of the securities from the seller to the buyer; and
- payment, requiring the transfer of funds from the buyer to the seller.

Figure 7.7 shows that the post-trading process starts with the confirmation of the terms of the securities transaction. This can be done either directly between the buyer and the seller ('over-the-counter' or OTC) or indirectly through the securities exchange or a clearing agent. In the end, the respective parties should clearly know what securities are bought or sold and at what price.

The next step is the clearing of the obligation of the counterparties resulting from the matching process. Clearance of a securities transaction establishes the respective obligations of the buyer and the seller and may be achieved on a gross (trade-for-trade) or a net basis (offsetting of mutual obligations). The latter reduces the number of actual transfers, thereby limiting the credit risk exposure. Clearance services can be provided by a clearinghouse, a national central securities depository (CSD), or an international central securities depository (ICSD).[2] The latter two also hold securities and allow them to be processed by book entry (rather than by physical movement of the securities between buyers and sellers).

Securities markets can also make use of central counterparties (CCPs), which are entities that interpose themselves between the buyers and the sellers of securities, i.e. buyers and sellers interact indirectly via the CCP. These entities can also offer netting arrangements, which facilitate the management of securities and payment transfers and reduce credit risk.[3]

The subsequent step is the *settlement* process, which involves the delivery of the securities and the payment of funds between buyers and sellers. The payment is usually made via a banking or payment system, while the delivery of securities is typically carried out in a CSD or an ICSD. According to the BIS (1992), the largest financial risks in securities clearance and settlement occur during the settlement process, especially when no mechanism exists to ensure that delivery occurs if – and only if – payment occurs. Without such a mechanism counterparties are exposed to *principal risk*, i.e. the risk that the seller of a security delivers but does not receive payment or that the buyer of a security makes a payment but does not receive the securities. A securities transaction is settled once the securities are delivered to the buyer and the seller has received the payment. However, often formal registration of the transfer of ownership by a CSD is needed to assure settlement.

Role of the Eurosystem

The smooth functioning of payment and security settlement systems is crucial for:

- a sound currency, i.e. stable and efficient payment systems are an essential condition for maintaining trust in the value of money;
- the conduct of monetary policy, as these systems play an important role in monetary policy operations;
- the functioning of financial markets, i.e. in the absence of a stable and efficient payment infrastructure, financial markets would not be able to process the current volume and value of transactions;
- the maintenance of financial stability, i.e. problems in financial institutions can manifest themselves in payment or security settlement systems. Moreover, these systems can act as a channel for transmitting problems from one institution to another.

For all these reasons, central banks have an interest in the design and management of payment and security settlement systems. The Eurosystem has the statutory task of promoting the smooth operation of payment and settlement systems. It fulfils this task by:

- providing payment and securities settlement facilities: the Eurosystem runs a settlement system for large-value payments in euros (TARGET2) and thereby functions as banker to the banks. The latter means that banks hold funds on their account at the central bank, and payments between banks are made by debiting and crediting central bank accounts. Moreover, the Eurosystem also provides a mechanism for the cross-border use of collateral in order to facilitate payments taking place when there is a deficit in the account of the paying bank;
- overseeing the euro payment and settlement systems: the Eurosystem applies internationally agreed standards to ensure the soundness and efficiency of systems handling euro transactions. It also assesses the continuous compliance of euro payment and settlement systems with these standards;
- overseeing compliance with the standards for securities clearing and settlement systems;
- ensuring an integrated regulatory and oversight framework for securities settlement systems;
- acting as a catalyst for change: the Eurosystem promotes efficiency in payment systems and securities markets by encouraging the removal of barriers towards integration.

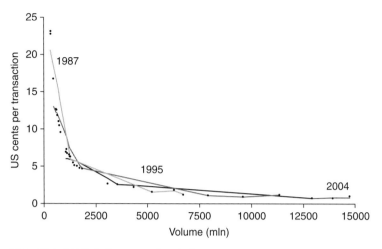

Figure 7.8   Economies of scale in the payment market
Source: Bolt (2007)

7.2 Economic features of payment and securities market infrastructures

Payment and securities market infrastructures are characterised by economies of scale and scope and network externalities.

Economies of scale arise when the cost per unit falls as output increases. This effect occurs when it is possible to spread fixed costs over a higher output. Schmiedel and Schönenberg (2005) argue that economies of scale are usually a result of the need for service providers to create a 'critical mass' of customers in order to reap the benefit of sizeable investments in information technology and communication networks. If securities infrastructure providers are successful in attracting a significant number of issuers and participants, these set-up costs may be spread over a wider number of transactions. Similarly, there are strong economies of scale in the production of payment services. In a European cross-country study, Humphrey *et al.* (2003) find that costs increase by 2 per cent when volumes rise by 10 per cent. Bolt and Humphrey (2007) estimate payment scale economies using a panel of payment and banking data for 11 European countries over 18 years. Their results show that doubling of payment volume would increase total costs by only 27 per cent. Figure 7.8 shows how unit payment costs vary with the total number of payment transactions.[4] The figure clearly shows that the costs of payments decline as the volume of payments that are processed increases.

Economies of scope refer to the reduction of the per-unit costs resulting from the production of a wider variety of goods and services (i.e. when it is cheaper to produce good A and good B together rather than separately). So, integrated financial infrastructures can develop new products and services at a lower unit cost. A precondition for economies of scope is that it is possible to share (certain) input factors for the production of different goods and services.

Economies of scope for CSDs and CCPs can stem from extending the number of financial instruments or trading platforms for which they provide services. Moreover, there is a strong complementary relationship between the various components of securities settlement (Kazarian, 2006). This entails that economies of scope can be obtained by integration along the value chain of a securities transaction, i.e. by combining trading, clearing, and settlement into one firm. Such a supplier can offer its services at lower cost than different suppliers providing these services separately. A good example of such a vertically integrated entity (or 'silo') is Deutsche Börse. Serifsoy and Weiß (2007) argue that one of the adverse effects of vertical integration is the leverage of a (natural) monopoly from one stage of the value chain upstream or downstream to other stages. An integrated supplier may cross-subsidise its trading costs – and thereby attract customers from other platforms – through its monopoly profits on the clearing and settlement stage, or vice versa. It may also foreclose the market for competitors as users can be forced to 'buy' another service from the same institution.

As for payment systems, economies of scope may exist when the system handles more than one type of payment instrument or service. This allows the operator of the system to spread out the fixed cost of the system over a wider range of payment instruments.

Generally, the demand for payment services is largely inelastic as payments in themselves do not generate value. A payment is made because of the purchase of a good or a service or to pay off a debt or a financial obligation. Payment services are therefore a convenience good rather than a primary good. However, payment service users may be (very) sensitive to relative payment prices (i.e. price differences between individual payment instruments).

Now we turn to network externalities. A *network* can be defined as a large system consisting of many similar (or complementary) parts that are connected to allow movement or communication between the parts or between the parts and a centre. The addition of a new participant in a network can increase the value of the network for all participants. This means that the value of the services and products offered to the participants depends on the number of other participants purchasing the same services and products (*network externalities*). As an example, consider a simple network

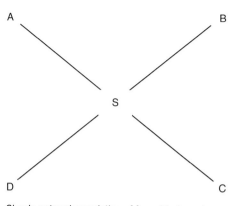

Figure 7.9   Simple network consisting of four side-branches

consisting of a central junction S and side-branches A, B, C, and D, as shown in Figure 7.9 (based on Economides, 1993). The goods in this network are composite goods, each comprising two complementary components – for example, ASB is comprised of the complements AS and SB. Imagine that the network would consist of the three side-branches A, B, and C. In this case the network would create six products (i.e. ASB, ASC, BSA, BSC, CSA, and CSB). Economides (1993) shows that the addition of a new side-branch to a network composed of *n* side-branches, creates *2n* new products. So the addition of another side-branch, say D, creates six new products. This is an economy of scope in consumption that is called a *network externality*. Network externalities can be found in a variety of industries, such as telecommunications, airlines, railroads, etc. (Shy, 2001). The externality directly increases consumer utility through the provision of new goods, and it may also affect consumers indirectly through price decreases.

Financial markets exhibit positive size externalities as increasing the size of an exchange market increases the expected utility of all participants. Higher participation of traders on both sides of the market decreases the variance of the expected market price and increases the expected utility of risk-averse traders. *Ceteris paribus*, higher liquidity increases traders' utility. Thus, financial exchange markets exhibit network externalities (Economides, 1996).

Payment and securities market infrastructures also have characteristics of network industries, as the benefits to one market participant using a specific platform or system increase when another participant also chooses to do business in that network. The nature of these networks creates scope for formal cooperation among market players. The European Commission (2007)

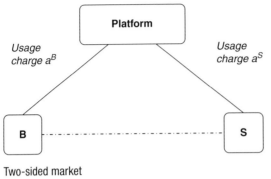

Figure 7.10 Two-sided market
Source: Rochet and Tirole (2006)

argues that certain types of cooperation (e.g. creating and operating common standards and platforms) may be necessary to generate efficiencies. However, cooperation extending to strategies, pricing, or selling policies could lead to collusion and limit competition and/or exclude third parties.

Networks can be *one-sided* or *two-sided*. A market is two-sided if the platform or system can affect the volume of transactions by charging more to one side of the market and reducing the price paid by the other side by an equal amount. In other words, the price structure matters, and platforms must design it so as to bring both sides on board (see Rochet and Tirole, 2006). To explain this further, consider a platform charging per-transaction charges a^B and a^S to the buyer and the seller side, respectively. The market for interactions between the two sides is one-sided if the volume V of transactions realised on the platform depends only on the aggregate price level $a = a^B + a^S$, i.e. V is insensitive to reallocations of this price between the buyer and the seller. However, if V varies with a^B while a is kept constant, the market is said to be two-sided (see Figure 7.10). Generally, payment and security settlement systems are two-sided markets. For example, Figures 7.4 and 7.5 show that the market for payment cards is two-sided, i.e. one side of the market is subsidising the other. This subsidy is made up of the *interchange* and *merchant fee*, which is paid by the acquiring to the issuing bank. Ultimately, these fees raise the price the merchant pays for a card transaction, while they reduce the price for the cardholder, thereby increasing the willingness of the cardholder to make use of a payment card. As a result, the volume of transactions within the card network is higher than would be the case if the cardholder would face higher (visible) costs.

While historically these platforms developed to ensure efficient cooperation in terms of standards and practices, and to share cost between suppliers, over time they created the opportunity to exploit the least elastic side of the market (the merchants originally). At a certain phase, however, the elasticity in the market may shift and it could well be necessary to shift the 'taxation'. This often leads to heavily 'skewed' prices in two-sided markets where the consumer pays a zero fee while the merchant pays a high fee (Bolt and Tieman, 2007).

The presence of network externalities often leads to oligopolies or monopolistic markets. This does not necessarily have to be a problem, as the marginal social benefits from network expansion may be larger than the benefits of having a perfectly competitive market. Perfect competition will generally lead to a network that is too small compared to the socially optimal size. However, given their dominance in certain markets, in practice network providers may be tempted to abuse their economic position and charge monopoly prices, leading to greater inefficiency than under perfect competition.

Finally, network industries are often characterised by *switching costs*, i.e. customers face substantial costs when they want to switch from one network provider to the other. In some situations, high switching costs may 'lock in' users and prevent them from switching to another network. As a consequence, high switching costs may obstruct innovation as users are prevented from making use of new and more efficient services.

7.3 Integration of financial market infrastructures

Given the opportunities to benefit from economies of scale and scope, one would expect substantial consolidation in the EU markets for payment and security settlement services. However, despite the Single Market initiative and the introduction of the euro, the internal market for (retail) payment and post-trading services remains relatively fragmented. This section will: (1) examine the current state of affairs in the payment and post-trading industry, (2) discuss the barriers to cross-border payment and security settlement services, and (3) highlight recent initiatives to promote further integration.

Current state of affairs and barriers to integration

Large-value payment systems

The integration of EU large-value payment systems (LVPSs) has been quite remarkable. Before the introduction of the euro in January 1999, LVPSs were organised domestically and almost all cross-border payments were made via correspondent banks. The latter means that banks (or other payment service providers) had individual arrangements under which one bank provided payment and other services to another bank (mostly on a cross-border basis), holding accounts at each other. These correspondent bank arrangements enabled financial institutions to operate cross-border payments without having a foreign branch or subsidiary.

This setting changed substantially in response to the launch of the euro, when the ESCB established TARGET, thereby connecting the existing domestic LVPSs and the ECB payment mechanism. Moreover, private banks introduced EURO1, a high-value payment system for cross-border and domestic transactions in euros between 70 participating banks operating in the European Union. In 2009, TARGET2 had a market share of 89 per cent by value and 60 per cent by number of payments processed in the two large-value payment systems in euro, with the remainder being accounted for by EURO1.

Another important global LVPS is the Continuous Linked Settlement (CLS) system for foreign exchange transactions. This specialised system, based in New York, provides global multi-currency settlement services for foreign exchange transactions, using a payment-versus-payment (PvP) mechanism (i.e. a foreign exchange operation is settled only if both counterparties simultaneously have a sufficient position in the currency they are selling). PvP has been introduced to prevent the Herstatt risk (or foreign exchange settlement or cross-currency settlement risk). The term *Herstatt risk* refers to the failure of Bankhaus Herstatt in 1974 as a result of incomplete settlement of foreign exchange transactions (see Box 7.2).

Retail payment systems

For retail payments, the EU still consists of 27 heterogeneous payment areas instead of one single payment market. According to Salo (2006), there are two important explanations for this. First, path dependence can explain the slow change of national payment habits. All national payment systems have their own membership criteria, standards, and practices. Second, critical mass or installed base of network facilities plays a crucial role in the start-up and growth of a network. Over time, national systems have been optimised to satisfy national-user preferences in the most efficient way. Since most payments take place nationally this is a very efficient outcome, but it prevents reaping European-scale benefits. Substituting the existing national systems with one European system does not only run the risk of not being able to satisfy all user requirements, it also means that substantial investments have to be made.

> **Box 7.2** The Herstatt crisis
>
> On 26 June 1974, the German authorities closed Bankhaus Herstatt, a medium-sized bank that was very active in foreign exchange markets. On that day, some of Herstatt's counter-parties had irrevocably paid large amounts of D-Marks to the bank but not yet received dollars in exchange, as the US financial markets had just opened for the day. Herstatt's closure started a chain reaction that disrupted payment and settlement systems. Its New York correspondent bank suspended all US-dollar payments from the German bank's account. Banks that had paid D-Marks to Herstatt earlier that day therefore became fully exposed to the value of those transactions. Other banks in New York refused to make pay-ments on their own account or for their customers until they had confirmation that their counter value had been received. These disruptions were propagated further through the multilateral net settlement system used in New York. Over the next three days, the amount of gross funds transferred by this system declined by an estimated 60 per cent. Bankhaus Herstatt's closure was the first and most dramatic case of a bank failure where incom-plete settlement of foreign exchange transactions caused severe problems in payment and settlement systems. Several other episodes occurred in the 1990s but they were less disruptive.
>
> *Source:* BIS (2002b)

This characteristic of networks can present a barrier to entry for new payment service providers. In fact, the start-up problem can be seen as a chicken-and-egg problem: consumers are not interested in purchasing the good or service when the installed base is too small, and the installed base is too small because an insufficiently small number of consumers have purchased the good or service (Economides and Himmelberg, 1995).

For now, the way in which cross-border retail transactions are settled varies widely across countries and types of institutions (Freixas and Holthausen, 2008). The first pan-European clearinghouse (PE-ACH) for retail payments is the STEP 2 system, which the Euro Banking Association launched in 2003. Payments may be settled on a bilateral basis between national clearinghouses. In case the payee and payer have an account with the same cross-border financial group, the payment may also be settled in house.

The current fragmentation upholds the inefficiency of some payment systems within the EU, with substantial differences in direct prices for payment services between EU Member States. Evidence suggests that the costs of payment services in these Member States are 0.3–0.5 per cent of GDP. The key determinant of the cost of payment systems is the use of cash, accounting for as much as 60–70 per cent of the total cost. The relatively low aggregated costs of payment services in, for example, the Benelux and Scandinavian countries are closely related to the relatively high usage of more efficient electronic payment instruments. At the national level, authorities have tried to minimise the cost of the payment system. This can be done by reducing the use of cash (the processing of which is very costly, particularly for banks) and by substituting paper-based payment instruments with electronic payments that can be automated from end to end.

According to the European Commission (2007), there are a number of competition concerns in the markets for payment cards and payment systems. Markets in many Member States are highly concentrated. Even though high concentration does not necessarily imply lack of competition, barriers to new entry exist especially in the market for payment cards where market parties charge high card fees (see Box 7.3).

There are large variations in merchant fees across the EU. For example, firms in Member States with high fees have to pay banks three or four times more of their revenue from card sales than those in Member States with low fees. There are also large variations in interchange fees between banks across the EU, which may not be passed on fully in lower fees for cardholders.

Box 7.3 Concentration in credit and debit card markets

According to the European Commission (2007), payment markets are still mostly fragmented, with little or no competition at the EU level. Market parties mostly compete domestically, with the rare exception of a few international network players, such as Visa, MasterCard, and AMEX, which compete at the European level. In some Member States, these international networks face strong competition from national debit networks, which sometimes account for up to 90 per cent of all card transactions. At the bank level, the picture is somewhat different. In most Member States, competition is strong among issuing banks while acquiring often remains a monopolistic or nearly monopolistic activity. The graphs in Figure 7.11 show the market structure in the EU markets for credit and debit cards using the so-called Herfindahl Index, which is defined as the sum of the squares of the market shares of all institutions in the sector ($HI = \sum_{i=1}^{n} s_i^2$, where s_i is the market share of institution i). The Herfindahl Index ranges between $1/n$ and 1, reaching its lowest value, the reciprocal of the number of institutions (n), when all institutions are of equal size, and reaching unity in the case of monopoly. The index as published by the European Commission has been rescaled and ranges between 0 (low concentration) and 10,000 (high concentration). As Figure 7.11 shows, the index in most Member States is (much) higher than 2,000, which is usually seen as an indication of a highly concentrated market.

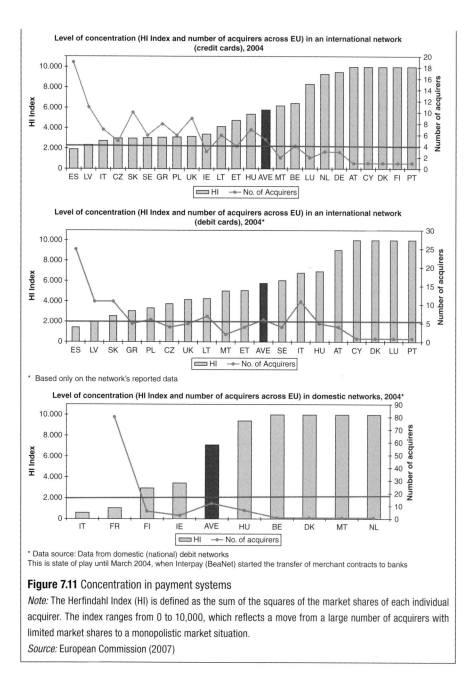

Figure 7.11 Concentration in payment systems

Note: The Herfindahl Index (HI) is defined as the sum of the squares of the market shares of each individual acquirer. The index ranges from 0 to 10,000, which reflects a move from a large number of acquirers with limited market shares to a monopolistic market situation.

Source: European Commission (2007)

High and sustained profitability (particularly in card issuing) suggests that banks in some Member States enjoy significant market power and can impose high card fees on firms and consumers. Furthermore, some rules and practices of market parties weaken competition at the retail level, for example by the blending of merchant fees and the prohibition of surcharging. Finally, the technical standards diverge across the EU, which may prevent many service providers from operating efficiently on a pan-EU scale.

These findings suggest that there is a need to address several barriers in order to strengthen competition in the EU retail payment market: technical, commercial, and legal barriers. It is crucial that common technical standards are developed and business models need to be aligned. As it is not clear to what extent market forces will initiate these changes, there may be a role for the European Commission to interfere and improve competition in the retail payment market through new legislative proposals. As for the commercial barriers, section 7.1 has shown that there are still substantial differences between user preferences and pricing structures in Europe. The adoption of the Payment Services Directive (PSD) in 2007 created the legal foundation for an EU-wide single market for payments. The fragmentation of retail payment infrastructures is being addressed in the context of the Single Euro Payments Area (SEPA) project. In SEPA, payment systems and infrastructures are expected to establish Europe-wide reach and become pan-European (see next section for further information).

Post-trading industry

As discussed in the previous section, CSDs/CCPs are characterised by economies of scale, economies of scope, and network effects. In principle, these characteristics are compatible with perfectly contestable markets (Schulze and Baur, 2006). However, investments made by CSDs/CCPs, both in human and technical capital, are very specific and therefore not easily recoverable. Moreover, users face substantial switching costs when changing CSDs/CCPs. Consequently, the national markets for post-trading services are far from being perfectly contestable. The EU post-trading industry has evolved into nationally based systems that tend to be monopolistic, i.e. all trades in a given type of security are cleared and settled by a single national entity.

Several studies have compared the post-trading costs of domestic versus cross-border transactions, as well as the costs of a domestic transaction in the EU and those in the US. Table 7.1 shows that these studies generally conclude that cross-border prices and costs are considerably higher than the corresponding costs and prices for domestic transactions. The studies by NERA Economic Consulting (2004) and Deutsche Börse Group (2005) also conclude that the costs of domestic transactions differ significantly among Member States. Moreover, post-trading costs per transaction in the EU are substantially higher than in the US.

Table 7.1 Studies examining post-trading costs per transaction for users

	EU cross-border	US	Ratio	EU domestic	US	Ratio
Lannoo and Levin (2001)	3.10	0.40	7.75	1.74	0.40	4.35
LSE/OXERA (2002)	3.41	0.53	6.43	2.04	0.53	3.85
Giovannini Group (2001)	2.86	0.46	6.22	1.49	0.46	3.24
NERA (2004)	n.a.	n.a.	n.a.	0.10–0.65	0.10	1.00–6.50
DBG (2005)	n.a.	n.a.	n.a.	0.30–0.60	0.10	1.50–3.00

Source: Schulze and Baur (2006)

The Giovannini Group (2001) concluded that fragmentation in the EU clearing and settlement infrastructure significantly complicates the post-trade processing of cross-border securities transactions relative to domestic transactions. Complications arise because of the need to access many national systems, whereby differences in technical requirements/market practices, tax regimes, and legal systems act as barriers to the efficient and safe delivery of post-trading services. The inefficiency that is created by these barriers is reflected in higher costs to pan-EU investors and is inconsistent with the objective of creating a truly integrated EU financial system. The Giovannini Group therefore called for the removal of a list of 15 barriers relating to: (1) technical requirements/market practice, (2) tax procedures, and (3) legal certainty. However, government-led initiatives have been set aside in the EU, in favour of a coordinated strategy that involves commitments from both private market participants and government authorities (see Giovannini *et al.*, 2008).

Integration of national systems may bring about various benefits. Among other things, opportunities to exploit economies of scale and scope and increased competition have the potential to lower the cost of post-trading activities and lead to a more efficient allocation of capital, thereby furthering economic growth (see Chapter 1). According to Schulze and Baur (2006), a more efficient EU post-trading system, leading to a lowering of transaction costs of 7–18 per cent, could result in a higher level of GDP (on average between 0.2 and 0.6 per cent).

Single Euro Payments Area

For retail payment systems, the introduction of the Single Euro Payments Area (SEPA) has the potential to remove a number of barriers discussed in the previous section. SEPA is a market-led initiative that aims to ensure that there are no longer any differences between national and cross-border payments within the euro area. It should give payment service providers the opportunity to benefit from economies of scale and scope.

SEPA is not merely aimed at improving the processing efficiency of the modest volumes of cross-border payments (EPC, 2006). It will lead to a major changeover of national payment markets in the euro area, as it will introduce new, common business rules and technical standards. Consequently, all electronic payments will be affected and existing national credit transfers, direct debits, and card payments will be phased out and gradually migrate to interoperable formats and processes. As of 2008, the new SEPA payment instruments (credit transfers, direct debits, and cards) operate alongside existing national processes, with sufficient critical mass expected to be achieved within a few years, making SEPA irreversible. After the full transition, purely national payment instruments will no longer exist. Next to this, the European banking community has defined a framework for the clearing and settlement of payments in SEPA. The framework defines the principles that infrastructure providers must comply with to ensure that they can process SEPA credit transfers and direct debits.

The ECB and the European Commission support the continued self-regulation by the industry. However, given the importance and size of the social and economic benefits of SEPA, the European Commission indicated that it reserves the right to introduce or propose necessary legislation to achieve it. As migration to SEPA products was lagging behind, the European Commission presented a legislative proposal in 2010 setting an end date for SEPA migration, thereby providing legal certainty, encouraging SEPA investment, and avoiding the cost of operating dual payments systems. At the time of writing, this proposal was being discussed by the European Parliament and the European Council.

Post-trading process: Code of Conduct and TARGET2-Securities

After calls from the European Commission to resolve the problems of EU cross-border clearings and settlement, the trading and post-trading infrastructure providers presented a Code of Conduct on Clearing and Settlement in 2006. The Code aims to enhance transparency and increase competition in the post-trading sector. For that purpose, the Code includes measures aimed at ensuring price transparency, access and interoperability, unbundling and accounting separation, and an independent monitoring process.

Next to this, the ESCB is working on an initiative to establish TARGET2-Securities (T2S), i.e. a platform for the cross-border and domestic settlement of securities against central bank money. According to ECB (2006), the objective of TARGET2-Securities is to maximise safety and efficiency in the settlement of euro-denominated securities transactions. Safety is achieved by making use of a delivery versus payment mechanism, while efficiency is strengthened by settling cash and securities on the same IT platform. The T2S project was initiated in 2006 and is scheduled to go live in 2014.

Post-trading: over-the-counter (OTC) derivatives

A derivative is a contract between two parties linked to the future value or status of the underlying to which it refers, e.g. the development of interest rates or of a currency value, or the possible bankruptcy of a debtor (European Commission, 2010). A derivative which is not traded on an exchange, but instead privately negotiated between two counterparts, is referred to as an over-the-counter (OTC) derivative (see Chapter 5).

The use of derivatives has grown significantly over the last decade. At the end of December 2009, the size of the OTC derivatives market by notional value equalled approximately $615 trillion, a 12 per cent increase with respect to the end of 2008. However, this was 10 per cent lower than the peak reached in June 2008.

The financial crisis of 2007–2009 highlighted the shortcomings in the functioning of the OTC derivatives market, where 80 per cent of derivatives are traded. In particular, participants in the OTC derivatives market do not collect sufficient collateral to mitigate counterparty credit risk, which refers to the risk of loss arising from one party not making the required payments when they are due.

Against this background, the European Commission (2010) launched a legislative initiative requiring standardised OTC derivatives to be cleared through central counterparties (CCPs). Since an OTC derivative contract cleared by a CCP usually involves the posting of higher amounts of collateral than an equivalent contract that is not cleared by a CCP, this will increase the amount of collateral held in the system (European Commission, 2010).

As collateral will be held in a few places, there is an argument that risk will be concentrated there. To avoid CCPs becoming a source of risk to the financial system in themselves, CCPs should be subject to stringent conduct of business, organisational and prudential requirements so that risks are properly managed. Furthermore, CCPs should have access to adequate liquidity. Such liquidity could result from access to central bank or to creditworthy and reliable commercial bank liquidity, or a combination of both.

In addition, policy initiatives have been launched to increase transparency in OTC derivative markets and reduce operational risk within CCPs.

7.4 Conclusions

Payment systems are composed of instruments, procedures, and transfer systems that ensure the transfer of money from one economic actor to the other. Relatively low-value and non-urgent mass payments are processed through retail payment systems, while wholesale payment systems process large-value and/or high-priority payments between financial institutions.

In securities markets, the clearing and settlement (or post-trading) process provides for the transfer of ownership and payment between buyers and sellers of securities. This process can be divided into four main activities: (1) the confirmation of terms of the trade as agreed by the buyer and the seller, (2) clearance, by which the respective obligations of the buyer and seller are established, (3) the transfer of the securities from the seller to the buyer, and (4) the transfer of funds from the buyer to the seller.

Payment and securities market infrastructures are characterised by economies of scale and scope, and network externalities. This means that the average costs of payment and post-trading services may fall considerably when the current fragmentation of EU financial infrastructures is overcome. In this respect, the introduction of SEPA should allow providers of payment services to benefit from economies of scale and scope, thereby increasing overall economic efficiency.

The integration of EU large-value payment systems has been quite remarkable, while retail payment systems and post-trading processes remain fragmented thus far. The latter has resulted in large variations in fees and higher costs and risks for cross-border transactions. Different initiatives have been launched to remove existing barriers for integration in these markets. In this respect, the ECB has played a prominent role.

NOTES

1 *Surcharging* refers to the situation in which a merchant passes on the costs of a payment by charging a fee for the use of the card. However, in most card networks the merchants are prohibited from applying higher prices to card transactions.

2 Examples of ICSDs are Euroclear and Clearstream International.

3 Netting can be carried out on either a bilateral or a multilateral basis. While bilateral netting is an arrangement between only two parties to net their bilateral obligations, multilateral netting is arithmetically achieved by summing each participant's bilateral

net positions with those of the other participants to arrive at a multilateral net position vis-à-vis all other participants (Kazarian, 2006).

4   Although the curves in Figure 7.8 are not average costs curves, they give a fair reflection of how payment unit costs change with payment volume. The curves refer to estimates for three different years.

SUGGESTED READING

Freixas, X. and C. Holthausen (2008), European Integration of Payment Systems, in: X. Freixas, P. Hartmann, and C. Mayer (eds.), *Handbook of European Financial Markets and Institutions*, Oxford University Press, 436–450.

Giovannini, A., J. Berrigan, and D. Russo (2008), Post-trading Services and European Securities Markets, in: X. Freixas, P. Hartmann, and C. Mayer (eds.), *Handbook of European Financial Markets and Institutions*, Oxford University Press, 540–567.

Kazarian, E. G. (2006), Integration of the Securities Market Infrastructure in the European Union: Policy and Regulatory Issues, IMF Working Paper 06/241.

Serifsoy, B. and M. Weiß (2007), Settling for Efficiency – A Framework for the European Securities Transaction Industry, *Journal of Banking and Finance*, 31, 3034–3057.

REFERENCES

Bank for International Settlements (1992), *Delivery Versus Payment in Securities Settlement Systems*, BIS, Basel.

(2001), *BIS Glossary No. 7*, BIS, Basel.

(2002a), *Policy Issues for Central Banks in Retail Payments*, BIS, Basel.

(2002b), *BIS Quarterly Review December 2002 – International Banking and Financial Market Developments*, BIS, Basel.

(2006), *General Guidance for National Payment System Development*, BIS, Basel.

Bergman, M., G. Guibourg, and B. Segendorf (2007), The Costs of Paying – Private and Social Costs of Cash and Card Payments, Sveriges Riksbank Working Paper 212.

Bolt, W. (2007), Retail Payments and Card Use in the Netherlands: Pricing, Scale, and Antitrust, *Competition Policy International*, 3(1), 257–270.

Bolt, W. and D. Humphrey (2007), Payment network scale economies, SEPA, and cash replacement, *Review of Network Economics*, 6(4), 453–473.

Bolt, W. and A. Tieman (2007), Heavily skewed pricing in two-sided market, *International Journal of Industrial Organisation*, 26(5), 1250–1255.

Brits, H. and C. Winder (2005), Payments Are No Free Lunch, De Nederlandsche Bank Occasional Studies, 3, No. 2.

Capgemini (2010), *World Payments Report*.

Deutsche Börse Group (2005), The European Post-Trade Market – An Introduction, White Paper.

Economides, N. (1993), Network Economics with Application to Finance, *Financial Markets, Institutions & Instruments*, 2(5), 89–97.

(1996), The Economics of Networks, *International Journal of Industrial Organization*, 16(4), 673–699.

Economides, N. and C. Himmelberg (1995), Critical Mass and Network Evolution in Telecommunications, in: G. Brock (ed.), *Toward a Comprehensive Telecommunications Industry: Selected Papers from the 1994 Telecommunications Policy Research Conference*, Lawrence Erlbaum Associates, New Jersey.

European Central Bank (2006), Speech by J.-M. Godeffroy: 'Ten Frequently Asked Questions About TARGET2-Securities' on 20 September 2006 at the British Bankers Association, London. Available at: www.ecb.int/paym/t2s/defining/outgoing/html/10faq.en.html (accessed 13 February 2012).

(2007), *Financial Stability Review*, ECB, Frankfurt am Main.

(2010), *A Single Currency – An Integrated Market Infrastructure* (T2, T2S, CCBM2, SEPA), ECB, Frankfurt am Main.

European Commission (2005), Annex to the Proposal for a Directive of the European Parliament and of the Council on Payment Services in the Internal Market – Impact Assessment, EC, Brussels.

(2007), *Report on the Retail Sector Inquiry*, EC, Brussels.

(2010), *Commission Proposal on OTC Derivatives and Market Infrastructures*, EC, Brussels.

European Payment Council (2006), *Making SEPA a Reality – Implementing the Single Euro Payments Area*, EPC, Brussels.

Freixas, X. and C. Holthausen (2008), European Integration of Payment Systems, in: X. Freixas, P. Hartmann, and C. Mayer (eds.), *Handbook of European Financial Markets and Institutions*, Oxford University Press, 436–450.

Giovannini, A., J. Berrigan, and D. Russo (2008), Post-trading Services and European Securities Markets, in: X. Freixas, P. Hartmann, and C. Mayer (eds.), *Handbook of European Financial Markets and Institutions*, Oxford University Press, 540–567.

Giovannini Group (2001), *Cross-Border Clearing and Settlement Arrangements in the European Union*, Brussels, November.

Harper, I., S. Rimes, and C. Malam (2006), The Development of Electronic Payment Systems, in: R. Cooper, G. Madden, A. Lloyd, and M. Schipp (eds.), *The Economics of Online Markets and ICT Networks*, Springer, New York, 25–40.

Humphrey, D. B., M. Willesson, T. Lindblom, and G. Bergendahl (2003), What Does It Cost to Make a Payment?, *Review of Network Economics*, June, 159–174.

Kazarian, E. G. (2006), Integration of the Securities Market Infrastructure in the European Union: Policy and Regulatory Issues, IMF Working Paper 06/241.

Khiaonarong, T. (2003), Payment Systems Efficiency, Policy Approaches, and the Role of the Central Bank, Bank of Finland Discussion Paper 1.

Lannoo, K. and M. Levin (2001), The Securities Settlement Industry in the EU – Structure, Costs and the Way Forward, CEPS Research Report.

London Stock Exchange/Oxera (2002), Clearing and Settlement in Europe – Response to the first report of the Giovannini Group.

NERA Economic Consulting (2004), The Direct Costs of Clearing and Settlement: An EU–US Comparison, City Research Series 1.

Rochet, J.-C. and J. Tirole (2006), Two-Sided Markets: A Progress Report, *The RAND Journal of Economics*, 35(3), 645–667.

Salo, S. (2006), Promoting Integration of European Retail Payment Systems: Role of Competition, Cooperation and Regulation, paper presented at the SUERF Seminar The Adoption of the Euro in New Member States: Challenges and Vulnerabilities on the Last Stretch, Malta, 4 May.

Schmiedel, H. and A. Schönenberg (2005), Integration of Securities Market Infrastructure in the Euro Area, European Central Bank Occasional Paper 33.

Schulze, N. and D. Baur (2006), Annex II of Economic Impact Study on Clearing and Settlement, EC, Brussels. Available at: http://ec.europa.eu/internal_market/financial-markets/docs/clearing/draft/annex_2_En.pdf (accessed 13 February 2012).

Serifsoy, B. and M. Weiß (2007), Settling for Efficiency – A Framework for the European Securities Transaction Industry, *Journal of Banking and Finance*, 31, 3034–3057.

Shy, O. (2001), *The Economics of Network Industries*, Cambridge University Press, New York.

8

Financial Innovation

The financial sector performs two main functions: (1) reducing information and transaction costs, and (2) facilitating the trading, diversification, and management of risk. Financial innovation ensures that the financial system can provide these functions more efficiently. Financial innovation is the act of creating and then popularising new financial instruments, as well as new financial technologies, institutions, and markets. As such, financial innovation can play an important role in fostering growth and economic prosperity. At the same time, financial innovations have been blamed for their role in the recent financial crisis. This chapter discusses the causes and consequences of financial innovation.

Two important drivers of financial innovation are regulation and deregulation, and technological advances. Regulation may forbid or otherwise restrain financial innovation so that deregulation may spur innovation. At the same time, several innovations have been the results of attempts to circumvent regulation. Technological advances made new instruments possible. The credit card is a good example of financial innovation driven by technological advance, including improvements in communications, data management, and credit scoring.

Financial innovations may improve payments, offer new savings and investment opportunities, and may increase risk sharing. The first part of this chapter examines the causes and consequences of financial innovation, while the second part analyses the pros and cons of financial innovation. This chapter also zooms in on the risks of financial innovation by offering two case studies. One of these case studies is about securitisation of subprime mortgages. Credit rating agencies (CRAs) play an important role in securitisations. The final part of this chapter therefore explains the recent debate about CRAs and outlines the recently introduced regulation of CRAs in Europe.

After you have studied this chapter, you should be able to:
- explain the causes and consequences of financial innovation
- understand the advantages and disadvantages of financial innovation
- explain the risks of financial innovation and the impact on financial fragility
- understand the role of credit rating agencies.

8.1 Financial innovation: causes and consequences

Financial innovation is the act of creating and then popularising new financial instruments, as well as new financial technologies, institutions, and markets. Financial innovations are sometimes divided into product or process innovations. Product innovations are exemplified by new derivative contracts, new corporate securities, or new forms of pooled investment products, while process improvements are typified by new means of distributing securities, processing transactions, or pricing transactions. In practice, however, this differentiation is not clear, because process and product innovations are often linked (Lerner and Tufano, 2011).

Financial innovation differs from other types of new product development in several ways (Lerner and Tufano, 2011). First, the financial system is highly interconnected. As a result, a financial innovation is likely to generate a complex web of externalities, both positive and negative. Therefore, assessing the social consequences of financial innovation can be very challenging. Second, financial innovations are very dynamic. As an innovation diffuses from pioneering adopters to more general users, these products frequently change in their underlying structure, the way that they are marketed, and how they are used. These transformations mean that the consequences of an innovation may change over time. Finally, many forms of innovation, such as pharmaceuticals, are subject to regulation. But the regulation of new financial products and services is particularly complex. This may ultimately lead to a cat-and-mouse game between the regulator and the industry, with several rounds of reregulation.

As explained in Chapter 1, the financial sector performs two main functions: (1) reducing information and transaction costs, and (2) facilitating the trading, diversification, and management of risk. Financial innovations enhance the efficiency of the financial system to provide these functions better. For instance, they provide households with new choices for investment and consumption and reduce the costs of raising and deploying funds. Similarly, financial innovations may enable firms to raise capital in larger amounts and at a lower cost than they could otherwise. At the same time, financial innovations have been blamed for the recent crisis (see Chapter 2). In one of his columns in the *New York Times*, Nobel Prize laureate Paul Krugman (2007) writes:

[T]he innovations of recent years – the alphabet soup of C.D.O.s and S.I.V.s, R.M.B.S. and A.B.C.P. – were sold on false pretences. They were promoted as ways to spread risk, making investment safer. What they did instead – aside from making their creators a lot of money, which they didn't have to repay when it all went bust – was to spread confusion, luring investors into taking on more risk than they realised.

This section reviews the literature on financial innovation, mainly drawing on Lerner and Tufano (2011) and Litan (2010). We focus on the consequences of financial innovation, but will first briefly dwell upon the causes of financial innovation.

Causes of financial innovation

Where does financial innovation come from? Generally, financial innovation is driven by investor demand for a particular set of cash flows. Intermediaries recognise this demand and engineer securities with the desired characteristics. By splitting up or combining cash flows of existing securities, the intermediaries can create profits for themselves and may increase social welfare (Lerner and Tufano, 2011). In the model of financial innovation of Gennaioli *et al.* (in press), a financial innovation can address the demand for clients for a particular set of cash flows and thus be socially beneficial. But these authors suggest that these investors may systematically underestimate the risks associated with these new products' cash flows. Once the investors suddenly realise these risks, there will be an exodus back to traditional, safer products. In this way, financial innovation can add to the fragility of the overall financial system.

Two particularly important drivers of innovation have been financial regulation and technological change. Regulation is one of the main drivers of financial innovation. This can be illustrated by the differences in the development of so-called *Exchange Traded Funds* (ETFs) between the US and Europe that will be explained in more detail in section 8.3. ETFs are investment vehicles that track an index (e.g. S&P 500). Whereas in Europe synthetic ETFs have developed very rapidly, in the US physical ETFs are dominant. *Physical ETFs* replicate the index by simply reconstituting the basket of physical securities underlying the index. *Synthetic ETFs* obtain the desired return through entering into an asset swap instead of replicating the index physically. One of the main factors explaining the difference between the US and Europe is difference in regulation. In Europe, regulators take a more liberal stance on the use of derivatives in investment funds. In contrast, the US regulator has adopted a more conservative approach, limiting de facto the development of synthetic ETFs (FSB, 2011).

However, generally the relationship between financial innovation and regulation is complex. Innovators look for opportunities that exploit regulatory gaps. A good example is that bank capital rules have encouraged banks to use off-balance sheet vehicles (see Chapter 2). So regulation may give rise to certain innovations, but then regulators frequently 'catch up' with the products, in a cat-and-mouse process. Under the new bank capital rules, opportunities for banks for using off-balance sheet vehicles have recently been limited. However, even a well-staffed regulatory agency is up against a world of potential entrepreneurs and innovators. Inevitably, regulation will therefore tend to react to innovations with a lag (Lerner and Tufano, 2011).

On the technological front, advances in information technology made the low-cost collection, processing, and dissemination of household and business financial data possible. This, in turn, allows for ever-faster evaluation of creditworthiness, identification of prospective borrowers, and management of existing accounts. A good example of how this may lead to financial innovation is the credit card (Bernanke, 2009). From the consumer's perspective, credit cards provide convenience, facilitate recordkeeping, and offer security from loss.

Consequences of financial innovation

Financial innovations may improve payments, offer new savings and investment opportunities, and may increase risk sharing. Drawing on Litan (2010), we will illustrate these consequences of financial innovation in turn. While most financial products described below are analysed throughout the book (e.g. derivatives in Chapter 5, payments in Chapter 7, and investments in Chapter 9), they are here analysed from the perspective of innovating the functions of the financial system.

Financial innovations: payments

Although the invention of the ATM machine was revolutionary, it was the advent of the networked ATM more than the machine itself that proved to be most useful for consumers. Once ATMs were networked, bank customers were free from not only having to wait in line at a bank, but in fact could get money any time across a wide geographical area. Clearly, ATMs have broadened access to financial services and been a major source of convenience for consumers. Moreover, by eliminating the need for tellers to dispense cash or take deposits, ATMs also have clearly improved productivity in the banking sector.

Another example of an innovation that has made payments easier are credit cards. They not only have become a means of payment, but also a source of credit. More recently, credit cards (along with newer forms of payment, such as PayPal, which are linked to credit cards) have found another use as an important form of payment for online purchases. They permit consumers both to pay and to borrow at the same time and enable consumers to pay without cash, and thus to reduce trips to the bank and/ or ATMs. They also offer a safer way to pay for things than money (which can be stolen).

Debit cards – which automatically deduct a customer's payment at a retail establishment from his or her bank account – are a natural outgrowth of both ATMs and credit cards. After the debit feature was added to ATM cards and as more merchants accepted debit transactions, debit cards grew in popularity.

The Internet has drastically changed the way consumers and businesses buy, and pay for, goods and services. Internet banking has enabled consumers to make payments or use other banking services anywhere in the world, at any moment. In addition, mobile and contactless payments are starting to take off, providing customers with new means of payments.

Financial innovations: savings and investments

Over the last four decades there has been a proliferation of new ways to save, like *mutual funds*. Mutual funds pool the savings of many small investors by selling them shares in the fund and using the proceeds to buy equity, bonds, money market instruments, or other securities. Mutual funds allow investors to buy or redeem shares on a daily basis at net asset value (NAV) that is calculated by dividing the fund's assets minus liabilities by the number of shares outstanding. This is usually calculated at the end of every trading day. There is a difference between *open-end* and *closed-end funds*. The shares of closed-end funds are listed on a stock exchange. Investors cannot sell their shares back to the fund as they can with an open-end fund but must sell their shares in the market. The price they receive may be significantly different from NAV. It may be at a 'premium', i.e. higher than net asset value, or, more commonly, at a 'discount', i.e. lower than net asset value. Open-end mutual funds have two advantages that contributed to the growth of mutual funds. First, as the fund agreed to redeem shares at any time, they are very liquid. Second, the open-end character allows the fund to grow as long as investors are willing to put money into the fund.

No doubt, mutual funds are one of the most successful financial innovations of the twentieth century, based on their growth rates, adoption rates, fraction of capital intermediated in the economy, or importance to household balance sheets (Lerner and Tufano, 2011).

One particular type of mutual funds are *money market funds* (MMFs). They gave ordinary people access to interest-bearing short-term assets that even had transaction-like features (one could write a cheque on them). MMFs came into being because of regulatory restrictions. In several countries banks were prohibited from paying interest on checking accounts. In addition, money market instruments can generally only be bought in large amounts. MMFs ingeniously avoided these restrictions and limitations by buying large batches of money market instruments and then sold shares to investors who could buy in with a limited amount of money.

Innovation also occurred in various kinds of financial limited partnerships: hedge funds, private equity funds, and venture capital funds. *Hedge funds* use investors' money to borrow still more money, and to make leveraged bets of various kinds, all in an effort to achieve for the investors a superior return adjusted for risk. The funds they use stem from so-called 'sophisticated investors' – wealthy individuals or institutions (pension funds or endowments). Hedge funds are like mutual funds, in that they place investors' money in markets for liquid financial instruments (stocks, bonds, derivatives). The liquid nature of their investments distinguishes hedge funds from *private equity funds*, which tend to buy large or controlling interests in companies, and to hold these positions for sale after several years. Today's typical private equity fund evolved from the leveraged buyout partnerships that were all the rage in the 1980s, and is still typically financed heavily with debt. According to Litan (2010), there is probably no more iconic financial innovation over the last four decades that has helped improve the allocation of savings towards productive investment than the rise of *venture capital funds*. The venture capital fund makes money by investing in young or emerging firms which usually have a novel technology or business model in high-technology industries. As these firms often have a limited operating history they cannot raise capital in the public markets and are unable to secure a bank loan.

One important financial innovation in the last two decades is the introduction of government bonds whose principal amounts are indexed to inflation. Such bonds were first sold by the British government in the 1980s; later also other governments have issued these instruments. Until such bonds were offered, investors had no (relatively) safe instrument that offered a hedge against inflation.

Financial innovations: risk sharing

A considerable portion of financial innovation over the past decades has come from the use of derivatives, which are financial contracts whose value is derived from some underlying asset. These assets can include equities, bonds, exchange rates, commodities, and residential and commercial mortgages. The more common forms of these contracts include options, forwards/futures, and swaps. The benefits of derivatives relate to:

(1) hedging and risk management;
(2) price discovery; and
(3) enhancement of liquidity.

As documented in Figure 5.15, the total value of derivatives in the world amounted to $650 trillion in 2010. This exceeds total global gross domestic product at $63 trillion in 2010 by a factor of ten. The use of financial derivatives has thus outpaced the real economy.

An innovation that is used overwhelmingly as a way of reallocating financial risks is the 'swap' arrangement. A swap is a contract arranging an exchange of cash flows between two parties. An *interest rate swap* involves the exchange of loan payments with a fixed rate of interest for another payment stream defined by a floating rate of interest. A *currency swap* involves the exchange of payments in different currencies (where both interest rates could be fixed, both variable, or one fixed and the other variable). Parties enter in such arrangements because they want to reduce or change their risk exposure from the assets on their balance sheets. Swaps enable them to do this without actually having to sell the underlying assets (Litan, 2010).

A more recent innovation is the *credit default swap* (CDS). It is an insurance instrument: the purchaser of a CDS receives money upon some defined event of default on a loan or a bond. The CDS market has become dominated by a handful of major banks, which use these instruments to hedge against the default of their borrowers, thereby reducing the amount of capital they are required to hold. Banks also trade these instruments among one other, for their own account or on behalf of customers who want to hedge against the possibility that their supplier or borrower might default, or speculate on this outcome.

A potential future innovation is *home equity insurance*. Shiller and Weiss (1999) have proposed insurance policies to enable individuals to protect themselves against the risks of declines in the prices of their homes, often people's most important asset. The risk of decline in the market value of homes is far greater than the risk of fire or other physical disaster; the potential significance of an insurance industry that protects market value of homes is much larger than that of the existing homeowner's property insurance industry. One predicate for this market is the creation of the Case–Shiller price index for real estate in major metropolitan areas of the US.

8.2 Pros and cons of financial innovation

In the aftermath of the 2007–2009 financial crisis, financial innovation has become controversial. Litan (2010) argues that there is a mix between good and bad financial innovations, although on balance he finds more good ones than bad ones. Individually and collectively, these innovations have improved access to credit, made life more convenient, and in some cases probably allowed the economy to grow faster. But some innovations, such as collateralised debt obligations (CDOs) and structured investment vehicles (SIVs) were poorly designed, while others, such as credit default swaps (CDSs) and adjustable rate mortgages, were misused and contributed to the financial crisis and/or amplified the downturn in the economy when it started.

Litan (2010) analyses the net impact of recent financial innovations, using three criteria:
(1) access to finance;
(2) convenience for users of financial services; and
(3) performance of productivity or total output.

This approach allows an impartial assessment of financial innovations. The fact that many financial innovations have been designed to get around financial regulation does not automatically make them bad. Indeed the opposite is true if the regulations are impeding productive activity. Some financial

Table 8.1 Net impact of recent financial innovations

	Access	Convenience	Productivity/GDP
Payments			
ATMs	++	++	+
Credit card expansion	++	++	+
Debit cards	++	++	+
Saving			
Money market funds	++	++	0
Exchange traded funds	+	+	0/+
Hedge funds	0	0	0/+
Private equity	0	0	+
Investment			
Credit scoring	++	++	0
Adjustable rate mortgages	++	+	-/ −
Asset-backed securities	++	++	-/+
CDOs*	++	++	−
SIVs*	++	++	−
Rise of venture capital	++	++	++ (but future not clear)
Risk bearing			
Options/futures exchanges	++	+	+/++
Interest/currency swaps	++	++	+/++
Credit default swaps	++	+	+

Notes: * The positive scores here were temporary.
Source: Litan (2010)

innovations have been useful for this purpose (Litan, 2010). Table 8.1 presents the net impact for financial products classified according to the different functions of finance (i.e. payments, saving, investment, risk bearing).

Most new financial products score positively on the criteria in Table 8.1. On the payments side, financial innovations have helped to move away from cash. On the saving side, new products offer more convenient, safer, and potentially rewarding ways of savings. According to Litan (2010), the net impact of money market funds (MMFs) on GDP is neutral, as it is not clear that MMFs benefit the economy. Hedge funds and private equity are organised as financial limited partnerships, and are therefore difficult to access for the mass. Private equity has a positive impact on economic growth. A typical private equity firm holds most of its investments longer than five years. While on average jobs fall at private equity-controlled firms during the first two years after they are acquired, employment grows thereafter. Moreover, private equity-controlled firms are good at controlling costs. Litan (2010) concludes that private equity contributes positively to productivity.

Moving to investment, credit scoring has improved banks' ability to assess credit risk. This allowed banks to price risk by reflecting it in the risk premium in the interest rate. Credit scoring has facilitated the extension of personal credit and credit to small businesses. While adjustable rate mortgages increase access to mortgages, they also add to the increase in overall household debt. In addition, underwriting standards on these mortgages were lapsing preceding the financial crisis. CDOs and SIVs permitted subprime mortgages to be originated and sold to investors, who did not fully appreciate the risks (see Chapter 2). This securitised mortgage credit allowed access and convenience to individuals who previously would not qualify for a regular mortgage. Cheap mortgage finance helped fuel the housing boom. The overall impact of the housing boom-bust is negative on GDP. Venture capital has helped to improve the allocation of savings to productive starts-ups, which have no access to bank loans or equity markets. So far, venture capital has financed the launch of famous companies, such as Google and Amazon, at an early stage. But venture capital investment is cyclical. In the aftermath of the financial crisis, the contribution of venture capital has dropped significantly.

Finally, derivatives help to spread or allocate risk to those most willing and able to bear it. Derivatives thus allow market participants and traders to manage their risks as well as to take positions. Putting aside the opportunities for traders and market makers in those instruments, derivatives enable firms producing real things in the economy to hedge risks, e.g. to lock in the price of oil, or the price they receive for their products, or to hedge against fluctuations in interest rates or currencies (Litan, 2010). Firms can thus reduce various financial risks to their businesses. This reduction risk may in turn lower their cost of capital. But it is important that firms have the financial skillls to understand the risk profile of derivatives. Otherwise derivatives may introduce unintended risks to their business.

Financial innovation and financial fragility

Financial innovation can turn into financial fragility. Some recent episodes of financial innovation share a common pattern (Gennaioli *et al.*, in press). It begins with a strong demand from investors for a particular, often safe, stream of cash flows. Some traditional securities in the market offer this pattern, but investors demand more, causing prices to rise. In response to demand, financial intermediaries create new securities offering the sought-after pattern of cash flows, usually by carving out of existing securities that are more risky. By virtue of diversification, tranching, insurance, and other forms of financial engineering, the new securities are believed by the investors, and often by the intermediaries themselves, to be good substitutes for the traditional ones. They are consequently issued and bought in great volumes.

At some point, news reveals that the new securities are vulnerable to some neglected risks, and in particular are not good substitutes for the traditional securities. Both investors and intermediaries are surprised by the news, and investors sell these false substitute securities, moving back to the traditional securities with the cash flows they seek. As investors fly for safety, financial institutions are stuck holding the supply of the new securities. The prices of traditional securities rise while those of the new ones fall sharply leading to financial fragility.

A recent example is the securitisation of subprime mortgages, which is discussed in section 8.3. Another example is the rise of money market funds (MMFs). The innovation of prime MMFs has arguably created much instability by giving investors the expectation of getting their money back on demand at par, even though it is invested in securities that are far from riskless. Gennaioli *et al.* (in press) suggest that it might be better to help investors form more realistic expectations by mandating that these funds be marked to market. With more realistic expectations of net asset value fluctuations, breaking the buck (i.e. suspending or stopping the return of money on demand at par) would no longer be a dramatic event that sparks a run on these funds and creates financial fragility.

When some risks are neglected, securities are over-issued. The reason is that neglected risks need not be laid off on intermediaries or other parties when manufacturing new securities. Investors thus end up bearing risk without recognising that they are doing so. Markets in new securities are fragile. A small piece of data that brings to investors' minds the previously unattended risks catches them by surprise, causes them to drastically revise their valuations of new securities, and to sell them in the market. The problem is more severe precisely because new securities have been over-issued.

Holmstrom (2010) illustrates the fragility of debt securities. As long as the value of the (underlying) assets is well above the default boundary (see Figure 8.1), the debt securities are perceived to be 'safe'. The value of securities is insensitive to new information. As Holmstrom (2010) puts it, 'the debt securities are fully liquid [in the information-insensitive region], there are no questions asked about the solvency'. Examples of such 'safe' securities are banknotes, US Treasuries, bank deposits, MMFs, and CDOs (prior to the emerging problems with subprime mortgages). Low volatility of the underlying

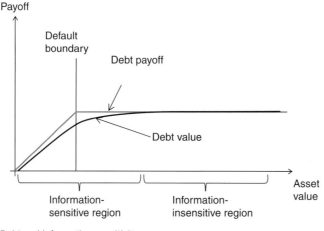

Payoff

Default
boundary

Debt payoff

Debt value

Asset
value

Information-
sensitive region

Information-
insensitive region

Figure 8.1   Debt and information sensitivity
Source: Holmstrom (2010)

collateral, such as mortgages, enhances the perceived safety. Once the assessment of the asset value drops towards the information-sensitive region in Figure 8.1 due to new information (on neglected risks), fragility comes into play. The safety of the debt securities starts to be questioned, and investors start to sell them off causing a drop in the value of these debt securities.

Gai *et al.* (2008) suggest that financial innovation and greater macroeconomic stability may have made financial crises in developed countries less likely than in the past. But should a crisis occur, its impact could be greater than was previously the case. Macroeconomic volatility is generally higher in developing countries than in advanced economies, but maximum loan-to-value ratios are invariably lower. Crises in emerging market economies should therefore be more frequent, but less severe than in developed countries. Hoggarth *et al.* (2002) find empirical evidence showing that crises in developed countries do indeed tend to be more costly than those in emerging market economies. While recent innovations have done damage, Box 8.1 suggests that the long-run story is that financial innovation is essential for economic growth.

8.3 Risks of financial innovation: two case studies

This section offers two case studies of financial innovation: first, one particular form of mutual funds, the so-called exchange traded funds, and second, the securitisation of subprime mortgages. We zoom in on the risks of these innovations.

Box 8.1 Financial innovation and long-run economic growth

According to Levine (2011), financial innovation is essential for growth. As firms become more complex, screening and monitoring firms becomes more difficult. Therefore, without corresponding innovations in finance that match the increases in complexity associated with economic growth, the quality of financial services diminishes, slowing economic growth. Several examples from history illustrate the crucial role of financial innovation in sustaining economic growth. Take the financial impediments to railroad expansion in the nineteenth century in the US. The novelty and complexity of railroads made pre-existing financial systems ineffective at screening and monitoring them. As only local investors with close ties to those operating the railroad provided capital for railroads during the early decades of this new technology, limited finance restricted growth. So financiers innovated. Specialised financiers and investment banks emerged to mobilise capital from individuals, to screen and invest in railroads, and to monitor the use of those investments. Based on their expertise and reputation, these investment banks mobilised funds from wealthy investors, evaluated proposals from railroads, allocated capital, and governed the operations of railroad companies for investors.

Another example provided by Levine (2011) is the information technology revolution of the twentieth century. As nascent high-tech information and communication firms struggled to emerge in the 1970s and 1980s, traditional commercial banks were reluctant to finance them because these new firms did not yet generate sufficient cash flows to cover loan payments. Furthermore, these firms were run by scientists with little experience in operating profitable companies. Conventional debt and equity markets were also wary because the technologies were too complex for investors to evaluate. Again, financiers innovated. Venture capital firms arose to screen entrepreneurs and provide technical, managerial, and financial advice to new high-technology firms. In many cases, venture capitalists had become wealthy through their own successful high-tech innovations, which provided a basis of expertise for evaluating and guiding new entrepreneurs. Venture capitalists typically took large, private equity stakes that established a long-term commitment to the enterprise, and they generally became active investors, taking seats on the board of directors and helping to solve managerial and financial problems.

A final example is the biotechnology revolution of the twenty-first century. Screening biotech firms is difficult because of the scientific breadth of biotechnologies, which frequently require inputs from biologists, chemists, geneticists, engineers, biuroboticists, as well as experts on the myriad of laws, regulations, and commercial barriers associated with successfully bringing new medical products to market. It was unfeasible to house all of this expertise in banks or venture capital firms. Yet again, financiers innovated. They formed new financial partnerships with the one kind of organisation with the breadth of skills to screen biotech firms – large pharmaceutical companies. Pharmaceutical companies employ, or are in regular contact with, a large assortment of scientists and engineers, have close connections with those delivering medical products to customers, and employ lawyers versed in drug regulations. According to Levine (2011), improvements in diagnostic and surgical procedures, prosthetic devices, parasite-resistant crops, and other innovations linked to biotechnology would almost certainly be occurring at a far slower pace without financial innovation.

Source: Levine (2011)

Exchange traded funds

Exchange traded funds (ETFs) are investment vehicles that track an index (e.g. S&P 500), trade continuously on exchanges, and are redeemable daily. So they offer low-cost diversification and liquidity and tradability. As there is a direct link between the security and its underlying components, ETFs do not require fund managers to choose securities. As a result, ETFs tend to have lower fees than other mutual funds. Like mutual funds, ETFs come in two forms: (1) unit investment trusts, which are like closed-end mutual funds in that they have a fixed number of shares, and (2) open-ended ETFs, which issue new shares as more investors want to invest in them. Most ETFs are listed on US and European exchanges, but they provide exposure to a much more diverse range of markets. For example, two of the three largest ETFs track emerging market indices. Since ETFs are traded on an exchange, investors can buy them as long as the exchange is open rather than being able to buy them only at the close of the market each day, as is the case with mutual funds. As ETFs are like stocks, investors must pay brokerage fees to purchase them and they must be purchased in a fixed number of shares (typically in round lots of a hundred). At the end of Q3 2010, the global ETF industry had $1.2 trillion in assets under management (see Figure 8.2). It has grown at an average of 40 per cent a year over the past ten years (FSB, 2011).

As Figure 8.2 shows, there are two types of ETFs. *Physical ETFs* replicate the index by simply reconstituting the basket of physical securities underlying the index (e.g. the basket of S&P 500 stocks) with appropriate weights. They are the dominant form of ETF, especially in the US, and are mainly provided by large independent asset managers. *Synthetic ETFs* obtain the desired return through entering into an asset swap, i.e. an OTC derivative, instead of

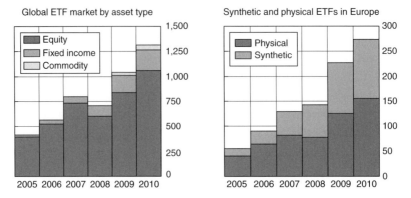

Global ETF market by asset type

Synthetic and physical ETFs in Europe

Figure 8.2   The ETF market: main characteristics and recent trends ($ billion)
Source: FSB (2011)

replicating the index physically. They have developed very rapidly in Europe to reach 45 per cent of that market (FSB, 2011). They are typically provided by asset management arms of banks. According to the FSB (2011), one factor supporting their growth resides in the synergies created within banking groups if the derivative trading desk acts as swap counterparty to the asset management arm providing the ETF. Another factor is the more liberal stance of European regulation on the use of derivatives in investment funds, while the US regulator has adopted a more conservative approach, limiting de facto the development of synthetic ETFs.

In a synthetic ETF (see Figure 8.3), the provider (typically a bank) sells ETF shares to investors in exchange for cash, which is then invested in a collateral basket, the return of which is swapped by the derivatives desk of the same bank for the return of an index. Since the swap counterparty is typically the bank also acting as ETF provider, investors may be exposed if the bank defaults. Therefore, problems at those banks that are most active in swap-based ETFs may constitute a powerful source of contagion and systemic risk. As there is no requirement for the collateral composition to match the assets of the tracked index, the synthetic ETF creation process may be driven by the possibility for the bank to raise funding against an illiquid portfolio that cannot otherwise be financed in the repo market (FSB, 2011).

Securitisation of subprime mortgages

Until the financial crisis, the benefits of securitisation had been unquestioned. Securitisation is the technology which encouraged unbundling of the

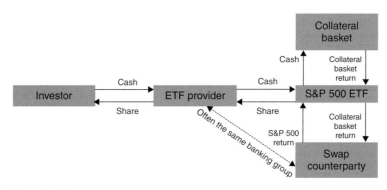

Figure 8.3   Simplified functioning of a synthetic ETF on the S&P 500
Source: FSB (2011)

production processes for many credit services, permitting separate financial institutions to originate, service, fund, and assume the credit or market risks of a portfolio of loans or other assets (Greenspan, 1997). Numerous types of assets were routinely securitised, including residential mortgages, commercial mortgages, auto loans, and credit card loans. By bundling illiquid loans into packages on which securities could be issued, securitisation was thought to considerably expand the supply of funds available for lending and to distribute the risks of lending throughout the financial system.

As pointed out by Litan (2010), the main reason that securitisation now has a bad name is because of the financial mutation known as the collateralised debt obligations (CDOs). CDOs permitted subprime mortgages to be originated and sold to investors because of an innovation in the way investors were paid. Subprime is lending to individuals with a high level of default risk, because they have a low income or a less than perfect credit history relative to the standards of 'prime' borrowers. The share of subprime in origination of all mortgages rose steadily between 2001 and 2006, from 7.2 to 20.1 per cent. When housing prices started declining while interest increased, losses on these loans rapidly increased. According to recent estimates, these losses amounted to $1.4 trillion in the course of 2008. Although these losses were huge, their magnitude was by no means unprecedented – the losses from the dotcom crash wiped out $5 trillion in the market value of technology companies between March 2000 and October 2002.

What led to the subsequent financial turmoil was the securitisation of these mortgages. Instead of passing through the principal and interest payments made on the underlying mortgages directly to all holders of the securities, as was common for MBSs, the CDO divides securities purchasers into groups or 'tranches' with different risks. The CDO structures a 'waterfall' of payments that flows first to the most risk-averse investors, and then in stages, to investors with higher risk appetites. To provide additional comfort to investors, especially those in the first tranche, insurance is often arranged via, for instance, credit default swaps (CDSs). By structuring the payments in a waterfall-like fashion and layering them with insurance, issuers of CDOs were able to take subprime mortgages that otherwise separately would have received low ratings by the ratings agencies, and to repurpose them into higher-rated securities, whose first tranche even typically received an AAA. CDOs were often purchased at market value by off-balance sheet vehicles.

As pointed out by Gorton (2008), when the housing price bubble burst, this chain of securities, derivatives, and off-balance sheet vehicles was so complicated that most investors could not determine the location and size of the risks. For CDO investors and investors in other financial instruments that have CDO tranches in their portfolios, it was impossible to penetrate the chain backwards and value the chain based on the underlying mortgages, i.e. information was lost because of the difficulty of penetrating to the core assets. In a similar fashion, it was impossible for those at the start of the chain to use their information to value the chain 'upwards'. So due to the complexity of the financial instruments that were sold, it was unclear who was actually affected by losses on these instruments and to what extent.

8.4 Credit rating agencies

Functions

Since John Moody started in 1909 with a small rating book, the rating business has developed into a multi-billion-dollar industry. Credit rating agencies (CRAs) play an important role in financial markets through the production of credit risk information and its distribution to market participants. CRAs essentially provide two services. First, they offer an independent assessment of the ability of issuers to meet their debt obligations, thereby providing 'information services' that reduce information costs, increase the pool of potential borrowers, and promote liquid markets. Second, they offer 'monitoring services' through which they influence issuers to take corrective actions to avert downgrades via 'watch' procedures.

CRAs have come under attack due to their role in the recent financial crisis. According to many observers, CRAs underestimated the credit risk associated with structured credit products. For instance, more than three-quarters of all private residential mortgage-backed securities issued in the United States from 2005 to 2007 that were rated AAA by Standard & Poor's are now rated below BBB–, i.e. below investment grade (IMF, 2010).

According to the Financial Stability Forum (2008), poor credit assessments of complex structured credit products by CRAs contributed to both the build-up and the unfolding of the financial crisis. With the benefit of hindsight, it is widely believed that CRAs assigned high ratings to complex structured subprime debt based on inadequate historical data and in some cases flawed models. Structured credit products are designed to take advantage of different risk preferences of investors. They are therefore structured for each tranche to achieve a particular credit rating. CRAs generally give these first tranches the highest ratings possible. If during this structuring process CRAs discuss with issuers the rating implications of particular structures, there is a clear potential for conflicts of interest. These conflicts are exacerbated when CRAs also sell consulting services to entities that purchase ratings. Investors have arguably over-relied on CRA ratings, not realising that an AAA rating of a structured instrument is very different from an AAA rating of, say, a government bond.

CRAs have also come under fire for their sovereign rating activities. CRAs were condemned for exacerbating the recent European debt crisis when they downgraded the countries in the midst of the financial turmoil, thereby exacerbating the fiscal problems of countries like Greece, Ireland, Portugal, and Spain. According to Barroso (2010), the President of the European Commission, 'ratings appear to be too cyclical, too reliant on the general market mood rather than on fundamentals – regardless of whether market mood is too optimistic or too pessimistic'.

CRAs assess credit risk of borrowers (governments, financial, and non-financial firms). A credit rating can be defined as an opinion regarding the creditworthiness of an entity, a debt or financial obligation, debt security, preferred share or other financial instrument, or of an issuer of such a debt or financial obligation, debt security, preferred share or other financial instrument, issued using an established and defined ranking system of rating categories. A rating only refers to the credit risk; other risks, like market risk (the risk due to unfavourable movements in market prices) or liquidity risk (the risk that a given security or asset cannot be traded quickly enough in the market to prevent a loss) are not covered.

There are around 150 CRAs, but the three largest competitors share roughly 95 per cent of the market. Standard & Poor's Ratings Services and

Interpretation	Fitch and S&P	Moody's
Highest quality	AAA	Aaa
High quality	AA+	Aa1
	AA	Aa2
	AA–	Aa3
Strong payment capacity	A+	A1
	A	A2
	A–	A3
Adequate payment capacity	BBB+	Baa1
	BBB	Baa2
	BBB–	Baa3
Likely to fulfil obligations, ongoing uncertainty	BB+	Ba1
	BB	Ba2
	BB–	Ba3
High-risk obligations	B+	B1
	B	B2
	B–	B3
Vulnerable to default	CCC+	Caa1
	CCC	Caa2
	CCC–	Caa3
Near or in bankruptcy or default	CC	Ca
	C	C
	D	D

Figure 8.4   Credit ratings
Source: IMF (2010)

Moody's Investors Service each have 40 per cent of the market while Fitch Ratings holds 15 per cent (White, 2010). While most CRAs are regional or product-type specialists, the three biggest players are truly global and broad in their product coverage. What is more, the sovereign rating coverage of the big three dwarfs that of other CRAs. As of 30 July 2010, Standard & Poor's rated 125 sovereigns, Moody's 110, and Fitch 107 (IMF, 2010).

Credit ratings are expressed on a scale of letters and figures (see Figure 8.4). The Standard & Poor's rating scale is, for example, as follows: AAA (highest rating), AA, A, BBB, BB, B, CCC, CC, C, D (lowest rating). Modifiers are attached to further distinguish ratings within classification. Whereas Fitch and Standard & Poor's use pluses and minuses, Moody's uses numbers. CRAs typically signal in advance their intention to consider rating changes, using 'outlooks' and rating reviews (so-called 'watchlists'). Whereas outlooks represent agencies' opinions on the development of a credit rating over the medium term, watchlists focus on a much shorter time horizon – three months, on average. The watch and outlook procedures are considered to be generally strong predictors of rating changes relative to other public data.

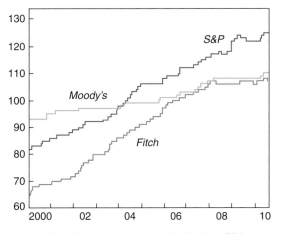

Figure 8.5   Total number of sovereigns rated by the big three CRAs
Source: IMF (2010)

Ratings play a crucial role in financial markets as investors use them to evaluate the credit risk of financial instruments. The assessment of these instruments requires specific knowledge and is highly time-consuming, making it attractive for individual investors to rely on the rating of the CRAs. The ratings have an important influence on the interest rate that borrowers have to pay. A downgrading generally leads quickly to a higher interest rate on loans. Portfolio manager performance is often benchmarked against standard indices that are usually constructed on the basis of credit ratings. This implies that a downgrade to below the investment-grade threshold (i.e. BBB-) often triggers immediate liquidation.

CRAs are mainly financed on the basis of an issuer-based compensation scheme, meaning that the agencies are paid by the issuers of these instruments to publish a rating. This may give agencies an incentive to overstate the creditworthiness of a particular product in order to build a good relationship with the issuer, thereby creating a conflict of interest. On the other hand, CRAs must safeguard their credibility with investors as their ratings would otherwise be of no value in the market. Yet, it is doubtful whether the potential loss of reputation sufficiently restrains CRAs and can indeed function as an effective form of sanction. CRAs may be manipulated by issuers which shop for a rating.

Sovereign credit ratings are an assessment by rating agencies of a government's ability and willingness to repay its public debt both in principal and in interests on time. These ratings are thus forward-looking qualitative measures of the probability of default. Figure 8.5 shows that the three major CRAs publish credit ratings for a high and increasing number of sovereigns.

Regulating CRAs

Until recently, CRAs were mainly governed by the International Organisation of Securities Commissions (IOSCO), which sets international standards for security markets. These standards come in the shape of the 'Code for Conduct Fundamentals for Credit Rating Agencies' (IOSCO code), which has been updated in the wake of the global financial crisis. However, this code is based on voluntary compliance and lacks enforcement mechanisms (self-regulation). CRAs were supposed to follow the code or explain why they did not do so (comply or explain). In the wake of the financial crisis, the EU has introduced regulation for CRAs, focusing on registration, enhanced oversight, and transparency. While the European Commission considers the revised IOSCO code to be 'the global benchmark', it maintained that its substance had to be made more specific, to make it easier to apply in practice, and more efficient. Therefore, it proposed a Regulation on Credit Rating Agencies (1060/2009/EC) that has been accepted by the Council and the European Parliament.

The newly created European Securities and Markets Authority (ESMA) is, among other things, responsible for the registration and ongoing supervision of registered credit rating agencies. The ESMA is an independent EU Authority that contributes to safeguarding the stability of the European Union's financial system by ensuring the integrity, transparency, efficiency, and orderly functioning of securities markets, as well as enhancing investor protection (see Chapter 12).

Under the EU Regulation, ratings for structured finance instruments must ensure that those credit rating categories that are attributed to structured finance instruments are clearly differentiated using a symbol, which distinguishes them from rating categories used for any other entities, financial instruments, or financial obligations. This should make it clear to investors that the ratings of structured finance instruments are different from the ratings of other financial instruments. CRAs are also obliged to disclose the methodologies, models, and key rating assumptions such as mathematical or correlation assumptions used in their credit rating activities as well as their material changes.

CRAs are obliged to disclose conflicts of interest in a complete, timely, clear, concise, specific, and prominent manner and record all significant threats to the rating agency's independence or that of its employees involved in the credit rating process, together with the safeguards applied to mitigate those threats. For instance, the administrative or supervisory board of a CRA must include at least one-third, but no less than two non-executive members who are independent with a non-renewable term in office not exceeding five years. At the same time, CRAs may no longer provide consultancy or advisory services to the rated entity or a related third party. Compensation arrangements of employees involved in the rating process may not be contingent on the amount of revenue that the CRA derives from the rated entities or related third parties to which the analyst or persons approving the credit ratings provide services.

Critics of the European Regulation argue that serious monitoring of the performance of CRAs is lacking. Goodhart (2009) has argued in favour of an independent institution, a CRA Assessment Centre (CRAAC), whose only task would be to assess the accuracy of CRA estimates and to publish comparative studies of such accuracy. All CRAs in all countries should be required to place with CRAAC a record of each product rated and a measure of the uncertainty of this rating. This might help competition as investors want forecast accuracy. At present, they have no simple or straightforward way of checking this, and therefore fall back on reliance on brand names, which reinforces oligopoly. At the same time, more competition may not lead to more reliable ratings, as more suppliers may give more opportunities for rating shopping. This is illustrated by a study of Becker and Milbourn (2010), who examine how the quality of ratings issued by Standard & Poor's and Moody's responded to the new competition presented by Fitch. These authors find that the ratings issued by Standard & Poor's and Moody's rose as competition increased, while the ratings are less informative about the value of bonds when raters faced more competition. Finally, the ability of firm level ratings to predict default became lower when Fitch got a higher market share.

8.5 Conclusions

Financial innovation is the act of creating and then popularising new financial instruments, as well as new financial technologies, institutions, and markets. Generally, financial innovation is driven by investor demand for a particular set of cash flows; financial regulation (e.g. opportunities to exploit regulatory gaps) or technological change. Financial innovations may improve payments, offer new savings and investment opportunities, and may increase risk sharing. Financial innovation can however also add to the fragility of the overall financial system.

In the aftermath of the 2007–2009 financial crisis, financial innovation has become controversial. While most innovations seem to have improved access to credit, made life more convenient, and in some cases even allowed the economy to grow faster, some innovations, such as collateralised debt obligations (CDOs) and structured investment vehicles (SIVs) were poorly designed, while others, such as credit default swaps (CDSs) and adjustable rate mortgages, were misused and contributed to the financial crisis and/or amplified the downturn in the economy when it started. Moreover, although financial innovation and greater macroeconomic stability may have made financial crises in developed countries less likely, it seems that innovations have made their impact greater than was previously the case.

Credit rating agencies (CRAs) play an important role in financial markets through the production of credit risk information on financial instruments (including new instruments) and its distribution to market participants. However, CRAs received heavy criticism over the past years due to: (1) the conflicts of interests inherent to their business model, (2) their role in the recent financial crisis, i.e. by underestimating the credit risk associated with structured credit products, and (3) their sovereign rating activities, i.e. when downgrading various EU Member States in the midst of the financial crisis, thereby exacerbating the fiscal problems of these countries.

SUGGESTED READING

Gennaioli, N., A. Shleifer, and R. Vishny (in press), Neglected Risks, Financial Innovation, and Financial Fragility, *Journal of Financial Economics*.

Lerner, J. and P. Tufano (2011), The Consequences of Financial Innovation: A Counterfactual Research Agenda, NBER Working Paper No. 16780.

Litan, R. (2010), In Defense of Much, But Not All, Financial Innovation, Wharton Financial Institutions Center, Working Paper No. 2010–06.

REFERENCES

Barroso, J. M. Durão (2010), Statement to the European Parliament prior to the meeting of the Heads of State and Government of the Euro Area, European Parliament Plenary, Brussels, 5 May.

Becker, B. and T. Milbourn (2010), How Did Increased Competition Affect Credit Ratings? Available at: www.hbs.edu/research/pdf/09-051.pdf (accessed 13 February 2012).

Bernanke, B. (2009), Financial Innovation and Consumer Protection, At the Federal Reserve System's Sixth Biennial Community Affairs Research Conference, Washington DC, 17 April.

Financial Stability Board (2011), Potential Financial Stability Issues Arising from Recent Trends in Exchange-Traded Funds (ETFs), 12 April.

Financial Stability Forum (2008), *Report of the Financial Stability Forum on Enhancing Market and Institutional Resilience*, 7 April, available at: www.fsforum.org/publications/r_0804.pdf (accessed 13 February 2012).

Gai, P., S. Kapadia, S. Millard, and A. Perez (2008), Financial Innovation, Macroeconomic Stability and Systemic Crises, *Economic Journal*, 118, 401–426.

Gennaioli, N., A. Shleifer, and R. Vishny (in press), Neglected Risks, Financial Innovation, and Financial Fragility, *Journal of Financial Economics*.

Goodhart, C. (2009), *The Regulatory Response to the Financial Crisis*, Edward Elgar, Cheltenham.

Gorton, G. (2008), The Subprime Panic+, Yale International Center for Finance Working Paper No. 08–25.

Greenspan, A. (1997), Remarks by the Chairman of the Board of Governors of the US Federal Reserve System, Mr Alan Greenspan, at the Conference on Bank Structure and Competition of the Federal Reserve Bank of Chicago.

Hoggarth, G., R. Reis, and V. Saporta (2002), Costs of Banking System Instability: Some Empirical Evidence, *Journal of Banking and Finance*, 26, 825–855.

Holmstrom, B. (2010), Comments on 'The Credit Rating Crisis', *NBER Macroeconomics Annual*, 24(1), 215–222.

IMF (2010), The Uses and Abuses of Sovereign Credit Ratings, Chapter 3 in the 2010 IMF Global Financial Stability Report.

Krugman, P. (2007), Innovating Our Way to Financial Crisis,. *New York Times*, 3 December.

Lerner, J. and P. Tufano (2011), The Consequences of Financial Innovation: A Counterfactual Research Agenda, NBER Working Paper No. 16780.

Levine, R. (2011), Finance, Long-run Growth, and Economic Opportunity, in: T. Beck (ed.), *The Future of Banking*, A VoxEU.org eBook, CEPR, London.

Litan, R. (2010), In Defense of Much, But Not All, Financial Innovation, Wharton Financial Institutions Center, Working Paper No. 2010–06.

Shiller, R. and A. Weiss (1999), Home Equity Insurance, *Journal of Real Estate Finance and Economics* 19, 21–47.

White, L. J. (2010), The Credit Rating Agencies, *Journal of Economic Perspectives*, 24, 211–226.

Part III

Financial Institutions

The Role of Institutional Investors

OVERVIEW

Over the last decades, the intermediation of financial assets has gradually shifted from banks towards institutional investors, such as pension funds, insurance companies, and mutual funds. In this process of re-intermediation, the assets of institutional investors of the EU-15 countries almost tripled from 49 per cent of GDP in 1990 to 141 per cent in 2009.

This chapter starts off with an overview of the growth of institutional investors over the last two decades. The development of the main types of institutional investors is documented. There is a small group of countries with large-scale funded pensions (Denmark, Ireland, the Netherlands, and the United Kingdom). Other countries rely more on life insurance and mutual funds. New types of institutional investment, such as hedge funds and private equity, are also discussed.

Both the demand side (growing investments by pension funds to cater for ageing, and by mutual funds to accommodate wealth accumulation of households) and the supply side (shift from bank-financing to market-financing) point to further growth of institutional investment. There is no substantial institutional investment yet in the new EU Member States, but institutional investors in these countries are expected to grow in line with economic development.

This chapter also analyses the impact of institutional investors on the functioning of the financial system. Institutional investors are pooling funds and transferring economic resources over different asset classes and countries. They also transfer resources over time. Moreover, they increase the efficiency of the financial system.

One would expect institutional investors to invest according to the principles of finance theory as implied by the international version of the Capital Asset Pricing Model (CAPM). This theory shows the gains of international diversification. However, there is a home bias in investments of institutional investors. Still, this bias declined from 1997 to 2004, especially in the countries in the euro area, a trend which can be attributed to the introduction of the euro. With the elimination of exchange-rate risk, investors based in the euro area have reallocated part of their portfolio from their home country to the wider euro area.

LEARNING OBJECTIVES

After you have studied this chapter, you should be able to:

- describe the different types of institutional investors and their functions
- understand the growth of institutional investment and the factors that explain this growth
- explain the theory of international diversification
- assess the home bias of institutional investments and the change in the home bias following the introduction of the euro.

9.1 Different types of institutional investors

This section describes the main types of institutional investors in the EU and their role in the EU financial system. *Institutional investors* are specialised financial institutions that manage collectively savings of small investors (Davis and Steil, 2001). The size of institutional investors differs across countries. Most countries in southern Europe are characterised by low institutional saving, while the role of institutional investors in north-western Europe is more important. The three most important categories of institutional investors are pension funds, insurance companies, and mutual funds. Table 9.1 illustrates the role of these institutional investors in the EU. For comparative purposes, Switzerland and the US are also included in this table.

Pension funds

Pension funds collect, pool, and invest funds contributed by sponsors (employers) and beneficiaries (employees and their family members) to provide for the future pension entitlements of beneficiaries.

In the EU, pay-as-you-go (PAYG) pensions are common to provide for some basic pension level (first tier). This system is not funded but based upon solidarity between generations, as the working generation has to pay for the pensions of the retired generation. Some countries have accumulated major pension assets, which provide beneficiaries with an additional pension (second tier). These funded pensions can be based on defined benefit or defined contribution (Davis and Steil, 2001 and Feldstein and Siebert, 2002). *Defined benefit (DB) funds* offer employees a guaranteed rate of return (the risk is borne by the employer) while the returns of *defined contribution (DC) funds* are solely determined by the market (the risk is borne by the employees).

Table 9.1 Assets of different types of institutional investors (% of GDP), 2009

	Pension funds	Life insurance companies	Mutual funds	Total
Austria	5	36	51	92
Belgium	4	65	28	97
Bulgaria	5	6	1	11
Cyprus	n.a.	n.a.	8	8
Czech Republic	6	10	3	19
Denmark	29	82	52	164
Estonia	7	6	4	18
Finland	0	30	25	55
France	n.a.	76	53	129
Germany	0	46	44	90
Greece	0	7	3	10
Hungary	15	9	8	32
Ireland	39	107	280	426
Italy	2	35	15	51
Latvia	1	3	1	4
Lithuania	4	4	0	8
Luxembourg	1	152	4,370	4,524
Malta	0	28	114	142
Netherlands	130	65	78	273
Poland	14	10	7	31
Portugal	13	32	20	65
Romania	1	2	2	4
Slovakia	6	10	3	19
Slovenia	4	15	6	26
Spain	8	25	18	52
Sweden	10	89	48	146
United Kingdom	83	123	40	247
EU-15	26	62	57	141
NMS-12	9	9	6	23
EU-27	25	58	53	132
Switzerland	96	85	71	252
United States	67	44	80	191

Notes: EU-15, NMS-12, and EU-27 are calculated as a weighted average; n.a. means not available.
Source: ECB, OECD

DC plans have gained popularity in recent years, as employers have sought to minimise the risk of their obligations, while employees desire funds that are readily transferable if they move from one job to another. A hybrid is the *collective defined contribution* (CDC) pension. This does not guarantee a certain return by the company, but employees are able to save collectively for their pension via their employer and to pool risks.

The role of pension funds in the financial system differs across countries. In countries with large pension assets (relative to GDP), such as the Netherlands, Switzerland, the UK, and the US, pension funds are an important vehicle for collective saving for retirement purposes (see Table 9.2). Pension funds in these countries are among the largest investors, with assets under management worth billions of euros (for example, the Dutch civil servants' pension fund ABP; see Box 9.1). Historically, some large EU countries (like Germany, France, and Italy) have relied on other forms of retirement funding. The lack of a funded pension system in these countries directed households towards life insurances and mutual funds.

Since early withdrawal of funds is usually restricted or forbidden, a pension fund has long-term liabilities resulting in a long-term oriented investment strategy. This allows a pension fund to hold high-risk/return instruments (for example, investments in commodities, hedge funds, and private equity). Clients of a pension fund have no (direct) influence on the investment process of the fund but are protected by regulation, since pension funds have to comply with the 'prudent person' rule (they should, for example, diversify their portfolios). Moreover, pension funds are under the scrutiny of financial supervisors (see Chapter 12).

Insurance companies

Life insurance companies offer a mix of long-term saving and insurance products. Historically, life insurance companies provided insurance for dependants against the risk of death, but life insurers increasingly also offer long-term saving products. Pension funds and life insurance companies therefore often have close ties. Life insurance companies offer annuities for guaranteeing pension benefits as well as guaranteed investment contracts that may be purchased by pension funds. *Non-life insurance companies* protect against risks such as accidents, illness, theft, and fire. As the asset base of life insurance is far larger than that of non-life insurance, the remainder of this section focuses on life insurance.

All EU-15 countries (except for Greece) have significant life insurance assets relative to GDP. Table 9.3 indicates that life insurance assets are concentrated in the UK, France, and Germany. The Netherlands and Italy also have a large life insurance industry. Life insurance companies function as retirement saving vehicles in countries with a weak pension sector (such as

Table 9.2 Assets of pension funds (in € billion and % of GDP), 2001–2009

	2001		2004		2007		2009	
	euro	%	euro	%	euro	%	euro	%
Austria	8	4	10	4	13	5	14	5
Belgium	14	6	12	4	14	4	12	4
Bulgaria	n.a.	n.a.	0	2	1	4	2	5
Cyprus	n.a.	n.a.	n.a.	n.a.	n.a.	n.a.	n.a.	n.a.
Czech Republic	2	3	3	4	6	5	8	6
Denmark	42	23	51	26	61	27	65	29
Estonia	0	0	0	2	1	5	1	7
Finland	0	0	0	0	0	0	0	0
France	n.a.	n.a.	n.a.	n.a.	n.a.	n.a.	n.a.	n.a.
Germany	0	0	0	0	1	0	1	0
Greece	0	0	0	0	0	0	0	0
Hungary	3	4	6	7	11	11	14	15
Ireland	51	44	62	42	87	46	64	39
Italy	10	1	18	1	26	2	23	2
Latvia	0	0	0	0	0	0	0	1
Lithuania	0	0	0	0	1	2	1	4
Luxembourg	n.a.	n.a.	n.a.	n.a.	0	1	1	1
Malta	0	0	0	0	0	0	0	0
Netherlands	451	101	522	106	763	134	743	130
Poland	6	3	15	7	39	13	44	14
Portugal	15	11	16	11	22	13	22	13
Romania	n.a.	n.a.	n.a.	n.a.	0	0	1	1
Slovakia	n.a.	n.a.	n.a.	n.a.	2	4	4	6
Slovenia	0	1	1	2	1	3	1	4
Spain	45	7	64	8	88	8	86	8
Sweden	59	24	72	25	29	8	28	10
United Kingdom	1,180	74	1,605	92	1,488	72	1,305	83
EU-15	1,875	25	2,433	29	2,592	27	2,363	26
NMS-12	10	3	26	4	63	7	76	9
EU-27	1,885	24	2,459	28	2,655	25	2,439	25

Notes: EU-15, NMS-12, and EU-27 are calculated as a weighted average; n.a. means not available.
Source: ECB

Belgium, France, Germany, and Italy). As life insurance companies offer a diverse range of products, they have different kinds of liabilities, which allows them a certain degree of diversification. Life insurance companies sell their products in a competitive market and compete both with each other

Box 9.1 ABP

The ABP (Algemeen Burgerlijk Pensioenfonds) is the Dutch pension fund for employers and employees of the government and the educational sector. It was founded by the government in 1922 and privatised in 1996. ABP provides its 2.8 million customers (employees, former employees, pensioners) with income security against pension, disability, and death.

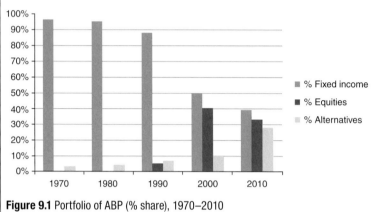

Figure 9.1 Portfolio of ABP (% share), 1970–2010
Source: ABP

ABP is the third largest pension fund in the world with around €240 billion of assets at the end of 2010. Given its objective to guarantee an adequate pension at all times at the lowest possible premiums, ABP's investment policy is geared towards a long-term risk-return profile. Diversification is a key element of that policy. The investment mix consists of 60 per cent in equities and alternative investments, such as real estate, private equity, and commodities, and 40 per cent in bonds. Over time, the share of equities and alternative investments has increased (see Figure 9.1). The geographical mix consists of 12 per cent of assets in the Netherlands, 41 per cent in the rest of Europe, and 47 per cent in the rest of the world.

and with pension funds and mutual funds. As a result, life companies may have a strong incentive for risk taking on the asset side.

From a customer point of view, the economic function of life insurance companies is (next to insurance for dependants) the provision of customised saving schemes. Saving and investing via life insurance is aimed not only at retirement but also at other long-term saving objectives (like the education of siblings), which makes them not only a substitute but also a supplement

Table 9.3 Assets of insurance companies (in € billion and % of GDP), 2001–2009

	2001		2004		2007		2009	
	euro	%	euro	%	euro	%	euro	%
Austria	58	27	68	29	88	32	98	36
Belgium	116	45	164	57	217	65	220	65
Bulgaria	n.a.	n.a.	0	2	1	4	2	6
Cyprus	2	18	4	28	n.a.	n.a.	n.a.	n.a.
Czech Republic	5	8	7	8	12	9	14	10
Denmark	97	54	124	63	163	72	183	82
Estonia	0	3	0	3	1	5	1	6
Finland	32	23	38	25	53	30	52	30
France	837	56	1,029	62	1,374	72	1,452	76
Germany	943	45	1,092	49	1,109	46	1,119	46
Greece	12	9	11	6	20	9	16	7
Hungary	3	6	5	7	9	8	9	9
Ireland	56	48	92	62	163	86	174	107
Italy	307	25	423	30	540	35	526	35
Latvia	0	2	0	2	1	2	1	3
Lithuania	0	1	0	2	1	3	1	4
Luxembourg	29	127	40	144	61	161	57	152
Malta	1	12	1	18	1	25	2	28
Netherlands	297	66	316	64	362	64	369	65
Poland	13	6	19	9	33	10	31	10
Portugal	27	21	36	25	53	31	54	32
Romania	n.a.	n.a.	1	1	2	1	2	2
Slovakia	1	6	2	7	5	9	6	10
Slovenia	1	6	2	9	4	12	5	15
Spain	149	22	204	24	243	23	263	25
Sweden	0	0	0	0	276	82	260	89
United Kingdom	1,740	109	1,629	93	2,098	102	1,923	123
EU-15	4,699	52	5,266	53	6,820	59	6,763	62
NMS-12	27	6	42	7	69	8	73	9
EU-27	4,726	50	5,308	50	6,889	56	6,836	58

Notes: EU-15, NMS-12, and EU-27 are calculated as a weighted average; n.a. means not available.
Source: ECB

to pensions. While pension schemes are more standardised, life insurance products can be tailored towards the needs of an individual. But this advantage comes at a price. The transaction and marketing costs of life policies are far higher than the costs of pension contracts.

Mutual funds

The mutual fund industry is among the most successful financial innovations (Khorana *et al.*, 2005). *Mutual funds* are investment vehicles whose underlying assets are identifiable and are marked to market on a regular (usually daily) basis. Moreover, the specific assets of the fund can be created or redeemed upon demand. Mutual funds contractually link investors' claims to the underlying asset. Investors can easily enter and exit the fund and pay or receive current market prices for their investments. Investors in mutual funds are residual claimants and bear all the risk of the fund.

The primary role of mutual funds is the pooling of funds. In contrast to pension funds, they do not necessarily transfer these funds over time. Many investors in mutual funds have a relatively short investment horizon, so the mutual fund is not specifically intended for retirement saving. The size of mutual funds differs sharply, ranging from small, specialised funds to major players like Fidelity Investments and Vanguard (having each about $1,500 billion of assets under management at the end of 2010). These larger funds also have important stakes in companies, which makes them prominent players in corporate governance.

Investors choose a fund with a specific investment objective (for instance, a bond fund, an equity fund, or an emerging market fund). The asset allocation of the fund is generally fixed by the prospectus, while the security selection process is either active or passive. Active asset managers try to 'beat the market' by picking stocks that they consider good investments. Passive funds 'track' the index and do not deviate from the market benchmark. They generally incur lower transaction costs and have lower investment fees.

Table 9.4 illustrates the growth of mutual funds between 2001 and 2009. Luxembourg and Ireland are outliers due to a favourable tax treatment of these funds. Remarkable is the large size of mutual fund investment in France. The new Member States have the smallest mutual fund market size relative to GDP. Also, in Italy and Spain this market is small.

Special types of institutional investors

In addition to the three main types of institutional investors described above, two other important institutional asset managers are hedge funds and private equity investors. During the last decade, they have gained popularity as they offer opportunities to diversify risk and increase expected returns.

Table 9.4 Assets of mutual funds (in € billion and % of GDP), 2001–2009

	2001		2004		2007		2009	
	euro	%	euro	%	euro	%	euro	%
Austria	98	45	123	53	161	59	141	51
Belgium	87	34	95	33	118	35	94	28
Bulgaria	n.a.	n.a.	n.a.	n.a.	1	2	0	1
Cyprus	n.a.	n.a.	0	3	1	8	1	8
Czech Republic	3	4	4	4	4	3	4	3
Denmark	38	21	77	39	137	60	116	52
Estonia	0	1	0	3	1	8	1	4
Finland	12	9	22	14	49	27	43	25
France	649	43	799	48	1,201	63	1,013	53
Germany	794	38	862	39	1,054	43	1,060	44
Greece	17	13	16	9	15	6	8	3
Hungary	3	5	4	5	10	9	8	8
Ireland	182	155	282	190	516	272	459	280
Italy	395	32	321	23	291	19	225	15
Latvia	0	0	0	1	0	1	0	1
Lithuania	0	0	0	0	0	1	0	0
Luxembourg	854	3,779	975	3,557	1,933	5,156	1,643	4,370
Malta	1	12	1	22	1	22	7	114
Netherlands	112	25	98	20	100	18	446	78
Poland	3	2	9	5	37	12	23	7
Portugal	26	20	31	22	40	23	33	20
Romania	n.a.	n.a.	1	1	4	3	2	2
Slovakia	n.a.	n.a.	2	5	2	4	2	3
Slovenia	3	11	2	8	4	12	2	6
Spain	158	23	208	25	299	28	194	18
Sweden	87	35	117	41	156	46	141	48
United Kingdom	362	23	410	23	684	33	627	40
EU-15	3,871	43	4,434	44	6,753	59	6,243	57
NMS-12	12	3	24	4	66	8	49	6
EU-27	3,883	41	4,458	42	6,819	55	6,292	53

Notes: Mutual fund data includes both UCITS (equity, bonds, balanced, money market, funds of funds, and other UCITS funds) and non-UCITS (real estate funds, special funds, and other non-UCITS). UCITS are collective investment schemes, which can operate freely throughout the EU on the basis of a single authorisation (see Chapter 12). EU-15, NMS-12, and EU-27 are calculated as a weighted average; n.a. means not available.

Source: ECB

Originally, *hedge funds* were eclectic investment pools, typically organised as private partnerships and often located offshore for tax and regulatory reasons. Since they operate through private placements and restrict share ownership to wealthy individuals and institutions, most disclosure and regulation requirements that apply to mutual funds and banks do not apply to hedge funds. Funds legally domiciled outside the main financial market countries are generally subject to even fewer regulations. Hedge-fund managers, who are paid on a fee-for-performance basis, are free to use a variety of investment techniques, including short positions and leverage, to raise returns and limit the investment risks. In contrast to investment funds, hedge funds concentrate more on absolute than on relative returns. The primary aim of most hedge funds used to be to reduce volatility and risk while attempting to deliver positive returns under all market conditions ('hedging'). However, the investment strategy of many funds has become more risky over the last decade, including the use of leverage. The aggressive investment style of some hedge funds can land them in financial trouble, as the bailout of the hedge fund LTCM in 1998 illustrates (see Box 9.2).

Box 9.2 The LTCM crisis

The hedge fund Long-Term Capital Management (LTCM) was founded in 1994. Its Board of Directors included Nobel Prize winners Myron Scholes and Robert Merton. The core strategy of LTCM was convergence trades, trying to take advantage of small differences in prices among closely related securities (Jorion, 2000). Compare, for example, a less liquid (called off-the-run) Treasury bond yielding 6.1 per cent versus 6.0 per cent for the more recently issued (called on-the-run) Treasury bond. The yield spread represents some compensation for the liquidity risk. Over a year, a trade that is long off-the-run and short on-the-run would generate a return of 10 basis points. The key is that eventually the two bonds converge to the same value at maturity. LTCM used this strategy in a variety of markets, such as spreads on different government bonds, mortgage-backed versus government securities, high-yielding versus low-yielding European bonds, equity pairs (stocks with different share classes), and so on. Most of the time, these trades should be profitable except for default or market disruption.

Such strategies generate tiny profits, so that leverage has to be used to create attractive returns. At the time of the crisis in 1998, LTCM had borrowed $125 billion compared with equity of $5 billion. This led to a *leverage ratio L*, defined as debt to equity, of 25. The following equation illustrates the impact of leverage: $r_{equity} = r_{assets} + L\,(r_{assets} - r_{debt})$. When the return on assets r_{assets} is higher than the return on debt r_{debt}, a large leverage would generate a high return on equity r_{equity}. But when the return on assets drops below that on debt, a large leverage would generate sizeable losses.

Initially, this strategy was very productive, with annual profits of almost 40 per cent. But losses occurred due to the Russian financial crisis in August 1998 when the Russian government defaulted on its bonds. Panicking investors sold Japanese and European bonds to buy US Treasury bonds. The profits that were supposed to occur as the value of these bonds converged became huge losses as the value of the bonds diverged. LTCM's equity capital dropped to around $600 million. The Federal Reserve Bank of New York organised a bailout of $3.6 billion by major creditors (14 leading investment banks) to avoid more collapses, without committing its own money. In return, the participating banks got a 90 per cent share in the fund. The fear was that there would be a chain reaction as LTCM liquidated its securities to cover its debt, leading to a drop in prices, which would force other companies to liquidate their own debt, creating a vicious cycle. The total losses amounted to $4.6 billion. After the bailout, the panic abated and the positions formerly held by LTCM were eventually even liquidated at a small profit to the bailers (Jorion, 2000). LTCM closed its books in 2000.

Critics have pointed out that this bailout increased moral hazard problems as financial institutions could take more risks because they suffer less in case of failure (Kho *et al.*, 2000). While central bankers typically argue that a bailout is necessary to prevent contagion and systemic threats, academics stress moral hazard. Furfine (2006) has estimated the potential costs of the Fed's intervention by examining the rates for interbank borrowing of large banks. The spreads on interbank borrowing go down if the market believes that these banks are 'too big to fail'.

Figure 9.2 illustrates the enormous growth of the hedge-fund industry. While there was a strong decline during the financial crisis in 2008, it is estimated that hedge funds in total managed around €1,400 billion in 2010. Total investment positions of hedge funds are even bigger as they can leverage their assets through borrowing money and through the use of derivatives, short positions, and structured securities. The growth of the hedge-fund industry was initially driven by investments by wealthy individuals and institutions looking for higher returns. However, during the last decade small investors have been able to invest via *funds of hedge funds*, which are investment funds that invest solely in hedge funds. Also, pension funds invest in hedge funds and funds of funds, as illustrated in Figure 9.3.

The distinctions between hedge funds and other types of funds are blurring. Hedge funds are characterised as unregulated private funds that can

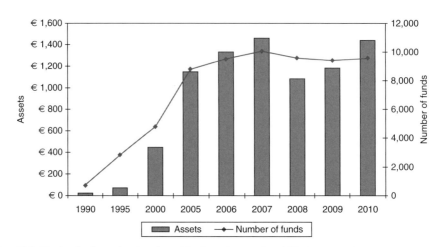

Figure 9.2 Global hedge funds market (number of funds and assets in € billion), 1990–2010
Source: TheCityUK (2011a)

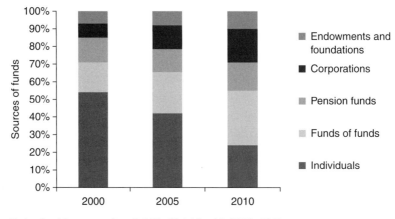

Figure 9.3 Hedge funds' sources of capital (% of total funds), 2000–2010
Source: TheCityUK (2011a)

take on significant leverage and employ complex trading strategies using derivatives or other new financial instruments. Although private equity funds are usually not considered hedge funds, they are also typically unregulated and often use leverage for their investments. However, new regulations for hedge funds and private equity were introduced in the aftermath of the financial crisis (see Chapter 12). Traditional asset managers also increasingly use derivatives or invest in structured securities that allow them to take leveraged or short positions.

Table 9.5 The most important countries with private equity investments (€ billion and %) in 2010

	Total investment value	Market share	As % of GDP
United States	60.6	45%	0.6%
United Kingdom	23.2	17%	1.4%
China	7.5	6%	0.2%
France	6.0	4%	0.3%
Australia	6.0	4%	0.9%
India	5.2	4%	0.4%
Germany	4.5	3%	0.2%
Japan	1.5	1%	0.0%
Others	19.5	15%	—
Total	134.0	100%	—

Source: TheCityUK (2011b)

In general, hedge funds provide liquidity and absorb risk. Moreover, due to their innovative trading strategies, they also play a role in financial innovation (see Chapter 8). Hedge funds thus improve the efficiency of the financial system. At the same time, they have the potential to amplify market price fluctuations if their investment behaviour becomes one-sided or if they concentrate on specific markets, in particular small-sized and low-liquidity markets.

Private equity investors invest in non-public companies and often finance these investments with a significant amount of debt, up to 90 per cent in the case of a leveraged buyout. By means of investment funds, which are open to certain institutions and wealthy individuals, they invest in companies and aim at annual returns of 20–25 per cent. This makes them attractive for institutional investors also. Some institutional investors invest in private equity by means of their own private equity branch. An example is AlpInvest, a private equity company owned until recently by two Dutch pension funds (ABP and PGGM, the Dutch pension fund for the healthcare and social work sector). In 2011 AlpInvest was sold to Carlyle Group.

Table 9.5 illustrates that the US and the UK have the biggest private equity markets. Relative to GDP, private equity markets are small. Still, these markets are growing rapidly, driven by the demand for risky assets and exposure to the non-public market. Private equity funds have become an important source of funds for start-up firms, private middle-market firms, firms in financial distress, and public firms seeking buyout financing (Smit, 2003).

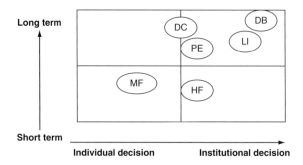

Figure 9.4   Investment horizon and decision power about asset allocation

Note: MF = mutual fund; DC = defined contribution pension scheme; DB = defined benefit pension scheme; LI = life insurance company; PE = private equity; HF = hedge fund.

Source: Bosch and Schoenmaker (2006)

Differences among institutional investors

Institutional investors differ from each other along three dimensions. First, the client base of the investor can be captive or can be determined via the market. In continental Europe, defined benefit pension funds often have a captive client base, as most employers use only one fund. In contrast, mutual funds must compete for clientele by means of low fees and/or an excellent track record.

Second, the investment horizon of institutional investors differs sharply. While pension funds have a very long investment horizon, mutual funds can have short-term investment objectives.

Third, the asset-allocation process differs across institutional investors. Mutual funds mainly focus on security selection or 'stock picking' and individual investors select the mutual fund that best matches with their risk preferences. Pension funds and life insurance companies take investment decisions concerning the percentage of equity and bonds in their portfolios, and diversify the risks within these asset classes. Figure 9.4 illustrates these differences.

9.2 The growth of institutional investors

Re-intermediation

Institutional investors have made banks less important as intermediaries of financial assets, a development which Rajan (2007) calls '*re-intermediation*'

Table 9.6 Bank and institutional intermediation ratios (in % of intermediated claims), 1970–2000

		1970	1980	1990	2000	Δ 1970–2000
France	*Bank*	94	68	82	65	**–29**
	Institutional	5	4	19	27	**22**
Germany	*Bank*	84	86	83	73	**–11**
	Institutional	10	12	17	23	**13**
Italy	*Bank*	98	98	95	64	**–34**
	Institutional	6	5	11	31	**25**
United Kingdom	*Bank*	58	64	55	44	**–14**
	Institutional	28	26	32	38	**10**
Canada	*Bank*	45	55	44	38	**–7**
	Institutional	23	19	25	35	**12**
Japan	*Bank*	45	36	38	24	**–21**
	Institutional	10	10	16	17	**7**
United States	*Bank*	58	58	42	21	**–37**
	Institutional	31	31	40	44	**13**
G7	***Bank***	**69**	**66**	**63**	**47**	**–22**
	Institutional	**16**	**15**	**23**	**31**	**15**

Notes: The intermediation ratio measures the share of the financial claims of banks and institutional investors as a percentage of total intermediated claims. The sum of bank and institutional ratios can be below 100, due to financial claims of other financial institutions, or over 100, due to double counting. Data for other EU Member States and time periods are not available, but the objective of this table is to show the shift from bank to institutional intermediation.
Source: Davis (2003)

(see Table 9.6). Also, in countries with a bank-dominated financial system, like France and Italy, the role of institutional investors has increased. This is mainly due to the growth of the mutual fund industry. However, Germany is still mainly bank-oriented. In the Anglo-Saxon countries, institutional investors are the most important financial intermediaries. The US is the prime example, where institutional claims are twice as large as bank claims. As Box 9.3 explains, re-intermediation is less important in the new EU Member States, as the role of institutional investors in those countries is currently rather limited.

Table 9.7 illustrates that the total claims of institutional investors in the EU-15 have increased enormously over the last two decades. The weighted average of assets to GDP rose from 49 per cent in 1990 to 141 per cent in 2009. In the US, institutional investment shows a similar trend, with an increase from 80 per cent of GDP in 1990 to 191 per cent in 2009. When the global stock markets tumbled after the Internet bubble in 2000 and the financial

Box 9.3 Institutional investment in the new EU Member States

Institutional investment can be seen as a luxury good. The most basic financial needs of households are the use of currency (coins and banknotes) and bank services (depositing and lending). Only when their income is increasing do households start to buy insurance and to save for retirement. This relationship is presented in Figure 9.5. Institutional investment starts to develop at a GDP per capita of around €5,000 and becomes meaningful beyond levels of €15,000. Greece and Portugal had a relatively low GDP per capita when they entered the EU in the 1980s. Figure 9.5 illustrates that their GDP per capita has gradually caught up with the EU average and that their institutional sector has also gradually developed. Currently, the new EU Member States have a very small institutional sector, but institutional investment in these countries is expected to grow in line with economic development.

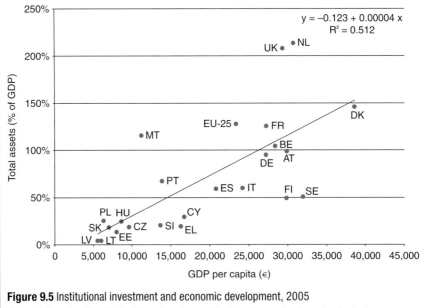

Figure 9.5 Institutional investment and economic development, 2005

Note: Total assets of institutional investment are defined as the assets of pension funds, insurance companies, and mutual funds. Ireland and Luxembourg are excluded, as they attract mutual funds from other countries due to a favourable tax regime.

Source: Own calculations based on ECB (2006)

Table 9.7 Assets of institutional investors (% of GDP), 1990–2009

	1990	1995	2000	2005	2009
Austria	22	35	71	99	92
Belgium	40	41	83	101	97
Denmark	53	69	103	149	164
Finland	6	16	43	52	55
France	49	76	127	120	129
Germany	34	45	81	94	90
Greece	1	12	32	20	10
Ireland	n.a.	53	199	366	426
Italy	12	26	63	61	51
Luxembourg	790	2,017	4,084	4,853	4,524
Netherlands	120	151	199	209	273
Portugal	8	35	52	65	65
Spain	n.a.	43	59	60	52
Sweden	47	65	109	157	146
United Kingdom	105	167	213	209	247
EU-15	49	73	125	136	141
Switzerland	107	141	224	248	252
United States	80	122	177	185	191

Notes: EU-15 is calculated as a weighted average; n.a. means not available.
Source: ECB, OECD

crisis in 2008, the assets of institutional investors declined sharply. The turmoil on the global financial markets reveals the vulnerability of institutional investors (with equity investments of up to 50 per cent of their portfolio) to such downward market pressures.

Drivers of growth of institutional investment

The growth of institutional investment can be explained by supply and demand factors. Institutional investors have become more efficient in their function as a financial intermediary, while households have an enhanced need for services provided by institutional investors. Institutional investors are well placed to perform the key functions of the financial system as identified in Chapter 1, i.e. trade, manage, and diversify risk, and reduce information and trading costs.

Supply-side factors

Institutional investors are pooling funds from individual households. Due to economies of scale, they are able to invest these funds more efficiently than individuals. Moreover, institutional investors are able to invest in assets that are indivisible (such as property) and therefore often not available to small investors. So, institutional investors provide diversified portfolios at low cost to households. For instance, a mutual fund requires a low level of minimum investment and offers households the possibility to invest in a diversified way. Costs of asset management are low as they are shared among many households, so that institutional investors offer an attractive risk-return profile.

Because of their policy to hedge exposure and to diversify their investments, institutional investors are increasingly using derivatives. Many of the new risk-management tools have been developed especially for institutional investors, increasing the efficiency of the financial system. Furthermore, when institutional investors adopt more active trading policies, they enhance the liquidity of markets, leading to higher efficiency and lower transaction costs. According to Davis (2003, p. 21), 'by demanding liquidity, institutional investors help to generate it'.

With respect to corporate governance, institutional investors have more 'bargaining power' than individual investors as they are often important shareholders in companies. However, the different types of institutional investors are not equally active in corporate governance. Gillan and Starks (2003) distinguish between pressure-sensitive and insensitive institutional investors. Pressure-sensitive investors are bankers and insurers who care about current or potential business relations with corporations in which they invest. They are more passive institutions. Pension funds and mutual funds are not sensitive to pressure and therefore are more active institutions. In particular, public pension funds are the pioneers in active corporate governance. Well-known examples are Hermes (the UK postal pension fund), CalPERS (California Public Employees' Retirement System), and ABP (see Box 9.1). More recently, hedge funds have become aggressive players in corporate governance.

Also, deregulation has spurred the development of institutional investors. For example, fees have been reduced and institutional investors have more freedom to investment internationally and to distribute their products to a wider public. Deregulation has also stimulated competition among asset management institutions, which has lowered costs for the end-user, i.e. households. The European Commission plays a crucial role in regulatory issues concerning institutional investors. Because of the ageing problems that the EU Member States face (see below), the Commission urged countries to reform their pension schemes. At the same time, the Commission proposed a number of directives that would impose severe restrictions on pension funds and life insurance companies ('quantitative portfolio regulations'). After lengthy negotiations between the Commission, the Member States, and the pension funds, a new Pension Directive has been adopted to stimulate the single European market for pension funds. This directive promotes prudential investing of pension funds applied to the portfolio as a whole rather than to individual investments (the 'prudent person' principle). No quantitative restrictions have been imposed on the portfolio composition of EU pension funds. EU pension funds are thus able to optimise their risk-return profile (see section 9.3 on international diversification).[1]

In contrast, insurance companies do face certain regulatory restrictions. The percentage of equity as well as the percentage of foreign assets in their portfolio is restricted. The new regulatory framework for the insurance industry, Solvency II, is supposed to remove most of these restrictions, which would be advantageous for the proper development of institutional investments in the EU. Chapter 12 explains the regulatory framework for financial institutions in Europe.

The final supply-side factor furthering the development of institutional investors consists of fiscal advantages. Pension funds benefit from deferred taxation (contributions and investment returns are not taxed, but payouts are taxed). Life insurance contributions also often benefit from deferred taxation, while mutual funds enjoy a favourable tax regime in some EU countries (such as Luxembourg and Ireland).

Demand-side factors

Demand-side factors also play an important role in explaining the vast growth of institutional investment. The need for saving via institutional investors is linked to the level of social security benefits to which households are entitled. Institutional investment is stimulated when social security provides only a minimum level of income after retirement. In that case, the remaining part of income is provided via some kind of institutional saving.

The demand for institutional savings is mainly fuelled by demographic developments. Figure 9.6 shows that the EU population is ageing. The need to save for retirement is thus increasing. Saving for retirement is done primarily via institutional investors. Which institutions benefit most from these demographic developments depends on the country-specific situation. In countries where pension funds are well established, like the Netherlands and the UK, retirement saving primarily takes place via pension funds. Employees

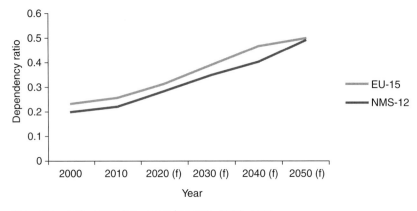

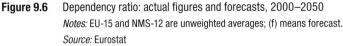

Figure 9.6   Dependency ratio: actual figures and forecasts, 2000–2050
Notes: EU-15 and NMS-12 are unweighted averages; (f) means forecast.
Source: Eurostat

in France, where pension funds are practically non-existent, save for their retirement via life insurance companies and mutual funds.

Demographic projections for the EU indicate that by 2050 the dependency ratio will be double that of today, moving from around 25 in 2010 to 50 in 2050. Note that the dependency ratios of the new and old Member States are converging. The *dependency ratio* is equal to the number of elderly persons of an age when they are generally economically inactive (aged 65 and over) divided by the number of persons of working age (from 15 to 64), expressed as a percentage. The increase in the dependency ratio can be explained by a decline in the fertility rates and increased life expectancy in the EU. Total fertility rates have declined dramatically over the past decades, falling from an average of 2.7 children per woman of child-bearing age in 1970 to 1.6 in 2008. At the same time, life expectancy in the EU-15 increased from 71 years in 1970 to 79.4 years in 2008. It is expected to increase further.

Finally, over the last two decades European households have become wealthier, which has resulted in an increase in their investment horizon. These household investors bother less about the liquidity of their investments, as they are better positioned to absorb liquidity shocks. Less liquid investments offer a higher return. So wealthier households will search for the highest risk-return profile in the medium to long run. This means a shift from the traditional savings accounts (which can often be withdrawn on demand) towards long-term investments. However, most retail investors are risk averse and do not feel very comfortable with making investment decisions. So investing via institutional investors instead of direct investment will be more convenient.

9.3 Portfolio theory and international diversification

Portfolio theory

According to the international version of the CAPM, investors should hold an internationally diversified portfolio since such a portfolio maximises returns given a certain risk profile. This can be explained by Figure 9.7 which plots the mean and standard deviation of annualised monthly returns from January 1980 to December 2005 for two different equity portfolios. The first is the MSCI (Morgan Stanley Capital International) USA Index, which is a proxy for the American stock market. The second is based on the MSCI Europe Index, which is a proxy for the European stock market. Moving along the curve from 100 per cent US stocks to 100 per cent European stocks, the line plots the mean returns and standard deviations. This is a simplified version of the so-called *efficient frontier*, i.e. the portfolio with the minimum standard deviation for a given return.

The mean of the MSCI USA is lower than portfolio C, which has the same standard deviation but includes a fraction of European stocks. In fact, as long as investors prefer higher returns and lower variance, the minimum-variance portfolio at point B (with 40 per cent European equity) is preferable to a portfolio consisting of US shares only. However, as will be explained in more detail in the next section, American investors hold only 7 per cent of European stocks in their equity portfolio, which is indicated by point A.

Figure 9.7 illustrates that it is beneficial for investors to diversify geographically. The formal international CAPM can be derived from the standard mean-variance framework modified to include foreign securities (Lewis, 1999). In the mean-variance framework, investors optimise their portfolio by increasing their return (i.e. the mean of their wealth) and decreasing their risk (i.e. the variance of their wealth). By introducing foreign stocks, investors have to choose the optimal mix of domestic and foreign stocks in their portfolio. Box 9.4 presents the international CAPM derived by Lewis.

International diversification

When investors diversify their portfolio internationally, they can generate an extra return and/or reduce risk. Lewis (1999) calculates that an American investor can generate an extra return of about 50 basis points per year while also decreasing risk (moving to point B in Figure 9.7), or 80 basis points per year with no change in risk (moving to point A' in Figure 9.7). Empirical

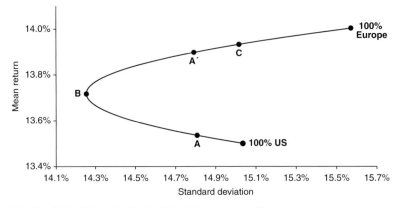

Figure 9.7   The simplified efficient frontier for US and European equities

Note: This graph is based on returns from the MSCI USA Index and MSCI Europe Index over the period 1980–2005.

Source: Bosch and Schoenmaker (2006)

Box 9.4 The international CAPM

Suppose that domestic investors have access to two risky assets, a domestic and a foreign stock. The domestic investor chooses the proportion of his wealth portfolio held in foreign stocks, x (with $0 < x < 1$). The investor's objective is to increase mean wealth, $E(W_1)$, and decrease the variability of wealth, $\text{var}(W_1)$. His objective function is given by:

$$\text{max} \qquad V = V(E(W_1), \text{var}(W_1)) \tag{9.1}$$

$$\text{subject to} \qquad V_1 > 0, \ V_2 < 0 \tag{9.2}$$

where W_1 = next-period wealth, and E = the expected value conditional upon information known at time 0. V_1 is the partial derivative of V with respect to the first term, and V_2 with respect to the second term. The one-period return is a combination of the foreign return earned on the fraction of foreign stocks, denoted by x, and the domestic return earned on the fraction of domestic stocks, denoted by $(1 - x)$, and is given by:

$$
\begin{aligned}
W_1 &= W_0(1 + x \cdot r^f + (1 - x) \cdot r^h) \\
&= W_0(1 + x \cdot (r^f - r^h) + r^h)
\end{aligned} \tag{9.3}
$$

where W_0 = current wealth, r^f = foreign return, and r^h = domestic return. The variance of the one-period return is given by:

$$
\begin{aligned}
\text{var}(W_1) &= \text{var}(W_0(1 + x \cdot (r^f - r^h) + r^h)) \\
&= W_0^2 \text{var}(1 + x \cdot (r^f - r^h) + r^h) \\
&= W_0^2(x^2 \ \text{var}(r^f - r^h) + 2 \cdot x \cdot (\rho_{fh} \cdot \sigma_f \cdot \sigma_h - \sigma_h^2) + \sigma_h^2)
\end{aligned} \tag{9.4}
$$

where $\sigma_h^2 = \text{var}(r^h) = $ the variance of the domestic stock return, $\sigma_f^2 = \text{var}(r^f) = $ the variance of the foreign stock return to the domestic investor, and $\sigma_{fh} = \rho_{fh} \cdot \sigma_f \cdot \sigma_h = \text{cov}(r^f, r^h) = $ the covariance between the domestic and foreign returns. The optimal fraction of foreign stock x^* can be calculated by deriving the first-order condition of the objective function V. The first-order condition is given by:

$$\frac{\delta V}{\delta x} = V_1 \cdot W_0 \cdot (r^f - r^h)$$
$$+ V_2 \cdot W_0^2 \cdot (2 \cdot x \cdot \text{var}(r^f - r^h) + 2 \cdot \sigma_{fh} - 2 \cdot \sigma_h^2) = 0 \tag{9.5}$$

Dividing by W_0 and arranging terms leads directly to:

$$x^* = \frac{r^f - r^h}{\text{var}(r^f - r^h)} \cdot \frac{-V_1}{2 \cdot V_2 \cdot W_0} + \frac{\sigma_h^2 - \sigma_{fh}}{\text{var}(r^f - r^h)}$$
$$= \frac{(r^f - r^h)/\gamma}{\text{var}(r^f - r^h)} + \frac{\sigma_h^2 - \sigma_{fh}}{\text{var}(r^f - r^h)} \tag{9.6}$$

where γ is the parameter of risk aversion $\frac{-2 \cdot V_2 \cdot W_0}{V_1}$. The interpretation of the demand function for foreign stock is straightforward. The first term on the right-hand side of equation 9.6 represents the demand arising from higher-potential returns from the foreign stock. The lower the risk aversion, γ, the greater the response of demand to higher expected returns. However, as γ increases, the importance of relative returns across countries declines. In the limiting case when γ equals infinity, i.e. investors are infinitely risk averse, the first term disappears. The demand for foreign stock then reduces to the second term, i.e. the portfolio share that minimises the variance of the wealth portfolio. This portfolio is illustrated by point B in Figure 9.7. Thus, in general, the demand for foreign stock depends on a combination of the risky portfolio share given by the first term and the minimum-variance portfolio given by the second term.

Source: Lewis (1999)

evidence for European investors shows an even stronger effect. Schröder (2003) finds that a British investor, holding the optimal portfolio of 80 per cent non-domestic assets instead of a portfolio of 20 per cent non-domestic assets, generates an extra return of 2.2 per cent per year. A German investor, holding the optimal portfolio, generates an extra return of 3 per cent per year. The excess return for European investors is larger than for American investors because the US market is very large so there is less upside potential from investing in foreign markets.

By the same token, international diversification reduces the cost of capital (Stulz, 1999). The expected return that investors require for investing in equity to compensate them for risk generally falls, resulting in lower cost of capital for companies.

The international CAPM is derived under the assumption that capital markets are perfect. Perfect capital markets imply a world without any barriers. However, several barriers may hamper international capital flows (Karolyi and Stulz, 2003). First, there are traditional barriers including capital controls and trading costs. While capital controls have been abolished in the EU over the past three decades (see Chapter 3); cross-border trading costs are still higher than domestic trading costs (see Chapter 7 on cross-border trading costs in the EU). Second, barriers can be related to different expectations about stock returns, volatilities, and covariances. In particular, investors can be more uncertain about the expected returns of foreign stock. An important risk in the cross-border setting is exchange-rate risk. The degree of risk aversion is captured by γ in equation 9.6. Finally, barriers can emerge from differences in information between local and foreign investors. According to the 'corporate insider theory', it is not possible for the home bias to fall sharply if it is optimal for insiders to have large ownership stakes in corporations in a specific country and foreign investors are not corporate insiders (Stulz, 2005). The existence of insider ownership thus limits the holdings of foreign investors.

The increasing importance of institutional investors may reduce the home bias. As professional parties, they may have better means to overcome the barriers to international investment. They employ, for example, analysts who can reduce the information asymmetries. Furthermore, due to their size, they can negotiate lower tariffs for large (cross-border) deals. Section 9.4 produces some empirical evidence on the impact of institutional investors on the home bias.

9.4 The home bias in European investment

Measuring the home bias

A *home bias* exists when investors underweight foreign assets in their portfolio while this might not be optimal from a diversification point of view. There is robust evidence across a large range of countries for the existence of such a home bias (Chan *et al.*, 2005). This section analyses to what extent (institutional) investors in Europe diversify their investments geographically.

By comparing the levels of the home bias between 1997 and 2004, it is possible to analyse whether the home bias has declined over time.

To derive the home bias, the international CAPM is used. The optimal portfolio with no bias can be calculated under strict assumptions (Elton *et al.*, 2007). In the international setting, these assumptions include fully integrated capital markets and purchasing-power parity. Fully integrated capital markets imply that investors can buy and sell securities in foreign markets without any restrictions or extra transaction costs. Under purchasing-power parity the long-run equilibrium exchange rates of currencies are equal to the currencies' purchasing power. It is based on the law of one price, which means that identical goods (including securities) in different markets must have the same price. When purchasing-power parity holds, exchange-rate risk is no longer relevant. If there are homogeneous expectations, all investors select the same optimal portfolio. Equilibrium in the international setting is achieved when all investors hold the world market portfolio in which each country portfolio is weighted by its market capitalisation.

The equity home bias, labelled EHB_i, is measured as one minus the *foreign asset acceptance ratio* which measures the extent to which the share of foreign assets in the portfolio of country i diverges from the relative share of foreign assets in the total world market portfolio (Ahearne *et al.*, 2004). The home bias is higher, the more the foreign asset acceptance ratio is below unity. The equity home bias is given by:

$$EHB_i = 1 - \frac{Foreign\ Equity_i}{Foreign\ Equity\ to\ Total\ Market_i} \qquad (9.7)$$

in which *Foreign Equity$_i$* = share of country i's holdings of foreign equity in country i's total equity portfolio (1 – share of domestic equity); *Foreign Equity to Total Market$_i$* = the share of foreign equity in the world portfolio available to country i (1 – share of country i in the total market capitalisation). The country portfolio is calculated as the domestic market capitalisation plus foreign equity holdings minus foreign owners of domestic equity.

Equation 9.7 measures to what extent domestic equity is overweighed compared with foreign equity in the investment portfolio. *EHB* will be equal to 0 if investors show no preference for equity issued domestically. If domestic investors have a preference for domestic equity, the ratio will be between 0 and 1. The home bias formula can be illustrated as follows. Country i investors allocate 15 per cent of their portfolio to foreign equity, while the total world market portfolio comprises 75 per cent of foreign equity and 25 per cent of domestic equity. Country i investors thus exploit international diversification to only one-fifth (15/75) and thus have a home bias of 0.8. EHB_i is 1.0 if domestic investors invest 100 per cent of their equity portfolio domestically. In a similar vein, the preference of investors for domestic debt securities can be measured. This home bias measure for bonds is BHB_i.

Finally, the *regional bias* can be measured. The question is whether European investors show a preference for European securities in their foreign securities portfolio in comparison with US securities. Within the part of the investment portfolio that is invested in foreign equity and bonds, EU investors should, according to the international CAPM, show no preference for either European or US equities and bonds.

Similar to the analysis of the domestic home bias, it can be tested whether European investors have a bias towards European equities and bonds. The regional bias for European investors is measured as one minus the US asset acceptance ratio. This ratio measures the extent to which the share of US assets in the foreign equity portfolio of country i diverges from the relative share of US assets in the total foreign market portfolio. The regional bias for equities is given by:

$$REB_i = 1 - \frac{US\ Equity_i}{US\ Equity\ to\ Foreign\ Market\ Portfolio_i} \qquad (9.8)$$

in which $US\ Equity_i$ = share of country i's holdings of US equity in country i's total foreign equity portfolio (1 – share of EU equity in foreign portfolio); *US Equity to Foreign Market Portfolio*$_i$ = share of US equity in the foreign-equity portfolio which is available for country i. The available foreign portfolio for country i is total domestic market capitalisation of EU and US minus domestic market capitalisation of country i.

The foreign market portfolio differs per country. For example, as the UK comprises a large part of total EU equity, the foreign equity portfolio for the UK is smaller than that of other countries. The same applies to the foreign bond portfolio. It is expected that the regional bond bias (RBB) is higher than the regional equity bias (REB) for the countries in the euro area, because there is no exchange rate risk involved, and international diversification of bonds primarily focuses on credit risk diversification.

Evidence on the home bias

Some recent empirical studies measure the development of the home bias in the EU-15 (Bosch and Schoenmaker, 2006; De Santis and Gérard, 2006).

Table 9.8 Equity and bond home bias, 1997–2004

	Equity home bias					Bond home bias				
	1997	2001	2004	Δ 97–01	Δ 97–04	1997	2001	2004	Δ 97–01	Δ 97–04
Austria	0.82	0.49	0.68	−0.33	−0.14	0.80	0.53	0.35	−0.27	−0.44
Belgium	0.86	0.73	0.69	−0.13	−0.17	0.84	0.63	0.56	−0.21	−0.28
Denmark	0.83	0.65	0.74	−0.18	−0.09	0.93	0.88	0.83	−0.05	−0.10
Finland	0.96	0.86	0.75	−0.10	−0.21	0.91	0.56	0.45	−0.35	−0.45
France	0.90	0.85	0.79	−0.05	−0.11	0.88	0.70	0.59	−0.18	−0.28
Germany	n.a.	0.77	0.77	n.a.	n.a.	n.a.	0.75	0.62	n.a.	n.a.
Greece	n.a.	0.99	0.97	n.a.	n.a.	n.a.	0.91	0.76	n.a.	n.a.
Italy	0.89	0.80	0.85	−0.09	−0.04	0.95	0.83	0.81	−0.12	−0.14
Netherlands	0.77	0.56	0.43	−0.21	−0.33	0.71	0.31	0.17	−0.40	−0.54
Portugal	0.94	0.89	0.85	−0.06	−0.10	0.84	0.62	0.58	−0.22	−0.27
Spain	0.95	0.89	0.93	−0.06	−0.02	0.96	0.76	0.63	−0.20	−0.33
Sweden	0.86	0.70	0.73	−0.16	−0.13	0.93	0.77	0.74	−0.17	−0.19
United Kingdom	0.84	0.80	0.80	−0.04	−0.04	0.61	0.49	0.38	−0.12	−0.23
United States	0.83	0.82	0.81	−0.01	−0.02	0.97	0.97	0.96	−0.00	−0.01
EU-13	0.86	0.78	0.78	−0.07	−0.08	0.84	0.69	0.60	−0.15	−0.24
Euro area	0.87	0.79	0.77	−0.08	−0.10	0.88	0.71	0.61	−0.17	−0.27
Non-euro area	0.84	0.78	0.79	−0.06	−0.05	0.72	0.60	0.53	−0.12	−0.19

Note: EU-13, euro, and non-euro area are calculated as a weighted average; n.a. means not available.
Source: Bosch and Schoenmaker (2006)

Table 9.8 gives an overview of the equity and bond home bias in 1997, 2001, and 2004.[2] All countries experienced a sharp decline of the equity home bias from 1997 to 2001. In most countries the home bias decreased further after 2001, but in some countries (such as Austria, Denmark, Italy, and Spain) the home bias increased after 2001. The Netherlands has the lowest home bias (0.43 in 2004); it also had the largest decline from 1997 to 2004. The southern European countries have a bias around 0.90. The equity home bias in the UK and the US decreased slightly from 1997 to 2004 but was still relatively high (0.80 and 0.81, respectively).

The weighted average bias for the EU-13 (EU-15 except for Ireland and Luxembourg) declined by 0.08 from 1997 to 2001, after which the bias remained stable at 0.78. It is interesting that the EU bias has decreased after the introduction of the euro, without a significant change of the US bias over this period. While the weighted-average bias for the countries in the euro area was higher in 1997 than the bias of the non-euro countries, the bias for the countries in the euro area decreased by 0.10 from 1997 to 2004 compared with 0.05 for the non-euro countries.

Table 9.8 also illustrates that the BHB has declined in all countries in the sample, and this reduction is in general larger than that of the EHB. In 2004, the BHB is the lowest for the Netherlands (0.17), followed by Austria and the UK. Denmark, Sweden, Greece, and Italy still exhibit a large BHB relative to the other EU Member States.

Compared with the EHB, the BHB is on average lower for the EU-13 countries. The weighted average BHB for the EU-13 was 0.60 in 2004, a reduction of 0.24 since 1997. The differences between the EU countries are larger for the BHB than for the EHB. The US has an exceptionally high BHB at 0.96. It can be concluded that US investors are very domestically focused within their long-term debt portfolios, and allocate only a small percentage of their bond portfolio to EU bonds. This is partly in line with theory. As the US economy is very large, there is more scope for US investors to diversify credit risk domestically without incurring exchange-rate risk.

For the EU, the largest decline has taken place in the period 1997 to 2001, which is related to the introduction of the euro. The decrease of the home bias for bonds from 1997 to 2004 is larger for the countries in the euro area (0.27) than for those outside the monetary union (0.19). The fact that the non-euro countries still have a lower BHB is fully driven by the UK. The reported results for the EHB and BHB are largely in line with the findings of De Santis and Gérard (2006). They also find a decline in the home bias from 1997–2001 for the countries in the sample.

As illustrated above, all countries in the sample exhibit a home bias towards domestic equities and bonds. Within the portfolio of foreign securities of the 14 countries in the sample, a distinction can be made between investments in European and US securities. If the home bias puzzle is mainly a geographical phenomenon, this implies that within their foreign portfolio European investors give too much importance to European securities.

Table 9.9 reports the output concerning the regional bias for equities and bonds. Investors in all European countries in the sample overweigh European relative to US equities. This means that the home bias also persists on a regional level. The weighted average REB for the EU-13 increased from 1997 to 2004. The split between countries inside and outside the euro area identifies an interesting pattern. The REB increased by 0.12 for the euro countries, while the bias declined by 0.09 for the non-euro countries.

Table 9.9 Regional equity and bond bias of European investors, 1997–2004

	Regional bias towards EU-13 equities					Regional bias towards EU-13 bonds				
	1997	2001	2004	Δ 97–01	Δ 97–04	1997	2001	2004	Δ 97–01	Δ 97–04
Austria	0.53	0.50	0.56	−0.03	0.03	0.68	0.82	0.86	0.14	0.18
Belgium	0.70	0.71	0.76	0.01	0.06	0.69	0.81	0.91	0.12	0.21
Denmark	0.58	0.42	0.39	−0.16	−0.19	0.75	0.71	0.65	−0.04	−0.10
Finland	0.69	0.61	0.73	−0.08	0.04	0.76	0.86	0.90	0.10	0.15
France	0.48	0.59	0.74	0.11	0.25	0.74	0.77	0.80	0.02	0.06
Germany	n.a.	0.59	0.62	n.a.	n.a.	n.a.	0.85	0.87	n.a.	n.a.
Greece	n.a.	0.44	0.23	n.a.	n.a.	n.a.	0.62	0.81	n.a.	n.a.
Italy	0.53	0.48	0.52	−0.05	−0.01	0.62	0.75	0.75	0.13	0.13
Netherlands	0.25	0.26	0.11	0.01	−0.14	0.81	0.70	0.74	−0.11	−0.07
Portugal	0.33	0.65	0.80	0.32	0.47	0.59	0.84	0.85	0.25	0.26
Spain	0.33	0.72	0.73	0.39	0.39	0.85	0.87	0.83	0.01	−0.02
Sweden	0.26	0.23	0.23	−0.03	−0.03	0.51	0.52	0.58	0.01	0.07
United Kingdom	0.47	0.53	0.38	0.07	−0.09	0.48	0.47	0.38	0.00	−0.10
EU-13	0.43	0.50	0.47	0.07	0.04	0.62	0.72	0.74	0.09	0.11
Euro area	0.41	0.52	0.53	0.11	0.12	0.73	0.79	0.82	0.06	0.09
Non-euro area	0.45	0.48	0.36	0.03	−0.09	0.43	0.49	0.41	0.06	−0.02

Notes: EU-13, euro, and non-euro area are calculated as a weighted average; n.a. means not available.
Source: Bosch and Schoenmaker (2006)

The Netherlands has the lowest REB of the EU-13 countries (0.11 in 2004), followed by Sweden and Greece (both 0.23). Denmark noticed the largest absolute decline (0.19) from 1997 to 2004. Portugal, Spain, Belgium, and France show a high preference for European equities in their foreign-investment portfolios. It is remarkable that the bias of Portugal, Spain, and France increased strongly from 1997 to 2004. Investors in these countries evidently moved to a euro-area investment strategy and thereby reduced their foreign (US) equity holdings.

Table 9.9 also reports the RBB of European investors. The weighted average for the EU-13 countries increased from 1997 to 2004. The increase in the RBB was driven by the euro countries. The RBB increased by 0.09 for the countries in the euro area and declined by 0.02 for those outside. The absolute value of the bias in 2004 was twice as large for the euro countries (0.82 vs. 0.41). The UK has the lowest RBB, followed by Sweden and Denmark (which are all non-euro countries). While the Netherlands had the lowest bias in

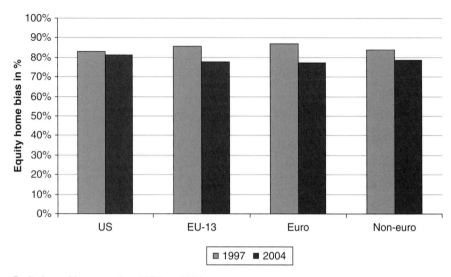

Figure 9.8   Equity home bias per region, 1997 vs. 2004

all previous tables, its RBB is equal to the EU-13 weighted average, at 0.74. Countries in the euro area, such as Austria, Belgium, and Finland, saw their RBB increase to around 0.90 in 2004. It can be concluded that for these countries the decline in the BHB is caused by a shift from domestic towards EU-13 bonds, and not to US bonds. These countries diversify the credit risk of the bond portfolio to a significant extent, but within the EU. The interest rate risk is hedged by investing primarily in EU bonds, which have interest rates which are almost identical (euro area) or linked (non-euro area) to domestic rates. Moreover, exchange-rate risk is largely eliminated.

The international diversification strategy of institutional investors is graphically illustrated in Figures 9.8–9.11. Data for 1997 and 2004 are compared for four regions: the US, the EU-13, the ten euro countries within the EU-13, and the three non-euro countries within the EU-13. Figures 9.8 and 9.9 illustrate that the decline in the home bias is larger for the EU than for the US. Within the EU-13 countries, the ten euro countries show a larger decline in the home bias than the three non-euro countries.

While the equity and bond home bias in the euro area have declined faster than in the non-euro countries (Figures 9.8 and 9.9), the reverse is true for the regional bias (Figures 9.10 and 9.11). In fact, this bias has increased for both equity and bonds in the euro area, but has decreased on average for the three non-euro countries. These results are consistent with the theory of economic integration. Since the introduction of the euro in 1999, investors in the

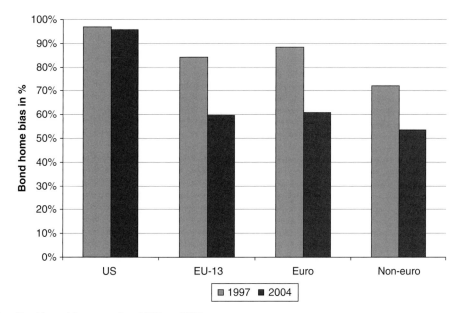

Figure 9.9   Bond home bias per region, 1997 vs. 2004

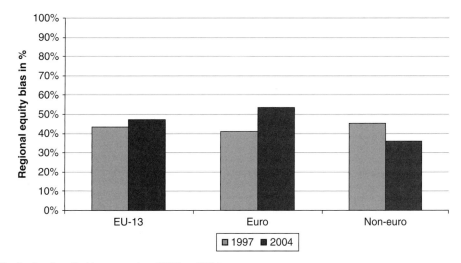

Figure 9.10   Regional equity bias per region, 1997 vs. 2004

euro countries have allocated a larger part of their portfolio to foreign assets than have non-euro countries and the US. At the same time, the regional bias of the euro area has increased, as investors in euro countries have invested their foreign assets mainly in their own region. Investors based in the euro area have thus shifted from a country-based investing strategy towards

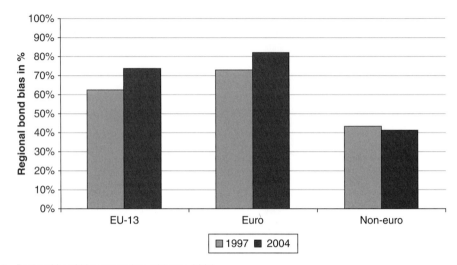

Figure 9.11   Regional bond bias per region, 1997 vs. 2004

a sector-based strategy. So there is a 'euro effect' as the euro has caused a decrease of the home bias but an increase of the regional bias. The regional bias decreased for the non-euro countries, which means that they partly shifted their foreign assets towards US assets compared with EU assets.

Explaining the home bias

If the gains of international diversification are positive and significant, why do (institutional) investors not hold the theoretically optimal portfolio? Table 9.10 explains which factors influence the size of the equity home bias.

The first factor is the ratio of total exports to GDP. This is a proxy for 'trade'. Investors in countries with a large export-to-GDP ratio have a lower need for international diversification, as the companies in these countries are already diversifying via their international business. However, this ratio could also be a proxy for the mindset of investors in a country indicating the openness of that country. If companies tend to do business abroad and diversify their business geographically, investors could act in the same manner.

Table 9.10 reports that export to GDP has a significant negative effect on the home bias. This supports the theory that countries with relatively large trade volumes can be considered as more 'open' and have a lower bias due to the *openness effect*. The domestic companies in these countries have significant exposure to the world market due to their level of international trade.

Table 9.10 Determinants of the equity home bias (OLS regression)

Independent variables	Expected sign	Coefficient	t-value
Constant		0.915***	17.3
Export	+/−	−0.324***	3.9
Institutional	−	−0.146**	2.4
Insider	+	0.127	1.3
Market cap	+	0.159*	2.0
N		42	
Adj. R^2		0.69	
F-statistic		16.25	

Notes: OLS panel regression using EHB_i as the dependent variable. Data for 1997, 2002, and 2004 for the EU-13 and the US are used for this analysis. Period-specific fixed effects are included in the regression. (***), (**), and (*) indicate statistical significance at the 1 per cent, 5 per cent, and 10 per cent levels, respectively.
Source: Bosch and Schoenmaker (2006)

However, investors in these countries are subject to a lower EHB, as they also tend to 'trade' (invest) internationally.

The second factor is the size of the institutional sector. Table 9.10 shows that the relative size of the institutional sector has a negative and significant effect on the home bias. Countries in which institutions manage a larger part of the financial assets exhibit larger international diversification. Indeed, this finding indicates that institutional investors, as professional asset managers, are subject to a lower home bias than non-financial corporations or households. This is the *professionalism effect.*

The third factor is the percentage of shares held by corporate insiders. Insider ownership is expected to increase the home bias in two ways. First, domestic investors hold shares that foreign investors cannot own. Second, domestic investors allocate a lower amount to foreign equity, as they have locked up a part of their portfolio in domestic assets. It should be noted, however, that the theory concerning insider ownership is developed to explain the bias towards a country (Stulz, 2005), but not necessarily the home bias of a country itself. The share of corporate insiders is the only variable that is not significant in Table 9.10, although it has the expected positive sign.

The fourth factor is the size of the domestic stock market to GDP. Table 9.10 illustrates that the relative size of the domestic stock market has a positive and significant effect on the home bias. Thus, investors are more domestically oriented if their domestic stock market is well developed. This indicates that investors are subject to the *availability effect*, which means that investors are more eager to invest in domestic assets when these domestic assets are readily available.

Finally, behavourial approaches may also explain the home bias. Behavioural finance draws upon psychological effects of individual behaviour. Huberman (2001), for example, argues that familiarity with domestic companies makes it easier for investors to invest in domestic equity. Campbell and Kräussl (2007) find that investors concerned with downside risk tend to hold a larger proportion of their portfolio in domestic equity, due to the greater downside risk from investing abroad.

9.5 Conclusions

The institutionalisation of the investment process, where professional market investors manage private savings, is a global trend. This chapter distinguishes three main types of institutional investors: pension funds, life insurance companies, and mutual funds. Both the demand side (growing investments by pension funds to cater for ageing and by mutual funds to accommodate wealth accumulation of households) and the supply side (shift from bank-financed companies to market-financed companies via equity and bonds) point to future growth of institutional investment.

As in many other financial sectors, distinctions between types of institutional investors are blurring. Mutual funds, in particular, are being used as a vehicle for retirement saving and are a specific asset class for pension funds. Private equity and hedge funds are alternative investments, which are increasingly added to the portfolio of pension funds. Insurance companies launch their own investment funds and are widely involved in pension provision, provision of annuities, and guaranteed investment contracts for pension funds, while also performing asset management for pension funds.

Institutional investors play an important role in monitoring companies in which they invest. This promotes good corporate governance. As dominant investors, institutions have the clout to influence the management of companies.

Finance theory suggests that investors should aim for international diversification of their investment portfolio to maximise returns given a certain risk profile. Nevertheless, there is a strong home bias in equity and bond portfolios. This chapter shows that the increasing professionalism of institutional investors (compared with individual investors) has led to a decline in the home bias in Europe. The elimination of exchange-rate risk following the introduction of the euro has led to a further decline of the home bias in the euro area.

NOTES

1 Davis and Steil (2001) discuss the two main approaches, namely *'prudent person rules'*, which enjoin portfolio diversification and broad asset-liability matching, and *'quantitative portfolio regulations'*, which limit holdings of certain types of asset within the portfolio. Both seek to ensure adequate portfolio diversification and liquidity of the asset portfolio, but in different ways.

2 Data concerning foreign equity and bond holdings are extracted from a country-level dataset of the IMF, the Coordinated Portfolio Investment Survey (CPIS). Luxembourg and Ireland are excluded from the EU-15 as they attract large amounts of foreign investment due to favourable tax policies, while the US is added to the dataset. This results in a sample of 14 countries. A proxy for the world market portfolio is the domestic market capitalisation of the EU-13 and the US. In this way, we analyse to what extent the EU-13 countries and the US overweight domestic equity in their portfolio compared with foreign equity.

SUGGESTED READING

Davis, E. P. and B. Steil (2001), *Institutional Investors*, MIT Press, Cambridge (MA).

Elton, E. J., M. J. Gruber, S. J. Brown, and W. M. Goetzmann (2007), *Modern Portfolio Theory and Investment Analysis*, 7th edition, John Wiley & Sons, New York.

Feldstein, M. S. and H. Siebert (eds.) (2002), *Social Security Pension Reform in Europe*, University of Chicago Press.

Gillan, S. L. and L. T. Starks (2003), Corporate Governance, Corporate Ownership, and the Role of Institutional Investors: A Global Perspective, *Journal of Applied Finance*, 13, 4–22.

Lewis, K. K. (1999), Trying to Explain Home Bias in Equities and Consumption, *Journal of Economic Literature*, 37, 571–608.

REFERENCES

Ahearne, A. B., W. Griever, and F. Warnock (2004), Information Costs and the Home Bias, *Journal of International Economics*, 62, 313–336.

Bosch, T. and D. Schoenmaker (2006), The Role and Importance of Institutional Investors in Europe, *Financial and Monetary Studies*, 24(3/4), SDU, The Hague.

Campbell, R. A. and R. Kräussl (2007), Revisiting the Home Bias Puzzle: Downside Equity Risk, *Journal of International Money and Finance*, 26, 1239–1260.

Chan, K., M. V. Covrig, and L. K. Ng (2005), What Determines the Domestic Bias and Foreign Bias? Evidence from Mutual Fund Equity Allocations Worldwide, *Journal of Finance*, 60, 1495–1534.

Davis, E. P. (2003), Institutional Investors, Financial Market Efficiency and Stability, The Pensions Institute (London) Working Paper PI-0303.

Davis, E. P. and B. Steil (2001), *Institutional Investors*, MIT Press, Cambridge (MA).

De Santis, R. A. and B. Gérard (2006), Financial Integration, International Portfolio Choice and the European Monetary Union, ECB Working Paper 626.

Elton, E. J., M. J. Gruber, S. J. Brown, and W. M. Goetzmann (2007), *Modern Portfolio Theory and Investment Analysis*, 7th edition, John Wiley & Sons, New York.

European Central Bank (2006), *EU Banking Structures*, ECB, Frankfurt am Main.

European Fund and Asset Management Association (2005), *Trends in European Investment Funds*, EFAMA, Brussels.

Feldstein, M. S. and H. Siebert (eds.) (2002), *Social Security Pension Reform in Europe*, University of Chicago Press.

Financial Stability Forum (2007), *Update of the FSF Report on Highly Leveraged Institutions*, FSF, Basel.

Furfine, C. (2006), The Costs and Benefits of Moral Suasion: Evidence from the Rescue of Long-Term Capital Management, *Journal of Business*, 79, 593–622.

Gillan, S. L. and L. T. Starks (2003), Corporate Governance, Corporate Ownership, and the Role of Institutional Investors: A Global Perspective, *Journal of Applied Finance*, 13, 4–22.

Hedge Fund Standards Board (2008), *Best Practice Standards*, HFSB, London.

Huberman, G. (2001), Familiarity Breeds Investment, *Review of Financial Studies*, 14, 659–680.

Jorion, P. (2000), Risk Management Lessons from Long-Term Capital Management, *European Financial Management*, 6, 277–300.

Karolyi, G. A. and R. M. Stulz (2003), Are Financial Assets Priced Locally or Globally?, in: G. M. Constantinides, M. Harris, and R. M. Stulz (eds.), *The Handbook of the Economics of Finance*, Elsevier, Amsterdam, 975–1020.

Kho, B. C., D. Lee, and R. M. Stulz (2000), US Banks, Crises, and Bailouts: From Mexico to LTCM, *American Economic Review*, 90, 28–31.

Khorana, A., H. Servaes, and P. Tufano (2005), Explaining the Size of the Mutual Fund Industry Around the World, *Journal of Financial Economics*, 78, 145–185.

Lewis, K. K. (1999), Trying to Explain Home Bias in Equities and Consumption, *Journal of Economic Literature*, 37, 571–608.

Organisation for Economic Co-operation and Development (2003), *Institutional Investors Statistical Yearbook*, OECD, Paris.

Rajan, R. G. (2007), Benign Financial Conditions, Asset Management, and Political Risks: Trying to Make Sense of our Times, in: D. D. Evanoff, G. G. Kaufman, and J. R. LaBrosse (eds.), *International Financial Stability: Global Banking and National Regulation*, World Scientific Publishing, Singapore, 19–28.

Schröder, M. (2003), Benefits of Diversification and Integration for International Equity and Bond Portfolios, ZEW Economic Studies 19, Heidelberg.

Smit, H. T. J. (2003), The Economics of Private Equity, ERIM (Erasmus University, Rotterdam) Report Series EIA-2002–13.

Stulz, R. M. (1999), Globalisation of Equity Markets and the Cost of Capital, NBER Working Paper 7021.

(2005), The Limits of Financial Globalisation, *Journal of Finance*, 60, 1595–1638.

TheCityUK (2011a), *Hedge Funds*, London.

(2011b), *Private Equity*, London.

10

European Banks

OVERVIEW

The traditional business of banking is the provision of long-term loans that are funded by short-term deposits. Banks have a comparative advantage against other financial institutions in providing liquidity. They have also developed technologies to screen and monitor borrowers in order to reduce asymmetric information between the lender and the borrower. These liquidity-providing and monitoring functions also give banks a key position in modern capital-market transactions, such as underwriting, trading, and derivatives transactions.

Risk is fundamental to the business of banking. Progress in information technology in combination with demands by supervisors has spurred the development of advanced risk-management models. This, in turn, has prompted the centralisation and integration of some management functions such as risk management, treasury operations, compliance, and auditing. This integrated approach to risk management aims to ensure a comprehensive and systematic approach to risk-related decisions throughout the banking group. Moreover, banks with an integrated risk-management unit can exploit diversification opportunities at the group level.

The European banking market is made up of 27 national banking systems. Each national banking system has its own characteristics, such as the number of banks, the level of concentration, and the intensity of competition. Some banking systems are highly concentrated, but this does not necessarily lead to a lack of competition. An important condition for competitive pressure is that the market is open to new entry (contestability). The European Commission therefore promotes the removal of remaining obstacles to cross-border mergers and acquisitions.

Domestic banking mergers used to be very common, while more recently the frequency of cross-border mergers has increased. While it is not possible yet to speak of an integrated banking market, the level of cross-border penetration has gradually increased.

LEARNING OBJECTIVES

After you have studied this chapter, you should be able to:

- explain the role of banks as liquidity providers to the economy
- explain the role of banks in screening and monitoring (potential) borrowers
- explain the use of risk-management models by modern banks and the centralisation of the risk-management function
- explain the dynamics of domestic and cross-border mergers and acquisitions in banking.

10.1 Theory of banking

Drivers of bank profitability

Banks perform multiple functions. The traditional business of banks is lending. Before a bank grants a loan, it screens the creditworthiness of a potential borrower. After the loan is granted, a bank monitors whether the borrower takes excessive risks. The lending business generates income for banks. As loans are funded with deposits, the difference (or spread) between the lending and borrowing rate determines a bank's profitability. Banks also make profits through various fee-earning activities, like capital-market transactions, such as underwriting and trading, and derivatives transactions. Banks use modern risk-management models to measure and control the risks arising from these transactions. These risk-management models are built on the monitoring technology that banks use in their lending business.

Lending business

Banks take deposits from the public and grant loans on their own account. These loans are typically held to maturity (the 'originate and hold' model). Banks are thus engaged in the transformation of liquid deposits into illiquid loans. The intermediation function of banks can be explained using a simple balance sheet (see Figure 10.1). On the liability side, banks fund themselves with many small deposits D from the public. The effective deposit rate r_D includes both the explicit interest paid and the cost of free services (for example, free access to ATMs). While deposits are redeemable on demand, depositors usually do not ask for their money back at the same time. Banks therefore hold only a fraction of these deposits in the form of liquid reserves

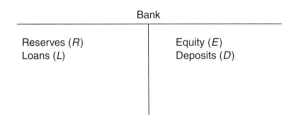

Figure 10.1   Simplified balance sheet of a bank

R that consist of balances with the central bank or readily tradable assets, such as Treasury securities, that pay the risk-free rate r_F.

Banks grant loans L on their own account. The expected loan rate r_L is different from the contracted rate on loans, as some borrowers default on their loan. Assuming a risk-neutral bank, the difference between the contracted or promised loan rate r_P and the expected loan rate r_L is given by:

$$E\left(1 + r_p\right) = \left(1 + r_p\right) \cdot \left(1 - p\right) + \left(1 + r_p\right) \cdot p \cdot \gamma = 1 + r_L \qquad (10.1)$$

where p is the probability of default and γ the recovery rate (the fraction of the principal and interest recovered in case of default). Equation 10.1 can be illustrated with a simple example. Assume a promised loan rate of 9 per cent, a probability of default of 5 per cent and a recovery rate of 80 per cent. The expected loan rate is 7.91 per cent, calculated as (1.09 * 0.95) + (1.09 * .05 * 0.8) = 1.0791.

The bank's profit π is the interest margin net of cost (C) and is given by:

$$\pi = L \cdot r_L + R \cdot r_F - D \cdot r_D - C \qquad (10.2)$$

An important determinant of bank profitability is the risk premium RP, i.e. the difference between the promised loan rate and the risk-free rate ($r_p - r_F$). The risk premium covers the expected loan losses (that are a function of p and γ), the cost of the loan business, and the reward for risk taking on the loans.

Fee-based business

Banks also make profits from fee-earning activities. These off-balance sheet activities are related to the traditional loan business and include securitisation of assets (see Chapter 1), credit lines, and guarantees, such as letters of credit. Off-balance sheet activities also encompass derivative transactions, such as forwards, options, and swaps. Nowadays, large banks are the key players in the derivatives markets.

Asset securitisation involves the sale of income-generating financial assets (such as mortgages, car loans, trade receivables, credit card receivables, and leases) by a bank, the originator of the financial assets, to a *special purpose vehicle* (SPV). The SPV finances the purchase of these financial assets by the issue of commercial paper, which is secured by those assets (see Chapter 8). Banks can thus liquefy their illiquid loans. The resulting 'originate and distribute' model separates the functions of granting loans and funding loans. When loans on their balance sheet are securitised, banks can provide new loans.

Finally, banks are increasingly involved in fee-earning capital-market and asset management activities. European banks deliver services like underwriting securities, advising on mergers and acquisitions (M&As), and managing assets. In this way, they have recovered part of the business lost due to dis-intermediation (see Chapter 9). Currently, non-interest income of banks in the EU amounts to 40 per cent of total income (ECB, 2010b).

Banks as liquidity providers

Banks have an advantage compared with other financial institutions in providing liquidity. This advantage is rooted in the structure of the banking system (Garber and Weisbrod, 1990). First, under normal circumstances there is an active and deep interbank market in which banks trade their liquidity surpluses and deficits so that liquidity shocks at individual banks can easily be offset. A bank with a surplus lends to a bank with a deficit, and vice versa. As shown in Chapter 5, the euro interbank market has worked smoothly from the first day of EMU until the crisis. Money market rates quickly converged to a single euro-wide money market rate. TARGET2 (the wholesale payment system of the National Central Banks and the European Central Bank) provide the infrastructure for transferring funds in real time (see Chapter 7).

Second, aggregate liquidity shocks are smoothed by the central bank. A central bank conducts open market operations to inject (withdraw) liquidity in the money market if there is an aggregate shortage (surplus). Banks are the usual counterparties of the central bank in these open market operations. If an individual bank cannot square its position at the end of the day, it can use facilities offered by the central bank. To stimulate banks to do their business as much as possible on the money market, the rates for these standing facilities are slightly off-market. The ECB's deposit rate is, for example, 0.75 per cent below the official refinancing rate for open market operations and the marginal lending rate is 0.75 per cent above the official refinancing rate (see Chapter 4).

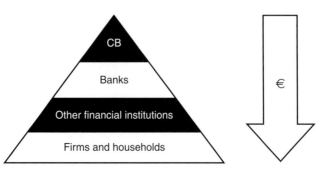

Figure 10.2 Liquidity pyramid of the economy

Note: CB = central bank. In this liquidity pyramid, the central bank provides liquidity to the banking system. Banks in turn provide liquidity to other financial institutions. Banks also provide liquidity to firms and households.

These features of the banking system enable banks to provide liquidity to other financial institutions if and when needed. More importantly, they are also the main provider of liquidity to households and firms. The liquidity pyramid in Figure 10.2 illustrates these relationships. The central bank is at the top of the pyramid, as it can create liquidity without limit by expanding its balance sheet (granting loans and taking deposits). As explained above, the central bank only provides liquidity to banks that in turn provide liquidity to the rest of the financial system and to households and firms. Especially during crises it is important that central banks act swiftly to provide liquidity. However, banks also play a crucial role under these circumstances, as the examples presented in Box 10.1 illustrate.

Banks as delegated monitor

Asymmetric information lies at the core of banking. A borrower has private information on the cash flow of an investment project, which is unobservable to outside lenders. Banks therefore monitor (potential) clients. Monitoring is defined here in a broad sense (Freixas and Rochet, 2008) as:

- screening projects ex ante (adverse selection);
- preventing opportunistic behaviour of the borrower during the project (moral hazard);
- auditing a borrower who fails to meet its contractual obligation (costly state verification).

Banks have a comparative advantage in monitoring (potential) borrowers if the following conditions are met (Diamond, 1984). First, a bank can develop economies of scale in monitoring by financing many investment

---

Box 10.1 Liquidity management during crises

On 19 October 1987 the US stock market crashed, with the S&P 500 stock market index falling about 20 per cent. The crash showed the vulnerability of the trading systems as they were not capable of processing so many transactions at once. Uncertainty about information contributed to a pull-back by investors from the market. Another factor contributing to the crash were *margin calls* to securities traders that accompanied the large price changes. When securities traders buy securities with borrowed money, they have to deposit a margin with the clearinghouse to cover the credit risk of the clearinghouse. As the value of securities declined, the clearinghouse called for extra margin. While necessary to protect the solvency of the clearinghouse processing the trades, the size of the margin calls reduced market liquidity as securities traders had drawn on their working capital to meet these margin calls and subsequently had difficulties in continuing trading. The Federal Reserve stepped in by providing highly visible liquidity support through massive open market operations. More importantly, the Federal Reserve also encouraged banks to extend liquidity support to securities traders (brokers and dealers). The extension of credit by banks to securities firms was key to their ability to meet their clearing and settlement obligations and to continue to operate in these markets.

Another example was the subprime mortgage market crisis in the summer of 2007. Many banks, including various large banks, such as Goldman Sachs, City Group, and Merrill Lynch, announced large losses due to this crisis. As it was unclear to what extent banks were exposed to these risks, banks were reluctant to provide short-term loans to each other. The ECB and the Federal Reserve therefore stepped in and provided massive liquidity support. The Bank of England (BoE), however, initially remained on the sidelines. On 12 September 2007 BoE governor Mervyn King said the Bank of England would be prepared to provide emergency loans to any bank that ran into short-term difficulties as a result of temporary market conditions. But he appeared to rule out following the lead of the ECB and the US Federal Reserve in pumping huge sums into the banking system to ease the liquidity drought. On 13 September, British bank Northern Rock, the country's fifth largest mortgage lender, applied to the BoE for emergency funds caused by liquidity problems. Concerned customers withdrew an estimated £2 billion in just three days; this was the first run on a British bank in more than a century. On 17 September, Chancellor Alistair Darling intervened to try to end the crisis by agreeing to guarantee all deposits held by Northern Rock.

---

projects. Second, the capacity of individual lenders is small compared to the size of many investment projects so that each project needs several lenders who would then need to monitor the borrowers. Finally, the costs of delegating this monitoring to a bank are small. Box 10.2 presents the Diamond model of delegated monitoring that shows that under these conditions it is efficient to delegate monitoring to a bank.

Box 10.2 When is it optimal to delegate monitoring to banks?*

Consider n identical borrowers who need funds for their investment projects. Each investment requires one unit of account and the returns of the investment are identically independently distributed. The cash flow $\tilde{y}$ that a borrower obtains from his investment is unobservable for lenders. The asymmetric information regarding the cash flow gives rise to moral hazard, which can be solved either by monitoring the firm at a cost K or by signing a debt contract with a cost C (in case of insufficient cash flow). It is assumed that monitoring is more efficient than using the debt contract: $K < C$. The next assumption is that each lender has only $\frac{1}{m}$ available for investment (i.e. lenders have a small capacity to lend). So each project needs m lenders. If small lenders provide the funds needed for the investment (direct lending), the total costs of monitoring all projects by all borrowers would amount to $n \cdot m \cdot K$.

Next, a bank is introduced. Facing the same trade-off between monitoring or signing debt contracts, the bank will also choose to monitor borrowers since $K < C$. The bank emerges as a delegated monitor, which monitors the borrowers on behalf of lenders. But who will monitor the bank? It is very costly for all lenders to monitor the bank. The solution is that the bank offers a debt contract (deposit). The lender is promised a nominal amount $\frac{r_D}{m}$ in return for a deposit $\frac{1}{m}$. The bank is liquidated if its announced cash flow $\tilde{z}$ falls below the total sum promised to depositors $n \cdot r_D$. Now, a mechanism is needed to ensure that a bank will truthfully reveal the realised cash flow $\tilde{z} = \sum_{i=1}^{n} \tilde{y}_i - n.K$. The threat of an audit in case of failure at a cost is used to make the contract incentive compatible.

Suppose that depositors are risk neutral and have access to outside investments with a return of r. The equilibrium repayment on deposits r_D is then determined by:

$$E\left[\min\left(\sum_{i=}^{n} \tilde{y}_i - n \cdot K, n \cdot r_D\right)\right] = n \cdot r \tag{10.3}$$

Equation 10.3 shows that the return r is equal to the minimum of the expected cash flow of the project minus monitoring costs and the expected unit return on deposits. In equilibrium, the expected unit return on deposits r_D equals r. Next, the total cost of delegation C_n is equal to the expectation of a costly audit in case of failure:

$$C_n = E\left[\max\left(n \cdot r_D + n \cdot K - \sum_{i=1}^{n} \tilde{y}_i, 0\right)\right] \tag{10.4}$$

Delegated monitoring is more efficient than direct lending if the combined cost of monitoring by the bank and delegation is lower than the cost of monitoring by all lenders:

$$n \cdot K + C_n < n \cdot m \cdot K \tag{10.5}$$

Dividing by n gives:

$$K + \frac{C_n}{n} < m \cdot K \tag{10.6}$$

Since $m > 1$, monitoring by bank is less costly than monitoring by all lenders if $\frac{C_n}{n}$ goes to zero when n goes to infinity. Dividing equations (10.3) and (10.4) by n produces:

$$E\left[\min\left(\frac{1}{n} \sum_{i=1}^{n} \tilde{y}_i - K, r_D \right) \right] = r \tag{10.7}$$

and

$$\frac{C_n}{n} = E\left[\max\left(r_D + K - \frac{1}{n} \sum_{i=1}^{n} \tilde{y}_i, 0 \right) \right] \tag{10.8}$$

According to the law of large numbers, $\frac{1}{n} \sum_{i=1}^{n} \tilde{y}_i$ converges to $E(\tilde{y})$. Since $E(\tilde{y}) > K + r$, equation (10.7) shows that $r_D = r$ when n goes to infinity. Substituting these results into equation (10.8) yields:

$$\lim_{n} \frac{C_n}{n} = \max\left(r + K - E\left(\tilde{y} \right), 0 \right) = 0 \tag{10.9}$$

So, the cost of delegation goes to zero when n goes to infinity.

Source: Freixas and Rochet (2008)

When the number of borrowers is large, it is efficient to delegate monitoring to one party. In the model shown in Box 10.2, a bank emerges as the delegated monitor for all lenders. Another party to whom lenders may delegate monitoring is a credit rating agency. A *credit rating agency* assigns credit ratings to firms and governments that issue debt obligations, such as bonds (see Chapter 8).[1] A credit rating measures the creditworthiness of a firm. It basically looks at the firm's ability to pay back a loan, which can be derived from observing the firm's cash flows. The resulting credit rating affects the interest rate charged for the bonds.

What determines the choice between direct and intermediated lending? In practice, direct lending in the form of issuing bonds at the capital market is less expensive than bank lending. So only those firms that cannot issue direct debt on financial markets will request bank lending (Freixas and Rochet, 2008). When the uncertainty about the firm's cash flows is relatively small (i.e. the asymmetric information between the firm and the lenders is limited), the firm can borrow on the market. As the uncertainty increases, banks come into play as they have more possibilities than credit rating agencies to ask for information and to intervene when necessary. When the uncertainty becomes too large, a firm cannot obtain finance. The resulting equilibrium is that large, well-capitalised firms with a track record of published annual reports finance themselves directly, while smaller, new firms have to turn to banks.

10.2 The use of risk-management models

Risk taking is fundamental to the business of banking. Only by taking calculated financial risks can a bank earn a rate above the risk-free rate of return. Banks unbundle and bundle financial risks. First, risks are decomposed so that they can be managed one by one. For example, the risk on a bank loan with a fixed interest rate can be separated into interest rate risk (i.e. the risk of loss because of rising interest rates) and credit risk (i.e. the risk of loss because of a default by a borrower). The bank can separately manage the interest rate risk (e.g. by buying an interest rate derivative with the same maturity as the bank loan) and the credit risk (e.g. by requiring collateral from the borrower). Next, risks are aggregated to reap the benefits of diversification. An example is a diversified portfolio of loans to companies from different sectors and/or geographic regions. The traditional role of banks in monitoring credit risk has evolved towards the use of advanced models to measure and manage risk. Risk management has been broadened from credit risk to market risk (i.e. the risk of loss because of unfavourable movements in market prices) and operational risk (i.e. the risk of loss from inadequate or failed internal processes, people or systems, or from external events). Progress in information technology has facilitated the development of risk-management models, which rely on statistical methods to process financial data. The financial services sector is one of the most IT-intensive industries (Berger, 2003).

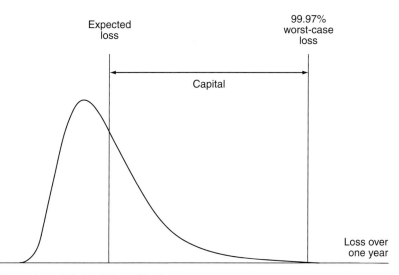

Figure 10.3   Economic capital of an AA-rated bank
Source: Hull (2009)

Modern risk management

The main risk types for a bank are credit risk, market risk, and operational risk. The concept of economic capital can be used for measuring different risks in a comparable way. *Economic capital* is defined as the amount of capital a bank needs in order to be able to absorb losses over a certain time interval with a certain confidence level. Banks usually choose a time horizon of one year. The confidence interval depends on the bank's objectives. A common objective for a large international bank is to maintain an AA credit rating (Hull, 2009). Companies rated AA have a one-year probability of default of 0.03 per cent. This results in a confidence level of 99.97 per cent. Figure 10.3 illustrates the calculation of economic capital.

Economic capital can be used to calculate the *risk adjusted return on capital* (RAROC) that is given by:

$$\text{RAROC} = \frac{\text{Revenues} - \text{Costs} - \text{Expected Losses}}{\text{Economic Capital}} = \frac{\pi}{E} \qquad (10.10)$$

Both the numerator and the denominator are adjusted for risk in the RAROC formula. This is an improvement compared with the widely used standard *return on equity measure* (ROE), defined as earned profit divided by available equity. An example can illustrate the working of RAROC. An

AA-rated bank estimates its expected losses as 1 per cent of outstanding loans per year on average. The worst-case loss at 99.97 per cent confidence is 4 per cent of outstanding loans. So the economic capital for €100 of loans is €3 (the difference between worst-case loss and expected loss). The numerator starts with the revenues: the spread between the promised loan rate and the risk-free rate is 2.20 per cent. The costs of the bank amount to 0.75 per cent of the loan. So RAROC is $\frac{2.20-0.75-1.00}{3.00} = 15$ per cent.

RAROC is emerging as the leading methodology for large banks (as well as other financial institutions, such as insurance companies) to measure and manage risk. The use of internal risk models has been stimulated by supervisors allowing banks to use their internal models to calculate capital requirements (see Chapter 12 for the Basel capital adequacy rules). Within the RAROC framework, banks first calculate the risk for credit, market, and operational risk and then aggregate the different risk types for the whole bank. To assess the overall risk profile of the bank, correlations across risk types have to be taken into account. But such a full approach that incorporates diversification effects between risk types is still in the early stages of development (Van Lelyveld, 2006).

The first type of risk is credit risk. *Credit risk* is defined as the risk of loss because of the failure of a counterparty to perform according to the contractual arrangement, for instance due to a default by a borrower.[2] In a modern bank, counterparties include not only the traditional counterparties on loans (borrowers) but also counterparties in derivatives transactions and in payment and settlement systems. Diversification is an important tool to manage credit risk. By lending to companies from different sectors, banks can diversify away the sectoral exposures in their loan portfolio. Similarly, international expansion would reduce the business-cycle risk. As long as business cycles across euro-area countries are not fully synchronised, there is scope for diversification within Europe. Clearly, geographic (and sectoral) diversification would not protect a bank against a worldwide economic downturn. A second tool to manage credit risk is monitoring counterparties.

The typical time horizon for credit risk is one year. This type of risk thus fits nicely into economic capital models that also use the one-year horizon. Figure 10.4 gives the loss distribution for credit risk. Its shape is quite skewed, as the vast majority of counterparties will repay (almost) in full and only a minority default (partly) on their payment obligation.

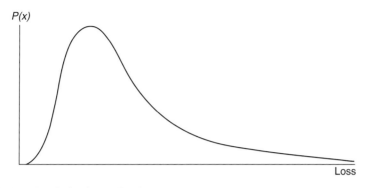

Figure 10.4 Loss distribution for credit risk

The second type of risk is market risk. *Market risk* is the risk of loss because of unfavourable movements in market prices like interest rates, foreign exchange rates, equity prices, and commodity prices. Market risk relates primarily to a bank's trading portfolio and focuses on changes in market value. Losses due to market risk materialise when an adverse price

---

Box 10.3 Value-at-Risk

A primary tool for measuring market risk is the *Value-at-Risk methodology*. The VaR measure summarises the expected maximum loss (i.e. Value-at-Risk) over a target horizon of N days within a given confidence interval of X per cent. As will be discussed in Chapter 12, the Basel capital framework calculates capital for a bank's trading book using the VaR measure with $N = 10$ and $X = 99\%$. This means that the bank is 99 per cent certain that the loss level over 10 days will not exceed the VaR measure. So only in 1 out of 100 trading days is the bank's loss expected to exceed the VaR measure.

The main advantage is that the risk of a portfolio comprising various financial assets is contained in a single measure, the VaR measure. Figure 10.6 illustrates VaR for the situation where the change in the value of a portfolio is approximately normally distributed. The basic VaR methodology assumes a normal (bell-shaped) distribution of returns. However, the returns on financial assets are non-normal with heavy tails (Daníelsson, 2011). So VaR underestimates the market risk of a portfolio. Extreme value theory, which uses extreme values (e.g. one-day losses of 5 per cent or larger) to measure the tails of a distribution more accurately, is typically applied to get a better estimation of the downside risk of a portfolio of assets. Alternatively, banks can complement the VaR methodology with stress-test scenarios to get a better picture of potential losses.

Source: Hull (2009)

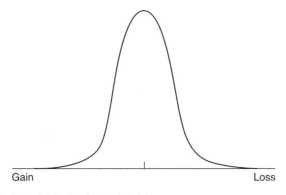

Gain   Loss

Figure 10.5 Loss distribution for market risk

movement causes the mark-to-market valuation of a trading position to decline. Banks typically manage their trading portfolio within a Value-at-Risk framework (VaR) with a ten-day time horizon (see Box 10.3). The rationale is that a bank can close its position (e.g. selling a security or taking an opposite position in a new derivative transaction) within ten business days. Under certain assumptions, the standard deviation of ten-day losses can be translated to the one-year horizon of economic capital models.[3]

A specific market risk occurs when assets and liabilities in the balance sheet are not matched. This risk is labelled *asset and liability management (ALM) risk*. The ALM risk of banks refers to the interest rate risk in the banking book, where long-term assets (loans) are funded by short-term liabilities (deposits). Insurance companies face the opposite problem: their liabilities have typically a longer maturity than assets (see Chapter 11).

The loss distribution for market risk is very different from that for credit risk. Figure 10.5 shows that the loss distribution for market risk is symmetrical. A good example is the price of equity. According to the efficient market hypothesis, all available information (including information on the future prospects of a company) is reflected in the equity price of a company. So today's stock price is the best predictor of tomorrow's stock price. The stock price will move only with the arrival of new information, which appears randomly. The stock price follows a random walk with equal likelihood of upward and downward movements.

More recently, operational risk has become part of risk management. *Operational risk* is defined as the risk of loss from inadequate or failed internal processes, people or systems, or from external events. A famous example of operational risk is the failure of Barings Bank in 1995. Nick Leeson, a trader for Barings in Singapore, made money by arbitraging between the Nikkei 225

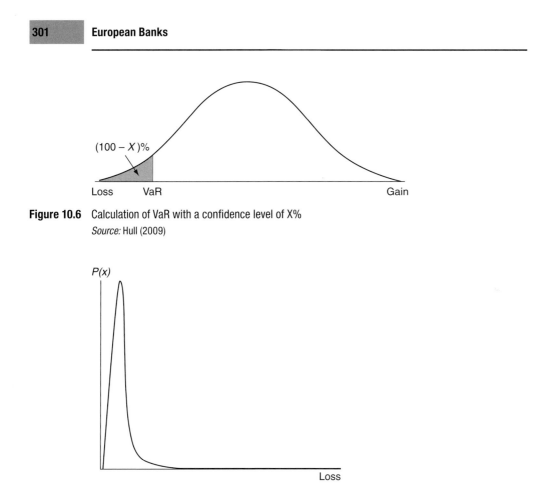

Figure 10.6   Calculation of VaR with a confidence level of X%
Source: Hull (2009)

Figure 10.7   Loss distribution for operational risk

futures on the Singapore and the Osaka exchanges. Barings had no effective risk limits in place and Nick Leeson could build up large positions. When the market moved against Leeson, Barings' total loss was close to $1 billion (Hull, 2009). A more recent example was the rogue trader scandal at Société Générale (SocGen) that cost the bank €4.9 billion. Jérôme Kerviel, a junior trader at SocGen, secretly built up huge and risky positions in the derivatives market. He was taking greater and greater risks over a period dating back to March 2007 for large amounts and to 2005 for smaller amounts. SocGen only discovered the fraud between 18 and 20 January 2008. Unwinding the positions over the subsequent three days cost the bank billions. The variety of concealment techniques used, a lack of systematic checks by staff when warning flags were raised, and shortcomings in the control systems all contributed to the late discovery of Kerviel's activities.

Other examples of operational risk are IT failures or terrorist attacks. The Barings and SocGen examples illustrate that operational risk can interact with credit and market risk. When a trader exceeds limits, losses result only if the market moves against the trader. Figure 10.7 provides the loss distribution for operational risk. The loss distribution is very skewed, even more skewed than the credit risk loss distribution. Most of the time, operational losses are modest, but occasionally they are very large.

While credit, market, and operational risk can threaten their solvency (and are therefore incorporated in the economic capital calculation), banks also incur liquidity risk. *Liquidity risk* arises when a bank has insufficient liquid resources to meet a surge in liquidity demand. (In Chapter 5, *market liquidity* is discussed and defined as the ease with which an investor can sell or buy a security immediately at a price close to the fair price.) The classical case of a surge in liquidity demand for a bank is the sudden withdrawal of deposits. Banks manage their liquid resources in two ways. The first way is maintaining a pool of liquid assets. Reserves at the central bank are the most liquid assets but generate a relatively low return. Other liquid assets are government bonds, which can be easily sold. But a bank typically holds only a fraction of its demand deposits in liquid assets. The remainder is invested in illiquid, but high-return, assets such as loans. These assets can be liquidated immediately only at low prices.

The second way banks can manage liquidity risk is by preserving a diversified funding base (also referred to as *funding liquidity*). As explained in section 10.1, banks can fund themselves in the interbank market. As long as banks have sufficient confidence in each other, a bank is able to borrow from other banks. Trust is therefore the most important 'asset' for a bank. When a bank loses the trust of other banks, it will face liquidity problems and possibly even failure. A case in point is the failure of Continental Illinois Bank in May 1984. This bank experienced funding difficulties in domestic markets and Continental therefore had to turn to more expensive Eurodollar deposits in London. Rumours that Continental was on the verge of bankruptcy resulted in a run on Continental's wholesale deposits by both domestic and foreign banks.

Centralisation of risk management

The organisational structure of international banks is moving from the traditional country model to a business-line model with integration and centralisation of key management functions (Schoenmaker and Oosterloo, 2008). These management functions comprise risk management, internal controls, treasury operations (including liquidity management and funding), compliance, and auditing. One of the most notable advances in risk management is the growing emphasis on developing a firm-wide assessment of risk. Such an integrated approach to risk management aims to ensure a comprehensive and systematic approach to risk-related decisions throughout the financial group. It allows senior management to have a full picture of the group's overall risk profile. RAROC provides the methodology to compare and aggregate different risks.

Moreover, financial groups with a centralised risk management unit in place could reap economies of scale in risk management. Nevertheless, these centralised systems still rely on local branches and subsidiaries for local market data. The potential capital reductions that can be achieved by applying the advanced approaches of the Basel framework (see Chapter 12) encourage banking groups to organise their risk management more centrally. A well-constructed risk and capital management framework can deliver significant benefits and substantially strengthen the competitive position of financial groups. The emergence of so-called chief risk officers (CROs) at the headquarters of large financial groups illustrates this trend towards centralisation.

The dominant approach among large international financial institutions is to adopt a 'hub and spoke' organisational model (Kuritzkes *et al.*, 2003). The spokes are responsible for risk management within business lines, while the hub provides centralised oversight of risk and capital at the group level. Activities at the spoke include the credit function within a bank, as local managers are familiar with the local conditions, such as the business cycle relevant for credit risk in a country. Moreover, aggregation across risk factors within a business line also typically takes place in the spokes.

While the hub is dependent on risk reporting from the spokes, in many cases it is also responsible for overseeing the development of an integrated economic capital framework (such as RAROC) that is then implemented within the spokes. The specific roles of the hub vary, but tend to include assuming responsibility for group-level risk reporting, participating in decisions about group capital structure, funding practices, and target debt rating, acting as liaison with regulators and rating agencies, and advising on major risk transfer transactions, such as collateralised loan obligations and securitisations.

10.3 The European banking system

Banking markets across Europe

The banking markets of most EU Member States are dominated by domestic banks. One way to assess the presence of foreign banks is *cross-border*

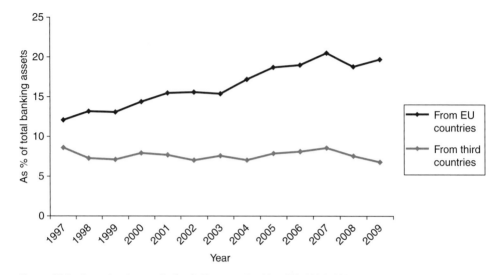

Figure 10.8 Cross-border penetration in European banking (%), 1997–2009

Note: Share of assets from other EU countries and third countries measured as a percentage of total banking assets. The share is calculated for the EU-27.

Source: Schoenmaker (2011)

penetration. This measure is defined as the assets of banks from other EU Member States (or third countries) as a percentage of the country's total banking assets. Average cross-border penetration in the EU gradually increased from 12 per cent in 1997 to 20 per cent in 2009 (Figure 10.8). Cross-border penetration from third countries was 7 per cent in 2009. However, the degree of cross-border penetration is very uneven across the EU Member States, as Table 10.1 shows. While the banking systems of the new Member States are dominated by banks from other EU countries (with a penetration rate of 63 per cent), average cross-border penetration in the EU-15 is only 19 per cent. With 84 per cent, Luxembourg has the highest cross-border penetration (reflecting the country's favourable tax regime), while the corresponding figures for France, Germany, the Netherlands, and Sweden are 10 per cent or less.

Table 10.1 also shows that the penetration by banks from third countries is well below 10 per cent for all EU Member States, except for the UK where it stands at 24 per cent, illustrating London's position as a major international financial centre. Most banking business in London is focused on large firms (i.e. wholesale). There is much evidence suggesting that EU wholesale banking markets are highly integrated, in contrast to retail banking, i.e. banking services delivered to consumers and SMEs. Most small customers receive their financial services from domestic suppliers, and the range and terms

Table 10.1 Cross-border penetration in EU Member States, 2009

	(1) Number of banks	(2) Total banking assets (in € billion)	(3) Assets of domestic banks (in % of (2))	(4) Assets of banks from other EU countries (in % of (2))	(5) Assets of banks from third countries (in % of (2))
Austria	790	1,037	81	15	5
Belgium	104	1,156	39	54	7
Bulgaria	30	38	16	82	2
Cyprus	155	139	63	33	4
Czech Republic	56	160	6	90	4
Denmark	164	1,105	80	18	2
Estonia	18	21	5	95	0
Finland	349	388	33	67	0
France	712	7,156	89	10	1
Germany	1,948	7,424	89	10	1
Greece	66	490	79	21	0
Hungary	190	126	41	56	3
Ireland	498	1,324	50	43	7
Italy	801	3,692	87	13	1
Latvia	37	30	31	63	6
Lithuania	84	26	17	83	0
Luxembourg	147	798	6	84	10
Malta	24	41	62	33	5
Netherlands	295	2,217	93	5	2
Poland	710	274	32	59	9
Portugal	166	520	77	22	1
Romania	42	86	24	76	0
Slovakia	26	55	4	96	0
Slovenia	25	53	71	29	0
Spain	352	3,433	90	10	0
Sweden	180	935	92	7	1
United Kingdom	389	9,421	48	27	24
EU-15	6,961	41,093	75	19	7
NMS-12	1,397	1,051	33	63	4
EU-27	8,358	42,144	74	20	7

Notes: Share of business from domestic banks, share of business of banks from other EU countries, and share of business of banks from third countries are measured as a percentage of the total banking assets in a country. The shares add up to 100 per cent. Figures are for 2009. EU-15, NMS-12, and EU-27 are calculated as a weighted average (weighted according to assets).
Source: ECB (2010a)

Box 10.4 Retail banking market integration

According to Dermine (2006), the 'law of one price', which represents the theoretical benchmark for integrated markets, is unlikely to hold in retail banking markets for various reasons. First, trust and confidence are important in these markets. Customers want to be sure that their money is in safe hands. Knowledge of the respective bank, the national legal system, language, cultural preferences, and geographical proximity may lead to a preference for a domestic bank, i.e. there are differentiated products. Second, retail customers generally buy a package of financial services from the same bank, rather than individual services. Therefore, the 'law of one price' may hold for the bundle of services, but not necessarily for each individual service. Third, asymmetric information in lending is quite important, and local knowledge can help to reduce this information asymmetry. Local banks may therefore be in a better position to lend to SMEs than foreign banks. Fourth, the 'law of one price' assumes the absence of transportation costs and regulatory barriers. But differences in legislation, like tax and consumer-protection rules, may create substantial barriers for foreign bank entry.

Still, there is evidence that EU retail banking markets also have become more integrated. Figure 10.9 shows that differences in EU retail banking interest rates have diminished substantially, but integration is still far from being perfect. In 2006 variation ranged from 20 per cent for loans to enterprises to 28.4 per cent for mortgage loans to households. Furthermore, using the beta- and sigma-convergence measures as explained in Chapter 6, Vajanne (2007) finds evidence for increased convergence in retail banking credit interest rates for households and non-financial corporations in the euro area between January 2003 and May 2006.

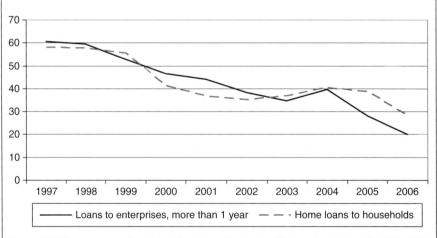

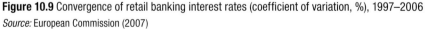

Figure 10.9 Convergence of retail banking interest rates (coefficient of variation, %), 1997–2006
Source: European Commission (2007)

Nevertheless, Kleimeier and Sander (2007) argue that integration in EU retail banking markets is still far from perfect, while integration has been strong in wholesale markets. In particular, they find that price stickiness is a major feature of European retail banking (i.e. banks are slow with lowering lending interest rates when the ECB reduces its interest rate). As a way forward, Kleimeier and Sander (2007) propose to foster integration of wholesale markets in conjunction with developing and preserving competitive banking markets. Competition can speed up the transmission of monetary impulses to retail bank lending interest rates. As the pass-through becomes faster and more homogeneous across countries, it will create a de facto integrated retail banking market.

under which products are available differ substantially across the EU Member States. Box 10.4 identifies some reasons why integration of retail banking markets is so difficult.

In 2009, there were nearly 8,400 banks in the EU. These banks can be segmented into three groups. The first, very large, group of banks consists of small banks operating in a region of a country. In particular, Germany and Austria have many small savings and cooperative banks, most of which have assets of less than €2 billion. About 20 per cent of German banks belong to public savings groups and about 60 per cent to the cooperative banking sector (Hackethal, 2004). The second group consists of medium-sized banks with assets ranging from €2 to €100 billion. These banks often operate on a country-wide scale. The third group are the large banks having assets up to €2,000 billion; they usually do a significant part of their business abroad.

Table 10.2 shows the biggest 30 banks in Europe, representing nearly half of the assets of the European banking system assets. Schoenmaker and Oosterloo (2005) split large banks in three categories, depending on the composition of their assets. A global bank has less than 50 per cent of its assets in the home country and less than 25 per cent in the rest of Europe. These banks include HSBC, Barclays and Standard Chartered from the UK, BBVA from Spain, UniCredit from Italy, and Credit Suisse and UBS from Switzerland.

A European bank has less than 50 per cent of its assets in the home country and more than 25 per cent in the rest of Europe. Some European banks focus on a specific region in the EU. The Nordea Group, for example, primarily operates in the Nordic countries. Other European banks operate Europe-wide; examples include BNP Paribas, Deutsche Bank, and ING.

Table 10.2 Biggest 30 banks in Europe in 2009

Banking groups	(1) Capital strength[a] (in € billion)	(2) Total assets (in € billion)	(3) Business in home country (as % of (2))	(4) Business in rest of EU (as % of (2))	(5) Business in rest of world (as % of (2))
Global banks[b]					
1. HSBC (UK)	85	1,641	27	17	56
2. Barclays (UK)	56	1,551	39	16	45
3. UniCredit (Italy)	39	929	41	24	35
4. BBVA (Spain)	27	535	41	2	57
5. Credit Suisse (Switzerland)	24	694	31	25	44
6. UBS (Switzerland)	21	903	39	5	56
7. Standard Chartered (UK)	17	303	15	0	85
European banks[c]					
1. BNP Paribas (France)	63	2,058	45	34	21
2. Santander (Spain)	57	1,111	31	30	39
3. Deutsche Bank (Germany)	34	1,501	30	33	37
4. ING (Netherlands)	34	1,164	43	37	20
5. Nordea (Sweden)	20	508	21	71	8
6. Dexia (Belgium)	18	578	36	47	17
7. KBC (Belgium)	15	324	47	36	17
Domestic banks[d]					
1. Royal Bank of Scotland (UK)	86	1,909	56	19	25
2. Lloyds Group (UK)	53	1,156	92	4	4
3. Crédit Agricole (France)	52	1,694	62	23	15
4. Groupe BPCE (France)	38	1,029	77	5	18
5. Société Générale (France)	35	1,024	56	27	17

6. Rabobank (Netherlands)	32	608	65	14	21
7. Banca Intesa (Italy)	30	625	79	19	3
8. Commerzbank (Germany)	30	844	72	20	8
9. Crédit Mutuel (France)	27	579	93	3	4
10. La Caixa (Spain)	16	272	100	0	0
11. Danske Bank (Denmark)	16	414	52	44	3
12. Landesbank Baden-Württemberg (Germany)	15	412	81	16	3
13. Bayerische Landesbank (Germany)	15	339	84	7	9
14. ABN AMRO (Netherlands)	14	260	84	12	3
15. DnB Nor Group (Norway)	12	219	81	12	6
16. Bank of Ireland (Ireland)	12	179	64	33	4

Notes:

[a] Top 30 banks are selected on the basis of capital strength (Tier 1 capital (see Chapter 12) as published in *The Banker*).

[b] Global banks: less than 50 per cent of assets in the home country and less than 25 per cent in the rest of Europe.

[c] European banks: less than 50 per cent of assets in the home country and more than 25 per cent in the rest of Europe.

[d] Domestic banks: more than 50 per cent of assets in the home country.

Source: Schoenmaker (2011)

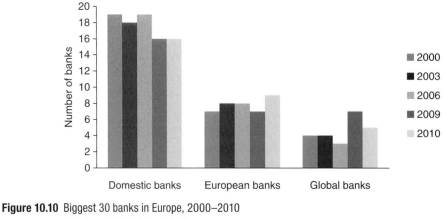

Figure 10.10 Biggest 30 banks in Europe, 2000–2010
Note: See Table 10.2 for definitions.
Source: Schoenmaker (2011)

Finally, a domestic bank has more than 50 per cent of its assets in the home country. Examples include Crédit Agricole in France, the Rabobank in the Netherlands, and the Royal Bank of Scotland in the UK. The latter took over ABN AMRO in 2007, together with Fortis and Santander.

Figure 10.10 shows that the number of European banks has increased from 7 in 2000 to 9 in 2010, while the number of domestic banks has declined from 19 in 2000 to 16 in 2010. The increased number of European banks is in line with the rising cross-border penetration shown in Figure 10.8.

International comparison

Turning to international banking, the geographical segmentation of large banks on the other continents, the Americas and the Asia-Pacific, can be compared with the geographical spread of the large European banks. Table 10.3 shows that European banks are the most international, with close to 50 per cent of business abroad. This may be due to the integrated European banking market. But even when looking at the business outside the region, European banks are the most international with more than 25 per cent of business in the rest of the world. The American banks are catching up; their business in the rest of the world rose from 14 per cent in 2006 to 21 per cent in 2009.

The picture is very different for the Asian-Pacific banks. They used to have a very domestic orientation (Schoenmaker, 2011), which has been reinforced over the last years. Business in the rest of the world has declined from 13

Table 10.3 Development of international banking by continent, 2006–2009

Continent	2006			2007			2008			2009		
	h	r	w	h	r	w	h	r	w	h	r	w
Europe	52	23	25	52	22	25	51	21	28	52	22	26
Americas	78	8	14	75	10	15	73	9	18	72	7	21
Asia-Pacific	82	5	13	83	6	11	82	7	11	85	7	8

Notes: Share of business in home country (h), rest of region (r), and rest of world (w) of the top banks by continent. The top 30 banks for Europe; the top 15 banks for Americas and Asia-Pacific. The shares add up to 100 per cent.
Source: Schoenmaker (2011)

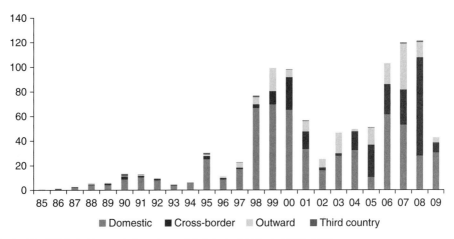

Figure 10.11 Banking M&As in Europe (value of completed deals, € billion), 1985–2009
Note: M&As exclude buyback, recapitalisation, and exchange offers. 'Cross-border' refers to intra-EU M&As; 'third country' denotes M&As by non-EU resident banks in the EU; and 'outward' stands for M&A activity of EU banks outside the EU.
Source: ECB (2010a)

per cent in 2006 to 8 per cent in 2009. The composition of the large Asian-Pacific banks is shifting from the major Japanese banks to the major Chinese banks. The Chinese banks have an even stronger domestic orientation than the Japanese banks.

Domestic and cross-border mergers and acquisitions

Mergers and acquisitions (M&As) have changed and will continue to change the European banking markets. It was widely expected that the Single Market initiative (see Chapter 3) would ease the path for cross-border M&As.

Instead, banks prepared themselves for the Single Market by merging with other domestic banks. Cross-border mergers increased only after the start of EMU (see Figure 10.11).

Boot (1999) argues that domestic banks in Europe were often protected as they were regarded as national flagships. A fundamental belief that national financial institutions should not be controlled by foreigners prevented almost any cross-border merger up to the late 1990s. The recent shift towards cross-border deals was caused by two factors. First, some national banking systems have become so concentrated that further domestic mergers would be blocked by the competition authorities. In principle, the European Commission (DG Competition) permits mergers up to the threshold of 2,000 for the Herfindahl Index (see below). Several countries are close to, or even above, this threshold.

Second, the European Commission (2005) reviewed obstacles to cross-border mergers and suggested remedies to remove them. The abuse of supervisory powers to block cross-border mergers was identified as a possible obstacle to cross-border mergers. New legislation has subsequently been passed to clarify and limit the criteria to assess possible M&As.

As the potential for domestic mergers is increasingly exhausted, the number of cross-border bank mergers has increased. Figure 10.11 illustrates that the cross-border share in total M&A deals has risen, accounting for over 30 per cent of the value of all deals in recent years, up from about 10 per cent in the 1990s. While early cross-border mergers in the 1990s created regional banks, such as Fortis in the Benelux countries and Nordea in Scandinavia, recent mergers are more widely spread across Europe. Examples are the takeover of Abbey National (UK) by Banco Santander (Spain) in 2004 and the takeover of Bank Austria Credit Anstalt (Austria) and HypoVereinsbank (Germany) by UniCredit (Italy) in 2005. One of the biggest acquisitions was that of the Dutch ABN AMRO Bank in 2007 by Fortis (Belgium), Royal Bank of Scotland (RBS) (UK), and Banco Santander (Spain), which resulted in the split of ABN AMRO into three parts. Already seen as having paid too high a price, both Fortis and RBS were among the first large European banks to be affected by the crisis in 2008. After the demise of Fortis, Fortis Netherlands and the Dutch part of ABN AMRO were nationalised and merged into a new bank named again ABN AMRO. BNP Paribas took over the remainder of Fortis (mainly the Belgian and Luxembourg parts). The increased financial integration within the EU thus led to larger and more multi-country banks. Important domestic deals after the crisis include the acquisition of Dresdner Bank by Commerzbank and HBOS by Lloyds TSB. Important drivers of cross-border

---

Box 10.5 The economics and performance of M&As

The classical motive for M&As in financial services is market extension (Walter, 2004). By merging with or acquiring another bank, it becomes possible to expand geographically into markets in which the acquiring bank has been absent or weak. The risk profile of the bank may be improved to the extent that business is spread across different macroeconomic environments. Or the bank wants to broaden its product range or client coverage because it sees profit opportunities that may be complementary to what it is already doing (see Chapter 11 for the expansion of banks into insurance activities).

A key issue is whether economies of scale exist in banking. In an information- and distribution-intensive industry with high fixed costs such as financial services, there may be potential for scale economies. In particular, domestic mergers offer scope for cost synergies, as overlapping branch networks can be rationalised. But there is also potential for diseconomies of scale attributable to disproportionate increases in administrative overheads or management of complexity. Recent empirical evidence finds economies of scale only in banks up to $25 billion in size (Saunders and Cornett, 2002).

Campa and Hernando (2006) examine the performance record of mergers and acquisitions in the European financial industry. Merger announcements imply positive excess returns to shareholders of the target company (the takeover premium), while the returns to shareholders of the acquiring firms are essentially zero around announcement. One year after the announcement, excess returns are not significantly different from zero for both targets and acquirers. Campa and Hernando (2006) also provide evidence on the operating performance. M&As usually involve target banks with lower operating performance than the average bank. The M&A transactions result in significant improvements in the target bank's performance beginning on average two years after the transaction is completed.

---

mergers are geographic diversification and a potential efficiency improvement (see Box 10.5 for further details). A good example was the takeover of Abbey National by Santander. The former had strategic problems as it was venturing into corporate banking without success and used outdated IT systems. The inefficiency of Abbey National was illustrated by a high cost-to-income ratio of 83 per cent and a negative return on equity of 10 per cent. In contrast, Santander had developed a new payment technology and had a cost-to-income ratio of 63 per cent. After the takeover, Santander successfully introduced this technology with new management at Abbey National to improve efficiency; in 2006, Abbey's cost-to-income ratio was 56 per cent.

Table 10.4 Market structure indicators, 1997 and 2009

	Size		Concentration				Competition
	Number of banks		CR5 (in %)[a]		Herfindahl Index[b]		H-statistic
	1997	2009	1997	2009	1997	2009	1990–2005
Austria	928	790	44	37	515	414	0.07
Belgium	131	104	54	77	699	1,622	0.54
Bulgaria	35[c]	30	52[c]	58	721[c]	846	n.a.
Cyprus	623	155	92	65	2,747	1,086	−0.11
Czech Republic	50	56	67	62	2,533	1,032	0.77
Denmark	213	164	70	64	1,431	1,042	0.30
Estonia	12	18	83	93	4,312	3,090	0.47
Finland	348	349	88	83	2,150	3,120	−0.24
France	1,258	712	40	47	449	605	0.58
Germany	3,420	1,948	17	25	114	206	0.65
Greece	55	66	56	69	885	1,184	0.47
Hungary	286	190	53	55	2,101	861	0.16
Ireland	71	498	41	59	500	881	1.11
Italy	909	802	25	34	201	353	0.08
Latvia	37	37	51	69	1,450	1,181	0.57
Lithuania	37	84	84	81	2,972	1,693	0.45
Luxembourg	215	147	23	28	210	288	0.31
Malta	29	24	98	73	4,411	1,246	0.72
Netherlands	648	295	79	85	1,654	2,032	0.80
Poland	1,378	710	46	44	859	574	0.10
Portugal	238	166	46	70	577	1,150	−0.14
Romania	39[c]	42	55[c]	52	1,251[c]	857	0.63
Slovakia	29	26	63	72	2,643	1,273	0.26
Slovenia	34	25	62	60	2,314	1,256	0.38
Spain	416	352	32	43	285	507	0.87
Sweden	237	180	58	61	830	899	0.48
United Kingdom	537	389	24	41	208	467	0.76
EU-15[d]	9,624	6,961	34	44	406	506	0.59
NMS-12[d]	2,589	1,397	63	58	1,985	972	0.31
EU-27[d]	12,213	8,358	35	45	445	518	0.59

Notes:
[a] CR5 is the share of the five largest banks, measured as a percentage of total assets.
[b] The Herfindahl Index is calculated as the sum of the squares of all the banks' market shares according to total assets, and rescaled from 0 to 10,000.
[c] The figure is for 2003.
[d] EU-15, NMS-12, and EU-27 are calculated as a weighted average (weighted according to assets).
n.a. means not available.
Source: Number of banks and concentration from European Central Bank (2004, 2010a) and Allen *et al.* (2006); competition from Bikker *et al.* (2006)

Market structure and competition

Table 10.4 shows some indicators of the structure of the EU banking sector. Between 1997 and 2009 the total number of banks in the EU decreased from 12,213 to 8,358, i.e. a reduction of over 30 per cent.[4] Due to the decline in the number of credit institutions the concentration in the national banking markets has increased. Table 10.4 presents two concentration measures: the market share of the biggest five banks (CR5) and the Herfindahl Index, which is defined as the sum of the squares of the market shares of all banks in the sector ($HI = \sum_{i=1}^{n} s_i^2$, where s_i is the market share of bank i). While the CR5 ratio is easily measurable, it does not take into account the remaining banks in the industry in contrast to the Herfindahl Index. The latter ranges between $1/n$ and 1, reaching its lowest value, the reciprocal of the number of banks (n), when all banks in a market are of equal size, and reaching unity in the case of monopoly. The index as published by the ECB has been rescaled and ranges between 0 and 10,000.

Table 10.4 shows that there are substantial concentration differences across the EU. In Austria, France, Germany, Ireland, Italy, Luxembourg, Spain, and the United Kingdom the concentration ratios in the banking markets are relatively low. The highest concentration ratios can be found in Belgium, Estonia, Finland, Lithuania, and the Netherlands.[5] From 1997 to 2009, the concentration ratios in the NMS-12 have gradually declined towards the level of the EU-15.

Another important feature of markets is the degree of competition. Panzar and Rosse (1977) have constructed a measure of competition, the so-called *H-statistic*, that is defined as the sum of the factor price elasticities of interest revenue with respect to borrowed capital, labour and physical capital. The value of H can be interpreted as follows. In case of a monopoly, H is lower than or equal to zero. This also applies to an oligopolistic market with cartels or complete imitation of each other's behaviour. A value of H between zero and one indicates monopolistic competition. A value equivalent to one points to perfect competition, as each change in input prices leads to a comparable change in output prices. The results of Bikker *et al.* (2006) as shown in Table 10.4 suggest that there is strong competition (i.e. values of H above 0.75) in the banking sectors of the Czech Republic, Ireland, the Netherlands, Spain, and the United Kingdom. France, Germany, Malta, and Romania have an intermediate level of competition (H around 0.60), while banking competition in Austria, Cyprus, Finland, Hungary, Italy, Poland, and Portugal is low.

The *structure-conduct-performance (SCP) paradigm* postulates a connection between market structure, banking behaviour, and profitability. The reasoning is as follows: in markets with a high degree of concentration, firms have more market power, which allows them to set prices above marginal costs and achieve higher profits. While earlier studies find a relationship between concentration and profitability, more recent studies suggest that there is no connection between the two (Claessens and Laeven, 2004; Jansen and De Haan, 2006).

Two alternative theories suggest that concentration does not necessarily reduce market competition. According to the *contestability theory*, a concentrated banking market can still be competitive as long as the entry barriers for potential newcomers are low. According to the *efficiency hypothesis*, the most efficient banks gain market share at the cost of less efficient banks. In other words, high concentration can be a result of fierce competition in a market (Bikker *et al.*, 2006).

Claessens and Laeven (2004) examine the competitiveness of a banking market in a large cross-section of countries and find no evidence that banking system concentration is negatively associated with competitiveness. In fact, they sometimes find evidence that more concentrated banking systems are more competitive.

Concentration is loosely related to bank size. Markets become more concentrated when the number of banks decreases or when the skewness of the size distribution of banks increases (i.e. the number of large banks increases). But the markets in some countries (e.g. Germany and France) have low levels of concentration and large banks. As Bikker *et al.* (2006) point out, large banks may have market power as they are probably in a better position to collude with other banks and may benefit from a more established reputation. Furthermore, they are in a better position than small banks to create new banking products due to economies of scale. Indeed, Bikker *et al.* (2006) report that market power increases with bank size. Their research covers 18,467 banks in 101 countries over a period of 16 years. In the aftermath of the 2007–2009 financial crisis, a debate emerged on whether banks are '*too big to fail*'. Box 10.6 summarises the discussion on the appropriate size of banks.

10.4 Conclusions

Banks are key players in the financial system, providing liquidity to other financial institutions and to firms and households. They have also developed

Box 10.6 What to do with big banks?

Following the 2007–2009 financial crisis there is much concern about the massive bailout costs of the financial sector. How can one reduce moral hazard and rein back expectations of future bailouts? The *too-big-to-fail* doctrine has been reinforced, if anything, by the handling of the financial crisis.

Demirgüç-Kunt and Huizinga (2011) develop measures for a bank's absolute size and its systemic size defined as size relative to the national economy. They examine how the extent to which a bank faces market discipline depends on both size measures. Despite too-big-to-fail subsidies, they find that systemically large banks are subject to greater market discipline as evidenced by a higher sensitivity of their funding costs to risk proxies, suggesting that they are often too big to save. The finding that a bank's interest cost tends to rise with its systemic size can also in part explain why a bank's rate of return on assets tends to decline with systemic size. These results cast doubt on the need to have systemically large banks. Poghosyan and De Haan (2011) examine whether bank earnings volatility depends on bank size and the degree of concentration in the banking sector. Using quarterly data for non-investment banks in the United States for the period Q1 2004–Q4 2009, they find that bank size reduces return volatility. The negative impact of bank size on bank earnings volatility decreases (in absolute terms) with market concentration. They also find that larger banks located in concentrated markets have experienced higher volatility during the recent financial crisis.

Several structural options to curtail the too-big-to-fail practice have been proposed. First, Avgouleas *et al.* (2012) argue that Living Wills might allow systemically important banks to fail or, at least, to be unwound in an orderly manner without imposing disproportionate costs on the taxpayer. The objective is to put in place, ex ante, conditions that would allow a wider range of options other than having the whole bank rescued. A Living Will is a recovery and resolution plan to be used when a bank may get into difficulties. At the time of writing, the Financial Stability Board is working on a proposal for Living Wills for all large banks.

Second, the Vickers Committee (2011) proposes structural reform of the large UK banks that combines domestic retail services with global wholesale and investment banking operations. Rather than full separation, the Committee recommends to ring-fence the retail operations, including separate, higher, capitalisation and a separate, independent, board. The ring-fencing should make it easier and less costly to resolve banks that get into trouble. Next, ring-fencing should help insulate retail banking from external financial shocks, including by diminishing problems arising from global investment banking.

Finally, the Financial Stability Board has proposed a capital surcharge for the biggest banks. This capital surcharge ranges from 1 to 2.5 per cent, depending on the bank's systemic importance.

technologies to monitor borrowers. Banks have expanded their business from traditional lending to modern capital-market transactions, thereby preserving their role in the financial system.

Banks use advanced models to measure, manage, and price market risk. The use of these advanced models has spurred the centralisation of risk management. While the business is done by the local bank managers who are familiar with the economic environment in which the local business units have to operate, the influence of the head office on the pricing of bank products is increasing.

Cross-border banking has gradually increased to 20 per cent in 2009. This chapter has documented the emergence of banks that operate Europe-wide. Nevertheless, retail banking markets are still segmented. Customers have a preference to do business with banks they 'know' and thus have a bias towards domestic banks. Cultural differences appear to be more important than regulatory differences. The policy of the European Commission is shifting from harmonising rules (Chapter 12) to ensuring effective competition (Chapter 14) in turn.

New evidence suggests that concentration does not necessarily reduce market competition. The contestability theory indicates that a banking market is competitive as long as the barriers for potential newcomers are low. Competition policy is important to open national markets: both to promote new entrants within a country and to promote foreign entry through cross-border mergers.

NOTES

1 There is, however, an important conflict of interest. Credit rating agencies are paid by the firms and governments whose securities they rate. This conflict is unavoidable due to the free-riding problem, i.e. ratings are valuable only if everybody knows them, but lenders (investors) have no reason to pay for information that is available to everyone else too.

2 A *counterparty* is a legal and financial term. It means a party to a contract.

3 Assuming a normal distribution, the time horizon of the standard deviation can be expanded by multiplying with $\sqrt{t}$. Given that there are 252 business days in the year, the standard deviation of the one-year loss distribution equals the standard deviation of the ten-day loss distribution multiplied by $\sqrt{25.2}$ (Hull, 2009).

4 The trend in the US is comparable, though slightly less pronounced. The number of US banks dropped from 10,923 in 1997 to 8,012 in 2009, i.e. a decline of around 27 per cent.

5 The European Commission investigates a proposed merger when the (rescaled) Herfindahl Index would pass the threshold of 2,000 after the merger (see Chapter 14).

SUGGESTED READING

Claessens, S. and L. Laeven (2004), What Drives Bank Competition? Some International Evidence, *Journal of Money, Credit and Banking*, 36, 563–583.

Freixas, X. and J. C. Rochet (2008), *Microeconomics of Banking*, 2nd edition, MIT Press, Cambridge (MA).

Hull, J. C. (2009), *Risk Management and Financial Institutions*, 2nd edition, Pearson Education, Upper Saddle River (NJ).

Schoenmaker, D. (2011), The European Banking Landscape after the Crisis, Duisenberg School of Finance Policy Paper 12.

REFERENCES

Allen, F., L. Bartiloro, and O. Kowalewski (2006), The Financial System of EU 25, in: K. Liebscher, J. Christl, P. Mooslechner, and D. Ritzberger-Griinwald (eds.), *Financial Development, Integration and Stability in Central Eastern and South-Eastern Europe*, Edward Elgar, Cheltenham, 80–104.

Avgouleas, E, C. Goodhart, and D. Schoenmaker D (2012), Bank Resolution Plans as a catalyst for global financial reform, *Journal of Financial Stability*, forthcoming.

Berger, A. N. (2003), The Economic Effects of Technological Progress: Evidence from the Banking Industry, *Journal of Money, Credit, and Banking*, 35, 141–176.

Bikker, J. A., L. Spierdijk, and P. Finnie (2006), The Impact of Bank Size on Market Power, DNB Working Paper 120.

Boot, A. W. A. (1999), European Lessons on Consolidation in Banking, *Journal of Banking and Finance*, 23, 609–613.

Campa, J. M. and I. Hernando (2006), M&As Performance in the European Financial Industry, *Journal of Banking and Finance*, 30, 3367–3392.

Claessens, S. and L. Laeven (2004), What Drives Bank Competition? Some International Evidence, *Journal of Money, Credit and Banking*, 36, 563–583.

Daníelsson, J. (2011), *Financial Risk Forecasting*, John Wiley and Sons, New York..

Demirgüç-Kunt, A. and H. Huizinga (2011), Do We Need Big Banks? Evidence on Performance, Strategy and Market Discipline, CEPR Discussion Paper 8276.

Dermine, J. (2006), European Banking Integration: Don't Put the Cart before the Horse, *Financial Markets, Institutions & Instruments*, 15(2), 57–106.

Diamond, D. W. (1984), Financial Intermediation and Delegated Monitoring, *Review of Economic Studies*, 51, 393–414.

European Central Bank (2004), *Report on EU Banking Structures*, ECB, Frankfurt am Main. (2010a), *EU Banking Structures*, ECB, Frankfurt am Main. (2010b), *EU Banking Sector Stability*, ECB, Frankfurt am Main.

European Commission (2005), *Cross-Border Consolidation in the EU Financial Sector*, SEC 1398, EC, Brussels. (2007), *European Financial Integration Report*, EC, Brussels.

Freixas, X. and J. C. Rochet (2008), *Microeconomics of Banking*, 2nd edition, MIT Press, Cambridge (MA).

Garber, P. M. and S. R. Weisbrod (1990), Banks in the Market for Liquidity, NBER Working Paper 3381.

Hackethal, A. (2004), German Banks and Banking Structure, in: J. P. Krahnen and R. H. Schmidt (eds.), *The German Financial System*, Oxford University Press, 71–106.

Hull, J. C. (2009), *Risk Management and Financial Institutions*, 2nd edition, Pearson Education, Upper Saddle River (NJ).

Jansen, D. J. and J. De Haan (2006), European Banking Consolidation: Effects on Competition, Profitability, and Efficiency, *Journal of Financial Transformation*, 17, 61–72.

Kleimeier, S. and H. Sander (2007), Integrating Europe's Retail Banking Markets: Where Do We Stand?, Research Report in Finance and Banking, Centre for European Policy Studies, Brussels.

Kuritzkes, A., T. Schuermann, and S. Weiner (2003), Risk Measurement, Risk Management, and Capital Adequacy in Financial Conglomerates, in: R. Herring and R. Litan (eds.), *Brookings-Wharton Papers on Financial Services: 2003*, Brookings Institution, Washington DC, 141–193.

Panzar, J. C. and J. N. Rosse (1977), Chamberlin vs Robinson: An Empirical Study for Monopoly Rents, Studies in Industry Economics, Research Paper 77, Stanford University.

Poghosyan, T. and J. J. De Haan (2011), Bank Size, Market Concentration, and Bank Earnings Volatility in the US, DNB Working Paper 282.

Saunders, A. and M. M. Cornett (2002), *Financial Institutions Management: A Risk Management Approach*, McGraw-Hill, Boston.

Schoenmaker, D. (2011), The European Banking Landscape after the Crisis, Duisenberg School of Finance Policy Paper 12.

Schoenmaker, D. and S. Oosterloo (2005), Financial Supervision in an Integrating Europe: Measuring Cross-Border Externalities, *International Finance*, 8, 1–27.

(2008), Financial Supervision in Europe: A Proposal for a New Architecture, in: L. Jonung, C. Walkner, and M. Watson (eds.), *Building the Financial Foundations of the Euro – Experiences and Challenges*, Routledge, London, 329–346.

Schoenmaker, D. and C. van Laecke (2006), Current State of Cross-Border Banking, London School of Economics FMG Special Papers 168.

Vajanne, L. (2007), Integration in Euro Area Retail Banking Markets – Convergence of Credit Interest Rates, Bank of Finland Discussion Paper 27/2007.

Van Lelyveld, I. (ed.) (2006), *Economic Capital Modelling: Concepts, Measurement and Implementation*, Risk Books, London.

Vickers Committee (2011), *Final Report: Recommendations, Independent Commission on Banking*, London.

Walter, I. (2004), *Mergers and Acquisitions in Banking and Finance: What Works, What Fails, and Why*, Oxford University Press.

11

European Insurers and Financial Conglomerates

OVERVIEW

The function of insurance is to protect individuals and firms from adverse events through the pooling of risks. Life insurance protects against premature death, disability, and retirement. Non-life insurance protects against risks such as accidents, illness, theft, and fire. Insurance is a risky business, as insurance companies collect premiums and provide cover for adverse events that may or may not arise somewhere in the future. The pattern of small claims, such as fire or car accidents, is fairly predictable. However, larger accidents or catastrophes (like hurricanes) involve high claims with low probability.

The insurance business is plagued by asymmetric information problems. There is a moral hazard problem when the behaviour of the insured, which can be only partly observed by the insurer, may increase the likelihood that the insurer has to pay. After signing the contract, the insured may behave less cautiously because of the insurance. Another problem is adverse selection. High-risk individuals (for instance, ill people) may seek out more (health) insurance than low-risk persons. The insurer may therefore end up with a pool of relatively high risks. Mechanisms to separate high from low risks are explained in this chapter.

Insurance companies tend to centralise risk management, using internal risk-management models at their headquarters. But there is still a role for local business units to capture factors that are location-specific. The same is true for asset management. As insurance companies are large asset managers, they can profit from economies of scale through the pooling of assets.

Insurance systems vary considerably across Europe. Life insurance is quite prominent in the EU-15, but far less so in the new EU Member States. Non-life insurance is more evenly spread across the EU. With the creation of the European single insurance market, insurers used mergers and acquisitions – at both the national and the European level – to become large enough to act at the European level. While it is still not possible to speak of an integrated insurance market, the level of cross-border insurance has gradually increased.

Finally, the chapter analyses financial conglomerates that combine banking and insurance. These conglomerates have the possibility of cross-selling insurance products through the bank and they may also gain from increased diversification possibilities. Yet it is difficult to manage a complex financial group that runs fairly different lines of business.

LEARNING OBJECTIVES

After you have studied this chapter, you should be able to:

- explain the nature of insurance business
- explain the economics of insurance risk
- explain the use of risk-management models by insurers and the centralisation of the risk-management function
- describe the structure of the European insurance market
- identify the characteristics of financial conglomerates and the role they play in the financial system.

11.1 Theory of insurance

Small vs. large claims insurance

The function of *insurance* is to protect individuals and firms against adverse events. Insurance companies are able to provide this protection through the pooling of individual risks. By combining the risks of various clients in a pool, insurance companies can spread the risks over this (large) group of clients. There are different types of insurance. *Life insurance* protects against premature death, disability, and retirement. While it is difficult to predict the death of an individual, death rates for large populations are fairly stable and therefore easier to predict. Other types of insurance are grouped under the name of *non-life insurance*, which protects against risks such as accidents, theft, and fire. Non-life insurance is sometimes also called property and casualty (P&C) or property and liability (P&L) insurance.

The risk dynamics of non-life insurance are more diverse than those of life insurance. Relatively small accidents (like car accidents) are fairly predictable and can easily be pooled by an insurance company. But larger accidents or catastrophes follow a different pattern: they are low-probability but high-impact events. A good example is Hurricane Katrina in New Orleans

Insurance company	
Assets (*A*)	Equity (*E*)
	Technical provisions (*TP*)

Figure 11.1   Simplified balance sheet of an insurance company

in 2005. The risk of such a catastrophe is too big for one insurance company and is therefore divided among different insurance and re-insurance companies.

The intermediation function of insurers can be illustrated with a simple balance sheet (see Figure 11.1). Insurers collect premiums *P* from clients and make payouts on claims *C* by these clients when the risk materialises. On the asset side, insurers invest the collected premiums in assets *A*, which earn a return R_A. On the liability side, insurers make technical provisions *TP* to cover expected future claims. In addition, insurers maintain a capital buffer *E* to cover unexpected claims.

Insurers evaluate the risk of prospective clients. If a client is accepted, the insurers have to decide how much coverage a client should receive and how much he should pay for it. The function of an underwriter is to acquire – or to 'write' – business that will bring the insurance company profits. The insurance business is viable only when the collected premiums exceed the payout on claims. When a claim is made, the insurer must determine the extent of the loss. Many insurers employ 'adjusters' who determine the liability of the insurer and the settlement to be made. The *claim ratio* measures the adjusted claims as a ratio to premiums earned, i.e. *C/P*. A claim ratio of less than 100 per cent means that premiums earned are sufficient to cover claims.

The insurance company also has to cover its expenses *Exp*. The biggest expenses are commissions paid to insurance agents for the acquisition of business. These acquisition costs are very high. To reduce their acquisition costs, insurers are increasingly selling insurance to the public directly (*direct writing*). The insurer must also gather information about potential clients to assess the underwriting risk and avoid adverse selection (see below). Finally, insurers incur administrative expenses. The *expense ratio* expresses total expenses relative to premiums earned, i.e. *Exp/P*.

A common economic measure to assess the profitability of non-life insurers is the combined ratio *CR*, which expresses claims and expenses relative to premiums earned:

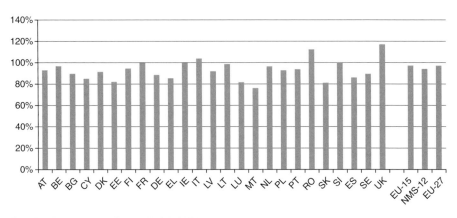

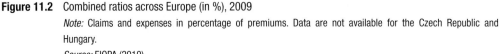

Figure 11.2   Combined ratios across Europe (in %), 2009

Note: Claims and expenses in percentage of premiums. Data are not available for the Czech Republic and Hungary.

Source: EIOPA (2010)

$$CR = C/P + Exp/P = \frac{C + Exp}{P} \tag{11.1}$$

Figure 11.2 shows the combined ratio for various EU Member States. The combined ratios for Romania and the United Kingdom are well above 100 per cent, indicating that the non-life insurance sector in these countries makes a loss. However, investment returns are not included (see below). In Estonia, Luxembourg, Malta, and Slovakia the combined ratio ranges between 75 per cent and 85 per cent, indicating a healthy profit. The combined ratio of the EU-25 average is 97 per cent. This results in a margin of 3 per cent.

The combined ratio provides an incomplete view of a non-life insurer's profitability. Premiums are invested before payouts are made. Investment returns R_A are therefore an important source of income for insurers. The *profitability* π, as a percentage of premium earned, is equal to the results on claims and expenses $(100 - CR)$ and the investment returns:

$$\pi = 100 - CR + R_A/P = 100 + \frac{R_A - C - Exp}{P} \tag{11.2}$$

Equation 11.2 illustrates that the successful management of an insurance company depends on making adequate investment returns and properly calculating underwriting risks while keeping a lid on acquisition and administrative expenses. This equation can be illustrated with a simple example.

Assume a claim ratio of 65 per cent of earned premiums, an expense ratio of 32 per cent, and allocated investment income of 9 per cent. The profit is 12 per cent of earned premiums (100 + 9 − 65 − 32 = 12).

The stochastic properties of large claims are very different from those of small claims. Small claims have a distribution with light tails (e.g. the normal distribution). In a large portfolio, the expected claim size approaches the average claim size according to the law of large numbers. Box 11.1 sets out the mathematics of calculating small claim risks in more detail.

In contrast, large claims are characterised by distributions with heavy tails. Insurance portfolios with heavy-tailed claim sizes are dangerous. Figure 11.4 shows the log-normal distribution, an example of a heavy-tailed distribution. In the tail on the right are events with a low probability but a large impact on the overall claim amount. We need extreme value statistics to model these large claims. The distribution needs to be fitted from a relatively small number of observations (the excesses over high thresholds). Embrechts *et al.* (1997) provide an overview of modelling extreme events.

Large losses are caused not only by nature (natural catastrophes) but also by man (man-made disasters). Table 11.1 provides an overview of the largest catastrophes over the last 40 years. Hurricane Katrina in New Orleans caused an insured loss of €54 billion, while the total loss (insured and uninsured) mounted to over €100 billion. The terrorist attack on the Twin Towers and the Pentagon in 2001 led to an insured loss of €17 billion. Europe has experienced several winter storms, such as Daria in 1990 and Lothar in 1999, causing an insured loss of close to €6 billion each. The highest insured losses are suffered in the US, Europe, and Japan due to the higher insurance density in the industrialised countries. Emerging markets generally have a lower insurance density, so that only a small proportion of victims benefit from insurance cover. An example was the tsunami in the Indian Ocean in 2004, which had a death toll of 220,000. Yet this extreme event is not taken up in Table 11.1 as only insured losses are counted.

Re-insurance

Individual insurers cannot bear these large losses on their own – their equity would be wiped out when an extreme event occurs. The risks (and premiums) of catastrophe insurance are therefore shared among insurers (Rejda, 2005). A common mechanism to share insurance risk is *re-insurance*, which is shifting part or all of the insurance originally written by one insurer to another insurer.[1] The insurer that originally writes the business is called the ceding

Box 11.1 The mathematics of small claims insurance*

This box abstracts from expenses, investment returns, and dividend payouts and focuses on the premium setting P and the claim process C. The premium setting follows the dynamics of the claim process. The pattern of small claims is different from that of large claims.

The stochastic properties of the small claim-size model can be derived formally following Mikosch (2004). The total size of the claims $C(t)$ is the product of the number of claims $N(t)$ over period t and the size of the claims X_i:

$$C(t) = \sum_{i=1}^{N(t)} X_i, t \geq 0 \tag{11.3}$$

where N is independent of the claim size. Both the number of claims and the size of claims are random variables. The claim numbers can often be described as a Poisson process. A Poisson process is a stochastic process, which is used for modelling random events that occur independently of one another. A variable following a homogeneous *Poisson process* has the property that the mean and variance of the distribution are the same. So for N it is possible to write: $\lambda = E(N) = \text{var}(N)$ where λ is the frequency of claims.

Equation (11.3) specifies the realised claims at time t. But an insurer needs to estimate the expected claims at the time of selling an insurance, i.e. $T = 0$. Exploiting the independence of the claim size sequence X_i and the claim number process $N(t)$, the expected total claim amount is given by:

$$E\big[C(t)\big] = E\left[E\left(\sum_{i=1}^{N(t)} X_i | N(t)\right)\right] = E\big[N(t) \cdot E(X_1)\big] = \lambda \cdot t \cdot E(X_1) \tag{11.4}$$

Equation 11.4 shows that the expected total claim amount grows linearly with t. Using the properties of the Poisson distribution, i.e. $\lambda \cdot t = E[N(t)] = \text{var}(N(t))$, the variance is denoted by:

$$\text{var}\big(C(t)\big) = \lambda \cdot t \left[\text{var}(X_1) + \big(E(X_1)\big)^2\right] = \lambda \cdot t \cdot E(X_1^2) \tag{11.5}$$

An insurer with a large portfolio is interested in the asymptotic behaviour of the total claim amount. Applying the law of large numbers, the mathematical foundation of insurance, the total claim amount is given by:

$$\lim_{t} \frac{C(t)}{t} = \lambda \cdot E(X_1) \tag{11.6}$$

The law of large numbers thus says that the total claim amount is the expected claim amount. Put differently, the number of claims is the average number of claims λ and the claim size is the average claim size $E(X_i)$. But the total claim amount may vary in practice. The risk of insurance is determined by the variance of the claims. The claim amount for a large population follows a normal distribution (i.e. a symmetric, bell-shaped curve).

Figure 11.3 visualises the law of large numbers for a portfolio of Danish fire insurance claims (Mikosch, 2004). The data cover the period 1980–1992 and include about 2,500 observations. Because the sample of fire insurance claims contains very large values, the ratio Cn/n converges to $E(X_i)$ very slowly in Figure 11.3.

Next, an insurer needs to set a premium $P(t)$ to cover the claims. As the total claim amount varies, it is necessary to choose a premium by loading the expected claim amount by certain positive number ρ. The premium is given by:

$$P(t) = (1+\rho) \cdot E\big[C(t)\big] \tag{11.7}$$

for some positive number ρ, called the safety loading. It is evident that the insurance business is more on the safe side the larger ρ. The safety loading can thus absorb fluctuations in the claim amount. But an overly large safety loading would make the insurance business less competitive.

The final step is to define the surplus or risk process of the portfolio. Following Mikosch (2004), $E(t)$ is the insurer's capital or equity balance at given time t (see also Figure 11.1) and is given by:

$$E(t) = E(0) + P(t) - C(t), \; t \geq 0 \tag{11.8}$$

where $E(0)$ is initial capital. A large initial capital is needed and reinforced by supervisors (see Chapter 12). When starting an insurance company, the supervisor requires a sufficiently large initial capital buffer to prevent the business from bankruptcy due to many small or a few large claims in the first period, before the premium income can balance the losses and the gains.

What is the risk for an insurer with a sufficient capital balance $E(0)$ and a sufficiently prudent premium rate ($\rho > 0$)? First, there may be an upward drift $\delta > 0$ in the claim amount which was not expected by the insurer at the time when setting the premium. The realised claim amount is thus larger than expected: $C(t) = (1 + \delta) \cdot E[C(t)]$. Examples of such a drift are a shorter life expectancy due to a new illness or more car accidents due to an unexpected shift in weather conditions (e.g. strong winters with frozen roads). The insurer will incur losses when $\delta > \rho$ and may go bankrupt when cumulative losses wipe out the capital balance $(\delta - \rho) \cdot E[C(t)] > E(0)$.

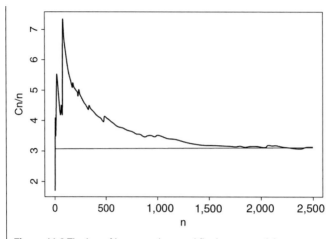

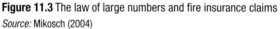

Figure 11.3 The law of large numbers and fire insurance claims
Source: Mikosch (2004)

Second, the principle of independence may be violated. A case in point is the accumulation of payouts on life policies by ING in the aftermath of the terrorist attack at the Twin Towers in New York on 11 September 2001. While it thought it had an adequate geographical spread of its life portfolio in the New York and New Jersey area, ING appeared to have a large concentration among people working in the Twin Towers.

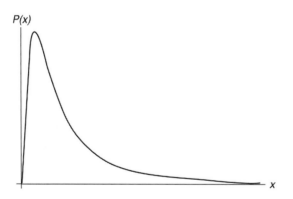

Figure 11.4   Heavy-tailed distribution

company. The insurer that accepts part or all of the insurance risk from the ceding company is the re-insurer. Finally, the re-insurer may in turn re-insure part or all of the risk with another insurer.

The insurance risk of extreme events is thus sliced in different layers and divided between different insurers. Re-insurance can be designed in different

Table 11.1 Catastrophes: the 25 most costly insurance losses, 1970–2010

Insured loss (in € billion, 2010 figures)	Victims (dead and missing)	Date (year)	Event	Country
54.1	1,836	2005	Hurricane Katrina: floods	US, Mexico
18.6	43	1992	Hurricane Andrew: floods	US, Bahamas
17.3	2,982	2001	Terror attack on WTC, Pentagon	US
15.4	61	1994	Northridge earthquake (M 6.6)	US
15.3	136	2008	Hurricane Ike: floods	US, Caribbean
11.1	124	2004	Hurricane Ivan: damage to oil rigs	US, Caribbean
10.5	35	2005	Hurricane Wilma: floods	US, Mexico
8.4	34	2005	Hurricane Rita: floods	US, Mexico
7.0	24	2004	Hurricane Charley	US, Cuba
6.8	51	1991	Typhoon Mireille	Japan
6.0	71	1989	Hurricane Hugo	US, Puerto Rico
6.0	562	2010	Earthquake (M 8.8) triggers tsunami	Chile
5.8	95	1990	Winter storm Daria	France, UK, Benelux
5.7	110	1999	Winter storm Lothar	Switzerland, UK, France
4.8	54	2007	Winter storm Kyrill: floods	Germany, UK, NL
4.5	22	1987	Storm and floods in Europe	France, UK, Netherlands
4.4	38	2004	Hurricane Frances	US, Bahamas
4.0	64	1990	Winter storm Vivian	Europe
4.0	26	1999	Typhoon Bart	Japan
3.5	600	1998	Hurricane Georges: flooding	US, Caribbean
3.3	—	2010	Earthquake (M 7.0)	New Zealand
3.3	41	2001	Tropical storm Allison: heavy rain	US
3.3	3,034	2004	Hurricane Jeanne: floods, landslides	US, Caribbean
3.1	45	2004	Typhoon Songda	Japan, South Korea
2.8	45	2003	Thunderstorms, tornadoes, hail	US

Notes: The losses include property and business interruption, but exclude liability and life-insurance losses. The losses are indexed to 2010.

Source: Sigma No.1, Swiss Re (2011)

ways. One format is *proportional re-insurance*. The insurer cedes a proportion of the premiums and the risks to a re-insurer. The remainder of the premiums and risks is retained by the ceding insurer (the retention amount). Another format, in particular used for catastrophe insurance, is *excess-of-loss re-insurance*. Losses in excess of a certain limit (i.e. the retention limit) are paid by the re-insurer up to some maximum limit. These amounts are expressed in money amounts. Excess-of-loss contracts allow for tailor-made slicing of the insurance risk. The terrorist attacks on 11 September 2001 show the importance of re-insurance. Re-insurers paid out at least half of the insured losses (Rejda, 2005).

In case of large catastrophes, traditional insurance and re-insurance may not suffice. The financial losses due to, for instance, a large flood can supersede the absorption capacity of individual insurers and re-insurers. Therefore, many countries have a government programme that covers part of the risk (see Box 11.2). However, government involvement gives rise to moral hazard, as private parties may seek to shift the risk to government (Loubergé, 2000; Kessler, 2008). There are several ways to mitigate this undesired effect. First, governments could provide cover for only the top layer of the risk. Private (re-)insurers are then taking the first layers of risk of the catastrophe and have an incentive to take appropriate precautionary measures, thereby reducing moral hazard. Second, governments should charge sufficiently high premiums, thereby pushing the insurance coverage back to the market as much as possible. Private (re-)insurers have a competitive motive to underbid the premium charged by the government. Only when the risk is too high in relation to the premium will private (re-)insurers drop out. In that case the government ends up providing residual coverage for catastrophes.

An alternative to traditional re-insurance and government insurance is securitisation of the risk. A recent example is the catastrophe bond (also known as cat bond). *Cat bonds* are corporate bonds that permit the issuer of the bond to skip or defer scheduled payments if a catastrophic loss beyond a certain threshold occurs. If insurers have built up a portfolio of risks by insuring properties in a region that may be hit by a catastrophe, they could create a special-purpose entity that issues the cat bond. Investors who buy the bond make a healthy return on their investment, unless a catastrophe (like a hurricane or an earthquake) hits the region; in that case, the principal initially paid by the investors is forgiven and is used by the sponsor to pay the claims of policy holders. The bonds pay relatively high interest rates and help institutional investors to diversify their portfolio, because natural disasters occur randomly and are not correlated with the stock market or other common factors (Rejda, 2005).

Box 11.2 Flood insurance

While flooding affects many people worldwide and often causes serious damage (see Table 11.1), insurance cover for the risk of flooding is not widespread. This box reviews (lack of) insurance solutions in some selected countries.

The oldest insurance scheme is found in the US. The National Flood Insurance Program (NFIP) that was set up in 1968 covers losses through river flooding. The maximum cover for residential buildings/contents is $250,000/100,000. Premiums are high and vary in line with the flood hazard. Prior to the Mississippi floods of 1993, 15–20 per cent of property in exposed areas was insured under NFIP. After the most recent floods, these figures went up markedly. There is no cap on insured losses, as NFIP is government funded.

In France, the insurance market is based on private insurers, but is statutorily regulated. The Caisse Centrale de Réassurance (CCR) is the main re-insurer and is guaranteed by the state. Insurance penetration is practically 100 per cent.

The United Kingdom has only private insurers and no state insurance. Insurance cover is generally included in homeowners' and household contents policies in conjunction with storm cover. Premium rates are often high for storm/flood and are broken down to individual postcodes. Insurance penetration is 95 per cent.

The Netherlands has an enormous loss potential. Some 70 per cent of property is at risk as vast areas lie below sea level (storm surge) and/or can be flooded by the Rhine or the Maas rivers. The Dutch insurers concluded a market agreement in 1965 to exclude flood cover. The result is that the state is expected to pay (partial) compensation in the event of a disaster. An example is the flooding of the Rhine and the Maas in 1995 with an economic loss of €900 million, of which €180 million was paid by the government.

Source: Swiss Re (1998)

Asymmetric information

Under the assumption of full information complete insurance is possible at actuarially fair premium rates. But complete coverage is not always available in insurance markets due to asymmetric information (Loubergé, 2000). Insurance is subject to moral hazard when the contract outcome is partly influenced by the behaviour of the insured and the insurer cannot observe, without costs, to which extent reported losses can be attributed to the behaviour of the insured. Complete coverage may not be attainable under moral hazard. This is due to the trade-off between the goal of efficient risk sharing, which is met by allocating the risk to the insurer, and the goal of efficient incentives, which requires leaving the consequences of decisions about care with the decision maker, i.e. the insured.

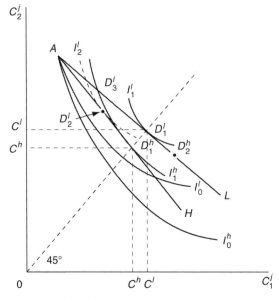

Figure 11.5   The Rothschild–Stiglitz model of the insurance market
Source: Spencer (2000), adapted from Rothschild and Stiglitz (1976)

Insurance is also subject to adverse selection. The ex-ante information asymmetry arises because the insured generally knows more about his risk profile than the insurer. The risk type of the insured cannot be determined ex ante by the insurer; the insurer can only charge the same premium rate based on aggregate risk. The high-risk types are the ones who are most eager to buy insurance, producing an undesirable outcome for the insurer.

While both types of asymmetric information (i.e. moral hazard and adverse selection) may lead to sub-optimal insurance outcomes, this section focuses on adverse selection, which is potentially a serious problem in any type of insurance market. Chapter 10 explains moral hazard in more detail. In a seminal paper, Rothschild and Stiglitz (1976) analyse adverse selection in the insurance market. They model the effect of two types of individuals under asymmetric information (i.e. the insurer does not know the type): the high-risk type H with accident probability P^h and the low-risk type L with accident probability P^l. We assume competitive insurance markets so that insurance is offered at actuarially fair premiums, as premiums are competed down to cost price. Following Spencer (2000), we define the premium ratio $B^l = (1 - P^l)/P^l$. If the contract with B^l is offered (represented by the fair-odds line AL in Figure 11.5), the insurer breaks even on the low-risk transactions at point D_1^l. This is the point of tangency between the budget line AL and the indifference curve of the low-risk individuals I_1^l. But the insurer loses on contracts with high-risk individuals who move to a point such as D_2^h on the fair-odds line AL. This is the adverse selection effect: high-risk individuals buy more insurance.

On the other hand, if a premium ratio of B^h is offered (represented by the fair-odds line AH), the insurer breaks even on contracts with high-risk clients at point D_1^h. But the insurer makes a profit on low-risk individuals. In this case, the best that the low-risk types can do is to move to a point such as D_2^l. This is the point of tangency between the budget line AH and the indifference curve of the low-risk individuals I_2^l (dashed) which lies between I_0^l and I_1^l.

Neither of these situations is consistent with the assumption of a contestable market. In the second case, another insurer can enter the market and offer a contract just to the left of the point D_3^l on the fair-odds line AL. Because this line lies to the left and below indifference curve I_1^h, the high-risk types will prefer the original contract and remain at D_1^h. However, because D_3^l lies above I_2^l, the new contract will be preferred to the original one by the low-risk individuals. This will give the new entrant all of the low-risk business at an actuarially fair premium (since D_3^l lies along AL, which is actuarially fair for low-risk types). The incumbent will be left with all high-risk individuals at the actuarially fair premium.

In equilibrium, the insurance market offers the two contracts simultaneously and clients self-select. This two-tier contract structure forces the low-risk types to distinguish themselves from the high-risk types in order to gain full insurance at an actuarially fair premium. The low-risk types get partial insurance at a fair premium. In practice, this partial insurance usually takes the form of a 'deductible' (i.e. own risk for the client) which reduces the scale of the compensation by a fixed amount. Alternatively, when losses are variable (rather than the fixed amount here), 'co-insurance' (fractional compensation) can be used. This two-tier market solution with self-selection is known as a *separating equilibrium*.

Box 11.3 provides some numerical examples to illustrate the working of the Rothschild–Stiglitz model. The application of a 'deductible' or 'co-insurance' is one way to separate high- and low-risk individuals. Another mechanism is screening. In the case of health insurance, the insurer can require the potential client to undergo a medical test. The insurer can also offer two contracts: one contract at a low premium for people who pass the medical test and a high premium for people who are not willing to do the test.

Finally, the government can impose compulsory insurance to enforce a pooling equilibrium (Spencer, 2000). It can bring in legislation stating that all individuals should take out full insurance. The compulsion prevents low-risk individuals breaking ranks and taking up a partial insurance offer from a rival

Box 11.3 Some numerical examples with high- and low-risk individuals

The working of the Rothschild–Stiglitz model can be easily illustrated with some numerical examples. The first example is with a relatively small proportion of high-risk individuals, so the insurer is still able to offer a single contract to all insured (high- and low-risk). The case where everybody can be charged the same premium is called a *pooling equilibrium*. Assume two types: healthy people with a low risk of illness at 1/1000 ($p^l = 0.001$) and unhealthy people with a high risk of illness 1/100 ($p^h = 0.01$). The cost of illness is €100,000 per episode. The population comprises 90 per cent healthy people and 10 per cent unhealthy people. Table 11.2 provides the details. The cost of insurance for the healthy is €100 ($= 100,000 * 1/1000$) and for the unhealthy €1,000 ($= 100,000 * 1/100$). The average cost is €190 ($= 0.90 * 100 + 0.10 * 1,000$). If insurance is offered at an actuarially fair premium of €190 for the whole population, both types will buy full insurance as the premium is below their reservation prices of €200, respectively €1,500.

In the second example, the proportion of healthy people is changed to 80 per cent (see Table 11.3). This has an impact on the average cost, which becomes €280 ($= 0.80 * 100 + 0.20 * 1,000$). Now, healthy people are unwilling to buy insurance at this premium as it is above their reservation price of €200. The pooling equilibrium breaks down; only the unhealthy people will buy insurance. Since the insurer knows that, it will charge a premium of €1,000. The result is that the 80 per cent healthy people are not insured.

In the third example, we assume that the insurer has enough market power to charge premiums above the actuarially fair premium. The figures are shown in Table 11.4. The average premium is €150 ($= 0.50 * 100 + 0.50 * 200$). Since healthy people are not willing

Table 11.2 Pooling equilibrium

Type	% of population	Risk of illness	Cost to insure	Willingness to pay
Healthy people	90	1/1000	€100	€200
Unhealthy people	10	1/100	€1,000	€1,500

Table 11.3 No equilibrium

Type	% of population	Risk of illness	Cost to insure	Willingness to pay
Healthy people	80	1/1000	€100	€200
Unhealthy people	20	1/100	€1,000	€1,500

Table 11.4 Separating equilibrium

Type	% of population	Risk of illness	Cost to insure	Willingness to pay	Cost of medical test
Healthy people	50	1/1000	€100	€140	€40
Unhealthy people	50	1/500	€200	€250	€150

to pay €150, there is again no pooling equilibrium. We now try to set up a separating equilibrium with two policies. The general policy is available for €240. In addition, the insurer offers an insurance policy for €100 to anyone who can pass a medical test, which costs €40. The healthy people will pick up the second contract. They pay €100 for the insurance and €40 for the medical test. Unhealthy people can pass the test only when they bribe the doctor, which is costly (€110). So unhealthy people will take the general policy at a premium of €240 rather than the second policy at a cost of €250 (€100 for the insurance and €150 for the test). This equilibrium with two different contracts and premiums is a separating equilibrium.

insurer. A typical example of such compulsory insurance is health insurance. As part of its social policy, a government may find it desirable that all citizens are fully insured in case of illness at an affordable premium. Without compulsion, low-risk individuals would have partial insurance and high-risk individuals would pay a high premium (the separating equilibrium).

11.2 The use of risk-management models

While the underwriting of risk is one of their core competencies, insurers are similar to banks when it comes to risk-management systems and practices (Von Bomhard, 2005). In fact, the banking industry imported risk-management skills from the insurance sector and developed them further. Several banking crises, like the financial crisis of 2007–2009 and the Scandinavian banking crisis in the 1990s (see Chapter 2), have underlined the importance of good risk and capital management for banks. Another reason are the similarities between traditional actuarial thinking that prevails in insurance companies and financial economic thinking that prevails in banks.

Modern risk management

The main risk types for an insurer are underwriting risk, market risk, credit risk, and operational risk. As explained in Chapter 10, economic capital has emerged as a 'common currency' for risk taking within financial institutions. *Economic capital* is defined as the amount of capital a financial institution needs to absorb losses over a certain time interval with a certain confidence level. Financial institutions usually choose a time horizon of one year.

The risk-adjusted return on capital for an insurer is given by:

$$\mathrm{RAROC} = \frac{\text{Revenues} - \text{Costs} - \text{Expected Claims}}{\text{Economic Capital}} = \frac{\pi}{E} \qquad (11.9)$$

The revenues consist of premiums P and investment returns R_A (see equation 11.2). Both the numerator and the denominator are adjusted for risk in the RAROC formula. RAROC divides profit by economic capital. RAROC can be used to assess past performance, but also to forecast future performance. It can thus be applied to determine whether activities should be discontinued or expanded.

RAROC is emerging as the leading methodology for large financial institutions to measure and manage risk. The use of internal risk models has been stimulated by supervisors, who allow insurers to use their internal models to calculate capital requirements (see Chapter 12 on the new Solvency II capital adequacy rules). Within the RAROC framework, insurers first calculate the risk for each risk type (underwriting, market, credit, and operational risk) and then aggregate these.[2]

The first type of risk is *underwriting risk*. Insurers make provisions for future claims. An unforeseen increase in the size and frequency of claims is a key risk factor for insurers. In life insurance, *longevity risk* is the risk that future trends in survival rates prove to be higher than projected. The payout period on annuities or pension contracts may thus be longer than expected. Insurance premiums to cover underwriting risk tend to follow a cyclical pattern. Several studies (e.g. Niehaus and Terry, 1993) identify the existence of an underwriting cycle in insurance markets. Box 11.4 explores different theories explaining the underwriting cycle.

The second type of risk is *market risk*. A specific market risk occurs when assets and liabilities in the balance sheet are not matched. This risk is labelled *asset and liability management risk*. In insurance companies, ALM risk is very important (Van Lelyveld, 2006). ALM risk increases when there is a significant

---

Box 11.4 The underwriting cycle

The *underwriting or insurance cycle* is a distinct pattern of upward and downward movements in insurance premiums and their subsequent impact on underwriting profitability. Cyclical patterns, typically running over a period of six to nine years, tend to be particularly pronounced in insurance markets. While both demand and supply of insurance varies over time, variations in supply are the more important. New financial capital can come into a market quickly to increase supply when premiums are high, and also can be withdrawn quickly when returns on insurance are low.

There are several theories explaining the underwriting cycle (see Niehaus and Terry, 1993). The first one is based on fluctuations in profits and assumes a competitive market. If profits are high, some insurers may reduce insurance premiums to attract more clients in expectation of these higher profits. Other insurers, not wishing to lose market share, may then also reduce premiums.

The second theory is founded on the availability and cost of equity capital. There are two main effects when stock markets rise markedly. First, the cost of capital falls for existing and new insurers. Second, rising share prices increase the value of an insurer's asset holdings and thereby also the value of equity. The increased availability and reduced cost of capital increases supply and hence exerts downward pressure on premiums.

The third theory holds that claims rather than capital-market effects are the key cause of underwriting cycles. It supposes that insurers tend to underestimate the potential for large claims when there are no large individual losses or accumulation of losses. However, when a very large loss occurs, premiums rise sharply. A case in point is car insurance. After a few 'soft' winters without frozen roads, the frequency of car accidents seems to be relatively low and premiums may decrease. But after a 'strong' winter with multiple car accidents, premiums tend to rise again. This theory assumes that insurers have a short memory. This theory also supposes that following a major loss, insurers will try to recover some of their losses. Of course, exceptionally large losses or accumulations of loss are likely to be more or less random in their timing, but their effects may appear to be cyclical.

---

mismatch between assets and liabilities. For life business, asset durations are generally shorter than liability durations. *Duration* is the effective maturity of an asset or liability. This duration mismatch will primarily cause an interest rate risk, as most assets consist of bonds.[3] Insurers also invest in equities and other investments to increase returns. While equities tend to generate a higher return than bonds in the long run (Dimson *et al.*, 2002), they also generate a considerably higher ALM risk. Insurers use advanced models to optimise their risk-return profile. The ability to invest in equities rather than

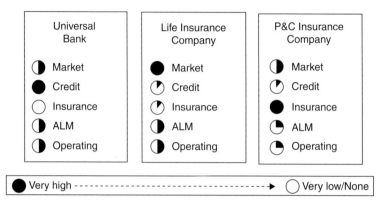

Figure 11.6   The relative role of risk types in banking and insurance
Source: Oliver, Wyman and Company (2001)

in bonds depends on the size of an insurer's capital buffer. The larger the capital buffer, the more risk (and thus equity investments) the insurer is allowed to take (see Chapter 12 for further details).

The third type of risk is *credit risk*. While banks grant loans, insurers typically invest in traded assets such as bonds. Credit risk is present because the value of bonds may decline as a result of an increase in the perceived likelihood that the issuer will not be able to meet scheduled payments in the future. For most banks, lending activities are typically the main source of credit risk. But a typical insurer attributes only 5–10 per cent of total risk capital to credit risk (Van Lelyveld, 2006).

The fourth type of risk is *operational risk*. This is the risk of loss from inadequate internal processes, people or systems, or from external events. While developments in the insurance industry generally follow those in banking, most insurers model external-event risk separately as an underwriting risk.

The impact of the various types of risk differs across banking and insurance. The main business of banks is granting loans. Credit risk is the most important risk driver in banking, followed by market and ALM risk. ALM risk is caused by long-term assets funded by short-term deposits. The main risk in life insurance is market risk related to the large asset portfolios. Life insurers collect premiums on life policies, which are invested over a long period. The next type of risk is ALM risk, which is opposite to banking ALM risk. Life insurers typically invest the premiums on their long-term policies in shorter-lived assets. Insurance or underwriting risk is the main risk driver for P&C insurers. Figure 11.6 illustrates the relative importance of the different types of risk.

Centralisation of risk management

The organisational structure of international financial firms is moving from the traditional country model to a business-line model with integration of key management functions. One of the most notable advances in risk management is the growing emphasis on developing a firm-wide assessment of risk. These integrated approaches to risk management aim to ensure a comprehensive and systematic approach to risk-related decisions throughout the financial firm. Once firms have a centralised risk-management unit in place, they may benefit from economies of scale in risk management. Nevertheless, these centralised systems still rely on local branches and subsidiaries for local market data. The potential capital reductions that can be achieved by applying the advanced approaches of the Basel II framework encourage banking groups to organise their risk management more centrally (see Chapter 10). The same is true for the future Solvency II framework for the European insurance industry (Drzik, 2005). Firms that implement a well-constructed risk- and capital-management framework can derive significant near-term business benefits, and substantially strengthen their medium-term competitive position.

Kuritzkes *et al.* (2003) provide evidence that internationally active financial conglomerates are putting in place centralised risk and capital-management units. The dominant approach is to adopt a so-called 'hub and spoke' organisational model. The spokes are responsible for risk management within business lines, while the hub provides centralised oversight of risk and capital at the group level. Activities at the spoke include the credit function within a bank, or the actuarial function within an insurance subsidiary or group, each of which serves the front-line managers for most trading decision making.

Schoenmaker *et al.* (2008) confirm the shift to a more holistic approach in the European insurance industry. Developments in the field of accounting (for instance the introduction of International Financial Reporting Standards (IFRS) and the Sarbanes Oxley Act in the US) and in supervision (Solvency II) contribute to the centralisation of risk- and capital-management processes. Moreover, as insurance groups operate in various countries, the need for a coherent policy regarding risk and capital management is increasing. This, in turn, has led to the adoption of chief risk officers in large insurance groups.

Hub functions

Applying the hub and spoke model to a sample of large European insurance companies, Schoenmaker *et al.* (2008) identify which functions are executed at the centre (hub) and which functions are performed at the local business units (spokes). The hub accommodates decisions and responsibilities for the group as a whole at a central level in the organisation. Although large insurance groups have a distinct central risk-management framework in place, there are great differences between the responsibilities and actual implementation of these frameworks. In some groups central risk- and capital-management processes are still in their infancy, while in other groups these processes are much more advanced and commonly accepted in the organisation.

All groups use their risk-management framework to get an overview and to monitor the group-wide risk exposure. The majority of the groups also use their risk framework for specifying their risk profile and setting risk management, control, and business-conduct standards for the group's worldwide operations (i.e. 'the rules of the game'). This group-wide risk profile specifies some risk-tolerance levels. Within these boundaries, the local units can act more or less independently. Furthermore, group-wide policies regarding risk management enable a broadly consistent approach to the management of risks at the business-unit level.

The risk-management framework encompasses several bodies with their own specific tasks. On top of the central risk-management framework is the group risk committee at the executive level, with the chief executive officer (CEO) or chief financial officer (CFO) bearing the ultimate responsibility. This committee is often responsible for setting the strategic guidelines and policies for risk management, for monitoring consolidated risk reports at group level, and for allocating economic capital to various entities of the group. Sometimes groups also have risk committees below the executive level. This may be the case in a financial group with both banking and insurance activities. The group risk committee is then responsible for the group as a whole, while banking and insurance risk committees reporting to the group risk committee are responsible for the risk management in banking and insurance, respectively.

Furthermore, many groups also have central or group risk-management teams. These teams are responsible for the development and implementation of the risk-management framework, for supporting the work of the risk committees, for reporting and reviewing risks, and for recommendations concerning risk methodologies. Many times, these central/group risk-management teams are headed by a CRO who oversees all aspects of the group's risk management and often reports to the CEO or CFO of the group and is present at meetings of the executive board.

Spoke functions

In the spokes, decisions are being taken on the level of the business/country unit. Insurance is very much a local business, with significant differences between the operational environment of the host countries in which the insurance group is active. Specific local knowledge is often required with respect to national rules and regulations (such as fiscal legislation, contracts, social security, consumer protection, or local risks), complicating the steering process at a central level. So a great number of decisions still have to be made by the local business units. In general, the actuary determines the specific risk at the local level. At the group level, these local models are subsequently monitored and assessed. Although the general conditions for determining local risk models are set at the central level, the local units carry the ultimate responsibility for their risk management.

So, despite the emergence of centralised risk management, the risk-management practices of the largest insurance groups are still to a large extent influenced by the risk-management policies of the local business units. Therefore, in general one could say that the 'rules of the game' are being determined at central level in the hub and that the local managers in the spokes determine 'how the game is actually being played' within the margins of these rules. This general principle is summarised in Figure 11.7 which gives an overview of the roles and responsibilities for each level of the organisation, whereby the spokes are placed within a field of jurisdiction-specific parameters in order to capture the location-specific factors that influence the business decisions.

11.3 The European insurance system

Insurance markets across Europe

The insurance markets vary significantly across Europe. This is illustrated by differences in the *insurance penetration*, i.e. insurance premiums as a percentage of GDP, which ranges from 1.5 per cent in Romania to 13.3 per cent in the Netherlands (see Table 11.5). There is a large difference between the new Member States of the EU and the EU-15. Whereas the prevalence of life insurance is 5.5 per cent in the EU-15, it amounts to only 1.5 per cent in the NMS-12. Life insurance is basically a savings product for the future, where the payout is linked to somebody's life. Life insurance may be considered as a 'luxury' good: only at high income levels do households start to save for retirement (Focarelli and Pozzolo, 2008).

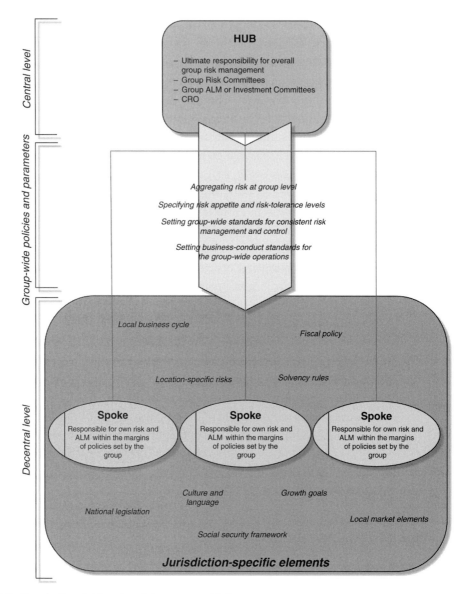

Figure 11.7 Organisation of risk and capital management in insurance groups
Source: Schoenmaker, Oosterloo and Winkels (2008)

Non-life insurance is less diverse across Europe. It looks more like a 'neces-sary' good offering basic protection against accidents, such as car accidents, fire, or illness. Non-life penetration is 3.3 per cent in the EU-15 and 2.1 per cent in the NMS-12. Also, at the country level the differences are less pro-nounced than for life insurance. The insurance penetration ranges from 1.1 per cent in Lithuania to 4.1 per cent in Slovenia.[4]

Table 11.5 Insurance penetration in the EU, 2009

	Number of insurers	Total premium income (in € billion)	Insurance penetration (in % of GDP)		
			Total	Life	Non-life
Austria	72	16.4	6.0	2.7	3.3
Belgium	148	28.4	8.4	5.4	3.0
Bulgaria	45	0.9	2.5	0.3	2.2
Cyprus	34	0.8	4.5	2.0	2.5
Czech Republic	52	5.2	3.9	1.5	2.3
Denmark	187	19.9	8.8	6.2	2.7
Estonia	20	0.4	2.6	1.0	1.7
Finland	63	16.2	9.2	7.3	1.9
France	452	200.1	10.3	7.1	3.2
Germany	604	171.3	7.1	3.5	3.6
Greece	82	5.0	2.1	0.9	1.2
Hungary	29	2.9	3.2	1.6	1.6
Ireland	236	12.1	7.4	5.5	1.9
Italy	234	117.9	7.7	5.3	2.4
Latvia	24	0.3	1.7	0.2	1.6
Lithuania	30	0.4	1.7	0.5	1.1
Luxembourg	96	1.9	5.2	3.3	1.9
Malta	54	0.3	5.1	3.4	1.7
Netherlands	320	76.4	13.3	4.2	9.1
Poland	65	14.6	4.7	2.3	2.5
Portugal	84	14.6	9.0	6.4	2.6
Romania	45	1.8	1.5	0.2	1.3
Slovakia	20	2.0	3.1	1.6	1.5
Slovenia	21	2.1	5.8	1.8	4.1
Spain	294	60.4	5.8	2.7	3.0
Sweden	381	23.2	7.9	6.1	1.8
United Kingdom	934	203.8	13.0	9.6	3.4
EU-15	4,187	967.6	8.8	5.5	3.3
NMS-12	439	31.6	3.6	1.5	2.1
EU-27	4,626	999.3	8.4	5.2	3.2

Notes: Insurance penetration is measured as premium income as a percentage of GDP. EU-15, NMS-12, and EU-27 are calculated as a weighted average (weighted according to total premium income).

Source: CEA (2010)

Table 11.6 Non-life premium income in the EU (in € billion), 1995–2009

	1995	2000	2005	2009
Motor insurance	78	98	119	121
Health insurance	51	66	88	101
Property insurance	47	54	74	80
Other non-life	48	51	72	107
Total non-life	224	269	353	409

Source: CEA (2010)

Table 11.6 illustrates the major business lines of non-life insurers. Motor insurance is the largest class of non-life business, but health insurance is catching up. The strong increase of health insurance reflects the privatisation of the healthcare sector in the Netherlands in 2006. Property insurance is increasing as well. Other non-life insurance includes general liability, marine, aviation, and transport insurance.

In 2010, some 4,600 insurance companies operated in the EU. Their number has declined since the creation of the European single market, due to mergers and acquisitions at both the national and the European level. Insurance companies aim for sufficient critical mass to be able to compete effectively at the European level.

The insurance market has a large number of small and medium-sized insurers with a very low market share and a small number of insurance groups with a high market share. The small insurers, with premium income below €10 million, are found in the non-life insurance sector in particular. Some 30 per cent of the smaller insurers are mutual companies (CEA, 2007). Large insurance groups have a premium income ranging from around €5 billion up to €100 billion. Table 11.7 shows the largest 25 insurers in Europe, amounting to over half of the premium income of the European insurance market.

Within the group of large insurance groups, Schoenmaker *et al.* (2008) define insurers as 'domestic' if they receive more than 50 per cent of their premiums in the home country. An example is the RBS Group in the UK. If 50 per cent or less of their premiums are collected in the home country and more than 25 per cent in other EU countries, the insurers are considered 'European'. Some European insurers focus on a specific region within Europe. Others, like Allianz, AXA, and Generali, operate Europe-wide. The remaining international insurers are 'global' insurers operating on a worldwide scale.

Table 11.7 Biggest 25 insurance groups in Europe in 2006

Insurance groups	(1) Premium income[a] in (€ billion)	(2) Total assets (in € billion)	(3) Premium income in home country (as % of (1))	(4) Premium income in rest of Europe (as % of (1))	(5) Premium income rest of world (as % of (1))
Global insurers[b]					
1. ING (Netherlands)	47	334	23	15	62
2. Aegon[e] (Netherlands)	25	315	18	31	51
3. Prudential (UK)	24	322	36	0	64
European insurers[c]					
1. Allianz (Germany)	91	1,053	35	46	20
2. AXA (France)	72	728	26	44	30
3. Generali (Italy)	63	378	38	58	5
4. Zurich Financial Services (Switzerland)	37	284	11	54	35
5. Old Mutual (UK)	21	191	20	28	52
6. Fortis (Belgium)	14	115	43	49	8
7. Swiss Life (Switzerland)	14	116	44	56	0
8. Royal & Sun Alliance (UK)	9	34	46	35	19
Domestic insurers[d]					
1. Aviva (UK)	50	436	51	38	11
2. CNP (France)	32	264	83	9	8
3. Crédit Agricole (France)	26	n.a.	90	5	5
4. Talanx (Germany)	19	93	53	26	21
5. HBOS (UK)	18	123	90	5	5
6. Ergo (Germany)	16	124	84	16	0
7. BNP Paribas (France)	16	97	51	30	19
8. Eureko (Netherlands)	14	86	89	11	0

Table 11.7 (*cont.*)

Insurance groups	(1) Premium income[a] in (€ billion)	(2) Total assets (in € billion)	(3) Premium income in home country (as % of (1))	(4) Premium income in rest of Europe (as % of (1))	(5) Premium income rest of world (as % of (1))
9. Groupama (France)	14	85	83	16	1
10. Fondiaria-Sai (Italy)	10	41	99	1	0
11. RBS Group (UK)	9	19	79	6	15
12. Unipol (Italy)	9	42	95	3	2
13. Lloyds TSB (UK)	7	270	90	5	5
14. Legal & General (UK)	6	324	86	8	6

Notes:
[a] Top 25 insurance groups are selected on the basis of gross written premium in 2006.
[b] Global insurers: less than 50 per cent of premium in the home country and less than 25 per cent in the rest of Europe.
[c] European insurers: less than 50 per cent of premium in the home country and more than 25 per cent in the rest of Europe.
[d] Domestic insurers: more than 50 per cent of premium in the home country.
[e] Since more than half of its activities are consistently collected in the rest of the world, Aegon is marked as a global insurance group.
n.a. means not available.
Source: Schoenmaker *et al.* (2008)

This group includes ING and Aegon from the Netherlands, and Prudential from the UK.

Figure 11.8 shows that the number of European insurers fluctuates around eight between 2000–2006, while the number of global insurers remains small at three.

In order to operate successfully in a foreign market, an insurer needs to know the legislation (e.g. on liability), fiscal treatment, and accident statistics (e.g. the number of car accidents) of that country. As these differ across EU countries, a major effort is required before entry of a foreign market. Cross-border insurance is therefore typically done by large insurance groups. The preferred method of entering a foreign market is through a subsidiary, usually by the acquisition of a local insurer. Figure 11.9 illustrates the cross-border

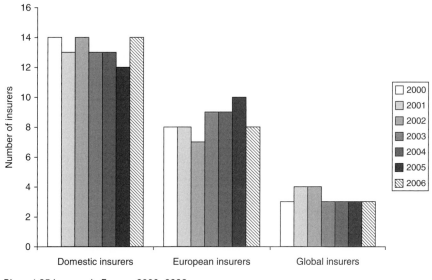

Figure 11.8 Biggest 25 insurers in Europe, 2000–2006
Note: See Table 11.7 for definitions.
Source: Schoenmaker *et al.* (2008)

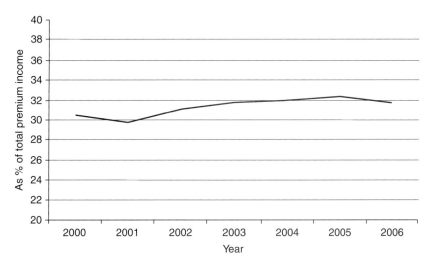

Figure 11.9 Cross-border penetration of top 25 EU insurers (%), 2000–2006
Note: Share of premium income from other EU countries measured as a percentage of total premium income. The share is calculated for the top 25 insurance groups in Europe, which represent more than half of total premium income for the EU-27.
Source: Schoenmaker *et al.* (2008)

penetration of the top 25 insurers in Europe. The cross-border penetration rose from 30 per cent to 32 per cent between 2000 and 2006. The corresponding figure for the largest 30 banks in Europe was an increase from 20 per cent to 23 per cent (see Chapter 10). Large insurance groups are thus more internationally oriented than their counterparts in banking.

Market structure and performance

Between 1994 and 2009 the total number of insurers in the EU decreased from 5,201 to 4,626 (see Table 11.8). This consolidation mainly reflects mergers or acquisitions of small and medium-sized domestic insurers. At the same time, some of the large insurers expanded domestically as well as cross-border.

There are different types of insurance companies. The main model is the limited-liability (or joint-stock) insurance company owned by shareholders, whose liability for losses is restricted to the share capital. The model of mutual insurer, owned by the policy holders, still counts for about 20 per cent of the European market (ACME, 2003). The significance of mutuals is large in some markets, such as France and Germany (about 30 per cent), and small in other markets, like the United Kingdom (about 10 per cent). There is a trend towards 'demutualisation', meaning that mutuals are converted into limited-liability insurance companies.

Again, there are substantial differences between the EU-15 and the NMS-12. First, the number of insurers in the EU-15 is substantially higher than in the NMS-12. This is largely due to the significant number of small insurers in countries, such as France, Germany, and in particular the United Kingdom.

Second, the trend in the number of insurers is different. On average, the number of insurers in the EU-15 declined by about 15 per cent over the 1994–2009 period, while in the NMS-12 the corresponding figure increased by nearly 35 per cent. The change in the number of insurers influences the degree of concentration in the different national insurance markets. Table 11.8 presents the CR5 ratio, which measures the market share of the top five insurers in the insurance industry. The table illustrates that the insurance markets in the NMS-12 are generally more concentrated than the markets in the EU-15. However, there is convergence. The concentration ratios in the EU-15 are increasing, while concentration in the NMS-12 is decreasing.

Overall, life insurance markets are more concentrated than non-life markets. That can be explained by the nature of the product. Life-insurance companies carry closely related (savings) products dependent on life expectancy. By contrast, non-life insurance is an industry with very different business

Table 11.8 Market structure indicators, 1994/95 and 2009

	Size		CR5 (in %)[a]				Competition
	Number of insurers		Life		Non-life		Combined ratio[b]
	1994	2009	1995	2009	1995	2009	2009
Austria	74	72	46	52	54	54	93
Belgium	252	148	64	73	52	61	97
Bulgaria	30	45	n.a.	72	n.a.	59	90
Cyprus	46	34	89	95	36	64	85
Czech Republic	27	52	97	73	93	81	n.a.
Denmark	250	187	57	50	63	69	91
Estonia	15	20	100	100	65	92	82
Finland	57	63	99	88	88	86	94
France	577	452	50	53	41	36	100
Germany	742	604	31	37	23	25	88
Greece	149	82	68	66	39	34	85
Hungary	13	29	93	60	96	81	n.a.
Ireland	122	236	61	46	50	53	100
Italy	265	234	45	33	34	44	104
Latvia	42	24	n.a.	100	n.a.	75	92
Lithuania	35	30	n.a.	89	n.a.	82	99
Luxembourg	76	96	67	84	82	84	82
Malta	24	54	n.a.	99	n.a.	75	76
Netherlands	492	320	68	56	35	36	96
Poland	34	65	100	68	90	71	93
Portugal	87	84	59	85	53	55	94
Romania	39	45	n.a.	71	n.a.	61	112
Slovakia	11	20	98	100	98	83	81
Slovenia	10	21	90	81	95	90	100
Spain	417	294	29	41	20	30	86
Sweden	494	381	74	69	77	62	89
United Kingdom	821	934	29	49	27	40	117
EU-15[c]	4,875	4,187	44	49	33	37	97
NMS-12[c]	326	439	96	73	91	75	94
EU-27[c]	5,201	4,626	44	49	34	39	97

Notes:
[a] CR5 is the share of the five largest life (non-life) insurers, measured as a percentage of total life (non-life) premium.
[b] Combined ratio is measured as claims and expenses in % of premium.
[c] EU-15, NMS-12, and EU-27 are calculated as a weighted average (weighted according to premium) for CR5 and the combined ratio.
n.a. means not available.
Source: CEA (2010) and EIOPA (2010)

lines (see Table 11.6). Among non-life insurers, there are many mono-liners that underwrite one type of insurance only. These specialised insurers are by definition smaller than multi-liner insurers that combine different business lines.

Measurement of competition in the insurance industry is still underdeveloped. There are no adequate indices of insurance prices that would allow comparison. An alternative approach is to rely on indirect measures, such as profitability (European Commission, 2007). A common economic measure to assess the profitability of non-life insurers is the combined ratio (see section 11.1). However, the use of the combined ratio has two major drawbacks. First, when claims are more likely to arise in the future, the matching principle of accounting is not satisfied. Clients pay, for example, their premium for their insurance in year 1, while the payout on claims may arise only in year 2 or 3. Second, investment returns are not included in the combined ratio. This is an important source of income, as premiums are invested in financial assets that are held until claims are paid.

The combined ratios are reported in the last column of Table 11.8. The figures indicate that the non-life insurance industry is competitive in Europe with a combined ratio of 97 per cent (EU-27) yielding a margin of 3 per cent. The margin is higher in the NMS with a margin of 6 per cent. At the country level, the picture is more diverse. The majority of EU Member States have a combined ratio between 90 per cent and 100 per cent. Some countries (Italy, Romania, and the United Kingdom) have combined ratios above 100 per cent and make a loss. Finally, a group of countries (Cyprus, Estonia, Germany, Greece, Luxembourg, Malta, Slovakia, Spain, and Sweden) have combined ratios between 75 per cent and 90 per cent. These ratios suggest a lack of competition, but the results should be interpreted with care and provide only an indication of lack of competition.

Insurance is sold through a variety of distribution channels. A growing share of insurance products is sold directly by employees of an insurance company or directly via the Internet channel (*direct writing*). Internet sales are expected to grow fast, particularly for simple non-life insurance products. Historically, insurance intermediaries in the form of brokers and agents play a dominant role. Brokers are fully independent, specialist insurance intermediaries. They are not tied to any specific insurance company. Insurance agents are typically less independent than insurance brokers. Agents can work exclusively for one insurance company, but may also offer competing products from a wide range of insurers. A final distribution channel is *bancassurance* (the combination of a bank and an insurance company within a financial institution), where insurance products are sold through the bank.

Life distribution channel 2008

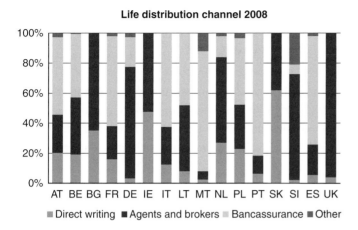

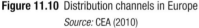

Non-life distribution channel 2008

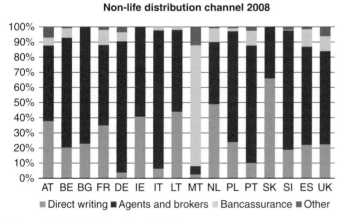

Figure 11.10 Distribution channels in Europe
Source: CEA (2010)

Distribution channels vary significantly across European countries. The distribution of life insurance is mainly driven by bancassurance networks (banking combined with assurance), with the exception of the United Kingdom and Ireland where brokers dominate the distribution of life products (see Figure 11.10). Bulgaria, Slovakia, and Slovenia also show a weaker role for banks. In non-life insurance, insurance products are principally distributed via agents in a large number of countries (Spain, France, Italy, Poland, Portugal, Slovakia, and Slovenia). The broker channel dominates in some other countries (the United Kingdom, Ireland, the Netherlands, and Belgium). The predominance of agents and brokers on almost every market finds its origin in the preference of the insured to benefit from proximity at the time of the contract and, above all, in the case of a claim. Direct writing is used more for non-life than for life products.

11.4 Financial conglomerates

Financial conglomerates combine banking and insurance activities. There are various arguments in favour of financial conglomerates: commercial integration, financial integration, and operational integration. First, commercial integration is related to cross-selling of multiple financial services to clients. The most important form of cross-selling is the provision of insurance services to the bank's customer base. This is called *bancassurance*. Cross-selling can also happen the other way round, when an insurer provides banking services to its clients. This is called *assurfinance*. Sharing of customer databases facilitates cross-selling. Cross-selling generates economies of scope through reduced client information and transaction costs and consequently higher prices and/ or transaction volumes for the financial group (Schmid and Walter, 2009).

Second, financial integration is an important driver of financial conglomerates. There is scope for financial diversification as the risk profile of the insurance activities is different from the risk profile of banking activities. These differences in risk profile are analysed in sections 10.2 and 11.2. The question is how stable these diversification benefits are. Diversification is particularly useful in bad times. The normal distribution underestimates the downside risk, since the return series of financial assets have a fat-tailed distribution. Slijkerman *et al.* (2012) apply extreme value theory, which gives a much better description of the downside risk than the normal approximation. For a sample of European financial conglomerates, they find evidence for diversification benefits (see also Box 11.5).

Third, operational integration can produce efficiencies in the back office. Operational integration generates economies of scope. Sharing of joint costs, such as IT platforms, across a diversified range of activities leads to higher levels of operating efficiency (Schmid and Walter, 2009). Another example is joint management of assets across the financial conglomerate.

There are also arguments against financial conglomerates. First, cross-subsidisation across business lines may lead to an inefficient allocation of capital and reduced performance. The profit in banking can be used for less-performing insurance activities, and vice versa. Second, opaque accounts may make it difficult to get a clear picture of the risk profile of financial conglomerates. As financial institutions report on a consolidated basis, it is difficult to detangle balance-sheet items as well as profit-and-loss items between banking and insurance business. This also gives scope for transfer of (risky) assets within a conglomerate (Schmid and Walter, 2009).

These arguments can be summarised under the heading of managerial complexity (Plantin and Rochet, 2007). A financial conglomerate is a portfolio of various business lines which require different expertise and give rise to different risks. It is very demanding to manage such a diversified firm in a coherent way. The empirical literature finds a significant (both in statistical and economic terms) discount for non-financial conglomerates, i.e. the shares of conglomerates seem to be structurally undervalued. Although one would expect mixed financial conglomerates to be formed mainly to create added value generated by the combination of banking and insurance, this added value has thus far not been transferred to the shareholders. The main arguments for this conglomerate discount are managerial complexity and the lack of focus.

Most studies on financial conglomerates focus on the US. The US definition of a financial conglomerate is a financial institution that is active in at least two of the following areas: commercial banking (lending), investment banking (capital-market transactions), insurance, and asset management. In practice, most financial conglomerates combine commercial and investment banking. Schmid and Walter (2009) and Laeven and Levine (2007) report a substantial and persistent conglomerate discount for US conglomerates. The market values of financial conglomerates that engage in multiple financial activities is about 10 per cent lower than those of comparable financial institutions that specialise in the individual activities.

Van Lelyveld and Knot (2009) focus specifically on the valuation of bank-insurance conglomerates. Using a dataset for 45 financial conglomerates, 45 banks, and 45 insurers, they compare the valuation of the three groups. Van Lelyveld and Knot (2009) do not find a structural diversification discount, but they observe considerable variability of the valuation. Large financial conglomerates face a larger discount, which is consistent with the hypothesis that larger conglomerates have more opportunities for inefficient cross-subsidisation.

On balance, the negative arguments present in financial conglomerates outweigh the positive elements. This is in line with recent market developments of large financial conglomerates. The Swiss bank, Credit Suisse, formed a financial conglomerate in 1997 with its acquisition of the insurer, Winterthur. However, in 2006, Credit Suisse sold Winterthur to the French insurer AXA. In 2010, ING announced it would separate its banking and insurance business by selling off the insurance parts. An example from the US is Citigroup, which grew out of a merger between Citicorp (banking) and Travelers (insurance)

> ## Box 11.5 Functional or geographical diversification?
>
> Financial firms can pursue different diversification strategies. Functional diversification is the combination of different activities, such as banking and insurance. Swiss Re (2007) indicates that Europe has the highest share of financial conglomerates. In particular, the combination of banking and life insurance accounts for more than half of the life-insurance market in Europe. In North America and Asia, the penetration of financial conglomerates is much lower than in Europe. This partly reflects the previously restrictive regulations on combining banking and insurance. In the US, the Gramm-Leach-Bliley Act of 1999 removed barriers between banks and insurance companies. The Japanese bancassurance market was fully liberalised only by the end of 2007.
>
> Geographical diversification aims to spread the activities over different regions. Schoenmaker and Van Laecke (2006) show that geographical diversification of European banks exceeds that of American and Asian banks.
>
> The two effects can be decomposed. Van Lelyveld and Knot (2009) do not find a structural discount for functional diversification, but they report that large financial conglomerates appear to trade at a discount. Functional diversification is thus predominantly value destroying for larger conglomerates. In contrast, Schmid and Walter (2009) report that geographically diversified financial firms trade at a small premium. Geographical diversification is thus value enhancing.

in 1998. Citigroup has, however, divested most of its insurance underwriting business over the last few years.

Financial conglomeration is facilitated by the strong demand for long-term savings products. Growth opportunities in life-insurance and pension products lead to increasing orientation of banks towards these areas. Table 11.9 indicates that the market share of financial conglomerates in banking and life insurance amounts to 27 per cent in the EU-15. While banks have acquired a large share of the life-insurance market, where bank-distribution channels are effective, penetration in non-life is less pronounced. The market share of financial conglomerates in non-life insurance is only 19 per cent.

Turning to the country level, it appears that financial conglomerates are prominent players in Belgium, Finland, and the Netherlands, with market shares well over 30 per cent. In the southern countries of Europe, such as Italy, Greece, Portugal, and Spain, conglomerates are almost non-existent.

Table 11.9 Market share of financial conglomerates (%), 2001

	Market share of financial conglomerates (in %)		
	Share of bank deposits	Share of life premium income	Share of non-life premium income
Austria	0	0	0
Belgium	87	71	46
Denmark	24	15	37
Finland	57	61	37
France	42	20	4
Germany	14	30	29
Greece	0	11	0
Ireland	29	46	0
Italy	17	7	7
Luxembourg	17	5	0
Netherlands	31	37	22
Portugal	0	0	0
Spain	0	0	11
Sweden	18	0	0
United Kingdom	14	19	24
EU-15	27	27	19

Notes: Financial conglomerates are defined as financial services groups that have at least 10 per cent of their financial activities in each of the sectors of banking and insurance.
Source: European Commission

11.5 Conclusions

Insurance seeks to protect individuals and firms from adverse events through the pooling of risks. The business lines are very diverse. Non-life insurance includes car, property, and liability insurance, while life insurance provides cover for premature death or retirement. Insurance companies collect premiums today and make payments when adverse events happen in the future. Insurance is thus a risky business. Indeed, risk is the essence of an insurance company. This chapter has shown that the pattern of small claims, such as fire or car accidents, is fairly predictable. But larger accidents or catastrophes (like hurricanes) involve high claims with low probability. The risk of catastrophes is too big for one insurance company and is therefore divided among different insurance and re-insurance companies. Insurance companies tend to centralise risk management using internal risk-management models. Insurers and banks are converging with regard to risk-management systems and practices.

The insurance markets vary considerably across Europe. Life insurance is quite prominent in the EU-15 and can be considered a 'luxury' good. Non-life is more evenly spread across the EU and is regarded as a 'necessary' good. The figures indicate that the level of cross-border insurance has gradually increased. Insurance is sold through a variety of distribution channels. A growing share of insurance products is sold directly through the Internet or by employees of an insurance company. Insurance intermediaries such as brokers and agents play a dominant role, which however is expected to decrease for simple non-life insurances. A final distribution channel for insurance products is bancassurance.

Financial conglomerates combining banking and insurance have emerged in Europe. They cover about 25 per cent of the banking and insurance markets. An important driver of financial conglomerates is the cross-selling of insurance products to banking customers. Another driver is financial-diversification benefits as the risk profile of banking and insurance activities is quite different. However, this chapter also indicates that it may be difficult for managers to run a diversified firm with different business lines.

NOTES

1 Re-insurance is also used for other reasons. First, it can be used to increase an insurer's underwriting capacity. It enables the insurer to pass on part of the risk. Second, it can be used to stabilise profits. It enables the insurer to level out the effects of poor loss performance.
2 To assess the overall risk profile of the insurance company, correlations across risk types should be taken into account, but incorporating diversification effects between risk types is still in the embryonic stage of development (Van Lelyveld, 2006).
3 In addition to interest rate risk, bonds are subject to credit risk. The credit risk of government bonds issued by developed countries is typically very low, while the credit risk of corporate bonds is usually higher.
4 The Netherlands, with a non-life penetration ratio of 9.1 per cent, is an outlier as health insurance is privatised in the Netherlands.

SUGGESTED READING

Dionne, G. (ed.) (2000), *Handbook of Insurance*, Kluwer, Dordrecht.
Drzik, J. (2005), At the Crossroads of Change: Risk and Capital Management in the Insurance Industry, *The Geneva Papers on Risk and Insurance – Issues and Practice*, 30, 72–87.

Mikosch, T. (2004), *Non-Life Insurance Mathematics: An Introduction with Stochastic Processes*, Springer-Verlag, Berlin.

Rees, R. (2008), Insurance and Re-insurance Companies, in: X. Freixas, P. Hartmann, and C. Mayer (eds.), *Handbook of European Financial Markets and Institutions*, Oxford University Press, 414–435.

Van Lelyveld, I. and K. Knot (2009), Do Financial Conglomerates Create or Destroy Value? Evidence for the EU, *Journal of Banking and Finance*, 33, 2312–2321.

REFERENCES

Association des Assureurs Coopératifs et Mutualistes Européens (2003), *Valuing Mutuality II*, ACME, Brussels.

Comité Européen des Assurances (2007), European Insurance in Figures, CEA Statistics, No. 31, CEA, Brussels.

(2010), European Insurance in Figures, CEA Statistics, No. 42, CEA, Brussels.

Dimson, E., P. Marsh, and M. Staunton (2002), *Triumph of the Optimists: 101 Years of Global Investment Returns*, Princeton University Press.

Drzik, J. (2005), At the Crossroads of Change: Risk and Capital Management in the Insurance Industry, *The Geneva Papers on Risk and Insurance – Issues and Practice*, 30, 72–87.

Embrechts, P., C. Klüppelberg, and T. Mikosch (1997), *Modelling Extremal Events for Insurance and Finance*, Springer, Heidelberg.

European Commission (2007), *Business Insurance Sector Inquiry: Interim Report*, EC, Brussels.

European Insurance and Occupational Pensions Supervisors Authority (2010), Statistical Annex 2009, EIOPA, Frankfurt am Main.

Focarelli, D. and A. F. Pozzolo (2008), Cross-Border M&As in the Financial Sector: Is Banking Different from Insurance?, *Journal of Banking and Finance*, 32, 15–29.

Kessler, D. (2008), Insurance Market Mechanisms and Government Interventions, *Journal of Banking and Finance*, 32, 4–14.

Kohn, M. (2004), *Financial Institutions and Markets*, 2nd edition, Oxford University Press.

Kuritzkes, A., T. Schuermann, and S. Weiner (2003), Risk Measurement, Risk Management, and Capital Adequacy in Financial Conglomerates, in: R. Herring and R. Litan (eds.), *Brookings-Wharton Papers on Financial Services: 2003*, Brookings Institution, Washington DC, 141–193.

Laeven, L. and R. Levine (2007), Is There a Diversification Discount in Financial Conglomerates?, *Journal of Financial Economics*, 85, 331–367.

Loubergé, H. (2000), Developments in Risk and Insurance Economics: The Past 25 Years, in G. Dionne (ed.), *Handbook of Insurance*, Kluwer, Dordrecht, 3–33.

Mikosch, T. (2004), *Non-Life Insurance Mathematics: An Introduction with Stochastic Processes*, Springer-Verlag, Berlin.

Niehaus, G. and A. Terry (1993), Evidence on the Time Series Properties of Insurance Premiums and Causes of the Underwriting Cycle, *Journal of Risk and Insurance*, 60, 466–479.

Oliver, Wyman and Company (2001), *Study on the Risk Profile and Capital Adequacy of Financial Conglomerates*, Oliver, Wyman and Company, London.

Plantin, G. and J.-C. Rochet (2007), *When Insurers Go Bust: An Economic Analysis of the Role and Design of Prudential Regulation*, Princeton University Press.

Rejda, G. E. (2005), *Principles of Risk Management and Insurance*, 9th edition, Addison Wesley, Boston.

Rothschild, M. and J. Stiglitz (1976), Equilibrium in Competitive Insurance Markets: An Essay on the Economics of Imperfect Information, *Quarterly Journal of Economics*, 90, 629–649.

Schmid, M. M. and I. Walter (2009), Do Financial Conglomerates Create or Destroy Economic Value?, *Journal of Financial Intermediation*, 18, 193–216.

Schoenmaker, D. and C. van Laecke (2006), *Current State of Cross-Border Banking, FMG Special Papers 168*, London School of Economics, London.

Schoenmaker, D., S. Oosterloo, and O. Winkels (2008), The Emergence of Cross-Border Insurance Groups within Europe with Centralised Risk Management, *Geneva Papers on Risk and Insurance – Issues and Practice*, 33, 530–546.

Slijkerman, J. F., D. Schoenmaker, and C. G. de Vries (2012), Systemic Risk and Diversification across Banks and Insurers, *Journal of Banking and Finance*, forthcoming.

Spencer, P. D. (2000), *The Structure and Regulation of Financial Markets*, Oxford University Press.

Swiss Re (1998), *Floods – An Insurable Risk? A Market Survey*, Swiss Re, Zurich.

(2007), Bancassurance: Emerging Trends, Opportunities and Challenges, *Sigma*, 5.

(2011), Natural Catastrophes and Man-Made Disasters in 2010: A Year of Devastating and Costly Events, *Sigma*, 1.

Van Lelyveld, I. (ed.) (2006), *Economic Capital Modelling: Concepts, Measurement and Implementation*, Risk Books, London.

Van Lelyveld, I. and K. Knot (2009), Do Financial Conglomerates Create or Destroy Value? Evidence for the EU, *Journal of Banking and Finance*, 33, 2312–2321.

Von Bomhard, N. (2005), Risk and Capital Management in Insurance Companies, *The Geneva Papers on Risk and Insurance – Issues and Practice*, 30, 52–59.

Part IV

Policies for the Financial Sector

Financial Regulation and Supervision

OVERVIEW

This chapter reviews the reasons for regulation and supervision of financial services. Regulation refers to the process of rule making and the legislation underlying the supervisory framework, while supervision refers to monitoring the behaviour of individual firms and enforcing legislation. The case for government intervention is based on market failures. A first market failure is rooted in asymmetric information: financial institutions are generally better informed than their customers. A second market failure is externalities: the failure of a financial institution may affect the stability of the financial system as a whole. A third market failure occurs when certain players in the market exert undue market power.

The chapter discusses financial supervision in more detail, distinguishing between prudential supervision and conduct-of-business supervision. Prudential supervision aims to protect consumers by ensuring the safety and soundness of financial institutions. As financial institutions are becoming more complex, supervisors are moving away from direct control to methods that provide incentives for financial institutions to behave prudently. Conduct-of-business supervision focuses on how financial institutions deal with their customers and how financial institutions behave in markets. For instance, information provisions aim to ensure that consumers get the right information about financial products. In addition, there are guidelines for objective and high-quality advice to protect the interests of customers. Conduct-of-business rules also promote fair and orderly markets.

This chapter also discusses the organisational structure of financial supervision, which is changing as most EU countries are moving from the traditional sector model (with separate banking, securities, and insurance supervisors) towards cross-sector models.

Finally, this chapter reviews the challenges for financial supervision in the EU. The newly emerging European financial landscape confronts the home and host authorities with complex coordination issues. It is therefore questionable whether national-based supervision is an adequate arrangement in an integrating market. The new European supervisory structure is analysed.

LEARNING OBJECTIVES

After you have studied this chapter, you should be able to:
- explain the main market failures in the financial system and the role of government intervention to remedy these failures
- understand the aims and instruments of prudential supervision
- understand the aims and instruments of conduct-of-business supervision
- describe the various supervisory structures
- understand the new European Supervisory Authorities and the need for European financial supervision in an integrated financial market.

12.1 Rationale for government intervention

Market failure

This section reviews the reasons for regulation and supervision of financial services. Regulation refers to the process of rule making and the legislation underlying the supervisory framework, while supervision refers to monitoring the behaviour of individual firms and enforcing legislation. The case for government intervention is based on market failures. A *market failure* occurs when the private sector if left to itself (i.e. without government intervention) would produce a sub-optimal outcome. Goodhart *et al.* (1998) identify three main reasons for government intervention in the financial sector:

1. *Asymmetric information*: customers are less informed than financial institutions. Financial supervision aims to protect customers against this information asymmetry. This chapter analyses how this can be done.
2. *Externalities*: the failure of a financial institution may affect the stability of the financial system. Systemic supervision aims to foster financial stability and to contain the effects of systemic failure. Chapter 13 discusses policies aimed at maintaining financial stability.
3. *Market power*: financial institutions or financial infrastructures, such as payment systems, may exert undue market power. Competition policy aims to protect consumers against monopolistic exploitation. Chapter 14 examines this topic.

Asymmetric information arises in two cases. First, customers are generally unable to properly assess the safety and soundness of a financial institution, because that requires extensive effort and technical knowledge. Establishing some sort of oversight may be needed, as financial institutions have an incentive to take too much risk. This is because high-risk investments generally bring in more revenues that accrue to the institution, while in case of failure a substantial part of the losses will be borne by the depositors. The information asymmetry creates problems of adverse selection (a riskier financial institution may make a more attractive offer to potential customers) as well as moral hazard (a financial institution may increase its risk after it has collected funds from customers). Prudential supervision aims to protect customers by ensuring the soundness of financial institutions. Moreover, governments provide direct protection to depositors through deposit insurance with a cover of €100,000 in the EU (see Chapter 3). However, a government safety net may provide banks with an even stronger incentive for risky behaviour. Prudential supervision is thus also needed to counter this incentive by ensuring the banks' soundness (Mishkin, 2000). Section 12.2 discusses prudential supervision in more detail.

Second, customers may not be in a position to assess properly the behaviour of a financial institution. This problem is common in professional services (Goodhart *et al.*, 1998). In most cases, private-sector mechanisms are used to mitigate this principal-agent problem. A disciplinary body of a privately run medical association can, for example, expel a member when it finds that this member has (repeatedly) failed to meet the minimum standards of the medical profession. Why, then, is government supervision of financial services needed? An important explanation draws on the fiduciary nature of financial services. A customer hands over his money today, while the service is rendered in the (sometimes far) future. For example, only after retirement does it become clear whether the advised pension savings scheme is appropriate to meet the financial needs of the retirees. Moreover, the amount of money at risk is typically larger in financial services than in other professional services. Conduct-of-business supervision focuses on how financial institutions conduct business with their customers and how they behave in markets. The focus is on the functions, regardless of the financial institution performing this function. Section 12.3 discusses conduct-of-business rules to mitigate the behaviour of financial institutions.

The second market failure that may give rise to government regulation is externalities. There is a risk that a sound financial institution may fail when another financial institution goes bankrupt (contagion). This externality is not incorporated in the decision making of the financial institution. The social costs of the failure of a financial institution thus exceed the private costs. In particular, banks are subject to contagion as their balance sheet contains illiquid assets financed by redeemable deposits. When rumours about the quality of a bank's assets spread, depositors may withdraw their deposits. The liquidity and subsequently the solvency of a bank will be threatened when it has to liquidate its assets at fire sale prices (i.e. prices well below prices under normal market conditions). The failure of multiple banks may lead to a banking crisis. Macroprudential supervision aims to foster financial stability and to contain the effects of systemic failure. The task of maintaining financial stability is usually assigned to a country's central bank. Chapter 13 explains in more detail why the financial system (and especially the banking sector) is more susceptible to systemic risk than other economic sectors and discusses the role of the central bank to contain systemic risk.

The third market failure is related to market power. In a monopoly (only one firm) or an oligopoly (a few firms which may collude), firms can raise and maintain the price above the level that would prevail under (perfect) competition. The exercise of market power by firms is to the detriment of consumers who face higher prices and less choice of products or services. Lack of competition occurs in many economic sectors. In the financial sector, economies of scale (incentive for mergers) and network economies (e.g. in payment systems (see Chapter 7) or stock exchanges (see Chapter 5)) may reduce competition. Competition policy aims to ensure effective competition by taking a strong line against price fixing, market-sharing cartels, abuse of dominant market positions, and anti-competitive mergers. Chapter 14 explains the EU competition policy for the financial sector.

Government failure

Government failure is the public sector analogy to market failure and occurs when government intervention causes a less efficient allocation of goods and resources than would occur without that intervention. There is thus a need to weigh problems of government failure against those due to market failure (Besley, 2007). There are various consequences of government intervention. First, government-induced protection may have a detrimental impact on incentives for consumers. Why should consumers be careful if they are protected against possible negative outcomes of their actions? Second, government regulation may lead to bureaucracy ('red tape') restricting the activities of financial institutions. Moreover, as supervisory agencies need information they generally have a more or less elaborate system of supervisory reporting in place which puts an administrative burden on the sector.

Some academics consider government failure to be a bigger problem than market failure. For instance, adherents of free banking challenge the justification for any form of government regulation of the financial system, arguing that there is nothing special about financial services that should make this sector an exception to the general rule of free trade (see, for instance, Dowd, 1996). In their view, a policy of *laissez-faire* for the financial sector is optimal as government intervention undermines the market forces that make the financial system safe. Other academics favour limited government intervention. For instance, Benston and Kaufman (1996) argue for some minimum prudential standards (in particular capital requirements) to counter externalities, but beyond these standards there is no special need for protection of customers.

12.2 Microprudential supervision

The current regulatory system in the EU is based on the principle of home-country control combined with minimum standards and mutual recognition. A financial institution is thus authorised and supervised in its home country and can expand throughout the EU by offering cross-border services in other EU Member States or establishing branches in these countries without additional supervision by host-country authorities (*home-country control*). The host country has to recognise supervision from the home-country authorities (*mutual recognition*), as minimum requirements for prudential supervision have been laid down in the respective EU Directives (*minimum standards*). However, financial institutions also operate through subsidiaries (separate legal entities) in other countries for reasons of taxation and limited liability (Dermine, 2006). These subsidiaries are separately licensed and supervised by the host-country authorities.

According to Lastra (2006), *microprudential supervision* can be understood as a process with four stages:

1. Licensing, authorisation, or chartering of financial institutions (i.e. the entry into the business). The objective of this stage is to establish whether a person is fit and proper, i.e. before a person may obtain a licence, supervisors determine a person's integrity, honesty, reputation, and capability to manage a financial services provider. In this respect, the Basel core principles for effective banking supervision state that 'the licensing process at a minimum should consist of an assessment of the ownership structure and governance of the bank and its wider group, including the fitness and propriety of Board Members and senior management, its strategic and operating plan, internal controls and risk management, and its projected financial condition, including its capital base' (BIS, 2006).

2. The ongoing monitoring of the health of financial institutions and the financial system, in particular the asset quality, capital adequacy,

liquidity, management, internal controls, and earnings. Supervision is exercised through a broad range of instruments, including off-site and on-site examinations (or inspections), auditing (internal unpublished audit and external published audits), analysis of statistical requirements, and internal controls. In case of distress in financial institutions, the supervisory authorities have to act. Box 12.1 discusses two different reactions to distress.

3. Sanctioning or imposition of penalties in case of non-compliance with the law, fraud, bad management, or other types of wrongdoing.

4. Crisis management, which comprises lender of last resort, deposit insurance, and insolvency proceedings (see Chapter 13 for an in-depth discussion of crisis management).

Box 12.1 Forbearance versus prompt corrective action

Once a supervisory authority finds out that a financial institution is in distress there are two possible ways to react. The supervisor can intervene and resolve the distressed institution by requiring capital injections, the sale of assets, a merger with a sound institution, or liquidation once the regulatory capital ratio falls below a predetermined threshold. Alternatively, the supervisor can choose to allow the distressed financial institution to continue operation even though it is unable to meet the minimum regulatory requirements. The first response is generally called *prompt corrective action* (PCA), while the second type of response is referred to as *forbearance*. While PCA has been prescribed in the US in the 1991 Federal Deposit Insurance Corporation Improvement Act (FDICIA), in the EU Member States supervisory authorities may choose forbearance. Forbearance may dilute banks' incentives to behave prudently and induce undue liquidity support.

In view of the emergence of large cross-border banking groups, the European Shadow Financial Regulatory Committee (2005) advocates the implementation of a system of PCA as part of the supervisory process in each Member State. These procedures would reduce the likelihood of a sudden banking crisis and contribute to host-country supervisors' trust in home-country supervisors. While similar procedures are recommended, the thresholds and measures foreseen do not have to be identical in each Member State and for all banks.

Nieto and Wall (2007) identify three important aspects of the philosophy underlying PCA: (1) the primary focus of banking supervisory authorities should be on protecting the deposit-insurance fund and minimising government losses; (2) banking supervisors should have a clear set of required actions to be taken as a bank becomes progressively more undercapitalised; and (3) any undercapitalised bank should be closed before the economic value of its capital becomes negative. Moreover, the authors identify several institutional prerequisites for PCA: supervisory independence and accountability, adequate authority, accurate and timely information, and adequate resolution procedures. Nieto and Wall conclude that substantial changes are needed in the Member States' institutional frameworks before PCA could be adopted in the EU.

According to the BIS (1997), banks face the following key risks (see Chapter 10 for an in-depth discussion):
- *credit risk*: the risk of a loss because of the failure of a counterparty to perform according to a contractual arrangement, for instance due to a default by a borrower;
- *country risk*: the risks associated with the economic, social, and political environments of the borrower's home country;
- *market risk*: the risk due to unfavourable movements in market prices;
- *interest rate risk*: the risk related to unfavourable movements in interest rates. This risk impacts both the earnings of a bank and the economic value of its assets, liabilities, and off-balance sheet instruments;
- *liquidity risk*: this risk arises when a bank has insufficient liquid resources to meet a surge in liquidity demand. In extreme cases, insufficient liquidity can lead to the insolvency of a bank;
- *operational risk*: the risk of loss from inadequate or failed internal processes, people or systems, or from external events;[1]
- *legal risk*: risks stemming from inadequate or incorrect legal advice, changes in laws affecting the bank, new types of transactions, etc.;
- *reputational risk*: this may arise from operational failures, failure to comply with relevant laws and regulations, or other sources. Reputational risk is particularly damaging as confidence is elementary in banking.

In order to cover the risks mentioned above, banks are required to hold a minimum level of own financial resources, i.e. *capital*. These capital requirements serve as a buffer against unexpected losses, thereby protecting depositors and the overall stability of the financial system. The challenge is to determine how much capital banks need to hold in order to ensure that they are sufficiently capitalised.[2] If capital levels are too low, banks may be unable to absorb potential losses but high capital levels are costly for banks.

The 1988 Basel I Accord presented the first set of global standards for bank capital adequacy, aimed at establishing a minimum base of own funds in every bank. Basel I required banks to ensure that 8 per cent of the risk-weighted assets on the balance sheet are backed by own funds in order to absorb losses that could not be absorbed by its creditors. The aim of *risk-weighted assets* is to move from a static capital requirement to a requirement based on the riskiness of a bank's assets. For example, commercial loans are weighted at 100 per cent, mortgage loans secured with collateral at 50 per cent, and OECD government bonds at 0 per cent.

Its successor, the Basel II Accord, tried to create a better link between minimum regulatory capital and risk as well as enhancing market discipline. The Basel II framework has a three-pillar structure:

- The first pillar covers the minimum capital requirements for credit risk, operational risk, and market risk. Unlike the Basel I accord, where capital requirements were specified in detail by supervisors, Basel II allowed banks to use their internal risk-management models for the calculation of the required amount of capital.
- The second pillar (supervisory review) entails supervisory authorities examining the activities and risk profile of the bank in order to see whether there is a need for banks to hold additional capital (on top of the level of capital calculated under Pillar 1).
- The third pillar aims at enhancing market discipline by increasing the transparency of the amount and composition of a bank's capital relative to its risk profile, thereby introducing incentives for banks to conduct their business in a safe, sound, and efficient manner.

Despite these efforts, the financial crisis of 2007–2009 revealed serious weaknesses in the way banks had been operating as well as the way in which their operations were regulated and supervised:

(1) Banks held too little capital and the capital they held was of poor quality and in effect not able to cover the losses banks were facing.

(2) Banks were not holding enough liquid funds and so faced a shortage of cash when they needed it most.

(3) Banks took on too many assets compared to their capital (i.e. banks were highly 'leveraged'). When the crisis hit, many of these assets fell in value. When banks tried to sell these assets at the same time, prices fell further and this contributed to making the crisis worse.

Against this background, the Basel Committee on Banking Supervision (BCBS) developed new international minimum standards on bank capital adequacy (Basel III), thereby introducing the following requirements (EC, 2011):

- Better and more capital: to increase loss absorbency, Basel III prescribes strict criteria that must be met by own funds instruments in order to be belonging to the highest quality category, i.e. Common Equity Tier 1 (CET1), in order to ensure that these own funds of the bank can effectively be used in times of stress. Basel III also raises the amount of capital of various categories that banks need to hold.

- More balanced liquidity: to make sure that banks do not lack liquid assets and liquid funding, Basel III requires bankers to manage their cash flows and liquidity much more intensely than before, to predict the liquidity inflows and outflows better than before, and to be ready for stressed market conditions by having sufficient liquid assets or funding available, both in the short and in the longer run.
- Leverage back stop: Basel III introduces a traditional back stop mechanism that limits the growth of the total balance sheet as compared to available own funds.
- Capital requirements for derivatives (counterparty credit risk): Basel III encourages banks to use central counterparties (CCPs) for clearing over-the-counter (OTC) derivatives.
- Conservation buffer: Basel III creates a capital conservation buffer, i.e. a fixed target buffer of 2.5 per cent, providing an additional layer of capital to better protect taxpayers against any future public bailouts.
- Countercyclical buffer: Basel III creates a buffer that is built up in good times, and used in economic downturns. The countercyclical buffer is meant to stabilise the supply of credit in an economy. Since dynamics can be very different across different markets, these buffers are determined on a national market base.
- Capital charges for systemically important financial institutions (SIFIs): global SIFIs must have higher loss absorbency capacity to reflect the greater risks that they pose to the financial system. The SIFI surcharge ranges from 1 per cent to 2.5 per cent, depending on a bank's systemic importance.

Figure 12.1 presents an overview of the Basel III framework, including the new capital buffers, i.e. the capital conservation buffer and the countercyclical buffer. In addition, capital surcharges may be added for systemically important banks. Furthermore, on top of these own funds requirements, supervisors may add extra capital to cover for other risks following a supervisory review process.

The Basel Committee has also proposed the introduction of liquidity standards, notably:

- The Liquidity Coverage Ratio (LCR) requiring banks to have enough cash (or cash equivalent securities) to meet net cash outflows over a short (30 day) period of acute stress. It aims to ensure that sufficient high-quality liquid resources are available for one-month survival in case of a stress scenario. This standard will be introduced in 2015.

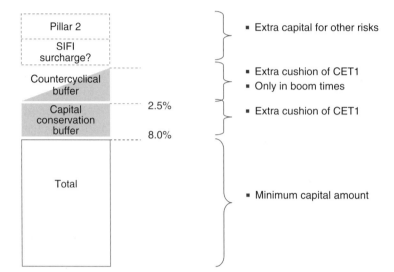

Figure 12.1 Basel III capital charges

- The Net Stable Funding Ratio (NSFR) requires banks to have longer term high quality funding (in relation to their liquidity profile) which can support operations over a longer (one year) period of less severe stress. It aims to limit over-reliance on short-term wholesale funding during times of buoyant market liquidity and encourage better assessment of liquidity risk across all on- and off-balance sheet items. This standard will be introduced in 2018.

It should be stressed that Basel III is not a legislative act, but rather the latest configuration of an evolving set of internationally agreed standards developed by supervisors and central banks. The European Commission transposes the Basel III rules into EU and national law. The Capital Requirements Directive IV package (SEC/2011/952) is a comprehensive review of the current Capital Requirements Directives (2006/48/EC and 2006/49/EC).

In Europe, a somewhat similar system for regulatory capital has been introduced for insurance companies as well. The so-called Solvency II Directive (2009/138/EC) establishes (more) sophisticated solvency requirements for insurers, in order to guarantee that they have sufficient capital to withstand adverse events, such as floods, storms, or major catastrophes. This will help to increase their financial soundness. The Solvency II Directive draws on the experiences from banking and follows the three-pillar approach of the Capital Requirements Directive.

Critics of the Basel framework argue that it has pro-cyclical effects. Financial regulation is inherently pro-cyclical, because capital requirements imply that financial institutions have to hold more capital when credit risk increases,

---

Box 12.2 Pro-cyclicality in bank lending?

The business cycle determines the prospects for business. The default rate of companies is low during an economic boom, while the default rate is high during a recession. The business cycle is thus an important driver of credit risk.

The probability of default and the related recovery rate (i.e. the part of the loan that is recovered in case of default) are not constant in time. In expanding economies, default probabilities decline and recovery rates improve. This results in declining rates on loans due to declining risk premiums. As loan rates go down, further loans are granted, fuelling the economic expansion. This is an example of pro-cyclicality. The reverse process can also happen. Increasing loan rates (due to rising default probabilities) in a recession cause a decline in new loans.

There is also a second effect. Losses in the loan book lower a bank's profitability. A bank's capital is then reduced as profits are added to capital and, worse, losses are deducted from capital. At the same time, capital requirements for loans increase as the credit risk on loans goes up. If banks are capital-constrained, they cannot grant new loans. This process could end in a full-blown 'credit crunch', where banks are no longer able to provide business with new credit.

The Basel Committee has recognised the problem of pro-cyclicality. The solution is to take the default probability (and related recovery rate) as an average of the default probability through the economic cycle, rather than an estimate at one point in time. However, when default probabilities are estimated in this manner the systemic component of default risk might be ignored. So except for an 'average year', regulatory capital will not reflect the actual risk and may overstate the true risk in economic booms and understate risk in an economic downturn. In addition, the new Basel III rules incorporate a countercyclical capital charge moving from 0 per cent (in bad times) up to 2.5 per cent (in good times).

The cyclical bias also has a psychological component. Guttentag and Herring (1984) have introduced the concept of 'disaster myopia', which means that the subjective probability of a major shock is a negative function of the time since the last shock happened. A good example is air travel. Passengers' feeling of safety decreases after one or more reported airplane crashes, while the safety feeling increases after a prolonged period with no major crashes. Similarly, it is possible that subjective probabilities of default decline during an economic boom (no major defaults), while actual probabilities remain constant.

---

which is generally the case in an economic downturn. If financial institutions have to increase capital, they can lend less to firms and households, thereby stimulating the downswing. The reverse reasoning applies in case of economic upswing (see Box 12.2 for a further discussion on pro-cyclicality in bank lending). Danielsson *et al.* (2001) argue that the Basel framework will exacerbate this tendency significantly. They argue that risk assessments, whether based on credit rating agencies' assessment or internal ratings, do not assess risk 'through the cycle'.

12.3 Conduct-of-business supervision

Conduct-of-business supervision focuses on how financial institutions conduct business with their customers and how they behave in markets, by prescribing rules about appropriate behaviour and monitoring behaviour that can be harmful to customers and to the functioning of markets. It is a relatively new activity, which became prominent after the liberalisation of financial markets. In the Big Bang in 1986, fixed commissions for trading at the London Stock Exchange were abolished. The Big Bang was the start of a process of liberalising financial markets across Europe. Liberalisation promotes entry of new players and may thereby lead to a wider choice of products and services (at lower prices). Conduct-of-business rules ensure a fair treatment of, in particular, retail customers in these liberalised markets.

The focus of conduct-of-business regulation is on the activities of financial institutions. The dividing lines between the sub-sectors of banking, insurance, and securities are blurring; the same type of product is increasingly offered by different financial institutions. Merton (1995) proposes a functional approach towards regulation to prevent regulatory arbitrage between different types of financial institutions. So, in his view the same conduct-of-business rules should apply to whoever (a bank, an insurer, or an investment firm) is offering, for example, long-term savings products to retail customers.

Protecting retail customers

Conduct-of-business rules protecting retail customers comprise the following elements (Llewellyn, 1999):[3]
- mandatory information provisions;
- objective and high-quality advice;
- duty of care.

Mandatory information provisions ensure that customers get the right information at the right time. Selecting an inappropriate product can have adverse consequences for retail customers and an important safeguard against this is proper disclosure and sufficient information (*transparency*). Good information helps customers to understand the key features of a financial product, including the risks, potential returns, and costs. Mandatory information provisions specify the (minimum) information needed to understand products. These provisions also require financial institutions to present this information in a consistent format to compare products.

Developing customers' literacy in financial matters is becoming increasingly important, as individuals take many decisions affecting their financial security and capital markets have become more accessible to consumers. The European Commission (2007) reports that international surveys demonstrate a low level of understanding of financial matters on the part of customers. There is a strong correlation between low levels of financial literacy and the ability to make appropriate financial decisions. Customers with poor financial literacy find it hard to understand and make use of the information they receive when purchasing financial services.

Conduct-of-business rules can also give guidelines for the quality and objectivity of advice. Providing advice is distinct from providing information. Whilst information merely describes the (essential) characteristics of a product or service, *advice* implies a recommendation to a given customer to opt for a specific product. A financial institution must take steps to ensure that a recommendation is suitable for its customer. This can, for example, be done by making a customer's profile containing information about the customer's knowledge and experience relevant to the specific type of financial product, financial situation, and investment objectives. When advice is given, it should be objective, based on the profile of the customer, and commensurate with the complexity of the products and the risks involved. The requirement of objectivity aims to minimise potential conflicts of interests when financial institutions are better informed than customers. Customers in some countries rely on independent advice to make appropriate decisions.

More generally, financial institutions have a duty of care towards their customers. A *duty of care* is an obligation imposed on financial institutions requiring that they adhere to a reasonable standard of care while dealing with customers. It aims to enhance responsible behaviour of financial institutions. A financial institution breaches its duty of care when it sells, for example, a high-risk investment product to a customer who cannot afford to bear the financial risk (e.g. a low-income household with limited savings).

To sum up, on the one hand conduct-of-business rules require proper information provision (transparency) to (potential) customers. This should enable customers to take better decisions. On the other hand conduct-of-business rules set minimum standards for advice and introduce a duty of care for financial institutions. The challenge for policy makers is to find the right balance between empowering customers by providing information and education (fostering financial literacy) and protecting customers by setting minimum standards for financial institutions' behaviour.

Since conduct-of-business rules are relatively new, they are not (yet) applied to all financial activities at the level of the EU. Until recently, rules for consumer credit and mortgage credit were largely left to the national authorities. There was an early Directive on Consumer Credit (87/102/EEC), which contained minimal common rules on consumer protection and permits Member States to add national rules. The new Directive on Consumer Credit (2008/48/EC) focuses on transparency and consumer rights. It provides for a comprehensible set of information to be given to consumers before the contract is concluded and also as part of the credit agreement. In order to enhance the comparability of different offers and to make the information better understandable, the pre-contractual information needs to be supplied in a standardised form, e.g. using the Annual Percentage Rate of Charge, which is a single figure, harmonised at EU level, representing the cost of the credit.

In the insurance markets, intermediaries play a vital role in selling insurance products. They also play a role in protecting the interests of insurance customers, primarily by offering them advice and assistance and by analysing their specific needs. At the same time, insurance intermediaries face incentives to sell products on which they earn a high commission, while these products are not always suitable for the customer. The Insurance Mediation Directive (2002/92/EC) contains rules to ensure a high level of professionalism and competence among insurance intermediaries whilst guaranteeing a high level of protection of customers' interests. In 2010, the European Commission started a public consultation on the revision of the Insurance Mediation Directive to enhance the framework and align the requirements with Solvency II (see section 12.2).

EU rules are most advanced in the field of securities. The Markets in Financial Instruments Directive (MiFID; 2004/39/EC), which replaced the Investment Services Directive (93/22/EEC), comprises a comprehensive set of operating conditions applicable to both banks and investment firms that regulates the relationship between these firms and their clients. This framework consists of a set of conduct-of-business, best-execution, and client-order-handling rules, as well as inducements and conflicts-of-interest provisions. Specific attention is paid to retail clients for whom a specific regime has been established, which entails reinforced fiduciary duties upon the firm. In 2011

€ trillion

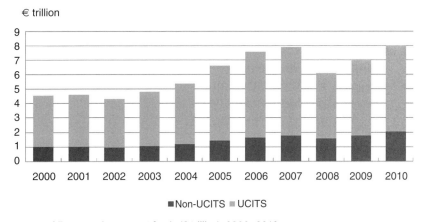

Figure 12.2 Assets of European investment funds (€ trillion), 2000–2010
Source: European Fund and Asset Management Association

the European Commission tabled proposals to revise MiFID in order to strengthen investor confidence and achieve MiFID's original objectives.

Another set of EU rules in the investment-services field is contained in the Undertakings for Collective Investments in Transferable Securities Directive (2009/65/EC). This Directive allows Undertakings for Collective Investments in Transferable Securities (UCITS) to operate freely throughout the EU on the basis of a single authorisation. A collective investment fund may apply for UCITS status in order to allow EU-wide marketing. Figure 12.2 illustrates that the vast majority of European investment funds are operating under a UCITS licence. In 2009 the European Commission completed a programme of improvements to the earlier UCITS Directive of 2001. These improvements aim at establishing a new standardised and harmonised disclosure document designed to empower investors to take more effective investment decisions as well as strengthening the rules for the conduct of UCITS management companies, including the prevention, management, and disclosure of conflicts of interest.

Market functioning

Conduct-of-business regulation promoting fair and orderly markets contains the following elements:
- transparency of trading;
- prohibition of insider trading and market manipulation;
- information requirements for issuers, including prospectus and financial reporting, and for shareholders.

Rules on the *transparency of trading* require disclosure of quotes, i.e. prices at which traders are prepared to sell or buy securities, and of prices at which trades have taken place. Potential investors can only analyse and compare trading conditions for securities when quotes (pre-trade transparency) are published. Post-trade transparency is also important to get timely insight into the movement of prices. The transparency requirements seek to achieve an adequate price-formation process, to ensure best execution and to provide for a level playing field between the different types of trade venue (see also Box 5.2).

Insider trading and market manipulation undermine the proper functioning and integrity of markets. *Insider-trading rules* put a ban on trading with inside information, i.e. material information on the firm that has not yet been made public. The use of this information by insiders, such as management or employees, may influence the price of the firm's securities. To speed up the release of new information (and thus reduce the potential for insider trading), insider-trading rules require listed firms to disclose inside information as soon as possible. It thus promotes transparency and equal treatment of investors. *Market-manipulation rules* prohibit the spread of rumours to influence (i.e. 'manipulate') the price of a security.

Firms that issue securities are required to publish information on a regular basis. First, firms have to publish a prospectus when they are issuing securities. A *prospectus* commonly provides investors with material information about the firm's business, financial statements, biographies of officers and directors, detailed information about their compensation, any litigation that is taking place, a list of material properties, and any other material information. Next, listed firms have to provide annual financial reports. In addition, half-yearly or quarterly financial reports may be required. The purpose of financial reporting is to ensure comparable, transparent, and reliable information about firms. Finally, shareholders have to disclose acquisitions (and disposals) of shareholdings beyond the 5 per cent threshold. In that way, firms can identify their major shareholders.

The conduct-of-business rules for markets are laid down in a raft of EU Directives. The Markets in Financial Instruments Directive (MiFID) (2004/39/ EC) contains inter alia rules on transparency of trading. MiFID expands trading from regulated markets (i.e. stock exchanges) to multi-trading facilities (MTFs), i.e. systems that bring together multiple parties (e.g. retail investors or other investment firms) that are interested in buying and selling financial instruments and enable them to do so. This has increased competition among exchanges, MTFs, and investment firms, giving them a single passport to operate throughout the EU on the basis of authorisation in their home Member State. MiFID also facilitates in-house matching. Under certain conditions regarding pre-trade transparency and best execution, banks and investment firms are allowed to 'match' trades of customers internally.

The Market Abuse Directive (2003/6/EC) harmonises the rules for insider trading and for market abuse. It requires closer cooperation and a higher degree of exchange of information between national authorities, thus ensuring the same framework for enforcement throughout the EU and reducing potential inconsistencies, confusion, and loopholes. The Prospectus Directive (2010/73/EC) requires that prospectuses provide investors with clear and comprehensive information. This directive makes it easier and cheaper for companies to raise capital throughout the EU on the basis of a single prospectus approved by a regulatory authority ('home supervisor') in one Member State.

Finally, the Transparency Directive (2004/109/EC) requires that all securities issuers must provide annual financial reports within four months of the end of the financial year. As for the contents of the financial reports, the EU has adopted the International Accounting Standards (IAS) – now referred to as International Financial Reporting Standards (IFRS) – through the IAS Regulation (1606/2002/EC). As explained in Chapter 3, the IAS provides a single set of comparable global accounting standards issued by the International Accounting Standards Board (IASB).

12.4 Supervisory structures

The organisational structure of financial supervision is in the process of change in most EU Member States. All countries used to have a sectoral model of financial supervision with separate supervisors for banking, insurance, and securities reflecting the traditional dividing lines between financial sectors. However, as documented in Chapter 11, financial conglomerates represent about 25 per cent of the banking market and the insurance market. Furthermore, financial products are converging. Banking as well as life-insurance products, for example, serve the market for long-term savings. Because of the blurring of the dividing lines between financial sectors, cross-sector models of supervision have emerged. There are two main cross-sector models of supervision: a functional (or 'twin peaks') model and an integrated model.

In the *functional model*, there are separate supervisors for each of the supervisory objectives: prudential supervision and conduct of business (see column (2) in Table 12.1). Referring to these two objectives, the functional model is also known as the 'twin peaks' model (Taylor, 1995). In some countries, especially in the euro area where central banks have transferred their responsibility for monetary policy to the ECB, the central bank is responsible

Table 12.1 Organisational structure of financial supervision

Countries	(1) Sectoral	(2) Cross-sector: Functional	Basic models	
			(3a) Cross-sector: Integrated without central bank role in banking supervision	(3b) Cross-sector: Integrated with central bank role in banking supervision
European Union	Bulgaria	Belgium (2011)	Denmark (1988)	Austria (2002)
	Cyprus	France (2003)	Estonia (2002)	Czech Republic
	Greece	Italy (1999)	Hungary (2000)	(2006)
	Lithuania	Netherlands (2002)	Latvia (2001)	Finland (2009)
	Luxembourg	Portugal (2000)	Malta (2002)	Germany (2002)
	Romania	United Kingdom	Poland (2008)	Ireland (2003)
	Slovenia	(2011)	Sweden (1991)	Slovakia (2006)
	Spain			
Outside EU		Australia (1998)	Japan (2000)	
		Canada (1987)		
		United States (1999)		

Note: In parentheses the year of establishment of the new cross-sector supervisor(s) is shown.
Source: Schoenmaker (2005) and ECB (2010)

for prudential supervision. In other countries (e.g. Australia), a separate agency is responsible for prudential supervision.

In the *integrated model*, there is a single supervisor for banking, insurance, and securities combined (or, put differently, one supervisor for prudential supervision and conduct of business combined). There are two modes of the integrated model. Denmark and Sweden have adopted a fully integrated model without central bank involvement in financial supervision (see column (3a) in Table 12.1). In Germany and Austria, the central bank still has a role in banking supervision. The findings of the central bank are provided to the integrated supervisor, who has final authority (see column (3b) in Table 12.1). Box 12.3 provides an overview of country experiences with the various models.

The functional model combines the objectives of systemic supervision and prudential supervision, leaving conduct-of-business supervision as a separate function. The integrated model combines the objectives of prudential supervision and conduct-of-business supervision, leaving systemic supervision (financial stability) as a separate function that is usually performed by the central bank.

Box 12.3 Country experiences

In 2002, the Netherlands adopted the functional model. In the Netherlands, the prudential and financial stability functions are delegated to the central bank, De Nederlandsche Bank (DNB). The Dutch model acknowledges the close linkage between systemic stability and prudential supervision of the larger financial institutions. A separate supervisor, Autoriteit Financiële Markten (AFM), is responsible for the conduct-of-business standards. In a similar way, France has merged its securities-market supervisors, Commission des Opérations de Bourse (COB) and Conseil des Marchés Financiers (CMF), into one agency, the Autorité des Marchés Financiers (AMF), while the prudential supervisors, the Commission Bancaire (CB) based at the Banque de France and the Autorité de Contrôle des Assurances et des Mutuelles (ACAM), merged into a single prudential supervisor, Autorité de Contrôle Prudentiel (ACP) linked to the Banque de France, in 2010. Italy has an objectives-based model of supervision, since the government changed the division of labour between CONSOB, the securities supervisor, and the Banca d'Italia (the Italian central bank) in 1999. In this new setting, CONSOB is responsible for transparency and proper conduct and the Banca d'Italia is responsible for prudential supervision of banks and securities firms as well as financial stability. The Banca d'Italia cooperates with the insurance supervisor, ISVAP.

The supervisory model in the US also has some features of the functional model (Padoa-Schioppa, 2003), although a sectoral orientation has been kept in place. The central bank is responsible for systemic stability and has extensive prudential supervisory responsibilities, while other agencies (notably the Securities and Exchange Commission (SEC) and the newly created Bureau of Financial Protection) are entrusted with the task of protecting the investor's interests. The overall supervisory landscape in the US is fragmented, with, for example, multiple supervisors for banks (the Federal Reserve, the Office of the Comptroller of the Currency, the Federal Deposit Insurance Corporation, as well as state banking supervisors). The new Bureau of Consumer Financial Protection was introduced by the Dodd–Frank Act of 2010. Canada also applies the functional model, with a prudential supervisor (OSFI) at the federal level and securities supervisors at the state level.

The integrated model started in Scandinavia in the late 1980s and early 1990s, while in the United Kingdom the Financial Services Authority (FSA) was established in 1997. The consolidation of financial supervision in the UK was a response to the scattered framework of nine different supervisors with overlapping responsibilities (including the Bank of England and the Building Societies Commission for banking supervision, the Securities and Investments Board with its multiple self-regulatory organisations for securities and conduct-of-business supervision, and the Department of Trade and Industry for insurance supervision). While the UK FSA was widely seen as the standard bearer of the single super-visor model, reform is underway to move to the twin peaks model (partly because of the lack of cooperation between the Bank of England and the FSA in the Northern Rock case). The prudential part will be moved to a new Prudential Regulation Authority, becoming a subsid-iary of the Bank of England, and a separate Financial Conduct Authority. Germany also used to have a sectoral framework: the Bundesaufsichtsamt für das Kreditwesen (in conjunction with the Bundesbank) was responsible for banking supervision, the Bundesaufsichtsamt für das Versicherungswesen for insurance supervision, and the Bundesaufsichtsamt für den Wertpapierhandel for securities supervision. These three supervisory agencies were merged into one agency, the new Bundesanstalt für Finanzdienstleistungaufsicht (BaFin), in 2002. Similarly, a single supervisor, the Finanzmarktaufsichtbehörde, was established in Austria. In the German and Austrian versions of the integrated model, the central bank still has some involvement in banking supervision.

Kremers *et al.* (2003) have developed a framework to analyse the trade-offs by listing the synergies and conflicts of supervisory interests of both models. Figure 12.3 summarises these potential synergies and conflicts. The first synergy in the left panel of Figure 12.3 results from combining systemic supervision and prudential supervision of financial institutions. The synergy between stability issues on a micro level (at the level of the financial institution) and a macro level (economy-wide) refers to the possibility to act decisively and swiftly in the event of a crisis situation. Crisis management usually requires key decisions to be taken within hours rather than days. Combining both micro- and macroprudential supervision within a single institution ensures that relevant information is available at short notice and that a speedy decision to act can be taken if necessary.[4]

The second synergy in Figure 12.3 is 'one-stop supervision', i.e. the synergy between prudential supervision and conduct of business. This relates to the fact that it confronts all types of financial institutions with one supervisor only for prudential and conduct-of-business supervision. Furthermore, syn-ergies in the execution of supervision are exploited by combining different supervisory activities within one institution.

The first potential conflict of interest between systemic supervision and pru-dential supervision relates to the possibility of lender-of-last-resort operations (LoLR) by the central bank. How to balance the pressure to extend the ben-efits of LoLR operations (avoiding systemic risk, like a financial panic or bank runs) to all financial institutions against its costs (moral hazard)? The answer adopted by many central banks is to limit the possibility of LoLR operations

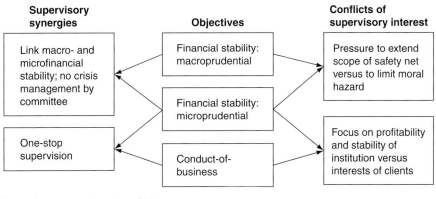

Figure 12.3 Supervisory synergies and conflicts
Source: Kremers *et al.* (2003)

to banks, which are subject to systemic risk (see Chapter 10). Then LoLR operations are not available to insurance companies. However, when financial groups integrate, it may become more difficult to separate the banking part of financial institutions that justify the possibility of LoLR operations.

The second potential conflict of interest between prudential supervision and conduct-of-business supervision relates to the different nature of their objectives. The prudential supervisor will be interested in the soundness of financial institutions including profitability, while the conduct-of-business supervisor will focus on the interests of clients. Mixing up both responsibilities of financial stability and conduct of business could lead to incentives for the supervisor to give prevalence to one objective over the other. By separating the supervisory functions, the conduct-of-business supervisor is ideally situated to supervise possible conflicts of interest between a financial institution and its clients, since it will focus only on the interests of the clients. Furthermore, the stability objective is consistent with preserving public confidence and may require discretion and confidentiality, which could be counter-productive to the transparency objective.

12.5 Challenges for financial supervision

A key element in the design of the institutional framework for financial supervision is the appropriate level of (de)centralisation. To date, national supervisory agencies in the EU Member States are in charge of the supervision of financial institutions. Until recently, they coordinated their activities through

European supervisory committees. The aim of these supervisory committees was to promote the convergence of supervisory standards and practices across the EU. While supervisors coordinated at the European level, they operated on the basis of a national mandate embedded in national legislation. This raised questions of efficiency and effectiveness. The three European supervisory committees had advisory powers and could only issue non-binding guidelines and recommendations. National supervisors of cross-border groups must cooperate within colleges of supervisors, but if they could not agree, there was no mechanism to resolve issues. Many technical rules were determined at Member State level, and there were considerable variations between Member States. Even where rules were harmonised, application could be inconsistent. This fragmented supervision undermined the Single Market, imposed extra costs for financial institutions, and increased the likelihood of failure of financial institutions with potentially additional costs for taxpayers.

Schüler and Heinemann (2005) have calculated the cost of fragmentation of financial supervision in the EU-15. Their results indicate increasing economies of scale in supervision. Comparing a structure with 15 national supervisors with a cost-efficient European supervisory framework, they predict cost savings of some 15 per cent.

Another drawback of national-based supervision is the potential for conflicts of interest among national supervisors. While large cross-border financial institutions increasingly operate on an integrated basis, with key decisions taken at headquarters, supervisors are still examining the national parts of these institutions. The home supervisor as consolidated supervisor is coordinating the national supervisory efforts to minimise the potential for regulatory and supervisory arbitrage. The national supervisors also perform joint risk assessments of the large cross-border financial institutions, resulting in a joint supervision plan. But there are no legally binding mechanisms to deal with potential conflicts of national interest.

An example of a potential conflict is the distribution of capital (or liquidity) in a financial services group. The host supervisor may request full capitalisation of the host subsidiary, while the home supervisor may request to maintain capital at the group level and to keep the capitalisation of subsidiaries at the minimum level. Supervisors may also have diverging views on how to remedy shortcomings of a financial institution. Supervisors can easily settle on a joint action when they agree. But when there are (lasting) differences, the various supervisors all have the legal power to take enforcement action under their national mandate and this may result in sub-optimal outcomes.

These coordination problems pose the question whether supervision should be done at the national level or the European level. The basic argument in

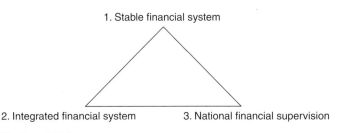

Figure 12.4 The financial trilemma
Source: Schoenmaker (2011)

favour of moving to a European structure is that it might be difficult to achieve simultaneously an integrated and a stable financial system, while preserving a high degree of national-based supervision and crisis management with only decentralised efforts at harmonisation (Thygesen, 2003). This is an application of the classical trilemma in monetary policy in which policy makers are confronted with three desirable, yet contradictory, objectives: fixed exchange rates, capital mobility, and independent monetary policy. Only two out of the three objectives are mutually consistent, leaving policy makers with the decision about which one they wish to give up: the 'trilemma'.

A similar trilemma occurs in financial supervision (Schoenmaker, 2011). Figure 12.4 illustrates the three incompatible objectives of the financial trilemma: (1) a stable financial system; (2) an integrated financial system; and (3) independent national financial supervision. An argument against moving to a European solution for financial supervision at the present time could be that the degree of financial integration does not yet justify such a move. However, as shown in previous chapters, many financial markets (in particular wholesale markets) are almost fully integrated. The infrastructures to support financial markets are also integrating, albeit at a slower pace. There is also evidence for increasing cross-border penetration of banks and insurers. Emerging pan-European financial institutions give rise to cross-border externalities arising from the (potential) failure of these institutions. The increasing presence of financial institutions from other EU countries undermines the capacity of host authorities to manage effectively the stability of their financial system (see Chapter 13 for more details).

European Supervisory Authorities

In October 2008 the European Commission mandated a High Level Group chaired by former managing director of the IMF, Jacques de Larosière, to give advice on the future of European financial regulation and supervision.

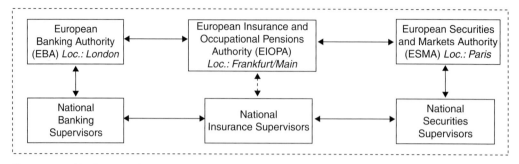

Figure 12.5 The European Supervisory Authorities (ESAs)

The Group presented its final report on 25 February 2009 and their recommendation provided the basis for the new European financial supervisory framework.

The de Larosière Report (2009) concluded that the supervisory framework needed to be strengthened to reduce the risk and severity of future financial crises. The de Larosière Group recommends creating a European System of Financial Supervisors, comprising three European Supervisory Authorities: one for the banking sector, one for the securities sector, and one for the insurance and occupational pensions sector. Although the de Larosière Report (2009, p. 48) mentions the twin peaks model (the functional model), it chooses to be neutral and adopts the sectoral model. As financial markets and institutions are operating on a cross-sector basis, it is regrettable that European supervision remains sectoral based. The Group also recommends establishing a European Systemic Risk Board (see Chapter 13).

Figure 12.5 illustrates the three new European Supervisory Authorities (ESAs) for the financial services sector: the European Banking Authority (EBA) based in London, the European Insurance and Occupational Pensions Authority (EIOPA) in Frankfurt, and the European Securities and Markets Authority (ESMA) in Paris. This framework provides the institutions to detect the risks at the European level which can accumulate across the financial system as witnessed during the financial crisis. The ESAs started their work in January 2011.

The three new ESAs work in a network and in tandem with the existing National Supervisory Authorities (NSAs) to safeguard financial soundness at the level of individual financial firms and protect consumers of financial services. The new European network combines nationally based supervision of firms with strong coordination at European level to foster harmonised rules as well as coherent supervisory practice and enforcement. The ESAs have the power to:

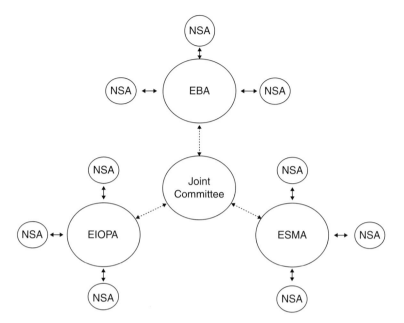

Figure 12.6 The European Supervisory Authorities work closely with the National Supervisory Authorities (NSAs)

- draw up specific rules for national authorities and financial institutions;
- develop technical standards, guidelines, and recommendations;
- monitor how rules are being enforced by the NSAs;
- take action in emergencies, including the banning of certain products;
- mediate and settle disputes between national supervisors;
- ensure the consistent application of EU law.

Where necessary, the ESAs have the possibility of settling disagreements between national authorities, in particular in areas that require cooperation, coordination, or joint decision making by supervisory authorities from more than one Member State. Mechanisms, such as Joint Committees, are introduced to ensure agreement and coordination between national supervisors of the same cross-border institution or in colleges of supervisors. For example, the EBA, the EIOPA, and the ESMA are to form a Joint Committee (see Figure 12.6) to oversee cooperation and coordination between national supervisors in the case of financial conglomerates.

The new European System of Financial Supervisors will execute day-to-day supervision close to the financial institutions and markets under supervision. So, day-to-day supervision is done at national level, close to the ground, where appropriate expertise can be found. The new system is a 'hub and spoke' type of network of EU and national bodies (Schoenmaker and Oosterloo, 2008). The new authorities act only where there is clear added value, and the areas where the authorities can act are strictly defined in European Regulations. The objective is for European and national bodies to work hand in hand. The new system has been designed in a way that it can be adapted to future developments in financial services. Every three years the European Commission will publish a wide-ranging report on the functioning of the new Authorities and assess whether further steps are needed to ensure the prudential soundness of institutions, the orderly functioning of markets and thereby the protection of depositors, policy holders, and investors. This may lead to proposals to change the structures or tasks of the Authorities.

The ESAs may need to override national authorities in certain cases. The ESAs can address decisions directly to national authorities in three areas: (1) in cases where they are arbitrating between national authorities both involved in the supervision of a cross-border group and where they need to agree or coordinate their position; (2) in cases where a national authority is incorrectly applying EU Regulations (EU Regulations are directly applicable and are not transposed into national law; see Chapter 3); and (3) in emergency situations declared by the Council.

The authorities are able to take decisions directly applicable to financial institutions as a last resort in the three cases just referred to above where the Authority has addressed a decision to the national supervisor but the national supervisor has not complied with it. This can be done only in cases where there is directly applicable EU legislation as defined above. It is crucial that this mediation power is legally binding (Schoenmaker and Oosterloo, 2008). In that way, the ESAs can make their mark. Given that national supervisors know that the ESA can overrule them in cases of disagreement, they have an incentive to cooperate and agree among themselves.

The ESAs also have direct supervisory powers. The ESMA supervises credit rating agencies (CRAs). Since rating services are not linked to a particular territory and the ratings issued by a CRA can be used by financial institutions all around Europe, there is a more centralised system for supervision of CRAs at EU level (see Chapter 8). The ESMA is entrusted with exclusive supervision powers over CRAs registered in the EU.

The Regulations establishing the new ESAs allow them to fulfil any other specific tasks, including supervisory tasks, conferred on them by EU Directives or Regulations. This may in particular be appropriate in the area of financial infrastructures. Another possible future task is the direct supervision of the largest cross-border banks and insurers by the EBA and EIOPA. Examples of such large European banks and insurers include BNP Paribas, Deutsche Bank, ING, UniCredit, Allianz, AXA, and Generali (see Chapters 10 and 11).

An important ingredient of an effective financial supervisory framework is decisive action in emergency situations. The new ESAs have emergency powers – which would only apply in exceptional circumstances (defined as a situation which seriously jeopardises the stability of financial markets). In the great majority of cases, the national and European level authorities will work hand in hand – sharing information, coordinating their work and taking decisions together (for example, on technical standards across the European banking sector so banks do not have to comply with different standards in different countries).

Even in emergencies, the first objective of any of the three ESAs is to facilitate and coordinate actions by national supervisors, without binding decisions. However, if deemed necessary, there is a procedure in place for ESAs to address binding decisions to national supervisors requiring them to take the necessary action to safeguard the orderly functioning and integrity of financial markets and the stability of the whole or part of the European financial system. So, the new Authorities have an important coordinating role and are able to adopt decisions requiring supervisors to jointly take action.

The new Authorities also contribute to and participate actively in the development and coordination of effective and consistent recovery and resolution plans, guarantee schemes, procedures in emergency situations, and preventative measures to minimise the systemic impact of any failure. The new Authorities should also ensure that they have a specialised and ongoing capacity to respond effectively to the materialisation of systemic risks.

The EU has adopted an evolutionary approach towards establishing a truly European supervisory framework. While some academics argue that the national supervisors are still in charge, others believe the role of the ESAs will increase over time. There are some pointers towards the latter. First, the ESAs have a legally binding power of mediation. Given that the ESA has the final say, game theory suggests that the national supervisors are expected to fall in line. National supervisors will want to avoid being overruled by the ESA. If that happens too often, their reputation will be hurt. Second, the ESAs have direct powers in emergency situations. Third, new tasks can be transferred from the national supervisors to the ESAs. Lee (2005), for example, argues that developments in securities markets will inevitably turn the ESMA into a strong European securities and markets supervisor, similar to the US SEC (see Box 12.4). Similarly, the financial trilemma suggests that the supervision of the large cross-border banks and insurers should be moved to the EBA and EIOPA, if financial stability is to be maintained in Europe.

> **Box 12.4 A European SEC?**
>
> Lee (2005) analyses the factors influencing whether a European Securities and Exchange Commission will be created. While public policy is determined by the trinity of economics, law, and politics, Lee argues that political factors matter most.
>
> First, there is a need for identical supervisory practices. A clear example is the oversight of international accounting standards. Under the IAS Regulation, European firms listed at a regulated market have to follow the same international accounting standards for financial reporting, as of January 2005. The oversight of these uniform standards is currently carried out by national supervisors, leaving scope for diverging supervisory practices. The political call for identical supervisory practices implies the need for a single supervisor.
>
> Second, the possible future models for regulating EU securities markets require that some power is centralised at the EU level. An example is the creation of Euronext, combining the stock exchanges (cash and derivatives) of Paris, Amsterdam, Brussels, Lisbon, and the derivatives market of London (see Chapter 5). The merger with the New York Stock Exchange reinforces the need for European supervisors to speak with one voice with their American counterpart, the SEC.
>
> Third, a majority of policy makers in the EU view the notion of regulatory competition as intrinsically harmful to the authority of supervisors. In particular supervisors in continental Europe are concerned that competition between regulatory regimes may encourage the adoption of Anglo-American practices and cultures in securities markets.
>
> Finally, Lee (2005) concludes that these factors will inevitably lead to the creation of a European SEC. He notes that the political support (e.g. in the European Parliament and France) for a European SEC is growing.

12.6 Conclusions

This chapter has identified three market failures in financial services that justify government intervention. First, consumers may be less informed than financial institutions. Financial supervision (both microprudential supervision and conduct-of-business supervision) addresses this problem of asymmetric information. Second, the malfunctioning of a part of the financial system may have an adverse impact on the financial system as a whole. Macroprudential supervision aims to foster financial stability and to contain the effects of systemic failure. Third, certain players in the market may exert undue market power. Competition policy seeks to protect consumers against exploitation of market power.

Microprudential supervision aims to protect consumers by ensuring the safety and soundness of financial institutions. As financial institutions are becoming more complex, supervisors are moving away from direct control to methods that provide incentives to financial institutions to behave prudently. The Basel capital adequacy framework allows banks to use their internal models to manage the risks and to assess the minimum capital required as a buffer against these risks. Conduct-of-business supervision focuses on how financial institutions deal with their customers. Information provisions ensure that consumers get the right information about financial products. In addition, there are guidelines for objective and high-quality advice to protect the interests of customers. Conduct-of-business rules also promote fair and orderly markets.

The organisational structure of supervision is changing across the EU. Countries are increasingly moving from the traditional sectoral structure (with separate banking, insurance, and securities supervisors) to a functional model (with a prudential and a conduct-of-business supervisor) or an integrated model (with only one supervisor). The functional and integrated models can better cope with market developments, such as the development of complex financial products and the emergence of financial conglomerates.

Finally, the European financial landscape is integrating. In response, financial supervision in the European Union (EU) has undergone a major reform. With the establishment of the new European Supervisory Authorities (ESAs), the balance seems to be shifting from national supervision to EU-based supervision. But day-to-day supervision remains with the national supervisors. So, they remain in the hot seat. Nevertheless, the chairs of the ESAs have some important mediation powers as well as special powers in emergency situations. It is to be expected that powers will move slowly to the emerging central bodies.

A major new task for the ESAs would be the direct supervision of the large European stock exchanges, banks, and insurers. A two-tier system could evolve with the large cross-border financial markets and institutions supervised at the European level and the smaller domestic ones at the national level. But that is not to be expected in the very near future.

NOTES

1 The €5 billion loss at Société Générale in 2007 due to the alleged fraud of a rogue trader is an exceptional example of the failure of internal controls in a bank.

2 While prudential supervision aims to minimise the risk of failure, it cannot eliminate the risk of a failing bank in a market economy.

3 The integrity and competence of financial institutions is not listed here as a specific conduct-of-business element. Fit and proper rules are general requirements that are applied in both prudential and conduct-of-business regulation. Section 12.2 explains these rules.

4 The Northern Rock crisis in 2007 indicates that crisis management by two institutions may not be very effective. According to Buiter (2007), the coordination between the Bank of England and the FSA has been wanting.

SUGGESTED READING

Goodhart, C. A. E., P. Hartmann, D. T. Llewellyn, L. Rojas-Suarez, and S. Weisbrod (1998), *Financial Regulation: Why, How and Where Now?*, Routledge, London.

Mishkin, F. S. (2000), Prudential Supervision: Why is It Important and What are the Issues?, NBER Working Paper 7926.

Schoenmaker, D. and S. Oosterloo (2008), Financial Supervision in Europe: A Proposal for a New Architecture, in: L. Jonung, C. Walkner, and M. Watson (eds.), *Building the Financial Foundations of the Euro – Experiences and Challenges*, Routledge, London, 337–354.

REFERENCES

Bank for International Settlements (1997), *Core Principles for Effective Banking Supervision*, BIS, Basel.

(2006), *Core Principles for Effective Banking Supervision*, BIS, Basel.

Benston, G. J. and G. G. Kaufman (1996), The Appropriate Role of Bank Regulation, *The Economic Journal*, 106, 688–697.

Besley, T. (2007), The New Political Economy, *The Economic Journal*, 117, 570–587.

Buiter, W. (2007), Lessons from the 2007 Financial Crisis, CEPR Discussion Paper 6596.

Danielsson, J., P. Embrechts, C. Goodhart, C. Keating, F. Muennich, O. Renault, and H. Song Shin (2001), An Academic Response to Basel II, London School of Economics FMG Special Papers 130.

de Larosière, J. (2009), Report of the High-level Group on Financial Supervision in the EU, European Commission, Brussels. Available at: http://ec.europa.eu/internal_market/finances/docs/de_larosiere_report_En.pdf (accessed 13 February 2012).

Dermine, J. (2006), European Banking Integration: Don't Put the Cart before the Horse, *Financial Markets, Institutions & Instruments*, 15(2), 57–106.

Dowd, K. (1996), The Case for Financial Laissez-Faire, *The Economic Journal*, 106, 679–687.

European Central Bank (2010), *Recent Developments in Supervisory Structures in the EU Member States*, ECB, Frankfurt am Main.

European Commission (2007), *Green Paper on Retail Financial Services in the Single Market*, EC, Brussels.

(2011), *CRD IV – Frequently Asked Questions*, Brussels.

ESFRC (2005), *Reforming Banking Supervision in Europe*, Statement No. 23, Frankfurt am Main.

Goodhart, C. A. E., P. Hartmann, D. T. Llewellyn, L. Rojas-Suarez, and S. Weisbrod (1998), *Financial Regulation: Why, How and Where Now?*, Routledge, London.

Guttentag, J. and R. Herring (1984), Credit Rationing and Financial Disorder, *Journal of Finance*, 39, 1359–1382.

Kremers, J. J. M., D. Schoenmaker, and P. J. Wierts (2003), Cross-Sector Supervision: Which Model?, in: R. Herring and R. Litan (eds.), *Brookings-Wharton Papers on Financial Services: 2003*, Brookings Institution, Washington DC, 225–243.

Lastra, R. M. (2006), *Legal Foundations of International Monetary Stability*, Oxford University Press.

Lee, R. (2005), Politics and the Creation of a European SEC, London School of Economics FMG Special Paper 161.

Llewellyn, D. (1999), The Economic Rationale for Financial Regulation, FSA Occasional Paper 1, Financial Services Authority, London.

Merton, R. C. (1995), Financial Innovation and the Management and Regulation of Financial Institutions, *Journal of Banking and Finance*, 19, 461–481.

Mishkin, F. S. (2000), Prudential Supervision: Why is It Important and What are the Issues?, NBER Working Paper 7926.

Nieto, M. J. and L. D. Wall (2007), Preconditions for a Successful Implementation of Supervisors' Prompt Corrective Action: Is There a Case for a Banking Standard in the EU?, Banco de España Working Paper 0702.

Padoa-Schioppa, T. (2003), Financial Supervision: Inside or Outside Central Banks?, in: J. J. M. Kremers, D. Schoenmaker, and P. J. Wierts (eds.), *Financial Supervision in Europe*, Edward Elgar, Cheltenham, 160–175.

Schoenmaker, D. (2005), Central Banks and Financial Authorities in Europe: What Prospects?, in: D. Masciandaro (ed.), *The Handbook of Central Banking and Financial Authorities in Europe*, Edward Elgar, Cheltenham, 398–456.

(2011), The Financial Trilemma, *Economics Letters*, 111, 57–59.

Schoenmaker, D. and S. Oosterloo (2008), Financial Supervision in Europe: A Proposal for a New Architecture, in: L. Jonung, C. Walkner, and M. Watson (eds.), *Building the Financial Foundations of the Euro – Experiences and Challenges*, Routledge, London, 337–354.

Schüler, M. and F. Heinemann (2005), The Costs of Supervisory Fragmentation in Europe, ZEW Discussion Paper 05–01.

Taylor, M. (1995), *Twin Peaks: A Regulatory Structure for the New Century*, Centre for the Study of Financial Innovation, London.

Thygesen, N. (2003), Comments on the Political Economy of Financial Harmonisation in Europe, in: J. J. M. Kremers, D. Schoenmaker, and P. J. Wierts (eds.), *Financial Supervision in Europe*, Edward Elgar, Cheltenham, 142–150.

Financial Stability

Against the backdrop of the 2007–2009 financial crisis, this chapter discusses the growing importance of macroprudential supervision, which focuses on the stability of the financial system as a whole and therefore on the monitoring and assessment of so-called systemic risks.

The chapter sets out the key features of the conceptual framework for macroprudential supervision, which consists of: (1) the monitoring and analysis of the financial system; (2) assessing potential threats to financial stability and deciding to take mitigating action, (3) implementing measures to actually mitigate vulnerabilities, and (4) evaluating these actions in order to ascertain to what extent vulnerabilities have indeed been diminished. Based on these elements, this chapter discusses the key indicators used by macroprudential authorities in search of potential vulnerabilities, as well as the main instruments available to address them. This chapter also discusses the emerging institutional architecture for macroprudential supervision in the EU and the US.

This chapter also touches upon the issue of crisis management and resolution, discussing the main reactive instruments that can be considered in crisis situations. Finally, this chapter discusses the key challenges related to the negative externalities caused by failure of cross-border institutions, including the need for ex-ante burden-sharing arrangements between Member States.

LEARNING OBJECTIVES

After you have studied this chapter, you should be able to:
- explain the concept of macroprudential supervision and the difference between micro- and macroprudential supervision

- explain the concept of systemic risk and describe what makes financial systems prone to this risk
- describe the key instruments used by macroprudential authorities to prevent the build-up of systemic risks
- describe the principal features of the crisis management and resolution tools
- explain why improvised cooperation leads to an insufficient level of recapitalisation in the case of a cross-border failure and why this calls for ex-ante burden-sharing arrangements.

13.1 Financial stability and macroprudential supervision

Macro- vs. microprudential supervision

Although microprudential and macroprudential supervision are closely related, the financial crisis of 2007–2009 highlighted the important distinction between both concepts (see Hanson *et al.*, 2011).

Microprudential supervision has traditionally been the key focus of supervisory authorities. The intermediate objective of microprudential supervision is to supervise and limit the distress of individual financial institutions, with the ultimate objective of protecting the customers of the institution in question. The fact that the financial system as a whole may be exposed to common risks is not (fully) taken into account. However, by preventing the failure of individual financial institutions, microprudential supervision aims to mitigate or prevent the risk of contagion and the subsequent negative externalities related to a possible fall in the confidence in the stability of the financial system.

Macroprudential supervision focuses on the soundness of the financial system as a whole. The intermediate objective of macroprudential supervision is to limit financial system-wide distress, with the ultimate objective of protecting the overall economy from significant losses in real output (see Table 13.1). While risks to the financial system can in theory arise from the failure of one financial institution, the much more important systemic risk arises from a common exposure of many financial institutions to the same risk factors.

Macroprudential analysis must therefore pay particular attention to common or correlated shocks as well as to shocks that may trigger contagious knock-on effects. Moreover, macroprudential supervision should take account of the interactions between financial institutions and their environment (i.e. other institutions, financial markets, infrastructure and the real economy) as well as the dynamics with which imbalances may build up over time.

Table 13.1 Macroprudential versus microprudential supervision

	Macroprudential	Microprudential
Intermediate objective	Limit financial system-wide distress	Limit distress of individual institutions
Ultimate objective	Avoid output (GDP) costs	Consumer (investor/depositor) protection
Correlations and common exposures across institutions	Important	Irrelevant
Characterisation of risk	Seen as dependent on collective behaviour ('endogenous')	Seen as independent of individual agents' behaviour ('exogenous')
Calibration of prudential controls	In terms of system-wide risks; top-down	In terms of risks of individual institutions; bottom-up

Source: Borio (2003)

As such, the macroprudential perspective assumes that the risk of a shock is (partly) generated and amplified within the system (i.e. the risk is *endogenous*), while the microprudential approach focuses on institutions' vulnerability to threats emanating from their environment (i.e. the risk is *exogenous*).

Moreover, in order to avoid financial system-wide distress, the macro-perspective takes a top-down approach to calibrating prudential controls by identifying risks in the system as a whole, calculating the contribution of each financial entity and then applying the relevant macroprudential tools. By contrast, the microprudential approach is bottom-up, setting the prudential controls in relation to the risk of each individual financial entity.

Systemic risk

Macroprudential analysis and supervision focuses, by definition, on the monitoring and assessment of so-called systemic risks within the financial system. The term *systemic risk* refers to the risk that an event will trigger a loss of economic value or confidence in a substantial part of the financial system that is serious enough to have significant adverse effects on the real economy.

In the absence of systemic risks, the financial system is stable, i.e. the financial system is in a condition in which it is capable of withstanding shocks and the unravelling of imbalances, thereby mitigating the likelihood of disruptions in the financial intermediation process which are severe enough to significantly impair the allocation of savings to profitable investment opportunities (ECB, 2007).

There are two key features of systemic risk: a structural and cyclical feature. First, as set out in Chapter 1, the financial system is composed of: (1) intermediaries, (2) financial markets, and (3) financial infrastructures. Intermediaries are connected with each other through direct transactions; through similar investment; and financing decisions with third parties. Financial markets, in turn, are connected with each other through the trading activities of financial intermediaries. From a structural perspective, systemic risk relates to the risk that these interconnections and similarities render emerging financial instability widespread in the system (ECB, 2009). Second, the complex network of financial connections is extended through the savings and financing needs of all economic actors. By reallocating savings from individuals and sectors with a surplus of funds to individuals and sectors in need of funds, the financial system plays a key role in the economy. From a cyclical perspective, systemic risk relates to the risk that financial imbalances – in the form of credit and liquidity cycles – can build up in a boom period leading to bubbles, which, when they burst, may translate into adverse effects on growth and welfare in the economy at large.

There are a number of additional features of financial systems that make them particularly prone to these forms of systemic risk (ECB, 2009):

(1) The possible negative externalities from risk taking by financial intermediaries. These arise when a financial institution does not take into account that if it takes more risk, and is thereby more prone to failure, it is more likely to impose costs on society. These costs may not only arise because of the failure of an individual institution, but in particular because of possible spill-over effects to other institutions and markets.

(2) Transactions in financial markets are subject to asymmetric information in which one party often does not know all that it needs to know about the other to make correct decisions (Mishkin, 1992). This may create problems in the financial sector in two ways:

  (i) Before the transaction enters into force there is the risk that potential borrowers who are most likely to produce undesirable (adverse) outcomes are selected (*adverse selection*), and

  (ii) After the transaction is entered into force, the borrower may have incentives to invest in projects with high risk in which the borrower does well if the project succeeds, but the lender bears most of the loss if the project fails (*moral hazard*).

(3) The financial system is characterised by powerful feedback and amplification mechanisms, which may reinforce shocks within the system. For example, illiquid assets, maturity mismatches between assets and liabilities and leverage amplify the force with which problems of one financial institution are pushed through the complex network of exposures. Moreover, sizeable amounts of debt relative to capital and short-term funding may have dramatic effects in stress situations.

How to address systemic risk?

Macroprudential vulnerabilities are addressed using three lines of defence (DNB, 2010):

- First, there is the possibility of eliminating threats to financial stability by identifying them in good time and subsequently mitigating them (see section 13.2). However, often, not all potential threats can be eliminated, as macroprudential imbalances are often fluid and hard to quantify. Moreover, the opportunities for mitigating action can be limited, as the means to address these threats cannot be directly influenced by the macroprudential supervisory authority or call for complex (inter)national coordination.
- Second, the relevant authorities may try to maintain and enhance the resilience of the financial system. This option can be pursued in situations where it is hard for the authorities to mitigate threats or where it is uncertain to what extent certain developments could undermine financial stability. If such a vulnerability becomes manifest, the financial system will have to be able to absorb it without losing its stability. One way of doing this is to foster the build-up in bank capital in good times, which can be released in bad times. The primary aim of these so-called *countercyclical buffers* is to use a buffer of capital to achieve the broader macroprudential goal of protecting the banking sector and the real economy from the system-wide risks associated with the boom-bust cycle in aggregate credit growth.
- Third, when hit by a crisis and the system is unable to absorb the shock, crisis management is the third and last line of defence to safeguard financial stability (see section 13.5). Potential instruments here are safety net arrangements – liquidity support, deposit guarantee schemes – and instruments permitting intervention at institutions in distress.

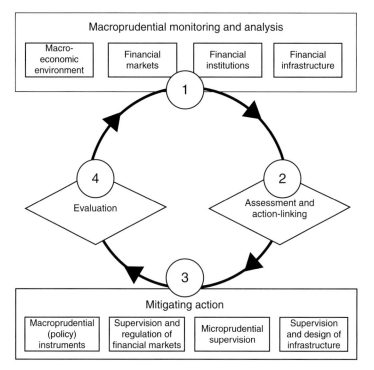

Figure 13.1   Conceptual framework of macroprudential supervision
Source: DNB (2010)

13.2 Macroprudential policy

Conceptual framework of macroprudential supervision

The macroprudential policy of framework consists of four stages: (1) the monitoring and analysis of the financial system in search of potential vulnerabilities, (2) assessing potential threats to financial stability and deciding to take mitigating action, (3) implementing measures to actually mitigate vulnerabilities, and (4) evaluating these actions in order to ascertain to what extent vulnerabilities have indeed been diminished (see Figure 13.1).

Macroprudential monitoring and analysis aims at reviewing potential threats to the stability of the financial system, stemming from the real economy, financial institutions, financial markets or financial infrastructures. This should enable the relevant authorities to gain better insight into the development of imbalances, such as asset price bubbles or vulnerabilities stemming from financial innovation, as well as the degree to which the financial system itself is capable of absorbing such risks.

The monitoring and analysis should in particular focus on (Borio, 2010):

- how aggregate risk evolves over time, i.e. the *time dimension*, and
- how risk is distributed in the financial system at a given point in time, i.e. the *cross-sectional dimension*.

The key issue in the time dimension is how system-wide risk can be amplified by interactions within the financial system as well as between the financial system and the real economy. This is what the cyclical dimension of systemic risk is all about. In good times, agents tend to underestimate risk and, subsequently, overinvest. This overinvestment is fuelled by credit. The credit cycle is in its upward swing. In bad times, the reverse happens: agents become more risk averse and reluctant to invest. In the extreme, this may accumulate in a credit crunch, where banks are withholding credit for new investment.

The key issue in the cross-sectional dimension is how to deal with the structural features of systemic risk, i.e. the common exposures across financial institutions. These arise either because institutions are directly exposed to the same or similar asset classes or because of indirect exposures associated with linkages among them (e.g. counterparty relationships). Common exposures are critical because they explain why institutions can fail together.

The monitoring process should pay specific attention to any sources of non-diversifiable/systematic risk in the financial system. Hence the importance of common exposures across institutions and of possible symptoms of generalised overextension in balance sheets during economic expansions and macro risks.

The subsequent assessment of risks consists of two stages. First, the potential risks are being ranked in order to see in which areas action is most needed. Second, the identified risks are being linked to possible mitigating policy instruments, which then have to be used. These actions may vary from one situation to the other, depending on the relevant risk.

Finally, evaluation is of importance to ensure that the mitigating action is actually followed up and, if necessary, adjusted.

Cyclical versus structural policies

The role of cyclical macroprudential policy is in mitigating the build-up of financial imbalances at an early stage. Herding behaviour can be individually rational, but lead to imbalances at the macro level. Financial markets are forward looking. As with monetary policy, the key to policy credibility will be in influencing expectations. Once market participants know that the central bank will step in to stabilise financial imbalances when they are building up, these imbalances may not build up in the first place. A further analogy with monetary policy is that effects of macroprudential policy will be uncertain and difficult to measure. Experience over time will help in the clarification of objectives and operating paradigms, as it has in the case of monetary policy (BIS, 2010a).

Structural policies are of an entirely different nature. They change the institutions of the economy, through discrete policy reforms, and ultimately aim to improve its long-term growth potential. Examples from outside the financial system include labour market reforms (e.g. changes in employment protection legislation or replacement rates) and tax reforms (e.g. reforms aimed at broadening the tax base or moving from direct towards indirect taxation). Examples from within the financial system include changes in the structure of financial institutions (see the discussion on the separation of retail banking from investment banking), static surcharges for systemically important financial institutions, and the deposit insurance system. Under this heading, one may also include reforms to the financial infrastructure, such as central counterparty (CCP) clearing and real-time gross settlement (RTGS).

What follows is that structural policies are more suitable for addressing the cross-section dimension of systemic risk that originates from externalities in the financial system. Spill-over effects can arise from interconnections within the financial system. Insofar as the spill-over effects are not internalised by financial institutions, they are called externalities. The underlying interconnections can be direct or indirect. Prime examples of direct interconnections are interbank exposures through the wholesale payment system or interbank market and, more broadly, counterparty exposures between financial institutions. An example of an indirect interconnection is common exposures. If financial institutions invest in the same asset, such as housing or the oil industry, they will be simultaneously hit by a housing or oil price shock.

Figure 13.2 illustrates the intermediate targets, or two pillars, of the macroprudential framework (Schoenmaker and Wierts, 2011). The first pillar is financial imbalances, for which a cyclical approach is appropriate. The second pillar is externalities, for which a structural approach is appropriate. The cyclical and structural pillars are not fully independent of each other. When the two-pillar strategy is applied, authorities must therefore do a cross-check when analysing financial stability developments. Shin (2010) shows, for example, that excessive asset growth and greater reliance on non-core liabilities (wholesale funding) are closely related to interconnections between

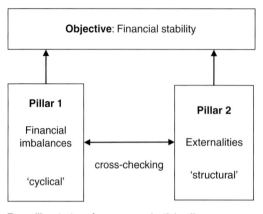

Figure 13.2   Two-pillar strategy for macroprudential policy
Source: Schoenmaker and Wierts (2011)

banks. In a boom when credit is growing rapidly, the growth of bank balance sheets outstrips available core funding (retail deposits), and asset growth is mirrored in the greater cross-exposure across banks (wholesale deposits).

13.3 Monitoring and analysing systemic risk

Indicators

As mentioned earlier, macroprudential supervision should take into account the interactions between financial institutions and their environment as well as the dynamics with which imbalances may build up over time. This entails that macroprudential supervisors should look at a wide range of indicators, stemming from different sectors. Table 13.2 summarises the quantitative measures commonly used, what they measure, as well as their signalling function (Gadanecz and Jayaram, 2010).

First, the *real sector* is described by GDP growth, the fiscal position of the government and inflation. GDP growth reflects the ability of the economy to create wealth and its risk of overheating. The fiscal position of the government mirrors its ability to find financing for its expenditures above its revenue (and the associated vulnerability of the country to the unavailability of financing). Inflation may indicate structural problems in the economy, and public dissatisfaction with it may in turn lead to political instability.

Table 13.2 Commonly used indicators

Sector	Measure	What do they measure?	Signalling function
Real economy	GDP growth	Strength of the macroeconomy, GDP is a key measure especially used in conjunction with measures such as credit expansion, fiscal deficit	Negative, or low positive values would indicate a slowdown; excessively high values may show unsustainable growth
	Fiscal position of government	Ability of government to find financing, vulnerability of sovereign debtor to unavailability of financing	High deficit values relative to GDP can mean unsustainable government indebtedness and vulnerability of the sovereign debtor
	Inflation	Rate of increase of various price indices	High levels of inflation would signal structural weakness in the economy and increased levels of indebtedness, potentially leading to a tightening of monetary conditions Conversely, low levels of inflation could potentially increase the risk appetite in the financial markets
Corporate sector	Total debt to equity	Corporations' leverage	Excessively high levels may signal difficulties in meeting debt obligations
	Earnings to interest and principal expenses	Corporations' ability to meet payment obligations relying on internal resources	Excessively low levels of liquidity may signal inability to meet debt obligations
	Net foreign exchange exposure to equity	Currency mismatch	High levels of this ratio may signal difficulties in the corporate sector arising from adverse currency moves
	Corporate defaults	Insolvencies in the corporate sector	High values can signal future problems in the banking sector, if insufficiently provisioned

Table 13.2 (*cont*)

Sector	Measure	What do they measure?	Signalling function
Household sector	Household assets (financial, real estate)	Assets and debt can be used to compute net household assets	Net household assets and disposable income can measure households' ability to weather (unexpected) economic downturns
	Household debts		
	Household income (labour income, savings income)	Income, consumption, and debt service payments can be combined to compute net disposable income	
	Household consumption		
	Household debt service and principal payments		
External sector	(Real) exchange rates	Over-/undervaluation of a currency	Over- or undervaluation of currency can trigger a crisis (capital outflows, massive inflows or loss of export competitiveness)
	Foreign exchange reserves	Ability of country to resist external shocks	Reserves below short-term foreign debt, or below three months' worth of exports can signal problems
	Current account/capital flows	Trade position of country	Significant trade deficits require large capital inflows in order to be financed; this raises sustainability issues about such inflows
	Maturity/currency mismatches	Disparity in the currency/maturity composition of assets and liabilities	Maturity and currency mismatches can expose the economy to adverse shocks in case of adverse currency movements or sudden reversals of capital inflows
Financial sector	Monetary aggregates	Transactions, saving, credit	Excessive growth can signal inflationary pressures

Indicator	Meaning	Significance
(Real) interest rates	Cost of credit, ability to attract deposits, sustainability of debt	Real interest rates above a threshold likely to exceed the trend rate of economic growth, making debt/GDP ratios explosive; negative real rates may mean banks will struggle to attract deposits
Growth in bank credit Bank leverage ratios NPLs Risk premia (CDS); credit risk component of 3-month LIBOR OIS spreads	Riskiness of the banking sector	Very rapid loan growth has often accompanied declining loan standards/greater risk. Excessively high loan losses, leverage ratios, and risk premia can foreshadow a banking crisis. Loan losses/GDP can measure cost of a banking crisis for economy
Capital adequacy	Banks' capital cushion size to address expected or unexpected losses	Excessively low levels of this ratio point to potential defaults and can be a forerunner of a banking crisis
Liquidity ratio	Ratio of banks' readily available short-term resources that can be used to meet short-term obligations	Excessively low levels of this ratio can lead to a systemic crisis
Stand-alone bank credit ratings	Individual strength of banks, after the effect of government or other guarantees has been taken into account	Possible coincident indicator of banks' condition, likely to influence their future funding costs
Sectoral/regional concentration, systemic focus	Concentration or diversification of banks' lending strategy	Can proxy for speed of propagation of shocks in the economy

Table 13.2 (*cont.*)

Sector	Measure	What do they measure?	Signalling function
Financial markets	Change in equity indices	Net worth of, present value of future cash flows of firms comprising the index	Above-trend growth in index, or very high levels of market to book value can be indicative of an equity price bubble
	Corporate bond spreads	Riskiness of debt compared to risk-free instruments	Spikes in spreads can suggest higher levels of risk, changes in risk appetite, changes in the incorporation of news into prices by the market
	Market liquidity	Price attached by the market to the ease with which liquid instruments can be traded	Spikes in these premia can reflect disruptions in market liquidity
	Volatility	Intensity of price movements on markets Ease of trade on the market	Low volatility can be indicative of a calm market, but also of failings in the price discovery process. High volatility can mirror a disruption of market liquidity
	House prices		House price bubble, consumption boom fuelled by equity withdrawals, potential losses to financial sector in case of downturn in prices

Source: Gadanecz and Jayaram (2010)

Second, the *corporate sector's* riskiness can be assessed by its leverage and expense ratios, its net foreign exchange exposure to equity and the number of applications for protection against creditors.

Third, the *household sector*'s health can be gauged through its net assets (assets minus liabilities) and net disposable income (earnings minus consumption minus debt service and principal payments). Net assets and net disposable earnings can measure households' ability to weather (unexpected) downturns.

Fourth, the conditions in the *external sector* are reflected by real exchange rates, foreign exchange reserves, the current account, capital flows, and maturity/currency mismatches. These variables can be reflective of sudden changes in the direction of capital inflows, loss of export competitiveness, and the sustainability of the foreign financing of domestic debt.

Fifth, the *financial sector* is characterised by monetary aggregates, real interest rates, risk measures for the banking sector, banks' capital and liquidity ratios, the quality of their loan book, standalone credit ratings, and the concentration/systemic focus of their lending activities. All these proxies can be reflective of problems in the banking or financial sector and, if a crisis occurs, they can gauge the cost of such a crisis to the real economy.

Finally, variables relevant to describe conditions on *financial markets* are equity indices, corporate spreads, liquidity premia, and volatility. High levels of risk spreads can indicate a loss of investors' risk appetite and possibly financing problems for the rest of the economy. Liquidity disruptions may be a materialisation of the market's ability to efficiently allocate surplus funds to investment opportunities within the economy.

Typically financial stability analysis would use several sectoral variables either individually or in combination. However, views on leading indicators diverge. According to the IMF (2011), the most frequently cited indicators are credit growth or the credit-to-GDP ratio, the ratio of banks' non-performing loans to total loans and changes in property or asset prices. However, threats to financial stability are often surrounded by major uncertainty and are therefore difficult to capture in a quantitative analysis. Even when a build-up of imbalances is being identified, that does not necessarily mean that a crisis will erupt, as most imbalances and excesses unravel without requiring an abrupt correction.

Systemically important financial institutions (SIFIs)

To compute the effect of potential threats to the system as a whole, macroprudential authorities also need to have a good understanding of what developments in the abovementioned indicators mean for the position of so-called *systemically important financial institutions* (SIFIs). These are financial institutions, whose disorderly failure, because of their size, complexity and systemic interconnectedness, may cause significant disruption to the wider financial system and economic activity.

SIFIs vary in their structures and activities, and hence in the nature and degree of the risks they pose to the international financial system. For example, the collapse of Lehman Brothers, which in itself was not considered to be 'systemic', demonstrated that the disorderly failure of a global financial firm has strong spill-overs across markets and affects financial stability and national economies around the world.

The assessment methodology for SIFIs comprises four broad categories:

(1) *Size:* looks at the amount of services provided by a financial institution and can be measured by its assets or equity, in absolute terms or as a proportion of GDP. It has long been thought that financial firms need to become large because of economies of scale and scope and need the size to be profitable and to compete globally. As such, size may serve as a first indicator of systemic relevance, although institutional size by itself is not sufficient to determine whether an institution is systemically relevant. For example, a large firm may not pose a systemic problem if it is not interconnected or if substitutes are available for its products. Therefore, interactions among the factors also are important in identifying systemically relevant institutions.

(2) *Interconnectedness*: looks at the possibility of financial distress in one institution or market spreading to others through provision of funds and services, funding, confidence factors or exposures through common risk factors.

(3) *Substitutability*: looks at the extent to which other institutions or parts of the financial system can provide the same services if one or more institutions were to fail. A lack of substitutability could pose a systemic threat if the services provided by the failed institution or institutions are of critical importance to the functioning of other institutions or the financial system (e.g. payment and settlement systems).

(4) *Complexity*: looks at the group structures and business models of financial institutions, as the complexity and integrated nature of many financial institutions makes it very difficult not only to manage and supervise SIFIs but also for orderly resolution in the event of their failure.

Stress testing

An important tool to enhance the authorities' understanding of possible vulnerabilities within individual institutions as well as the overall system is to execute a so-called stress test. At the level of individual financial institutions, a stress test is a way of revaluing a portfolio using an extreme scenario. The results of such a test show the sensitivity of the portfolio to one or more shocks. Stress tests can be useful because historical data often does not provide sufficient information about the behaviour of markets under extreme events (Hilbers and Jones, 2004).

System-wide stress tests measure the sensitivity of a group of institutions or even an entire financial system to common shocks. The objective is to identify common vulnerabilities across institutions that could undermine the overall stability of a financial system. The focus is also more macroeconomic in nature, because authorities are often interested in understanding how major changes in the economic environment may affect the financial system as a whole.

These system-wide tests can complement stress tests conducted by individual institutions, while also acting as a cross-check for other types of analysis.

13.4 Macroprudential instruments and architecture

Macroprudential authorities do not have a concrete set of instruments at their disposal. Often, if not always, they have to rely on instruments that are primarily intended to serve other policy objectives, mostly microprudential supervision and monetary policy. These objectives may be compatible, but they may also be conflicting, e.g. a natural starting point to influence the price of credit is the interest rate, but this would lead to close interference with monetary policy.

A key part of developing macroprudential instruments is to adapt existing microprudential tools, such as strong prudential standards and limits on activities that increase systemic vulnerabilities and risks. These standards and limits might be occasionally varied, or adjusted in a countercyclical manner, especially with a view to leaning against the financial cycle (BIS, 2010a).

Cyclical pillar

Table 13.3 specifies the cyclical pillar (Schoenmaker and Wierts, 2011). It contains time-varying instruments for effectively stabilising financial imbalances that cause risks to financial stability. The intermediate target of financial

Table 13.3 Cyclical pillar strategy

Intermediate target	Financial imbalances		
Sub-target	Aggregate credit	Credit: Housing	Maturity mismatch
Time-varying instrument	Countercyclical capital buffer	LTV ratio	Liquidity charge

imbalances is divided into sub-targets for credit and liquidity (or maturity mismatch) cycles, which dominate the literature. Alternatively, one could also specify the first sub-target in terms of leverage, i.e. the extent to which imbalances are financed by debt instead of equity (Bank of England, 2009). If asset growth is debt financed (i.e. credit), declining asset values will trigger default when the value of the asset drops below the level of debt. This first default may trigger further defaults. By contrast, if assets are equity financed, falling asset prices may be absorbed by the investors without necessarily triggering a default (e.g. the dotcom bubble of 2000).

On instruments, a natural starting point would be to influence the price of credit, which is the interest rate. But this would lead to close interference with monetary policy. Attention therefore naturally turned to prudential measures. Indeed, the Basel III agreement already specifies the countercyclical capital buffer. The idea is to build up additional capital buffers when the credit-to-GDP ratio is above its long-term trend. The Basel Committee decided to focus this instrument on increasing resilience (building up a buffer for bad times), and not on stabilising the credit cycle (putting a brake or speed limit on credit growth in good times). Such a cautious approach is understandable given limited experience with the instrument. Going forward, one may need an instrument that can effectively stabilise the aggregate credit cycle.

For the housing market, many authors stress the *loan to value* (LTV) ratio, i.e. the ratio of money borrowed on a property to the property's fair market value. When house prices increase (upswing), the LTV ratio is reduced. The LTV ratio is increased when house prices decline. The evidence presented by Crowe *et al.* (2011) suggests that LTV ratios can be effective in addressing a leveraged housing cycle. To prevent regulatory arbitrage, LTV ratios should be applied to all financial institutions that provide mortgages. Another option would be to use risk weights on real estate exposures. There is, however, less experience with its application and fewer countries support its use, according to IMF (2011). Moreover, risk weights are only applied in banking capital rules, while a financial system-wide instrument is needed.

Table 13.4 Structural pillar strategy

Intermediate target	Externalities		
Sub-target	Systemically important financial institutions	Markets	Infrastructure
Instrument	Capital surcharge	Collateral-based tools	Improvements to resilience

Liquidity cycles relate to the excessive build-up of short-term wholesale funding in good times. A strong consensus on the best tool for addressing this sub-target still needs to emerge. Perotti and Suarez (2009) propose a liquidity risk charge, or a levy, on non-core liabilities, for correcting negative externalities caused by banks' excessive reliance on short-term debt. The levy can be increased in good times when imbalances are building up (leaning against the wind). However, even if the levy is held stable it will operate as an automatic stabiliser and increase proportionally with non-core liabilities during the boom (Shin, 2010).

There is at least some experience with the use of this instrument. The UK has a bank tax related to wholesale liabilities, whereby short-term liabilities get the full charge and liabilities for longer than one year get half the charge. Germany only taxes wholesale liabilities up to one year. Another option would be to align the liquidity instrument with the Basel III agreement. This would amount to adding a time-varying element to the net stable funding ratio (NSFR) and/or the liquidity coverage ratio (LCR) as described in Chapter 12.

Structural pillar

Table 13.4 specifies the structural pillar (Schoenmaker and Wierts, 2011). It contains instruments for effectively addressing risks to financial stability due to externalities within the financial system, i.e. within financial institutions, market transactions, and financial infrastructures.

The first sub-target concentrates on systemically important financial institutions (SIFIs). Because of their size, complexity, and systemic interconnectedness, the failure of such institutions would imply large risks to financial stability (FSB, 2010). The second sub-target relates to externalities in markets. The market mechanism can transmit shocks, through the effects of changes in prices, on similar assets classes elsewhere in the financial system. This is relevant from a systemic perspective when markets become dysfunctional and prices move from their equilibrium value. This happened during the last crisis due to fire sales, or forced sale of assets at a dislocated price (Shleifer and Vishny, 2010; Kashyap *et al.* 2011). The third sub-target concerns externalities within the financial system infrastructure. The design and oversight of large-value payment and securities systems are relevant here in particular. The oversight role of central banks is usually considered an integral element of its function in ensuring financial stability (BIS, 2005).

The FSB (2010) recommends that SIFIs should have higher loss-absorbency capacity than the minimum levels agreed in Basel III. Ideally, such capital surcharges should be based on the risks that SIFIs pose due to their systemic position within the financial system. Another structural instrument for SIFIs to reduce the moral hazard of 'too big to fail' are the newly developed resolution plans. The explicit objective of resolution plans is to put in place ex-ante conditions that would allow a wider range of options other than having the whole bank rescued (Avgouleas *et al.*, 2012). A resolution plan is to be used when a bank may get into difficulties.

The FSB and Basel Committee on Banking Supervision (BCBS) have examined the macroeconomic costs and benefits of proposals for higher loss absorbency for global systemically important banks (G-SIBs). They conclude that the transition to stronger capital standards on G-SIBs is likely to have at most a modest impact on aggregate output, while the benefits from reducing the risk of damaging financial crises will be substantial. Raising capital requirements on an illustrative group of potential G-SIBs by one percentage point over eight years is estimated to lower GDP by less than one one-hundredth of a percentage point per year during the implementation period. The primary driver of this macroeconomic impact is an estimated increase of lending spreads of between 5 and 6 basis points. The overall impact of the Basel III proposals (which apply to all banks) and the G-SIB framework is also quite small, with GDP at the point of peak impact projected to be lower by 0.34 per cent relative to its baseline level. Roughly four one-hundredths of a percentage point are subtracted from annual growth during this period, while lending spreads rise by around 31 basis points. The benefits arise from the reduced likelihood of systemic crises that can have long-lasting effects on the economy. It is estimated that the Basel III and G-SIB proposals combined contribute a permanent annual benefit of up to 2.5 per cent of GDP.

Another potential instrument for SIFIs is legal restrictions on activities (see also Box 10.6). The best-known example is probably the legal separation between investment banking and retail banking. The US and the UK consider allowing macroprudential authorities to break up financial institutions when a threat to systemic stability cannot otherwise be constrained (IMF, 2011).

Regarding markets, increasing margin calls and haircuts in a crisis are seen as a destabilising element in causing fire sales. The valuation of collateral could therefore be based on through the cycle margins and haircuts (BIS, 2010b). There is, however, little evidence on the potential effectiveness of this instrument: the empirical literature has not yet investigated the causality between haircuts and asset prices (BIS, 2010b).

For the infrastructure, the discussion traditionally focused on spill-over effects through large-value payment and settlement systems. Measures to include resilience against failure include real-time gross settlement, delivery versus payment, and payment versus payment. After the crisis (and in particular with resolving AIG), the focus is shifting to clearing houses for OTC derivatives. Furthermore, the MIFID directive increases possibilities for parallel structures of trading and clearing and settlement. Such innovations again underline the need for activity-based regulation.

Macroprudential architecture

One of the key lessons from the 2007–2009 financial crisis was that the supervisory arrangements had placed too much emphasis on the supervision of individual firms, and too little on the macroprudential side. In order to strengthen the supervisory arrangements on both sides of the Atlantic, the EU and US authorities established new bodies responsible for macroprudential supervision, i.e. the European Systemic Risk Board (ESRB) in the EU and the Financial Stability Oversight Council (FSOC) in the US. Moreover, at the global level G20 leaders decided to establish the Financial Stability Board (FSB).

European Systemic Risk Board (ESRB)

The ESRB is responsible for the macroprudential oversight of the EU's financial system, defined as contributing to the prevention or mitigation of systemic risks that arise from developments within the financial system and taking into account macroeconomic developments, so as to avoid periods of widespread financial distress.

The ESRB comprises a General Board as its decision-making body, a Steering Committee which sets the agenda and prepares the decisions, a Secretariat, as well as an Advisory Technical Committee and a Scientific

Committee. While all relevant stakeholders are represented within the ESRB, a prominent role has been granted to central banks, i.e. the majority of the voting members of the General Board are central banks, the Chair is the ECB President, and the ECB also provides the Secretariat as well as analytical, statistical, administrative and logistical support to the ESRB.

The ESRB tasks include: (1) the collection and analysis of all information relevant for macroprudential oversight; (2) the identification and prioritisation of systemic risks; (3) the issuance of warnings where such risks are deemed to be significant; (4) the issuance of recommendations for remedial action; (5) the monitoring of the follow-up to warnings and recommendations; (6) cooperation with the European Supervisory Authorities (ESAs), including the development of indicators of systemic risk and the conduct of stress-testing exercises; (7) the issuance of confidential warnings on emergency situations addressed to the European Council; and (8) coordination with the IMF and the FSB, as well as other macroprudential bodies. Although ESRB recommendations are not binding, the parties addressed are obliged to respond under the principle of 'comply or explain'. In other words, they must follow the recommendation, or explain why they are not doing so.

Developments in EU Member States

Within the various Member States different initiatives have been launched to strengthen macroprudential supervision at the national level. While in some Member States the legal mandate for macroprudential policy is still relatively vague and does not contain explicit authorisations to use macroprudential instruments, others have been more ambitious. For example, in the UK a new Financial Policy Committee (FPC) is created in the Bank of England, with primary statutory responsibility for maintaining financial stability. Unlike in the previous system, which did not provide the Bank of England with tools for maintaining financial stability, the FPC is provided with control of macroprudential tools to ensure that systemic risks to financial stability are dealt with.

The majority of the FPC's members are executives of the Bank of England. But the FPC also includes external members – including from other regulatory bodies, and from the markets themselves – to ensure that wider perspectives are fed into the Committee's work. The FPC also includes the head of the new Financial Conduct Authority (FCA) as well as the Treasury, with the latter as a non-voting member. The FPC is accountable to the British Parliament.

Financial Stability Oversight Council (FSOC)

As established under the Dodd–Frank Act, the Financial Stability Oversight Council (FSOC) in the US should provide comprehensive monitoring to ensure the stability of the nation's financial system. The Council is charged with identifying threats to the financial stability of the United States; promoting market discipline; and responding to emerging risks to the stability of the United States financial system. It is chaired by the Secretary of the Treasury and the members comprise representatives from the Federal Reserve, the federal financial regulators, as well as state regulators (the latter being non-voting members).

The tasks of the FSOC may be summarised as comprising three sets of powers (Enria and Teixeira, 2011):

(1) Coordination powers: the FSOC has the duty to support coordination and information sharing among its members;

(2) Advisory powers: the FSOC may issue recommendations for regulatory policy. In particular, it may recommend new or stricter standards for interconnected institutions including non-banks, as well as financial products and markets posing a threat to financial stability. The FSOC may also issue recommendations to the US Congress to close regulatory gaps;

(3) Systemic powers: the FSOC has the possibility to require consolidated supervision of non-bank financial institutions and to designate specific financial market infrastructures (e.g. payment, clearing and settlement) as systemic, so as to make them subject to regulatory oversight. Finally, the FSOC also plays a role in the possible breaking up of institutions that pose a 'grave threat' to financial stability.

The ESRB and the FSOC have a number of broad similarities. They both have analytical functions regarding the monitoring of the emergence of systemic risks and in this context the ability to share and collect information on the financial system. However, the main difference between the two is the ability to intervene directly in the financial system. The ESRB does not have such powers, while the FSOC can bring institutions and market infrastructures within the scope of regulatory oversight and determine whether the Federal Reserve can act in the context of its important new power to break up financial institutions.

Financial Stability Board (FSB)

The FSB has been established by G20 leaders at their summit of April 2009 to coordinate the work of national financial authorities and international standard-setting bodies and to develop and promote the implementation of effective regulatory, supervisory, and other financial sector policies. It gathers national authorities responsible for financial stability in significant international financial centres, international financial institutions, sector-specific international groupings of regulators and supervisors, and committees of central bank experts.

The FSB was established as the successor to the Financial Stability Forum (FSF), with a broadened mandate to promote financial stability.

13.5 Crisis management and resolution

If supervision fails to prevent or spot the build-up of systemic risks and a financial crisis occurs, an effective crisis management framework needs to be available to deal cost-effectively with failing systemic financial institutions, markets or infrastructures.

There is however not a single set of instruments that can be used in all crisis situations. Crises are generally never exactly alike and options differ as to which particular approach is 'best' for resolving them. Although there is no blueprint for crisis resolution, generally four reactive instruments can be considered:

(1) private-sector solutions;
(2) liquidity-support measures;
(3) public-intervention tools; and
(4) winding down.

Private-sector solutions

Each financial institution is responsible for its own safety and soundness. So if financial losses occur, the shareholders should bear the costs and the management should suffer the consequences. In principle, each financial institution should be allowed to fail. If this is not possible for stability reasons, authorities often try to involve the private sector as much as possible in its resolution.

These private solutions can be organised on an ad hoc basis, such as liquidity provision, a merger or acquisition (capital infusion), or other rescue operations, which may be considered in case of an emergency. These solutions can be promoted by the authorities acting as honest broker, especially given the time constraints under which most crises have to be solved and the potential information asymmetries that then exist. In other cases there can be prede-termined private sector mechanisms aimed at preventing spill-over effects of financial crises.

If a private-sector solution is not immediately at hand, the public author-ities can bridge the gap between failure and resolution by a third party (*bridge banking*).

Liquidity-support measures

According to Frydl and Quintyn (2000), liquidity support from the public authorities to troubled financial institutions starts long before the systemic nature of a banking crisis has been recognised. When one or more banks start experiencing substantial withdrawals from depositors and creditors, and they cannot borrow directly (or only at high rates) in the interbank mar-ket, the public authorities (usually the central bank) can become their lender of last resort (LoLR).

In principle, central banks should support only illiquid, but still solvent banks. Yet during the early stages of an unfolding crisis, it is very difficult to distinguish illiquidity from insolvency. It often turns out that banks resort-ing to the central bank for liquidity support have been insolvent for a while, without this being known. In a crisis situation it is hardly possible to distin-guish between illiquidity and insolvency. So, the LoLR interventions by the public authorities mostly involve high-risk loans, which eventually may lead to huge costs to the taxpayer.

Apart from liquidity support to individual financial institutions, liquid-ity support can also be given to the market as a whole. Emergency assist-ance to the market as a whole is provided temporarily to relieve market pressure following an adverse exogenous shock (for example, the 9/11 ter-rorist attacks and the financial crisis of 2007–2009). In the euro area, this is typically a task of the ECB.

Decisions to provide emergency liquidity assistance to individual bank-ing groups are up to the National Central Banks in the respective countries where they are licensed and operate.

Public-intervention tools

Facilities such as deposit-insurance schemes may act as stabilisers to the financial system. There are two rationales for deposit insurance (MacDonald, 1996):

- consumer protection: deposit insurance protects depositors against the consequences of the failure of a bank. It is difficult for (potential) depositors to assess the financial health of banks. Only a small part of the information necessary to make an effective assessment of a bank is publicly available and even then the general public may have difficulties in interpreting such information;
- reducing the risk of a systemic crisis: without deposit insurance, uninformed depositors might remove their deposits from sound banks in reaction to problems at a single bank (bank run). In order to meet these withdrawals, banks have to liquidate their asset portfolio at a loss, and eventually might fail. If depositors know their money is safe because of the insurance, they will have no reason to withdraw it. Deposit insurance can thus be seen as a preventative instrument as well. However, this requires a high coverage level and rapid payout.

In reaction to the 2007–2009 financial crisis the EU Member States decided that the level of deposit protection should be increased in the EU. A Directive adopted in March 2009 requires coverage to be increased from a minimum of €20,000 to at least €50,000 by June 2010 and to a uniform level of €100,000 by the end of 2010.

When the failure of a financial institution could create systemic problems, the government may decide to recapitalise (or even nationalise) the institution. During the 2007–2009 financial crisis, EU Member States were forced to bail out significant parts of their banking sector. This option can only be optimal if the costs of recapitalisation are lower than the social benefits of preserving financial stability. Recapitalisation may consist of a direct capital injection or the purchase of troubled assets. As the provision of solvency support puts taxpayers' money at risk, the decision to recapitalise is normally taken by the government and not by the central bank. Initially, the fiscal costs of nationalisation will be relatively high, but the government can try to sell the nationalised institution at a later date. A so-called Banking Restructuring Agency (BRA) can be established to restore the health of the banking system. To protect it from political interference, such agencies should arguably be functionally independent from the government and publicly accountable.

Winding down

When systemic risks are negligible, or when the costs of intervention are higher than the potential social benefits, the authorities will opt for the winding down of the troubled institution. However, the closure of a financial institution creates potential for disruption, especially to market functioning and liquidity. Therefore, the authorities should ensure that the winding down is managed in an orderly manner. One way to contain the negative effects is by liquidity support to other intermediaries. However, when financial distress has been broad-based or has involved systemically important institutions, liquidation has rarely been the preferred option (OECD, 2002). The expectation that large financial institutions are 'too big to fail' may give rise to moral hazard, i.e. the risk that once institutions know there is some sort of safety net or insurance they take greater risk than they would do without this protection.

In reaction to the financial crisis of 2007–2009, the European Commission launched an initiative to equip national authorities with common and effective tools and powers to tackle bank crises at the earliest possible moment, and avoid costs for taxpayers. This toolbox of measures will include: (1) preparatory and preventative measures, (2) powers to take early action to remedy problems before they become severe, and (3) resolution tools (see Box 13.1 below).

13.6 Challenges for maintaining financial stability

Cross-border externalities

Especially in Europe, an important challenge for maintaining financial stability arises from cross-border banking. The interaction of highly penetrated banking systems with national regulations and burden allocation might be a dangerously weak institutional feature (Goodhart, 2005). The reason is that national authorities have a mandate for maintaining financial stability in their own system and they may therefore be reluctant to help solve problems in other EU Member States, thus neglecting cross-border externalities caused by financial institutions under their jurisdiction. Current national-based arrangements may therefore undervalue externalities related to the cross-border business of financial institutions. To formalise this issue, two different models of recapitalising banks are examined: a single-country and a multi-country model.

Single-country model of bailout

Freixas (2003) presents a model of the costs and benefits of a bailout. The model considers the ex-post decision whether to recapitalise or to liquidate

Box 13.1 An EU framework for crisis management in the financial sector

The 2007–2009 financial crisis highlighted the need for more robust national crisis management arrangements, as well as the need to put in place arrangements to better deal with cross-border failures.

For a long time, many felt that crisis management was best dealt with at the national level, mainly because of possible budgetary implications and the link between crisis measures and national insolvency regimes. As a result, the crisis management frameworks in place in the EU varied greatly between Member States. The crisis showed the need for action at the EU level, demonstrating that uncoordinated, ad hoc national solutions, are less effective in resolving the situation and may prove more costly for the taxpayers.

The overriding objective of a European crisis management and resolution framework should therefore be that ailing institutions of any type and size, and in particular systemically important institutions, can be allowed to fail without risk to financial stability whilst avoiding costs to taxpayers. The introduction of such a framework would be desirable to: (1) reduce the systemic impact of a potential failure; (2) afford control to the authorities; (3) shift the financial burden away from the taxpayer; (4) let losses be borne by existing shareholders; and (5) reduce moral hazard and increase market discipline (Čihák and Nier, 2009).

The principal features of a resolution framework should: (1) allow the authorities to take control of the financial institution at an early stage of its financial difficulties; (2) empower the authorities to use a wide range of harmonised tools to deal with a failing financial institution, without the consent of shareholders or creditors; (3) establish an effective and specialised framework for liquidation of the institution; (4) ensure clarity as to the objectives of the regime and define clearly the scope of judicial review; and (5) promote information sharing and coordination among all authorities involved in supervision and resolution. A framework for prevention, crisis management, and resolution is therefore being developed, comprising three classes of measures (EC, 2009), i.e. preparatory and preventative measures, early supervisory intervention, and resolution tools and powers.

Preparatory and preventative measures

Failures in effective supervision often proceed and contribute to financial shocks. Robust and intrusive supervision is therefore the starting point for any effective preparatory and preventative measures.

Recovery and resolution plans are a key element of planning for the failure of major institutions and are widely regarded as a necessary component of an effective crisis management regime. The objective of a recovery plan should be to set out how a bank may react to a whole range of stresses and the steps that it could plausibly take to head off the impact of these stresses in order to avoid formal resolution actions in the event of failure. Recovery plans should encompass contingency funding plans and the use of contingent capital instruments as well as the sale of assets and/or business lines. They would be expected to be detailed and realistic, and should not assume access to any support from public funds. The relevant (supervisory) authorities may also be granted with preventative powers which may be applied in cases where there may be impediments to the resolution of an institution. This should enable them to require institutions to adopt measures, including changes to business operations and corporate structure, necessary to ensure that resolution is viable. Such preventative powers can include requirements to limit or modify exposures; to increase reporting; to restrict or prohibit certain activities; or to change to group structures.

Early supervisory intervention

Early intervention covers any action by supervisory authorities aimed at restoring the stability and financial soundness of an institution when problems are developing, together with intra-group asset transfer between solvent entities for the purposes of financial support. Such actions are taken before the thresholds conditions for resolution are met, and before the institution is insolvent or likely to become so.

Resolution tools and powers

Resolution covers the measures taken by the relevant authorities to manage a crisis in a financial institution, to contain its impact on the stability of the financial system and, where appropriate, to facilitate an orderly winding up of the whole or parts of the institution. Such powers may include: (1) powers to facilitate or effect a private sector acquisition of the failing bank or its business; (2) powers to transfer the business of a failing bank to a temporary 'bridge bank' in order to preserve it as a going concern with a view to sell it to a private sector purchaser; (3) powers to separate 'clean' and 'toxic' assets between 'good' and 'bad' banks through a partial transfer of assets and liabilities; and (4) powers to write down the debt of a failing bank, or to convert it to equity, as a means of restoring the institution's capital position ('bail in'). This would allow the bank to be restructured as a going concern or wound down in an orderly manner, and may provide an additional resolution tool that would give authorities further flexibility to deal with the failure of complex institutions.

a bank in financial distress. The choice to continue or to close the bank is a variable x with values in the space $\{0, 1\}$. Moreover, θ denotes the social benefits of a recapitalisation and C its costs. The benefits of a recapitalisation include those derived from avoiding contagion and maintaining financial stability. The direct cost of continuing the bank activity is denoted by C_c and the cost of stopping its activities by C_s and the difference is $C = C_c - C_s$. The case $C < 0$ is obviously possible, but is a case where continuing the bank's operations is cheaper than closing it, so that continuation is preferred and the recapitalisation decision is simplified. In this situation, private-sector solutions are possible and the central bank can play the role of 'honest broker'.

The optimal decision for the authorities will be to maximise:

$$x^*(\theta - C)$$

so that x^*

$$\begin{cases} x^* = 1 \ if \ \theta - C > 0 \\ x^* = 0 \ if \ \theta - C < 0 \end{cases} \tag{13.1}$$

This simple model shows that a bank will be recapitalised whenever the total benefits of an intervention are larger than the net costs. In the case of a bailout, the authorities will contribute C.

Multi-country model of bailout

In the multi-country model, Freixas (2003) considers the case where the mechanism is set in such a way that the bank is recapitalised only if a sufficient contribution from the different countries can be collected. This is an interpretation of improvised cooperation: the different countries meet to find out how much they are ready to contribute to the recapitalisation, denoted by t. If the total amount they are willing to contribute is larger than the cost, the bank is recapitalised. The decision is:

$$\begin{cases} x^* = 1 \ if \ \Sigma_j(t_j - C_j) > 0 \\ x^* = 1 \ if \ \Sigma_j(t_j - C_j) < 0 \end{cases} \tag{13.2}$$

and the objective for country j will be to maximise:

$$x^*\left(\theta_j - t_j\right) \tag{13.3}$$

This game may have a multiplicity of equilibria and, in particular, the closure equilibrium $t_j = 0$, $x^* = 0$ will occur provided that for no j we have:

$$\theta_j - \sum{}_j C_j > 0 \tag{13.4}$$

that is, no individual country is ready to finance the recapitalisation itself. Obviously, if this equilibrium is selected, the recapitalisation policy is inefficient as banks will almost never be recapitalised.

That in most cases the closure equilibrium will occur can be explained by the fact that part of the externalities fall outside the home country (although it is safe to assume that in the current setting the country with the highest social benefits of a recapitalisation is the home country). The countries are grouped as follows: the home country denoted by H, all other European countries denoted by E, and all other countries in the world denoted by W. The social benefits can then be decomposed into the social benefits in the home country ($h \cdot \theta = \theta_h$), the rest of Europe ($e \cdot \theta = \theta_e$), and the rest of the world ($w \cdot \theta = \theta_w$):

$$\sum_{j=1}^{w} \theta_j = \theta_h + \sum_{j \notin h}^{e} \theta_{e,j} + \sum_{j \notin e}^{w} \theta_{w,j} \qquad (13.5)$$

In this equation h, e, and w are indexes for the social benefits (i.e. externalities caused by the possible failure of a financial institution) in the home country, the rest of Europe, and the rest of the world. The sum of h, e, and w is 1. When the total social benefits are close (or equal) to the social benefits of the home country (θ is close to θ_h, so h is close to 1), the home country will be willing to bail out the financial institution. In all other cases ($h < 1$), the home country will deal with the social benefits only within its territory, while host countries expect the home country to pay for (a part of) the costs in the host country. Current national-based arrangements undervalue externalities related to the cross-border business of financial institutions. As a result, insufficient capital will be contributed and the financial institution will not be bailed out. This model pinpoints the public-good dimension of collective bailouts and shows why improvised cooperation will lead to an underprovision of public goods, that is, to an insufficient level of recapitalisations. Countries have an incentive to understate their share of the problem so as to incur a smaller share of the costs. This leaves the largest country, almost always the home country, with the decision whether to shoulder the costs on its own or let the bank close and possibly be liquidated.

Burden sharing

Some authors argue in favour of explicit burden-sharing arrangements to cover potential losses in bailout operations (see Goodhart and Schoenmaker, 2009).

As the funding for recapitalisation is exclusively available at the domestic level, no one knows how the loss burden arising from the failure of a cross-border financial group might be handled. To counter moral hazard, crisis-management arrangements for LoLR and solvency support could not be specified in advance. Constructive ambiguity regarding the decision whether or not to recapitalise can be useful to contain moral hazard. However, it is clear that ambiguity over burden sharing will lead to fewer recapitalisations than is socially optimal. It is therefore desirable to attain the same clarity at the European level as currently exists at the national level, where the financial risk of support operations is carried by the Ministry of Finance and the central bank. Clarity at the European level about how to share the costs among treasuries (and central banks) does not increase moral hazard.

In designing ex-ante mechanisms for burden sharing, the following issues arise. First, should all countries join in the burden sharing (in a banking crisis, every country pays relative to its size) or only the countries involved (countries pay relative to the national presence of the problem bank)? Second, should the burden be shared according to a fixed or a flexible key (accommodating the specific circumstances)?

The general-fund mechanism is an example of generic burden sharing by countries. An example of a general fund is the European Stability Mechanism (see section 2.4 in Chapter 2). Under this mechanism, the costs of recapitalisation are distributed among the participating countries, irrespective of the location of the failing bank. However, there are two substantial problems with such a mechanism. First, this construction will lead to international transfers between countries (a country may have to contribute its share to the recapitalisation of a problem bank that does not operate in its jurisdiction). Second, general burden sharing generates adverse selection and moral-hazard problems. Countries with weak banking systems will profit from such a scheme and countries with strong banks are therefore less inclined to sign up (adverse selection). As the link between payment for a recapitalisation and responsibility for supervision is weakened, supervisory authorities may have fewer incentives to provide an adequate level of supervisory effort.

Alternatively, the burden may be shared only by countries in which a failing bank is present. Each country involved pays part of the burden that reflects the relative presence of the bank in the country concerned. An important advantage of specific burden sharing arrangements is that there are almost no international transfers. The specific sharing scheme is also incentive compatible: the fiscal authorities (the principal) will require from the supervisor (the agent) adequate supervision.

Finally, there are some concerns regarding both burden-sharing mechanisms. First, burden-sharing arrangements face a free-rider problem.

Countries that do not sign up to burden sharing still benefit from it, as the stability of the European financial system is a public good. Second, there is a concern with foreign banks in small countries. If such a bank is systemic in the host country but not in the home country, the bank might not be rescued. This could be a problem for the new EU Member States in particular. Third, it could be difficult to organise burden sharing for truly international banks, which have a large part of their business outside Europe. Moreover, such mechanisms fail to address crisis problems caused by the failures of banks headquartered outside Europe. Fourth, a common agreement on burden sharing will need political commitment. The appetite of European politicians for adopting explicit burden-sharing arrangements is currently, however, limited (Pauly, 2008).

13.7 Conclusions

The 2007–2009 financial crisis highlights the crucial importance of effective macroprudential supervision focusing on the soundness of the financial system as a whole.

As a rule, macroprudential supervision focuses on risks that may trigger a loss of economic value or confidence in a substantial part of the financial system that is serious enough to have significant adverse effects on the real economy. This requires the monitoring and analysis of the way in which: (1) risk is distributed in the financial system at a given point in time, i.e. the cross-sectional dimension, and (2) aggregate risk evolves over time, i.e. the time dimension.

Several indicators are being used for financial stability analysis, with key variables being credit growth or the credit-to-GDP ratio, the ratio of banks' non-performing loans to total loans and changes in property or asset prices.

Particular attention is being paid to monitoring possible risks within systemically important financial institutions (SIFIs), whose disorderly failure, because of their size, complexity and systemic interconnectedness, may cause significant disruption to the wider financial system and economic activity. Stress tests can be an important tool in this process, measuring the sensitivity of a group of institutions or even an entire financial system to common shocks.

Various efforts have been launched at the national and regional level to strengthen macroprudential arrangements, often by establishing new bodies responsible for macroprudential supervision, e.g. the European Systemic

Risk Board (ESRB) in the EU, the Financial Policy Committee (FPC) in the UK, and the Financial Stability Oversight Council (FSOC) in the US.

In the absence of a blueprint for crisis resolution, generally four reactive instruments can be considered: (1) private-sector solutions; (2) liquidity-support measures; (3) public-intervention tools; and (4) winding down. Against the background of the 2007–2009 financial crisis, efforts have been launched in the EU to better allow the relevant authorities to take control of the financial institution at an early stage of its financial difficulties and empower the authorities to use a wide range of harmonised tools to deal with a failing financial institution.

Finally, the potential for a pan-European crisis raises the thorny issue of dividing the fiscal costs of possible bailouts between the Member States involved. As countries have an incentive to understate their share of the problem in order to have a smaller share in the costs, negotiations on burden sharing will likely lead to an underprovision of recapitalisations. This leaves the largest country, generally the home country, with the decision whether to bear the costs on its own or to let the bank close. An alternative to negotiations after a crisis has occurred is to agree ex ante on some burden-sharing mechanisms, be it generic or specific burden sharing.

SUGGESTED READING

Borio, C. (2010), Implementing a Macroprudential Framework: Blending Boldness and Realism, Bank for International Settlements, Basel.

Hanson, S. G., A. K. Kashyap, and J. C. Stein (2011), A Macroprudential Approach to Financial Regulation, *Journal of Economic Perspectives*, 25(1), 3–28.

Schoenmaker, D. and P. Wierts (2011), Macroprudential Policy: The Need for a Coherent Policy Framework, Duisenberg School of Finance Policy Paper 13.

REFERENCES

Avgouleas, E., C. Goodhart, and D. Schoenmaker (2012), Bank Resolution Plans as a catalyst for global financial reform, *Journal of Financial Stability*, forthcoming.

Bank for International Settlements (2005), *Central Bank Oversight of Payment and Settlement Systems, Committee on Payment and Settlement Systems*, BIS, Basel.

(2010a), *Macroprudential Instruments and Frameworks: A Stocktaking of Issues and Experiences*, CGFS Papers 38, BIS, Basel.

(2010b), The Role of Margin Requirements and Haircuts in Procyclicality, CGFS Papers 36, BIS, Basel.

Bank of England (2009), *The Role of Macroprudential Policy*, A Discussion Paper, BoE, London.

Borio, C. (2003), Towards a Macroprudential Framework for Financial Supervision and Regulation?, *CESifo Economic Studies*, 49(2), 181–216.

    (2010), Implementing a Macroprudential Framework: Blending Boldness and Realism, Bank for International Settlements, Basel.

Čihák, M. and E. Nier (2009), The Need for Special Resolution Regimes for Financial Institutions – The Case of the European Union, IMF Working Paper 09/200.

Crowe, C., G. Dell'Ariccia, D. Igan, and P. Rabanal (2011), How to Deal with Real Estate Booms: Lessons from Country Experiences, IMF Working Paper 11/91.

de Larosière, J. (2009), Report of the High-level Group on Financial Supervision in the EU, European Commission, Brussels. Available at: http://ec.europa.eu/internal_market/finances/docs/de_larosiere_report_En.pdf (accessed 13 February 2012).

De Nederlandsche Bank (2010), *Towards a More Stable Financial System*, DNB, Amsterdam.

Enria, E. and P. G. Teixeira (2011), *A New Institutional Framework for Financial Regulation and Supervision*, University of Milan.

European Central Bank (2007), Progress Towards a Framework for Financial Stability Assessment, speech by José-Manuel González-Páramo, Member of the Executive Board of the ECB, OECD World Forum on 'Statistics, Knowledge and Policy', Istanbul, 28 June.

    (2009), *Text of the Clare Distinguished Lecture in Economics and Public Policy by Mr Jean-Claude Trichet,* President of the European Central Bank, organised by Clare College, University of Cambridge.

European Commission (2009), *An EU Framework for Cross-Border Crisis Management in the Banking Sector*, EC, Brussels.

Financial Stability Board (2010), *Reducing the Moral Hazard Posed by Systemically Important Financial Institutions*, FSB, Basel.

Freixas, X. (2003), Crisis Management in Europe, in: J. J. M. Kremers, D. Schoenmaker, and P. Wierts (eds.), *Financial Supervision in Europe*, Edward Elgar, Cheltenham, 102–119.

Frydl, E. and M. Quintyn (2000), The Benefits and Costs of Intervening in Banking Crises, IMF Working Paper 00/147.

Gadanecz, B. and K. Jayaram (2010), *Measures of Financial Stability – A Review,* IFC Bulletin 31, Bank of International Settlements, Basel.

Goodhart, C. A. E. (2005), How Far Can a Central Bank Act as a Lender of Last Resort Independently of Treasury (Ministry of Finance) Support?, paper presented at the Norges Bank conference on Banking Crisis Resolution – Theory and Policy, 16–17 June, Oslo.

Goodhart, C. A. E. and D. Schoenmaker (2009), Fiscal Burden Sharing in Cross-Border Banking Crises, *International Journal of Central Banking*, 5(1), 141–165.

Hanson, S., A. Kashyap, and J. Stein (2011), A Macroprudential Approach to Financial Regulation, *Journal of Economic Perspectives*, 25(1), 3–28.

Hilbers, P. and M. Jones (2004), *Stress Testing Financial Systems*, International Monetary Fund, Washington DC.

International Monetary Fund (2011), *Macroprudential Policy: An Organizing Framework*, Background Paper, IMF, Washington DC.

Kashyap, A., R. Berner, and C. Goodhart (2011), The Macroprudential Toolkit, *IMF Economic Review*, 59, 145–161.

MacDonald, R. (1996), *Deposit Insurance*, Centre for Central Bank Studies, Bank of England, London.

Minsky, H. (1982), *Can 'It' Happen Again? Essays on Instability and Finance*, M.E. Sharpe Inc., Armonk (NY).

Mishkin, F. S. (1992), Anatomy of a Financial Crisis, NBER Working Papers 3934.

Organisation for Economic Co-operation and Development (2002), Experiences with the Resolution of Weak Financial Institutions in the OECD Area, OECD, *Financial Market Trends*, 82.

Pauly, L. W. (2008), Financial Crisis Management in Europe and Beyond, *Contributions to Political Economy*, 27, 73–89.

Perotti, E. and J. Suarez (2009), *Liquidity Risk Charges as a Macro Prudential Tool*, CEPR Policy Insight 40, CEPR, London.

Schoenmaker, D. and P. Wierts (2011), Macroprudential Policy: The Need for a Coherent Policy Framework, Duisenberg School of Finance Policy Paper 13.

Shin, H. (2010), Macroprudential Policies Beyond Basel III, Policy Mimeo, Princeton University.

Shleifer, A. and R. Vishny (2010), Unstable Banking, *Journal of Financial Economics*, 97, 303–318.

Turner, A. (2009), *The Turner Review – A Regulatory Response to the Global Banking Crisis*, Financial Services Authority, London.

European Competition Policy

OVERVIEW

This chapter provides a concise overview of European competition policy, with a focus on financial services. The chapter first defines competition and describes the objectives of EU competition policy, i.e. the maintenance of competitive markets in the EU, as well as the single-market objective. The ultimate goal of competition is to offer consumers greater choice of products and services at lower prices (i.e. to enhance consumer welfare).

The second part of the chapter analyses the economic rationale for competition policy by examining the difference between a perfectly competitive market and a monopoly. In a competitive market, prices are 'competed' down and goods or services are produced in the least costly way. Firms are price takers. In a monopoly, there is a single seller in the market who can exert undue market power. The monopolist thus has significant power over the price and is a price setter.

The third part of the chapter elaborates on the four tools of EU competition policy, i.e. the elimination of agreements that restrict competition and abuse of a dominant position, the control of mergers and acquisitions, the liberalisation of monopolistic sectors, and control of state aid. The application of the state aid rules in the 2007–2009 financial crisis is reviewed.

The fourth part of the chapter discusses a framework for investigating abuse of dominance. One of the elements of this framework is the so-called 'Small, but Significant Non-transitory Increase in Prices' (SSNIP) methodology, which is used to define the smallest market in which a hypothetical monopolist would be able to impose a small but significant non-transitory price increase (the relevant market). The relevant market for various financial services is discussed.

The final part of the chapter provides a brief description of the dual legislative and enforcement system for competition policy in the EU.

LEARNING OBJECTIVES

After you have studied this chapter, you should be able to:
- describe competition and competition policy
- explain the economic arguments for having competition policy
- reproduce the different tools of EU competition policy and explain how these relate to financial markets
- describe the process of assessing a dominant position
- understand the institutional structure of competition policy in the EU.

14.1 What is competition policy?

Competition can be defined as a market situation in which firms or sellers independently strive for the patronage of buyers in order to achieve a particular business objective, e.g. profits, sales, and/or market share (OECD, 1993). Competition forces firms:
- to become (more) efficient;
- to offer greater choice of products and services; and
- to offer these products and services at lower prices.

Ultimately, competition gives rise to increased consumer welfare and allocative efficiency (the latter will be discussed in more detail in section 14.3). Moreover, the level of competition is an important aspect of financial-sector development and, in turn, economic growth (Claessens and Laeven, 2005).

Generally, *competition policy* aims to ensure that competition in the marketplace is not restricted in a way that is detrimental to society (Motta, 2004). In practice, authorities establish a set of rules and policies aimed at safeguarding competition, as a means of enhancing economic welfare and ensuring efficient allocation of resources. However, the aim of competition policy should not be to eliminate market power, as the prospect of enjoying market power is an important driver for innovation and efficiency. Still, as will be discussed in section 14.4, firms are prohibited from abusing market power.

Competition policy is one of the pillars of the EU's internal market policy. By combating distortions of competition between firms, competition policy creates the preconditions for the proper market functioning with the aim to enhance overall consumer welfare. Moreover, safeguarding competition in the EU is an important instrument to promote further market integration, e.g. by taking away barriers for entry or exit, and the application of non-discrimination principles for new entrants. The objective of EU competition policy is therefore twofold (European Commission, 2000). The first objective of competition policy is the maintenance of competitive markets. Competition policy serves as an instrument to encourage industrial efficiency, the optimal allocation of resources, technical progress, and the flexibility to adjust to a changing environment. In order for the Community to be competitive on worldwide markets, it needs a competitive home market. Thus, the Community's competition policy has always taken a very strong line against price-fixing, market-sharing cartels, abuses of dominant positions, and anti-competitive mergers. It has also prohibited unjustified state-granted monopoly rights and state aid measures which do not ensure the long-term viability of firms, but distort competition by keeping them artificially in business. The second is the single-market objective. An internal market is an essential condition for the development of an efficient and competitive industry. The Commission has used its competition policy as an active tool to prevent this (i.e. the erection of barriers to trade), prohibiting, and fining heavily the parties to two main types of agreement: distribution and licensing agreements that prevent parallel trade between Member States, and agreements between competitors to keep out of one another's 'territories'. The provisions of the Treaty on the Functioning of the European Union (TFEU) specifically require EU policy makers to 'act in accordance with the principle of an open market economy with free competition, favouring an efficient allocation of resources'. Roeller and Stehmann (2006) argue that with the progress made towards realisation of the internal market, the relative importance of the market integration goal has declined. As a result, policy statements increasingly focus on efficiency, consumer welfare, and competitiveness. Nevertheless, competition policy may be an effective instrument to strengthen integration in certain segments of the financial market.

At the EU level, competition law is enforced by the European Commission (more specifically, the Directorate General for Competition), while at the national level the national competition authorities are responsible. Section 14.5 will discuss the organisation of EU competition policy in more detail.

14.2 The economic rationale for competition policy

According to Motta (2004), the basis of competition policy is the idea that monopolies are 'bad'. Although this might sound somewhat simplistic, examining the difference between perfect competition and a monopoly (i.e. the two extremes in a marketplace) is useful to explain the economic rationale for competition policy.

A *monopoly* can be defined as a situation where: (1) there is a single seller in the market, (2) there are no (close) substitute products or services, and (3) there are barriers to entry for potential sellers. As a result of these characteristics, a monopolist has significant power over the price, i.e. he or she is a *price setter* rather than a price taker. The ability of a monopolist to raise and maintain a price above the level that would prevail under (perfect) competition is referred to as *market* or *monopoly power*. Generally, the exercise of market power leads to reduced output and loss of economic welfare. However, monopolies do not necessarily have to be a bad thing. A good example is a *natural monopoly* where a single firm can produce at lower costs than a situation in which there are two or more firms. According to the OECD (1993), natural monopolies are characterised by steeply declining long-run average and marginal-cost curves such that there is room for only one firm to fully exploit available economies of scale and supply the market.

Figure 14.1 shows the welfare effects of market power, by comparing the total surplus at the monopoly price with that at the perfect competitive (marginal-cost) price.[1] Under perfect competition, the price of the goods or services produced equals marginal cost (P_c = MC) and the goods or services will be produced in the least costly way. At the opposite, the monopolist sets output at the level where marginal cost equals marginal revenue (MC = MR) in order to maximise its profits. Tirole (1988) shows that the total surplus is equal to the sum of the consumer surplus and the producer surplus (or profit), or to the difference between total consumer utility and production costs. In Figure 14.1 this surplus is represented by the area DGAD under marginal-cost pricing and by the area DEFAD under monopoly pricing. The difference between the total surplus under monopoly and the surplus under marginal-cost pricing is the *welfare* or *deadweight loss* (given by triangle EFG in Figure 14.1). This welfare loss represents the overall opportunity costs to society arising from monopoly pricing. In addition, part of the consumer surplus under perfect competition, BCEH, is transferred to the monopolist in the form of excess profits.

So what does this entail in practice for competition policy? Figure 14.1 shows that having one firm (or very few firms) serving the market generally leads to a welfare loss for society. Competition policy should, however, not try to maximise the number of firms that operate in a market, because firms will then not be able to optimise the scale or magnitude of their output,

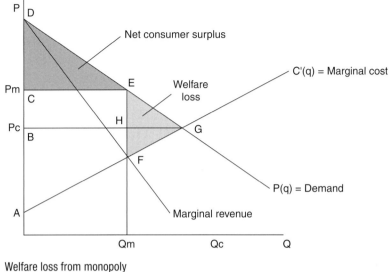

Figure 14.1   Welfare loss from monopoly
Source: Tirole (1988)

which results in an average cost per unit of output that is higher than would be the case in a more concentrated market. Motta (2004) stresses that:

(1) competition policy is not concerned with maximising the number of firms; and

(2) competition policy is concerned with defending market competition in order to increase welfare, not defending competitors.

Should competition authorities then strive for perfect competition? Since the notion of perfect competition can in practice be highly restrictive in terms of policy making (OECD, 1993), the goal of competition policy should be a more realistic target such as *workable competition*, i.e. trying to create the preconditions for the proper operation of markets and ensure that firms do not abuse a dominant position. Although there is no generally accepted definition of workable competition, all authorities involved in competition policy seem to make use of some version of this concept. According to the OECD (1993), workable competition is a notion which arises from the observation that since perfect competition does not exist, theories based on it do not provide reliable guides for competition policy. Criteria for judging whether competition was workable are wide ranging, e.g. the number of firms should be at least as large as economies of scale permit, promotional expenses should not be excessive, and advertising should be informative.

For competition authorities it is important to have insight into the market power of firms and the level of competition in a specific market. There are various ways to quantify the level of market power. A well-known indicator is the *Lerner Index* (LI), which measures the degree to which a firm is able to price its products above marginal costs. The Lerner Index is a more accurate measure of market power than concentration measures (such as the Herfindahl Index and the CR5 ratio). Nevertheless, it poses some challenges. For instance, if the LI is relatively high it may still be hard to judge whether this indicates market power or superior efficiency. Moreover, in practice the LI is hard to calculate as information on marginal costs is often not readily available. The LI is given by the following formula:

$$LI = (Price - Marginal\ Cost)/Price = 1/\varepsilon \tag{14.1}$$

where ε is the price elasticity of demand [$\varepsilon = -(\Delta Q/\Delta P)(P/Q)$]. The key determinant of market power is the elasticity of demand. The greater ε is, the greater will be the reduction in quantity demanded when the price rises. This entails that the higher the elasticity of demand, the lower the market power of the respective firm. In the case of perfect competition, P = MC and the LI equals zero. The higher the value of the LI, the greater is the firm's market power.

Schaeck and Čihák (2008) show a slight upward trend for bank market power in the period 1995–2005 (see Figure 14.2). The banking systems in Luxembourg, Switzerland, and Germany exhibit on average the lowest values for the Lerner Index, indicating that banks in these markets do not wield much market power.

A method to assess competition in a market is the H-statistic of Panzar and Rosse (1987). This test statistic examines the relationship between a change in a firm's input prices and the revenue earned. The basic idea behind this indicator is that firms employ different pricing strategies in response to changes in input costs depending on the market structure in which they operate. Back in Chapter 10, the last column of Table 10.4 provides an overview of the level of competition in the EU banking sector in the period 1990–2005. (See Bikker and Bos (2008) for a further discussion on competition and concentration in the banking sector.)

Even in the absence of a monopoly, dominant positions might arise (Motta, 2004). The latter can, for example, be due to *sunk costs*, i.e. costs which, once incurred, cannot be (easily) recovered. Sunk costs lead to barriers to entry as well as to exit, as the existence of these costs increases an incumbent's

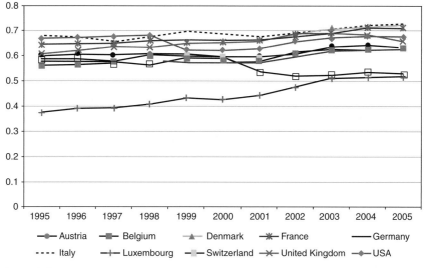

Figure 14.2   Lerner indices
Source: Schaeck and Čihák (2008)

commitment to the market and may signal a willingness to respond aggressively to entry (OECD, 1993). In this respect, offering financial services via the Internet or via intermediaries has the potential to improve contestability of markets by lowering sunk costs and barriers.

In other cases a dominant position may arise as a result of *lock-in effects* or *switching costs*. These are costs that customers face when changing from one supplier to the other. The higher these costs, the more difficult it becomes to switch. The existence of switching costs can give substantial market power to existing suppliers. For example, the absence of account number portability increases switching cost of customers who would like to change banks. Finally, dominant positions can be a result of *network effects*. As shown in Chapter 7, the addition of a new participant to a network increases its value for all participants. This means that the value of the services and products offered to the participants depends on the number of other participants purchasing the same services and products. The existence of network externalities can lead to lock-in effects and make it hard for potential competitors to successfully enter the market.

According to Motta (2004), competition policy is also needed because firms may resort to actions that increase their profits but harm society. One example of such behaviour is *collusion*, which refers to any formal or informal agreements to raise or fix prices or to reduce output in order to increase profits. When explicitly formalised, these agreements are referred to as *cartels*. Firms may also display *predatory behaviour*, which refers to the situation in which one firm drives out its competitors by setting very low prices (sometimes even below costs). As soon as the predatory firm has driven out its competitors and has discouraged new entry into the market, it can raise prices and earn higher profits. Other types of *exclusionary behaviour* include investing in extra capacity, foreclosing access of rivals to crucial inputs, tying and bundling, and price discrimination. *Tying* refers to the practice of making the purchase of product A conditional on the purchase of product B. *Bundling* refers to the practice of selling two or more products or services in a package. *Price discrimination* occurs when customers in different segments are charged different prices for the same good or service, for reasons unrelated to costs (OECD, 1993). However, this type of exclusionary behaviour is effective only if customers cannot profitably resell the goods or services to other customers. Finally, as will be discussed in the next section, mergers and acquisitions may also reduce competition.

14.3 Pillars of EU competition policy

The objective of EU competition policy was first set out in the Treaty of Rome (1957), where it was indicated that one of the activities of the Community includes establishing 'a system ensuring that competition in the internal market is not distorted'. In general, EU competition policy has the following objectives:

- the elimination of agreements which restrict competition and of abuses of a dominant position (*antitrust*);
- the control of mergers and acquisitions between firms;
- the liberalisation of monopolistic economic sectors; and
- the control of state aid.

Antitrust

The two main pillars of EU competition law are Articles 101 and 102 TFEU. Article 101 prohibits agreements and concerted practices with an anticompetitive object or effect on the market, while Article 102 prohibits abuse of a dominant position.

The Treaty on the Functioning of the EU (TFEU) prohibits 'all agreements between undertakings, decisions by associations of undertakings and concerted practices which may affect trade between Member States and which have as their object or effect the prevention, restriction or distortion of competition within the common market'. Actions prohibited under Article 101 can take the form of:

- direct or indirect fixing of purchase or selling prices or any other trading conditions;
- limiting or controlling production, markets, technical development, or investment;
- sharing markets or sources of supply;
- applying dissimilar conditions to equivalent transactions with other trading parties, thereby placing them at a competitive disadvantage; or
- making the conclusion of contracts subject to acceptance by the other parties of supplementary obligations which, by their nature or according to commercial usage, have no connection with the subject of such contracts.

Box 14.1 provides two decisions in the domain of Article 101. The first example is the decision of the European Commission to prohibit MasterCard's multilateral interchange fees[2] (see Chapter 7 for a discussion on interchange fees). The second example is related to the price measures by the Groupement des Cartes Bancaires in France that – according to the Commission – hindered the issuing of cards at competitive rates.

Article 101 applies to horizontal as well as vertical agreements. *Horizontal agreements* are made between competitors in the same product market, while *vertical agreements* are made between firms operating at different stages of a certain production or distribution chain. However, exceptions can be made for those agreements that improve the production or distribution of goods or that promote technical or economic progress. Moreover, such agreements should benefit consumers and should not unnecessarily eliminate competition.

Article 102 prohibits abuse of a dominant position. This article states that '[A]ny abuse by one or more undertakings of a dominant position within the common market or in a substantial part of it shall be prohibited as incompatible with the common market in so far as it may affect trade between Member States'. A firm is in a dominant position if it has the ability to:

- set prices above the competitive level;
- sell products of an inferior quality; or
- reduce its rate of innovation below the level that would exist in a competitive market (European Communities, 2003).

Box 14.1 Article 101 cases: MasterCard and the Groupement des Cartes Bancaires

MasterCard's intra-EEA multilateral interchange fees

Chapter 7 indicated that the use of interchange fees is the subject of several regulatory and antitrust investigations. In December 2007, the European Commission published its findings on the multilateral interchange fees (MIFs) for cross-border payment card transactions with MasterCard and Maestro branded debit and consumer credit cards in the European Economic Area. The Commission concluded that MasterCard violated EC Treaty rules on restrictive business practices, as its MIF inflated the cost of card acceptance by retailers without leading to proven efficiencies. It was, however, stressed that MIFs are not illegal as such. According to the Commission, a MIF in an open-payment card scheme such as MasterCard's is compatible with EU competition rules only if it contributes to technical and economic progress and benefits consumers. In 2008 the European Commission also opened formal antitrust proceedings against Visa in order to establish whether its MIF constituted infringements of Article 81 (now Article 101 TFEU).

Price measures by the Groupement des Cartes Bancaires

In 2007 the Commission decided that the Groupement des Cartes Bancaires (France) had infringed the EC Treaty rules prohibiting practices which restrict competition. The Groupement had adopted price measures that hinder the issuing of cards in France at competitive rates by certain member banks, thereby keeping the price of payment cards artificially high to the benefit of the major French banks. According to the Commission, consumers were the victims of this illegal practice, depriving them of cheaper cards and a more diversified product offering. The decision ordered the Groupement to annul the measures concerned with immediate effect and to avoid taking any measures with a similar purpose or effect in the future.

Source: European Commission (2007a, 2007b)

However, it is not illegal under EU competition law to hold a dominant position, since this can be obtained by legitimate means of competition. Still, competition rules forbid companies to abuse their dominant position. The next section will discuss a framework for investigating abuse of dominance. A well-known example of an Article 102 case was the decision of the European Commission that Microsoft had abused its dominant market position by leveraging its near monopoly in the market for PC operating systems onto the markets for work-group-server operating systems and for media players (European Commission, 2007c). Microsoft was fined €497 million for infringing the EC Treaty rules on abuse of a dominant market position. Because of non-compliance with certain requirements set out by the European Commission, the fine was subsequently raised to €899 million in 2008.

Examining mergers

The second element of the EU's competition policy is the examination of mergers, in order to assess whether they may lead to less competition. Merger control regulation has existed since 1989. The EC Merger Regulation[3] adopted in 2004 sets out rules for mergers and acquisitions of companies, which could have the possibility to restrict competition. In this respect, Article 2(3) of the Regulation states that: '[A] concentration which would significantly impede effective competition, in the common market or in a substantial part of it, in particular as a result of the creation or strengthening of a dominant position, shall be declared incompatible with the common market.' *Dominance* has been defined by the European Court of Justice (ECJ) as 'a position of economic strength enjoyed by an undertaking which enables it to prevent effective competition being maintained on the relevant market by affording it the power to behave to an appreciable extent independently of its competitors, customers and ultimately of its customers'.[4] However, the new EC Merger Regulation prohibits every merger which significantly impedes effective competition, i.e. the ban is not confined to 'dominant firms'. It therefore takes account of the argument that even in the absence of a dominant position a merger may also have serious anti-competitive effects.

As for the enforcement of merger rules, general principles have been established to ensure an efficient division of work. Mergers with a Community dimension are investigated by the European Commission. The main requirement for a merger having a Community dimension is that the combined aggregate worldwide turnover of the merging companies is over €5 billion and that the aggregate Community-wide turnover of each of at least two of the undertakings concerned is more than €250 million.

A merger may also have a Community dimension if the following turnover criteria are met: the combined aggregate worldwide turnover of all undertakings is more than €2.5 billion, and the aggregate Community-wide turnover of each of at least two of the undertakings concerned is more than €100 million, and in each of at least three Member States the combined aggregate turnover of all the undertakings concerned is more than €100 million, and in each of at least three of these Member States the aggregate turnover of each of

Table 14.1 Community dimension – threshold I

Undertaking	A	B	A + B
Worldwide turnover			> €5 billion
Community turnover (CT)	> €250 million not 2/3 of CT in one and the same Member State	> €250 million not 2/3 of CT in one and the same Member State	

Table 14.2 Community dimension – threshold II

Undertaking	A	B	A + B
Worldwide turnover			> €2.5 billion
Community turnover (CT)	> €100 million not 2/3 of CT in one and the same Member State	> €100 million not 2/3 of CT in one and the same Member State	
Turnover Member State 1	> €25 million	> €25 million	> €100 million
Turnover Member State 2	> €25 million	> €25 million	> €100 million
Turnover Member State 3	> €25 million	> €25 million	> €100 million

at least two of the undertakings concerned is more than €25 million. A merger of such a dimension can subsequently be assessed in a single procedure by the European Commission (one-stop-shop principle), instead of different assessments by the Member States involved.

But if each of the undertakings involved achieves more than two-thirds of its Community-wide turnover within one and the same Member State, the merger is in principle examined by the competition authority of that country (as it is supposed to be better placed to examine the potential effects). Both merger-regulation thresholds are summarised in Tables 14.1 and 14.2. Below these thresholds, the national competition authorities in the EU Member States may review the merger. However, the European Commission can also examine mergers, which are referred to it by the national competition authorities or the undertakings involved. In the latter case, agreement of all relevant national competition authorities is needed.

Apart from competitive reasons, potential mergers and acquisitions between financial institutions may also be blocked for prudential reasons.

The *'prudential carve-out'* allows supervisory authorities to block proposed mergers and acquisitions if the 'sound and prudent management' of the targeted firm(s) could be put at risk. Initially, the margins of this requirement were defined rather broadly and on several occasions the carve-out was used in a protectionist manner. After the takeover battle for the Italian bank Antonveneta in 2005, in which then-governor of the Italian Central Bank Antonio Fazio tried to block the purchase of Antonveneta by ABN AMRO, the Council and the European Parliament endorsed a proposal in 2007 to tighten the procedures that supervisory authorities have to follow when assessing proposed mergers and acquisitions. The new directive (2007/44/EC) comprises a list of criteria on the basis of which prudential supervisory authorities should assess the acquiring company, e.g. reputation of the proposed acquirer, reputation and experience of the management, financial soundness, compliance with EU Directives, and risks related to money laundering and terrorism financing. Moreover, the assessment period is reduced from three months to 30 days.

Liberalisation of monopolistic economic sectors and state aid

Governments can also introduce restrictions on competition by granting national businesses exclusive rights to provide certain goods or services, or by providing public aid to businesses.

Based on Article 106 TFEU, the European Commission is responsible for monitoring public undertakings and undertakings to which Member States grant special or exclusive rights (thereby establishing monopolistic sectors). The European Commission also has the power to address government actions which may distort competition in the internal market. Under this heading, the European Commission plays a pivotal role in opening up markets such as transport, energy, postal services, and telecommunications to competition.

Firms receiving support from their government are likely to obtain an unfair advantage over their competitors. State aid is therefore forbidden by the Treaty, unless it is justified by reasons of general economic development. The rules concerning state aid have been laid down in Articles 107, 108, 109 TFEU. The objective of state aid control is to ensure that government interventions do not distort competition and trade inside the EU. It strives to find the right balance between on the one hand the advantage for the aid recipient and the achievement of a policy objective (e.g. economic development, job creation, financial stability) and on the other the competitive distortion created in the market (i.e. the disadvantage for the competitors). In this respect,

Table 14.3 Government support to banks and central banks' balance sheets; measures taken in the 2007–2009 crisis, € billion, unless stated otherwise

	US	Euro area	UK
Government support **banks**			
Capital injected	369	187	83
Asset relief	385	407	385
Debt guaranteed	274	498	152
Total in % GDP	9.3	16.6	36.5
Central bank balance sheet **expansion ($/€/£ bn)**			
Securities purchases	818	18	172
Open market operations & special credit facilities	462	243	18
Total in % GDP	8.8	4.0	13.0

Note: Government support for banks in the euro area is the sum of support in DE, FR, SP, NL, BE, and IE. Position as at mid-2010. Central bank balance sheet expansion based on increase of assets between July 2007 and October 2009.
Source: Van den End *et al.* (2009)

state aid is defined as an advantage in any form whatsoever conferred on a selective basis to undertakings by national public authorities. Therefore, subsidies granted to individuals or general measures open to all enterprises are not covered by TFEU and do not constitute state aid. In order to ensure that these rules are respected and exemptions are applied equally across the EU, the European Commission is in charge of monitoring state aid.

During the 2007–2009 financial crisis, Member States took several measures to support the European financial sector (see Table 14.3 and Figure 14.3). Some of these measures were directed towards individual institutions (capital injections, asset solutions), while others were general (guarantee schemes, liquidity operations). They reduced the default risks among financial institutions and thus helped to safeguard financial stability. However, the interventions had distortionary effects, because the rapid unfolding of the crisis and market failures complicated the proper design of support policies.

Since the beginning of the 2007–2009 financial crisis, the European Commission has provided detailed guidance on the criteria for the

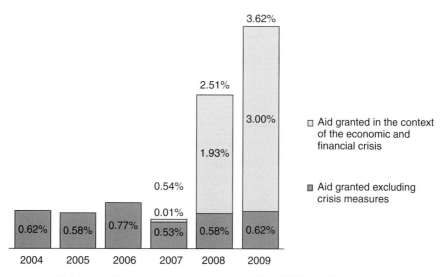

Figure 14.3 Evolution of total state aid granted by Member States as % of GDP in the EU, 2004–2009
Source: European Commission (2011)

compatibility of temporary crisis-related support measures with Article 107 TFEU. Through the application of state aid rules, the Commission tried to ensure that distortions of competition within the internal market were limited to a minimum despite the important amounts of state aid and that beneficiary banks were restructured when necessary.

Restructuring followed three main principles: (1) the return to long-term viability without state aid, based on a sound restructuring plan; (2) burden sharing between the bank/its stakeholders and the state; and (3) limitation of competition distortions, usually through structural (divestitures) and behavioural measures (acquisition bans or limitations on aggressive commercial behaviour).

Van den End *et al.* (2009) argue that setting conditions for support cannot always prevent that the level playing field between supported and non-supported institutions is affected and that undesirable shifts in capital flows occur. Moreover, it cannot be ruled out that interventions damage the confidence of market participants, also with regard to the financial strength of support-providing governments and central banks. To reduce such negative side effects of support, it is important that the support policies are market compatible, unambiguous and timely withdrawn through an appropriate exit strategy.

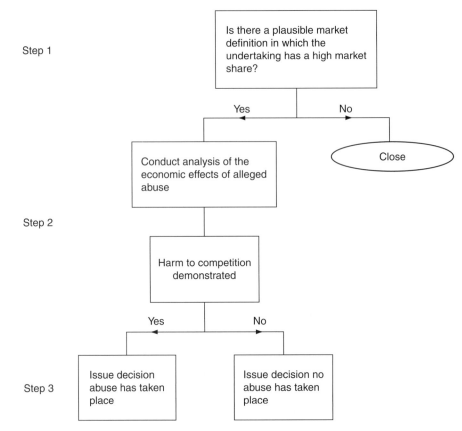

Figure 14.4 Flowchart for undertaking abuse-of-dominance investigations
Source: Office of Fair Trading (2001)

14.4 Assessment of dominant positions

Under Article 102 TFEU and the EC Merger Regulation, competition authorities need to examine abuse of dominance. This section discusses how competition authorities may examine (potential) abuse of dominant positions, using a framework suggested by the UK Office of Fair Trading (OFT, 2001). This approach consists of three steps (see Figure 14.4):

1. Assess whether there is a plausible market definition under which the firm under investigation has a high market share.
2. If there is a plausible market in which the firm might be dominant, conduct a full analysis of the economic effects of the practice under investigation.
3. If competition is likely to have been significantly damaged or if there is a prospect of such damage, issue a decision that describes and demonstrates

the adverse economic effects of the business practice. Alternatively, if the conduct is not harmful, issue a decision giving the reasons why the business practice under investigation does not constitute an abuse of a dominant position.

The three steps will be discussed in more detail. Although Figure 14.4 depicts an ex-post investigation of possible abuse of dominance, similar investigations can be done ex ante in case of a proposed merger or acquisition.

Step 1: Identify the relevant market

The main purpose of market definition is to identify in a systematic way the competitive constraints that the firms involved face. A market is defined in both its product and geographical dimension (European Commission, 1997). The relevant *product market* is said to 'comprise all those products and/or services which are regarded as interchangeable or substitutable by the consumer, by reason of the products' characteristics, their prices and their intended use'. Moreover, the relevant *geographical market* 'comprises the area in which the undertakings concerned are involved in the supply and demand of products or services, in which the conditions of competition are sufficiently homogeneous and which can be distinguished from neighbouring areas because the conditions of competition are appreciably different in those areas'.

A very common methodology to define the relevant geographical market is the *Small, but Significant Non-transitory Increase in Prices* methodology (European Commission, 2004). The SSNIP methodology is used to examine whether some goods produced within a specific area constitute their own relevant geographical market. The first step is to assume that the respective goods or services are produced by a hypothetical monopolist. Subsequently, the question is asked whether it is likely that this monopolist can earn a profit by increasing prices by 5–10 per cent (i.e. small but significant) for a period of not less than 12 months (i.e. non-transitory).

If the answer is yes, then the candidate goods form their own relevant geographic market. If the answer is no, because consumers substitute away from the candidate markets as they are able to purchase the same good in neighbouring regions or because producers from other regions enter the market, then the relevant geographical market is larger than the goods for the candidate market. The thought experiment is subsequently repeated with a larger geographical area and continued until the answer to the question posed is affirmative. At that stage, the relevant geographical market is composed of all areas included in the last experiment. When it is difficult to assess whether goods which meet the same needs of the consumer belong to the same market or not, price tests (looking at price co-movements) can be used to evaluate the extent of the relevant candidate market.

Whether or not a price increase is profitable depends on the sales volume that is lost following the price increase, i.e. the extent to which a consumer can substitute away from the candidate market (see Box 14.2 which explains the algebra of the SSNIP methodology). The quantity of lost sales depends on the following two aspects:

- the availability of substitute products (i.e. *demand-side substitutes*); and
- the ability of other firms to supply these products (i.e. *supply-side substitutes*).

Once the relevant market has been defined, market shares and concentration indices have to be calculated. There are no thresholds for defining dominance set by law, but the ECJ has argued that dominance can be presumed in the absence of evidence to the contrary if a firm has a market share persistently above 50 per cent. However, a firm with lower market shares may also be dominant, particularly if it faces competitors that are much smaller. The OFT (2001) stresses that despite having a high market share, a firm may not be dominant if one or more of the following conditions hold:

- there are very low barriers to entry into the relevant market and the threat of potential entry is sufficient to discipline firms with high market shares;
- the nature of competition within the market is such that very intense competition exists even where there are very few players; and
- the nature of the buyers in a market and the volumes that they purchase are such that they can exert significant countervailing power against a firm with a high market share.

Also, a high concentration ratio does not necessarily point towards a lack of competition. Claessens and Laeven (2004) estimate competitiveness indicators for banks in a large cross-section of countries and find no evidence that banking-system concentration is negatively associated with competitiveness. In fact, they find some evidence that more concentrated banking systems are more competitive. The latter may be the result of fierce competition in the preceding period, as a result of which the overall banking system has become relatively efficient. Claessens and Laeven (2004) conclude that a contestable system may be more important to assure competitiveness than a system with low concentration (see Chapter 10).

Box 14.2 Algebra of the SSNIP methodology*

Profits (π) beforehand (denoted with subscript 0) are equal to revenue (price (P) times quantity (Q)) minus total costs (average costs (C) times Q):

$$\pi_0 = (P_0 - C_0)Q_0 \tag{14.2}$$

A change in the price ($\Delta P = P_1 - P_0$) leads to a change in quantity demanded ($\Delta Q = Q_1 - Q_0$) and may also lead to a change in the average costs of production ($\Delta C = C_1 - C_0$). This gives a new level of profits:

$$\pi_1 = (P_1 - C_1)Q_1 \tag{14.3}$$

The change in profit is given by:

$$\begin{aligned} \Delta \pi = \pi_1 - \pi_0 &= (P_1 - C_1)Q_1 - (P_0 - C_0)Q_0 \\ &= \Delta P Q_1 + (P_0 - C_0)\Delta Q - Q_1 \Delta C \end{aligned} \tag{14.4}$$

Note that when $\Delta P > 0$, it is expected that $\Delta Q < 0$. The issue is when $\Delta\pi$ will be less than zero. It is convenient to rewrite (14.4) by dividing through P_0 (note that this does not matter as $\Delta\pi < 0$ if $\Delta\pi/P_0 < 0$), yielding:

$$\frac{\Delta\pi}{P_0} = \frac{\Delta P}{P_0}Q_1 + \frac{P_0 - C_0}{P_0}\Delta Q - \frac{Q_1}{P_0}\Delta C. \tag{14.5}$$

Suppose average costs is constant (i.e. it does not depend on the amount produced) so that $\Delta C = 0$. Then,

$$\frac{\Delta\pi}{P_0} = \frac{\Delta P}{P_0}Q_1 + \frac{P_0 - C_0}{P_0}\Delta Q \tag{14.6}$$

Thus, a price rise will be profitable if:

$$\frac{\Delta P}{P_0}Q_1 > \frac{P_0 - C_0}{P_0} - \Delta Q \tag{14.7}$$

that is, if the increased price charged on the new (lower) quantity is greater than the lost margin on the decrease in quantity. If there are economies of scale, it is also necessary to work out:

$$\frac{Q_1}{P_0}\Delta C. \tag{14.8}$$

If for example, $\Delta C > 0$ when $\Delta Q < 0$, the increase in price on the new quantity needs to be greater than the lost margin on the decreased quantity plus the higher costs of the new quantity.

Source: Geroski and Griffith (2004)

Step 2: Abuse of dominance?

Once it is clear that a market can be defined in which the respective firm has a dominant position, the economic effects of (possible) abuse should be examined. Abusive conduct generally falls into one of the following categories (OFT, 2004):

- conduct which exploits customers or suppliers (for example, through excessively high prices); or
- conduct which amounts to exclusionary behaviour, because it removes or weakens competition from existing competitors, or establishes or strengthens entry barriers, thereby removing or weakening potential competition.

In the first case, it may be possible to identify abuse by analysing the profitability of the respective firm. However, profitability figures may be hard to interpret (OFT, 2003). For example, when are profits too high or too low, and what is the relevant time period to consider? And if high profits are found, are they due to market power or to superior efficiency? Profitability figures should therefore be cautiously interpreted and other economic indicators – such as productivity, the advertise-to-sale ratio, prices, and the level of innovation – should also be analysed.

The economic impact of exclusionary behaviour on the market requires a detailed analysis of, among other things, barriers to entry and switching costs. The challenge is to make a distinction between what can be seen as behaviour under normal competition and what can be labelled as abusive practices. In this respect, the OFT (2001) distinguishes between conduct that inflicts harm to competition and conduct that inflicts harm to competitors. Demonstrating harm to competitors is important only when it leads to adverse impacts on consumers. Harm to competitors does not necessarily have an adverse impact on competition. It must therefore be determined whether the conduct represents normal business practice (i.e. lawful competitive behaviour) or abusive behaviour.

Step 3: Issue decision

If no harm to competition can be demonstrated, competition authorities refrain from any intervention. However, if (possible) harm to competition can be proven, competition authorities may impose administrative sanctions, like imposing a fine, prohibiting a proposed merger or acquisition, or requiring additional concessions for the proposed merger or acquisition.

An interesting example of the latter is the proposed merger between the two Swedish banking groups FöreningsSparbanken and SEB in February 2001. The merger of these two banking groups would have created Sweden's leading financial group with market shares in a number of markets in the range of 40–60 per cent. According to the European Commission (2001), the merged entity's large customer base and extensive branch network would have placed it well ahead of its closest competitors in Sweden. In reaction to the preliminary views of the European Commission set out in its Statement of Objections, FöreningsSparbanken and SEB announced in September 2001 that they would withdraw their merger application, claiming that the concessions (e.g. forcing the banks to significantly reduce their market shares) would jeopardise the value of the proposed merger. The European Commission (2001) argued that it should not have been a surprise that it had considered the market as national.

To define the market for banking services to households and SMEs as national is standard practice for antitrust regulators worldwide. In previous cases involving banking mergers the European Commission has raised concerns where market shares were considerably lower (30–35 per cent). Moreover, in 2001 the UK authorities blocked a merger between Lloyds and Abbey National which presented significantly lower combined market shares (27 per cent for household accounts). The subsequent takeover of Abbey National by the Spanish banking group Banco Santander in 2004 did not raise any competition concerns as these banks were (mostly) active in different countries.

Table 14.4 provides some indications on the relevant geographical market for various financial services. The relevant market for retail banking and insurance is national. Retail banking consists of banking services for consumers (e.g. payment services, consumer credit, and mortgages) and SMEs (e.g. payment services and loans). Retail insurance for consumers and SMEs is also very much a local business with significant differences between countries. The relevant rules for retail insurance products, such as the fiscal treatment, the social security framework, and the liability legislation, are national.

Table 14.4 Relevant geographical market for financial services

National	European	Global
Retail banking & insurance		
	Wholesale banking & insurance	
		Re-insurance
	Stock exchanges	
		Investment banking

The relevant market for motor and health insurance is thus clearly national. Markets for wholesale banking and insurance for large firms are European or even global. Corporate customers are looking for tailor-made solutions for their business and are approached by banks and insurers across Europe. There is a shift to global solutions for more specialised services for large firms. Re-insurance, for example, is a global business. A small group of large re-insurance companies from Europe (in particular Germany and Switzerland) and the United States dominate the global market. Investment banking is also a global business. Leading investment banks – located primarily in New York and London – offer underwriting services and advice for mergers and acquisitions. Finally, the relevant geographic market for stock exchanges is shifting. Not too long ago, each country had its own stock exchange where nearly all domestic companies were listed. The market is consolidating at the European (Euronext, OMX) as well as the global level (for instance, the merger between the NYSE and Euronext; see Chapter 5).

The borderline between geographical markets may in practice be less distinct than is suggested by Table 14.4, e.g. the relevant geographical market for large firms can also be defined at the national rather than at the European level.

14.5 Institutional structure

The enforcement of EU competition policy remained largely unchanged from 1962, when a highly centralised authorisation system for all restrictive agreements was established (Monti, 2003a). However, since May 2004 the enforcement system has become more decentralised as the national competition authorities and national courts have become (increasingly) involved in the enforcement of Community competition law. Figure 14.5 gives an overview of the dual legislative and enforcement system in the EU.

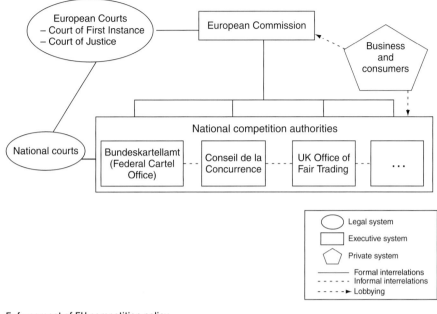

Figure 14.5   Enforcement of EU competition policy
Source: Based on Budzinski and Christiansen (2005)

Before the introduction of the Community competition law in 1958, most Member States did not have a competition policy regime in place. Competition policy has been established at the Community level, and many Member States created their own legislation and enforcement agencies, while gradually obtaining more enforcement powers originating from EU legislation. This centralised approach in competition policy differs from the enforcement of financial supervision, where supervision has traditionally been organised at the national level. Box 14.3 discusses the issue of decentralisation vs. centralisation in more detail.

Within the current EU competition policy system, the Community institutions (still) occupy a central position. The European Commission enjoys the right of initiative in the legislative process, which confers agenda-setting power to it (Schmidt, 2000). Moreover, as shown in section 14.4, the Commission has specific powers in enforcing Community competition law. The application of EU competition law is supervised by the European Court of First Instance (ECFI) and the ECJ. The ECFI is an independent court attached to the ECJ which rules on competition cases in the first instance. Decisions of the ECFI can be appealed to the ECJ.

Box 14.3 Which level of (de)centralisation?

The appropriate level of centralisation is an important issue for policy making. National policies offer the flexibility to adapt policies to local circumstances. In addition, policy competition between countries can be beneficial. But when there are externalities (i.e. spill-over effects of national policy from one country to another country) it may be useful to centralise policy making. Another reason for centralisation can be economies of scale. It is, for example, more efficient to examine a merger between two EU-wide operating companies at the central level than to have up to 27 separate examinations by national authorities.

The *principle of subsidiarity* states that matters ought to be handled by the smallest (or the lowest-level) competent authority. Subsidiarity means that a central authority should perform only those tasks which cannot be performed effectively at a more local level (Gelauff *et al.*, 2008).

Figure 14.6 illustrates the degree of centralisation for the three main policy areas in financial services. As discussed in Chapter 12, the competent authorities for financial supervision are national. There is some coordination within the new European Supervisory Authorities, but the national supervisors are still operating on the basis of a primarily national mandate. Large European banks often complain about duplications in the supervision of their European activities. Steps have been taken to work towards a European mandate forcing national supervisors to cooperate with other EU supervisors and to promote convergence within the EU.

Chapter 13 indicates that National Central Banks are primarily in charge of financial stability. The lender-of-last-resort function for individual banks is the responsibility of the NCBs. Financial stability is typically an area where externalities are important. The central authority, the ECB, is allowed to contribute to the policies of the NCBs only to promote financial stability. The ECB is slowly expanding its role by maintaining the liquidity of the overall financial system in times of crisis (but not of individual banks) and publishing a Financial Stability Review. The new European Systemic Risk Board (ESRB) is meant to strengthen European coordination in the area of financial stability.

This chapter illustrates that competition policy is highly centralised: the European Commission (DG Competition) is in charge. In 2004, the European Competition Network, consisting of the European Commission and national competition authorities, was created to facilitate cooperation and delegate activities to national authorities where possible.

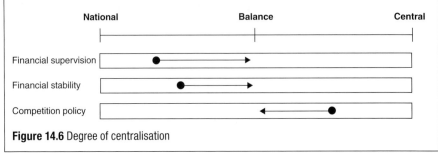

Figure 14.6 Degree of centralisation

Effective enforcement of EU antitrust rules requires close cooperation between the Community and national institutions. According to Smits (2005), they have to cooperate in finding evidence for infringements and inform each other about investigations, so as to ensure both an efficient division of work and an effective and consistent application of EC competition rules. For this reason, the European Competition Network (ECN) was established in 2004. Within this network, EU competition authorities work together, exchange information, and allocate cases. Monti (2004) argues that the ECN reflects that in an integrated economy collaborative competition enforcement is more effective than isolated efforts. Given the dual structure of EU enforcement, general principles have been established to ensure an efficient division of work (Monti, 2003b):

- as a rule, competition authorities of the Member States will be well placed to deal with cases that have a major effect on the territory of their Member State;
- where a suspected infringement has its main effects in the territory of two or three Member States, these authorities should consider working together on a case;
- where a suspected infringement has larger geographical scope, the Commission is likely to be best placed to deal with a case.

As for the sanctioning regime, Smits (2005) argues that the absence of a clear regime to impose sanctions for infringements with out-of-state effects is an omission which requires close collaboration among national competition authorities. Another element which needs to be remedied according to Smits (2005) is the absence of a common leniency platform, as currently individual applicants need to approach as many authorities as the number of markets that may be affected. However, in 2006 the ECN Model Leniency Programme was introduced. Although it does not provide for a one-stop shop, it diminishes discrepancies and allows for summary applications in case of applications in multiple jurisdictions, notably with the European Commission.

The EU's competition policy is different from that in other countries. Box 14.4 illustrates this by comparing competition policies in the US and the EU.

14.6 Conclusions

Competition policy is one of the pillars of the EU's internal market policy. By combating distortions of competition between firms, competition policy

---

Box 14.4 Antitrust policy in the EU and the US

Ginsburg (2005) argues that Sections 1 and 2 of the US Sherman Act cover largely the same ground as Articles 81 and 82 of the Treaty of Rome (now Articles 101 and 102 TFEU). Moreover, the US Clayton Act is roughly comparable to the EC Merger Regulation. In practice, EU and US competition policy are exhibiting more and more similarities. In this respect, Martin (2005) poses that the EU is moving along the same path trod by US antitrust a quarter of a century ago: from a reliance on maintaining the ability of equally efficient competitors to compete as a way of getting good market performance towards an explicit, case-by-case assessment of the impact of a business practice on market performance, or of a proposed merger/structural change on expected market performance.

Still, there are important differences between antitrust policies in the US and the EU. According to Rosch (2007), one of the main explanations for these differences is that the policies are based on different schools of thought. While US antitrust policies are based on 'Chicago School economics', those of the EU policies are built on 'post-Chicago School economics'. The basic assumption of the first is that markets are by their nature efficient and that a monopolist will never be able to keep out competitors. Chicago School scholars therefore argue that: (1) firms alleged to be engaged in predatory pricing are more likely to be engaged in profit-maximising conduct that is efficiency-enhancing instead of efficiency-impairing, and (2) even if a firm is trying to engage in predatory conduct, the market is likely to adjust. However, according to post-Chicago School scholars, firms do engage in strategic behaviour to undermine (potential) rivals and active antitrust policies are therefore needed. In addition, Rosch (2007) argues that where the Chicago School tends to advocate a hands-off approach, post-Chicago scholars favour a 'light-touch' regulatory approach. In practice, this entails that EU enforcement agencies challenge certain actions of monopolists, while US agencies and courts rarely (successfully) challenge certain exclusionary practices, such as vertical restraints and predatory pricing.

---

aims to create the preconditions for the proper functioning of markets. Moreover, safeguarding competition is an important instrument to promote further market integration, also within the financial system.

Competition forces firms to become (more) efficient, offer greater choice of products and services, and offer these products and services at lower prices. Ultimately, this gives rise to increased consumer welfare and allocative efficiency. The level of competition is also an important aspect of financial-sector development and, in turn, economic growth. However, firms can benefit from anti-competitive behaviour and may try to scale down competition. The European Commission and the National Competition Authorities therefore aim to:

- eliminate agreements which restrict competition;
- prevent abuse of a dominant position;
- make sure that mergers and acquisitions do not harm competition;
- liberalise monopolistic economic sectors; and
- prevent illegitimate state aid, as witnessed during the 2007–2009 financial crisis.

As for the prevention of abuse of a dominant position, this chapter discusses a framework for abuse of dominance investigations. One of the elements of this framework is the 'Small, but Significant Non-transitory Increase in Prices' (SSNIP) methodology, which is used to define the smallest market in which a hypothetical monopolist would be able to impose a small but significant non-transitory price increase (the so-called relevant market). Finally, the institutional structure of EU competition policy is explained. It is shown that enforcement of EU competition policy has become more decentralised and the dual enforcement system requires close cooperation between the European Commission and the National Competition Authorities.

NOTES

1 The OECD (1993) defines perfect competition using four conditions: (1) there is such a large number of sellers and buyers that none can individually affect the market price, (2) there are no barriers to entry and exit, (3) buyers and sellers are perfectly informed about production and consumption decisions, and (4) products are homogenous.
2 The multilateral interchange fee is a fall-back option, which can be used when the issuing and acquiring banks are not able to bilaterally agree on an interchange fee.
3 Council Regulation (EC) No 139/2004 of 20 January 2004 on the control of concentrations between undertakings.
4 Case 27/76 *United Brands Co and United Brands Continental BV v Commission* [1978] 1 CMLR 429.

SUGGESTED READING

Bikker, J. A. and J. W. B. Bos (2008), *Bank Performance: A Theoretical and Empirical Framework for the Analysis of Profitability, Competition and Efficiency*, Routledge, London.

Monti, M. (2004), Competition Policy in a Global Economy, *International Finance*, 7(3), 495–504.

Motta, M. (2004), *Competition Policy; Theory and Practice*, Cambridge University Press.

REFERENCES

Bikker, J. A. and J. W. B. Bos (2008), *Bank Performance: A Theoretical and Empirical Framework for the Analysis of Profitability, Competition and Efficiency*, Routledge, London.

Budzinski, O. and A. Christiansen (2005), Competence Allocation in EU Competition Policy as an Interest-Driven Process, *Journal of Public Policy*, 25(3), 313–337.

Claessens, S. and L. Laeven (2004), What Drives Bank Competition? Some International Evidence, *Journal of Money, Credit and Banking*, 36, 563–583.

(2005), Financial Dependence, Banking Sector Competition, and Economic Growth, *Journal of the European Economic Association*, 3(1), 179–207.

European Commission (1997), *Commission Notice on the Definition of the Relevant Market for the Purposes of Community Competition Law*, EC, Brussels.

(2000), *XXIX Report on Competition Policy*, EC, Brussels.

(2001), *Commission Takes Note of Merger Withdrawal by Swedish Banks (SEB/FSB)* (press release), EC, Brussels.

(2004), *The Internal Market and the Relevant Geographical Market – The Impact of the Completion of the Single Market Programme on the Definition of the Relevant Geographical Market*, Enterprise Papers No. 15, EC, Brussels.

(2007a), *Antitrust: Commission Prohibits MasterCard's Intra-EEA Multilateral Interchange Fees* (press release), EC, Brussels.

(2007b), *Anti-trust: Groupement des Cartes Bancaires Restricts Competition by Hindering the Issuance of Cards at Competitive Prices* (press release), EC, Brussels.

(2007c), *Antitrust: Commission Welcomes CFI Ruling Upholding Commission's Decision on Microsoft's Abuse of Dominant Market Position* (press release), EC, Brussels.

(2011), *Report on Competition Policy 2010*, EC, Brussels.

European Communities (2003), *Glossary of Terms used in Competition Related Matters*, EC, Brussels.

Gelauff, G., I. Grilo, and A. Lejour (eds.) (2008), *Subsidiarity and Economic Reform in Europe*, Springer, Berlin.

Geroski, P. and R. Griffith (2004), Identifying Antitrust Markets, in: M. Neumann and J. Weinand (eds.), *International Handbook of Competition*, Edward Elgar, Cheltenham, 290–305.

Ginsburg, D. H. (2005), Comparing Antitrust Enforcement in the United States and Europe, *Journal of Competition Law and Economics*, 1(3), 427–439.

Martin, S. (2005), US Antitrust and EU Competition Policy: Where Has the Former Been, Where is the Latter Going?, University of Aveiro Working Paper in Economics 27.

Monti, M. (2003a), The New Shape of European Competition Policy, Speech given at the Inaugural Symposium of the Competition Policy Research Center, How Should Competition Policy Transform Itself?, Tokyo.

(2003b), *EU Competition Policy after May 2004, Fordham Annual Conference on International Antitrust Law and Policy*, New York.

(2004), Competition Policy in a Global Economy, *International Finance*, 7(3), 495–504.

Motta, M. (2004), *Competition Policy; Theory and Practice*, Cambridge University Press.

Office of Fair Trading (2001), *The Role of Market Definition in Monopoly and Dominance Inquiries*, OFT, London.

(2003), Assessing Profitability in Competition Policy Analysis, OFT Economic Discussion Paper 6.

(2004), *Abuse of a Dominant Position – Understanding Competition Law*, OFT, London.

Organisation for Economic Co-operation and Development (1993), *Glossary of Industrial Organisation Economics and Competition Law*, OECD, Paris.

Panzar, J. and J. Rosse (1987), Testing for 'Monopoly' Equilibrium, *Journal of Industrial Economics*, 35, 443–456.

Roeller, L.-H. and O. Stehmann (2006), The Year 2005 at DG Competition: The Trend Towards a More Effects-based Approach, *Review of Industrial Organization*, 29, 281–304.

Rosch, J. T. (2007), I say Monopoly, You say Dominance: The Continuing Divide on the Treatment of Dominant Firms, is it the Economics?, paper presented at the International Bar Association Antitrust Section Conference in Florence. Available at: www.ftc.gov/speeches/rosch/070908isaymonopolyiba.pdf (accessed 13 February 2012).

Schaeck, K. and M. Čihák (2008), How Does Competition Affect Efficiency and Soundness in Banking? New Empirical Evidence, ECB Working Paper 932.

Schmidt, S. K. (2000), Only an Agenda Setter? The European Commission's Power over the Council of Ministers, *European Union Politics*, 1(1), 37–61.

Smits, R. (2005), The European Competition Network: Selected Aspects, *Legal Issues of Economic Integration*, 32, 175–192.

Tirole, J. (1988), *The Theory of Industrial Organization*, MIT Press, Cambridge (MA).

Van den End, J. W., S. Verkaart, and A. Van Dijkhuizen (2009), Distortionary Effects of Anti-crisis Measures and How to Limit Them, *DNB Occasional Studies*, 7(3).

Index